IMAGINING REALITY

also by Kevin Macdonald

EMERIC PRESSBURGER:
The Life and Death
of a Screenwriter

IMAGINING REALITY

*The Faber Book
of the Documentary*

Kevin Macdonald
and Mark Cousins

faber and faber
LONDON · BOSTON

First published in 1996
by Faber and Faber Limited
3 Queen Square London WC1N 3AU

Photoset by Parker Typesetting Service Ltd
Printed in England by Clays Ltd, St Ives plc

This collection © Kevin Macdonald and Mark Cousins, 1996
Photographs © BFI Stills, Posters and Designs except for photograph of *Hoop Dreams*
courtesy of The Feature Film Company and photograph of *Crumb* courtesy of Artificial Eye
Film Company Ltd

Kevin Macdonald and Mark Cousins are hereby identified as author of this
work in accordance with Section 77 of the Copyright,
Designs and Patents Act 1988

A CIP record for this book
is available from the British Library

ISBN 0–571–17723–9

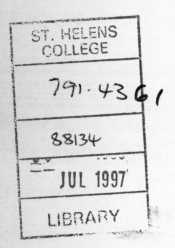
2 4 6 8 10 9 7 5 3 1

Contents

List of Illustrations

Introduction

John Grierson has a lot to answer for. Not only was he the populariser of that most dreary and off-putting of terms, 'documentary', but he proceeded to convince us that the only type of documentaries worth making were the type that he approved of: utilitarian, pedagogic and impersonal. In Britain, Canada, the United States and various other parts of the world, we've been suffering from a Griersonian hangover ever since; suspicious, if not down-right dismissive, of all other forms of documentary. The primary aim of this book is to demonstrate how diverse and fascinating our documentary heritage really is, and to encourage today's film-makers to continue to explore the imaginative possibilities of cinema's most flexible, but least appreciated, genre.

We have structured the book chronologically, but it does not aspire to be a comprehensive history of the documentary. Although we have tried to cover many of the major film-makers and movements, we have been restricted by lack of space and, in some cases, by the absence of appropriate pieces of writing. It was more important to us to include pieces that were readable, exciting and inspiring than ones that merely represented some notional high-point in documentary history, but were of dubious quality. If no good pieces existed to cover a particular area (or we couldn't find them) then we were forced to leave those subjects out. Among the topics that we would like to have included were: Chinese documentary, ethnographic film-making, nature documentaries and the effects of the digital revolution.

It was noticeable that the nearer to the present day we came in our research, the harder it was to find intelligent and stimulating pieces accessible to the general reader. Outside of a few exemplary American critics, very few people are writing about contemporary documentary. Particularly frustrating was the absence of material on the myriad forms of the British television documentary. The television critics who ought to be writing about these films usually dismiss them in a couple of glib lines. With one or two notable exceptions none of the British television critics seems to have any historical or practical knowledge of the documentary. No other step would do as much to improve the quality of the debate around the documentary as having decent critical discussion in the newspapers.

Wherever possible we have given precedence to pieces written by, or interviews with, film-makers themselves. It seemed important to keep the book as close to the actual films as possible. It is remarkably difficult for enthusiasts to see even the most famous British and American documentaries, let alone the more obscure titles from Asia or Eastern European cinema. Short of establishing an international documentary distribution network, there is little that can be done about that. But perhaps this book can serve as some sort of substitute for the experience of the films themselves.

Part 1

1 The Kingdom of Shadows

INTRODUCTION

Even in its infancy, when films were composed of a single shot and lasted less than a minute, cinema was divided into two camps: those who looked to the real world for their subject matter, and those who filmed performances. At the forefront of the latter group was Thomas Edison. His first film – *the* first film? – was *Fred Ott's Sneeze*, a brief record of his assistant pretending to sneeze. Among Edison's other early titles, all shot in a tiny studio known as 'the Black Maria' in upstate New York, were *Anabelle Butterfly Dance*, showing the celebrated dancer Anabelle Moore in a diaphanous dress, gyrating against a black background, and a more risqué film of a belly-dancer called *Fatima*. When these films were first shown, the *New York Journal* (4 April 1896) ran the headline: 'Lifeless Skirt Dancers In Gauzy Silks They Smirk and Pirouette at Wizard Edison's Command.' For Edison, film-making was a matter of contrivance and control.

On the other side of the divide, were the Lumière brothers. If Edison was the originator of the fiction film, they were the fathers of documentary. The audiences who came to see their first *cinématographe* programme in Paris in December 1895 were confronted not by exotic performances, but by vignettes and incidents from everyday life: workers passing through factory gates, a train pulling into a station, a baby being fed, a small boat leaving harbour.

Judging from contemporary reports, the Lumière films made a more profound impression on audiences than their Edison counterparts. Famously, Parisian spectators panicked and dodged aside when a train projected on the screen appeared to be heading towards them. Nothing as dramatic happened at early Edison screenings; the Americans merely marvelled at the 'life-like' quality of the moving images ('So true to life were the figures . . . that the spectator would almost believe that the girls were real and that the machine which clicked and sputtered had nothing to do with the performance,' wrote the man from the *New York Journal*).

1 *The first documentary. Workers leaving the Lumière factory (1895).*

A more subtle and telling reaction to the Lumière's proto-documentaries – one which the Edison films singularly failed to provoke – was recorded by the future film-maker Georges Méliès, a guest at an early screening. Referring to the film *Le Déjeuner de Bébé*, in which Auguste Lumière and his wife are seen feeding their baby, Méliès noted that the spectators were transfixed, not by the animated figures themselves, but by the rustling foliage in the background. Similarly, in *A Boat Leaving a Harbour*, it was the random movement of the waves which attracted their attention, and in *Demolishing a Wall*, the free-floating brickdust that filled the air. Why? Méliès suggests that the audience readily accepted the movements of photographed people because they were accustomed to the theatre, and to the idea of performers colluding in an illusion. But the brickdust, the rustling leaves and the waves were astonishing because they showed that the Lumière films were not an illusion, or a performance, but a grey, flickering mirror of a *past reality*. The cinema, unlike any previous art form, was able to represent the *spontaneous* – the very essence of life itself.

Even today the Lumière films of 1895–1900 retain much of their freshness and peculiar sense of 'naturalness'. They certainly make for more compelling viewing than the simplistic dumb show of most early fiction films. Purely from an historical point of view, it *is* fascinating to see how Paris, Peking or Piccadilly looked in the 1890s, to see how people dressed, how they walked and how the horse-drawn trams passed through the streets. But there is also something undeniably poignant about seeing moments from the relatively distant past preserved, knowing that everyone who appears in those films is long dead and buried. 1895, the year the cinema is said to have truly begun, was also, coincidentally, the year H.G. Wells published *The Time Machine*. The cinema is still the closest we can come to travelling in time.

Of course, for all their sense of spontaneity, of 'life caught as it is', the Lumière films (like every documentary to come) tampered with, and organized, 'reality'. Most of their films were, literally, 'set up': subjects can sometimes be seen responding to a signal from behind the camera before starting their activities; often, as in *A Train Arrives at the Station* the people involved were not anonymous members of the public, as one might think, but members of the Lumière family, obviously rehearsed and positioned and then told to ignore the camera and *act naturally*.

On a more subtle level, even when these, almost the simplest films we can imagine, are not actually 'set up', they do what all art does: they give form to the chaos of life and make it meaningful. Take, for example, *The Workers Leaving the Factory*. Unlike the 'reality' from which it is drawn, the film is discrete; it has a beginning and an end and it is carefully structured so that it begins with the big, wooden gates of the factory opening and ends as they are about to close again. It has a circular narrative. And then there's the framing. What are we not seeing? Where is this factory situated? Once a segment of 'reality' has been chosen, isolated and recorded it takes on significance and we are tempted to interpret it. Take *Le Déjeuner de Bébé*. Its themes are perhaps parenthood, familial joy and nourishment. Even in the simplest non-fiction film, the relationship between film and reality is not a straightforward or literal one, but that of a metaphor.

For almost a decade after the Lumières, the cinema was infatuated with reality. Fiction films remained comparatively rare. Up until as late as 1903, seventy-five per cent of films were so called *actualities*. Initially, subjects were chosen almost indiscriminately – the only important thing being that the films contained plenty of movement. Gradually, however, as the length of the films increased from one minute to five or more, subjects were chosen more carefully, designed to inform or entertain in their own right. They included topical events (disasters, parades and battles), famous personalities, scenic views from around the world and sporting fixtures; boxing films were the most popular.

But the dominance of factual cinema was short lived. Around 1903 fiction film-makers began to develop the techniques of editing, allowing ever more complex and effective stories to be told in an ever more subtle and sophisticated manner. The possibilities for creating tension and comedy in particular were enormous, and the popularity of fiction films grew astronomically.

Suddenly, films of unmanipulated reality seemed very dull indeed, and *actualities* were relegated to the bottom of the bill. Non-fiction film-makers had failed to advance their techniques since the days of the Lumières. A single shot was still deemed sufficient to cover an entire event. Their films lacked a strong, engaging narrative and characters with whom an audience could empathize. In the open market, only the most spectacular factual footage could now compete with the pleasures of fiction.

The Kingdom of Shadows
MAXIM GORKY

In April 1896 the young writer Maxim Gorky (1868–1936) attended one of the first Lumière *Cinématographe* shows in Russia in his home town of Nizhni-Novgorod. He wrote the following report for the local newspaper.

Last night I was in the Kingdom of Shadows.

If you only knew how strange it is to be there. It is a world without sound, without colour. Everything there – the earth, the trees, the people, the water and the air – is dipped in monotonous grey. Grey rays of the sun across the grey sky, grey eyes in grey faces, and the leaves of the trees are ashen grey. It is not life but its shadow, it is not motion but its soundless spectre.

Here I shall try to explain myself, lest I be suspected of madness or indulgence in symbolism. I was at Aumont's and saw Lumière's *cinématographe* – moving photography. The extraordinary impression it creates is so unique and complex that I doubt my ability to describe it with all its nuances. However, I shall try to convey its fundamentals.

When the lights go out in the room in which Lumière's invention is shown, there suddenly appears on the screen a large grey picture, *A Street in Paris* – shadows of a bad engraving. As you gaze at it, you see carriages, buildings and people in various poses, all frozen into immobility. All this is in grey, and the sky above is also grey – you anticipate nothing new in this all too familiar scene, for you have seen pictures of Paris streets more than once. But suddenly a strange flicker passes through the screen and the picture stirs to life. Carriages coming from somewhere in the perspective of the picture are moving straight at you, into the darkness in which you sit; somewhere from afar people appear and loom larger as they come closer to you; in the foreground children are playing with a dog, bicyclists tear along, and pedestrians cross the street picking their way among the carriages. All this moves, teems with life and, upon approaching the edge of the screen, vanishes somewhere beyond it.

And all this in strange silence where no rumble of the wheels is heard, no sound of footsteps or of speech. Nothing. Not a single note of the intricate symphony that always accompanies the movements of people. Noiselessly, the ashen-grey foliage of the trees sways in the wind, and the grey silhouettes of the people, as though condemned to eternal silence and cruelly punished by being deprived of all the colours of life, glide noiselessly along the grey ground.

Their smiles are lifeless, even though their movements are full of living energy and are so swift as to be almost imperceptible. Their laughter is soundless, although you see the muscles contracting in their grey faces. Before you a life is surging, a life deprived of words and shorn of the living spectrum of colours – the grey, the soundless, the bleak and dismal life.

It is terrifying to see, but it is the movement of shadows, only of shadows. Curses and ghosts, the evil spirits that have cast entire cities into eternal sleep, come to mind and you feel as though Merlin's vicious trick is being enacted before you. As though he had bewitched the entire street, he compressed its many-storied buildings from rooftops to foundations to yard-like size. He dwarfed the people in corresponding proportion, robbing them of the power of speech and scraping together all the pigment of earth and sky into a monotonous grey colour.

Under this guise he shoved his grotesque creation into a niche in the dark room of a restaurant. Suddenly something clicks, everything vanishes and a train appears on the screen. It speeds straight at you – watch out! It seems as though it will plunge into the darkness in which you sit, turning you into a ripped sack full of lacerated flesh and splintered bones, and crushing into dust and into broken fragments this hall and this building, so full of women, wine, music and vice.

But this, too, is but a train of shadows.

Noiselessly, the locomotive disappears beyond the edge of the screen. The train comes to a stop, and grey figures silently emerge from the cars, soundlessly greet their friends, laugh, walk, run, bustle, and . . . are gone. And here is another picture. Three men seated at the table, playing cards. Their faces are tense, their hands move swiftly. The cupidity of the players is betrayed by the trembling fingers and by the twitching of their facial muscles. They play . . . Suddenly, they break into laughter, and the waiter who has stopped at their table with beer laughs too. They laugh until their sides split but not a sound is heard. It seems as if these people have died and their shadows have been condemned to play cards in silence unto eternity . . .

This mute, grey life finally begins to disturb and depress you. It seems as though it carries a warning, fraught with a vague but sinister meaning that makes your heart grow faint. You are forgetting where you are. Strange imaginings invade your mind and your consciousness begins to wane and grow dim . . .

But suddenly, alongside of you, a gay chatter and a provoking laughter of a woman is heard . . . and you remember that you are at Aumont's, Charles Aumont's . . . But why of all places should this remarkable invention of Lumière find its way and be demonstrated here, this invention which affirms once again the energy and the curiosity of the human mind, forever striving to solve and grasp all, and – while on the way to the solution of the mystery of life – incidentally builds Aumont's fortune? I do not yet see the scientific importance of Lumière's invention but, no doubt, it is there, and it could probably be applied to the general ends of science, that is, of bettering man's life and the developing of his mind. This is not to be found at Aumont's where vice alone is being encouraged and popularized. Why then at Aumont's, among the 'victims of social needs' and among the loafers who here buy their kisses? Why here, of all places, are they showing this latest

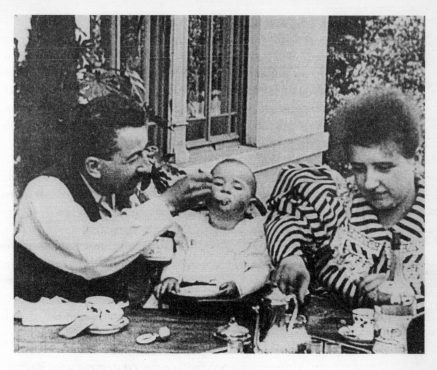

2 *Auguste Lumière and his wife feeding their baby (1895).*

achievement of science? And soon probably Lumière's invention will be perfected, but in the spirit of Aumont-Toulon and Company.

Besides those pictures I have already mentioned, is featured *The Family Breakfast*, an idyll of three. A young couple with its chubby first-born is seated at the breakfast table. The two are so much in love, and are so charming, gay and happy, and the baby is so amusing. The picture creates a fine, felicitous impression. Has this family scene a place at Aumont's?

And here is still another. Women workers, in a thick, gay and laughing crowd, rush out of the factory gates into the street. This too is out of place at Aumont's. Why remind here of the possibility of a clean, toiling life? This reminder is useless. Under the best of circumstances this picture will only painfully sting the woman who sells her kisses.

I am convinced that these pictures will soon be replaced by others of a genre more suited to the general tone of the Concert Parisien. For example, they will show a picture titled: *As She Undresses*, or *Madam at*

Her Bath, or *A Woman in Stockings*. They could also depict a sordid squabble between a husband and wife and serve it to the public under the heading of *The Blessings of Family Life*.

Yes, no doubt, this is how it will be done. The bucolic and the idyllic could not possibly find their place in Russia's markets thirsting for the piquant and the extravagant. I also could suggest a few themes for development by means of a *cinématographe* and for the amusement of the market place. For instance: to impale a fashionable parasite upon a picket fence, as is the way of the Turks, photograph him, then show it.

It is not exactly piquant but quite edifying.

Sources: A review of the Lumière programme at the Nizhni-Novgorod Fair, as printed in the *Nizhegorodski listok* newspaper, 4 July 1896, and signed 'I. M. Pacatus' – a pseudonymn for Maxim Gorky. This translation comes from *Kino* by Jay Leyda, Allen and Unwin Ltd., London, 1960, translated by Leda Swan.

George Méliès and the Illusion of Reality

George Méliès (1861–1938), master of cinematic special effects and trickery and creator of the celebrated fantasy *Le Voyage dans La Lune* (1902), is often referred to as the progenitor of imaginative, illusionist cinema. However, during his first few years of production, Méliès' work was firmly naturalistic.

The following extract from Méliès' autobiography, written in the third person, towards the end of his life, describes the production and exhibition of one of his first films in 1896.

Having filmed in the studio a number of short comic or artistic scenes, Méliès wanted to take some sea views on the spot, in order to enhance his program with some scenic views, or documentaries, as we call them now. Very determined, he left for Trouville and Le Havre, loaded like a donkey. Two excruciating working days were in store for him. A storm was raging, as Méliès had chosen on purpose a period of bad weather, so as to obtain more attractive effects. His camera could hold only twenty metres of film and films could not be inserted or removed in the open air, therefore he had to spend the whole day in gymnastics, taking down his set-up after each shot, carrying all his equipment to a photographer's shop to get it ready for his next shot. As he was alone he did not dare to leave anything on the shore, being afraid that somebody might touch his equipment and perhaps take away parts of it. It is easy to imagine the fatigue produced by such manoeuvres, especially if they are repeated twenty times in a day, usually walking miles on sandy beaches into which he often sank up to his knees, heavily loaded as he was. Nothing could stop him, however, as he was dedicated ('*avait le feu sacre*'). He was tired when he came home, but he triumphantly brought back to Paris about fifteen glorious shots which had a prodigious effect on the spectators. Nothing of that kind had ever been seen before; the assault of raging waves on the cliffs of Sainte Adresse, the foam, the seething waters, foam sprayed into the air, the eddies and spindrifts which were flitting about. As banal as all this might appear today, it fascinated the public then, as it was used to standard representations of the sea in the theatre which was realized by means of painted canvas surfaces shaken by kids crawling underneath it. It was the rigorously exact representation of nature – a complete novelty at that time – which thrilled the public. The ones who were familiar with the sea exclaimed, 'That's it, exactly!' and the ones who had never seen the sea felt they were standing on its shore.

Sources: Méliès' memoirs *La Vie et l'oeuvre d'un des plus anciens pionniers de la cinématographie mondiale – Georges Méliès, createur du spectacle cinématographique*. First published in *Georges Méliès* by Mageby Maurice Bessy and Lo Duca, Paris, 1945 & 1961.

1896: Censorship of News Footage in Imperial Russia
FRANCIS DOUBLIER

Early in 1896, in order to take full advantage of what they thought would be the short commercial life of the cinema, the Lumière brothers trained up four of their workmen as cameramen/projectionists and sent them on world tours, with strict instructions not to reveal the secrets of the cinematograph to anyone – even royalty. In each new place they visited the operators shot topical events and scenic views, which were included in their nightly shows. These locally produced films attracted large audiences – everyone was desperate to see their own town or city projected on the screen – before being sent back to the burgeoning Lumière archive in Lyon. In this way films were made and shown in almost every country by 1898 – just three years after the first cinema show in Paris.

Among the original Lumière cinematograph operators was the seventeen-year-old Francis Doublier, who is visible wearing a straw hat and riding a bicycle in the Lumière's very first film *Workers Leaving the Factory*. After visiting Madrid in 1895 to film a bullfight and giving Lumière shows in Brussels, Paris and Amsterdam, Doublier initiated film production in Russia on 14 May 1896 when he shot the coronation of Tsar Nicholas II. Two days later Doublier was present at a feudal ceremony at which the new Tsar was presented to his subjects. Doublier and his assistant, Moisson, set up their camera on the roof of an unfinished building near the Tsar's stand. What happened next was almost certainly the first instance of film censorship. Doublier recalled:

We arrived about eight o'clock in the morning because the ceremony was due to take most of the day, and the Tsar was to arrive early. When I saw some of the souvenirs being handed out ahead of time, I got down and pushed through the very dense crowd to the booths, about 150 feet away. On the way back, the crowd began to push, impatient with the delay and by the time I got within twenty-five feet of our camera, I heard shrieks behind me and panic spread through the people. I climbed on to a neighbour's shoulders and struggled across the top of the frightened mass. That twenty-five feet seemed like twenty-five miles, with the crowd underneath clutching desperately at my feet and biting my legs. When I finally reached the roof again, we were so nervous that we were neither able to guess the enormity of the tragedy nor to turn the camera crank. The light boarding over two large cisterns had given way, and into these and into the ditches near the booths hundreds had fallen, and in the panic thousands more had fallen and been trampled to death. When we came to our senses we began to film the horrible scene. We had brought only five or six of the sixty-foot rolls, and we used up three of these on the shrieking, milling, dying mass around the Tsar's canopy where we had expected to film a very different scene. I saw the police charging the crowd in an effort to stop the tidal wave of human beings. We were completely surrounded and it was only two hours later that we were able to think about leaving the place strewn with mangled bodies. Before we could get away the police spotted us, and added us to the bands of arrested correspondents and witnesses. All our equipment was confiscated and we never saw our precious camera again. Because of the camera we were particularly suspect, and we were questioned and detained until the evening of the same day, when the Consul vouched for us.

Source: Jay Leyda, *Kino: A History of Russian and Soviet Film*; George Allen and Unwin Ltd., London, 1960.

Boleslaw Matuszewski and the Documentary Idea

The Pole Boleslaw Matuszewski (1856 – 1929?) was almost certainly the first person to seriously consider and write about the *documentary* possibilities of cinema. As early as 1898 he suggested the foundation of a film archive for films of documentary importance.

Little is known of Matuszewski's life, but it seems his first contact with cinema was through the Lumière operation in St Petersburg. In January 1898 when the President of France visited Russia, Bismarck almost created an international incident by protesting that the Frenchman had failed to salute a march past in his honour. Matuszewski's film of the event proved otherwise and a diplomatic incident was averted.

The following extract is taken from Matuszewski's pamphlet *Une nouvelle source de l'histoire*, published in Paris in 1898.

Sir, allow me to call to your attention a project which is ready for implementation and which I would like to interest you in. It is about providing a suitable repository for a collection of cinematographic documents . . .

Inevitably restrained to begin with, this collection will expand rapidly as our curiosity about moving pictures goes beyond simple recreations of scenes and fantastical images, towards actions and spectacles with a documentary interest, and scenes of unusual individuals and events are replaced by animated photography of aspects of public or national life. The simple pastime of animated photography will then become an acceptable process for the study of the past, and moreover it will give it a clear view and will remove, at least on certain important points, the need to investigate or study.

Perhaps the cinematograph does not give the whole story, but at least what it gives is unquestionable and of an absolute truth. Ordinary photography allows retouching which can go as far as transformation, but try retouching in an identical way each shape on the thousands of almost microscopic plates! One can say that animated photography has an authentic character and a unique exactness and precision. It is the true eyewitness and is infallible. It can control oral tradition and if people contradict each other it can prove who is right and silence the liar. Let us imagine a military or naval manoeuvre each phase of which has been filmed by the cinematograph. A debate begins. It can soon be resolved. With a mathematical exactness it can give the distances between two scenes in view. Often it indicates very clearly the hour of the day, the season and the climactic conditions in which the event occurs. From the first far-off appearance on the horizon, it can capture the unnoticed movement of something as it moves to the point closest to the screen. In summary, one would wish that other historical documents could have the same degree of accuracy of evidence and certainty.

Source: Boleslaw Matuszewski's pamphlet *Une nouvelle source de l'histoire*, first published in Paris in 1898. Translated by Rachel Davison and Annalene Hursthouse.

Taking the Camera to War
ALBERT E. SMITH

Albert E. Smith and J. Stuart Blackton co-founded the *American Vitagraph Company* in New York in 1897. Originally the youthful pair merely showed Edison films as part of a Vaudeville act but soon Smith, a talented engineer, constructed his own camera and projector and they went into production.

In 1898 Smith and Blackton took their camera to Cuba to film the Spanish–American war. This was long thought to be the first occasion a moving picture camera was taken into battle, until it was recently discovered that the flamboyant English war correspondent Fredric Villiers got there first, taking shots of the Greco-Turkish war of 1897 and the battle of Omdurman in the Sudan the following year.

In his autobiography Smith recounts how difficult it was to get satisfactory shots of the fighting in Cuba and how, when they got back to New York, they realized that they had completely missed the biggest engagement of them all, the Battle of Santiago Bay.

Once in our office, we knew we were in trouble. Word had spread through New York that Vitagraph had taken pictures of the Battle of Santiago Bay! To caller after caller we said we had not developed any of the film, that we were not sure what we had, that it would be some time yet inasmuch as the film had to be processed in order. We sat down and looked at each other. How to get out of this one? Vitagraph, not too well off as things were, could ill-afford to reverse itself.

Blackton said we could fake a sea battle and I said he was insane, but as the minutes passed the idea got better and better. Why not?

At this time street vendors in New York were selling large sturdy photographs of ships of the American and Spanish fleets. We bought a set of each and we cut out the battleships. On a table, topside down, we placed one of artist Blackton's large canvas-covered frames and filled it with water an inch deep. In order to stand the cut-outs of the ships in the water, we nailed them to lengths of wood about an inch square. In this way a little 'shelf' was provided behind each ship, and on this shelf we placed pinches of gunpowder – three pinches for each ship – not too many, we felt, for a major sea engagement of this sort.

For a background, Blackton daubed a few white clouds on blue-tinted cardboard. To each of the ships, now sitting placidly in our shallow 'bay', we attached a fine thread to enable us to pull the ships past the camera at the proper moment and in the correct order.

We needed someone to blow smoke into the scene, but we couldn't go too far outside our circle if the secret was to be kept. Mrs Blackton was called in and she volunteered, in this day of non-smoking womanhood, to smoke a cigarette. A friendly office boy said he would try a cigar. This was fine, as we needed the volume.

A piece of cotton was dipped in alcohol and attached to a wire slender enough to escape the eye of the camera. Blackton, concealed behind the side of the table furthermost from the camera, touched off the mounds of gunpowder with his wire taper – and the battle was on. Mrs Blackton, smoking and coughing, delivered a fine haze. Jim had worked out a timing arrangement with her so that she blew the smoke into the scene at approximately the moment of explosion. Brave soul though she was, Mrs Blackton turned and fled with each blast of gunpowder. Jim waited until she returned, whereupon he would ignite another mound and Mrs Blackton would blow in the smoke, then flee. Consequently, the lapse between Mrs Blackton's flight and return made it impossible for Blackton to 'shoot' in rapid-fire order. We knew this was a serious compromise of the real battle, but it was hardly a time to weigh deceptions.

The boy on the other side of the table was not faring as well, the cigar quickly proving too much for him, though he held to his post in fine military fashion. Blackton was the busiest – setting off the powder, drawing one ship then another into the scene, and stirring up little waves.

It would be less than the truth to say we were not wildly excited at what we saw on the screen. The smoky overcast and the flashes of fire from the 'guns' gave the scene an atmosphere of remarkable realism. The film and the lenses of that day were imperfect enough to conceal the crudities of our miniature, and as the picture ran only two minutes there was not time for anyone to study it critically. Deception though it was then, it was the first miniature and the forerunner of the elaborate 'special effects' technique of modern picturemaking.

Pastor's and both Proctor houses played to capacity audiences for several weeks. Jim and I felt less and less remorse of conscience when we saw how much excitement and enthusiasm were aroused by *The Battle of Santiago Bay* and the thirty-minute-long *Fighting with Our Boys in Cuba*. Almost every newspaper in New York carried an account of the showings, commenting on Vitagraph's remarkable feat in obtaining on-the-spot pictures of these two historic events.

Source: *Two Reels and a Crank*, Doubleday and Company, Inc., Garden City, New York, 1952.

2 Going to Extremes

INTRODUCTION

Non-fiction films never regained the popularity they had during cinema's first decade, but, in one form or another, they continued to be produced in great quantities throughout the silent period.

Newsreels, devised by Pathé Frères in France in 1910 and rapidly imitated around the world, were the most ubiquitous, if least ambitious, non-fiction form. Essentially a development of the early 'topicals', they provided the often illiterate working classes with a palatable weekly dose of current affairs.

On the whole, however, audiences were no longer interested in seeing their own world reflected back at them, and heartily resisted films which had a mission to improve. A 'scenic' or 'educational' was often thrown in by a distributor as part of a film programme, but the money invested in them was limited and the public held them in contempt. In order to secure any sort of popular appeal, proto-documentary-makers were forced to film the extremes of human experience. That usually meant either going to war or travelling to exotic corners of the globe.

War footage had been a cinema staple since the Spanish-American conflict of 1898. Distributors had always understood the blend of morbid voyeurism and patriotism which made war films so popular, but it was only with the First World War that governments fully realized the propaganda value of cinema and supported the medium. In Britain the best of the resulting films included *Battle of the Somme*(1916) and *Sons of the Empire* (1917) and in Germany, *The Battle of Przemsyl*(1915) and *Germany and its Armies of Today* (1917). In France, *Paris in the Third Year of the War* (1917) was notable in not showing soldiers at all, but concentrating – with surprising realism – on the difficult living conditions on the home front.

First World War films were usually compilations, often utilizing old, irrelevant or downright fake footage. To a modern viewer much of the material is tedious: an endless round of marching troops, royal inspections and artillery firing at invisible targets. There is little or no sign of death, destruction and carnage – cameramen were forbidden by the military to take long lenses to the front and by all accounts what little combat footage they obtained was eliminated by the censors. Occasionally, there are spectacular moments, as in the 1918 German film *Kriegflieger an der Westfront* [*Fighter Pilots on the Western Front*] which – apart from an unexpected glimpse of Herman Goering in his days as an air ace – has an astonishing, perhaps unique, shot of a real dogfight in action, taken by an automatic camera perched on the German plane's wing.

Early travel-films fell into three approximate categories. Travelogues, invented and popularized by Burton Holmes, provided picturesque views of exotic climes and were often little more than the visual accompaniment to genteel lectures. The second category of travel films were the genuine ethnographic and expeditionary films. As early as 1901 the Baldwin–Spencer expedition in Australia took along a camera to record tribal rituals.

The final type of travel film was that made to record – and often ultimately to fund – amateur expeditions. At their worst these films were vulgar and self-serving, glorifying the dubious exploits of obtuse, solar-topee-clad westerners searching out adventure in the wilds of Africa or Asia, without the slightest interest in the local people or surroundings. Some amateur expeditionary films did, however, record remarkable adventures, from sailing down the length of the Yangtse river in 1909, to being shipwrecked on a cannibal island off Borneo.

But however good the raw material for early travel and war films could be, the film-makers rarely had a clear idea of how to shape it by shooting or editing. Neither lectures nor the fiction film offered a satisfactory model. Audiences wanted drama, tension and characters with whom they could empathize, but how could they find those in factual footage? Some travel film-makers attempted to satisfy the audience by having the 'natives' act out simple fictional plots, while retaining the 'authentic background'. The results were absurd – like crossing a Mary Pickford film with an ethnographic essay.

It was not until Robert Flaherty and *Nanook of the North* (1922) that a satisfactory synthesis was found. Flaherty adopted both the editing style and dramatic structure of the fiction film, while taking his characters and plot from the life of the Inuit Eskimos he was filming. Because Flaherty had known and lived with the Eskimos for years before he made his famous film, he understood and respected their culture, and perhaps most crucially, looked beyond cultural differences to a common humanity. The film may romanticize but it rarely patronizes.

Flaherty's film *Nanook* was not about the Great White Explorer, but about the fascinating way of life of an isolated people battling for survival against the elements. The central drama is: will they or will they not survive the harsh environment? Flaherty realized that if a scene was shot and edited like a fiction film, he could create tension and expectation around almost any process, from building an igloo to harpooning a walrus.

Ironically, in order to find its first really successful model, the documentary had to move further away from reality and adopt the dramatic and technical features of the fiction film.

A Woman at War
JESSICA BORTHWICKE

In 1913–1914 twenty-two year old Jessica Borthwicke spent a year in the Balkans filming the First and Second Balkan Wars.

After only three days of instruction from motion picture camera manufacturer Arthur Newman, and citing 'curiosity' as her motivation, Jessica Borthwicke set off for the front. This account of her adventures appeared in *The Bioscope*.

The difficulties of taking cinematograph pictures on the battlefield, especially when you are alone and unaided by any assistant, are, as you can imagine, tremendous. The use of a tripod is a particular embarrassment. Things happen so quickly in time of war that, unless one can be ready with one's camera at a few seconds' notice, the episode one wishes to record will probably be over. During the Serbian war in Macedonia, my tripod was smashed by a shell, and although the camera was intact, the film . . . got hopelessly jumbled up and had to be cut away from the mechanism.

Another great difficulty was the want of a darkroom. One day, while taking films in the Rhodope Mountains, I came to a strange village of wooden huts inhabited by a nomadic race called Vlaques. Something went wrong with my camera, and I tried to make the people understand that I wanted some place which would serve as a darkroom. It was impossible to get them to grasp what I meant, however, until eventually I found a man making rugs out of sheeps' wool. After much persuasion, I induced him to cover me up with his rugs, and in this unusual and very stuffy 'darkroom' I managed to open my camera in safety. Having no film box with me at the moment, I wrapped the negative up in pieces of paper and stowed it away in my pocket, carrying it thus for fifteen days until I returned to Sofia. Occupied with other matters, I forgot the film and handed my coat to a servant who, being of an inquisitive nature, unwrapped the negative, and finding it uninteresting, put it back in the pocket without the paper, afterwards hanging up the coat to air in the sun. Subsequently I developed the film – and found it one of the best I had.

The want of a technical dictionary, combined with the natives' ignorance of photography, brought about several rather amusing situations. On one occasion, in Adrianople, I lost a screw from my tripod. There were shops of most other kinds, but no ironmongers, and at last, in despair, I tried to explain to an officer what I wanted in dumb show, not knowing the word for 'screw'. Having followed my actions for some moments with apparent intelligence, he suddenly hailed a cab and bundled me hastily in. We drove right across the city, until eventually we entered some massive gates and drew up – inside the prison. However, I turned the misconception to advantage by securing some excellent snapshots and having some very interesting talks with the prisoners. One convict – a German of considerable education – invited me to go and see him hanged the next morning. I saw two executions in that prison.

During the cholera rage in Adrianople, everything connected with that terrible disease was painted black. The carts in which the dead bodies were carried away were black, for example, as were the coffins in which cholera victims were buried. While the scourge was at its height, I went down into the gypsy quarter to take a film. The people in this part of the city had never seen a camera before, and when they saw me pointing my black box at various objects they thought I was operating some wonderful new instrument for combating the disease which was destroying them. Quickly surrounding me, they came and knelt upon the ground, kissing my feet and clothing, and begging with dreadful pathos that I should cure them. It was a task as sad as it was difficult to explain that their hopes were mistaken, and that I was impotent to help them . . .

Sources: Kevin Brownlow, *The War, The West and The Wilderness*, Knopfler, New York, 1979. Original quotation From *The Bioscope*, 7 May 1914.

In the Land of the Head Hunters
EDWARD S. CURTIS

The American ethnographic photographer and writer Edward S. Curtis (1868–1952) is best remembered today for his stunning twenty-volume study of vanishing Indian culture, *The North American Indian*, published between 1907 and 1930. Less well known is that Curtis had ambitions as a film-maker, and in 1912 founded the Continental Film Company, with the intention of making a series of films to 'document' Indian tribal life. Ultimately, only one film in this projected series was completed: *In The Land of The Head Hunters* (1914), featuring the Kwakiutl Indians of the Pacific North-West.

Perhaps naïvely, Curtis hoped his films would both 'meet the demands of the scientists and students' and appeal to 'the masses, or those who are looking for amusement only'. Like Robert Flaherty's *Nanook* almost a decade later[1], *In The Land of The Head Hunters* is set in an idealized period before the white man's influence undermined traditional tribal life. It is a peculiar mixture of detailed anthropological reconstruction – using original costumes, rituals etc. – and a preposterous, Hollywood-style story.

This piece is from the Continental Film Company's prospectus, issued in 1913, and almost certainly penned by Curtis. It contains the first known use of the term 'documentary' in the English language – predating John Grierson by thirteen years.

The question might be raised as to whether the documentary material would not lack the thrilling interest of the fake picture. It is the opinion of Mr Curtis that the real life of the Indian contains the parallel emotions to furnish all necessary plots and give the pictures all the heart interest needed. In this respect it is as important that we take into consideration the Indian's mental processes as it is to picture his unique costume.

---

1 Flaherty saw *In The Land of Head Hunters* in New York in 1915. It almost certainly influenced his film-making ideas.

To do the work in a way creditable to the subject and to the nation would require a vigorously conducted campaign covering a period of five to fifteen years, this presumably to include Central and South America. All pictures made should be classed among the educational, and should be preserved as a part of the documentary material of the country. It is needless to say that such a collection of material would be an important national asset, and would from the beginning have the encouragement of every educational institution.

In making such pictures, the greatest care must be exercised that the thought conveyed be true to the subject, that the ceremony be correctly rendered, and above all, that the costumes be correct. It must be admitted that the making of such a series of pictures would be the most difficult thing attempted in motion photography, but it can be done, and will be one of the most valuable documentary works which can be taken up at this time.

The Indians and the Indian life do now and will for all time furnish an important part of the literature, art, and drama of our country.

As to motion pictures and their bearing on the subject, it is safe to say that properly produced under proper and permanent arrangement, they can be made of more importance than books or printed illustrations.

Source: A prospectus for the Continental Film Company issued in 1913, reproduced in *Edward S. Curtis* by Holm and Quimby.

Pancho Villa Fights for the Camera
TERRY RAMSAYE

This piece, on the celebrated Mexican revolutionary Pancho Villa's yearning for movie stardom, is from Terry Ramsaye's ground-breaking film history *A Million and One Nights*.

Villa, like every military conqueror, was a dramatist. It was the physical excitement and emotion of war which lured him on. Modern wars are won by book-keeping and the strategy of maps on flat-top desks. But Villa's generalship was of the feudal age, when valor was efficiency. Villa rode to battle and conquest because he loved the vision of himself on horseback.

And Villa ahorseback, in consequence of his propaganda of glory, became a figure of striking dramatic interest in the motion picture. Never of the slightest importance to the screen, he lighted it for a moment with the flare of his ambition. He did not, after all, tell the world of the glories of the great Pancho, but he tried.

The year of 1914 had just dawned when agents of Villa in El Paso on the border let it be known that the conquistador could be approached for the motion picture rights of his war.

The Kings of Babylon graved their conquest of the Hittites in tablets of stone. Trajan had his column, and Pancho Villa would inscribe his glories in the living shadows of the screen and let the theatre proscenium be his Arc de Triomphe. Meanwhile, in an immediately practical sense, pictures of the success of Villa would make Villa more powerful in taking tribute of those foreign interests which could use the friendship of an Mexican government whatsoever.

The El Paso representatives of a number of motion picture concerns sent wires away to their home offices in New York. New York home offices in the motion picture industry usually let telegrams from such inconsequential persons as El Paso branch exchange managers ripen on the desk. Fate, however, entered.

And Harry E. Aitken, president of the Mutual Film Corporation, read his mail and messages that morning. There was an appeal to the ever-glowing imagination of Aitken in this daring idea. Saturday, 3 January 1914, Frank M. Thayer, acting for the Mutual Film Corporation, signed a contract with Villa in Juarez, taking over the screen rights to the Villa version of the salvation of Mexico by torch and Mauser. It was agreed that Villa was to fight his battles as much by photographic daylight as possible. He was to share on a percentage basis the earnings of his pictures. He received in hand pay, in most excellent gringo money, $25,000.

. . . Villa delayed his projected attack on the city of Ojinaga until the Mutual could bring up its photographic artillery. When the cameras had consolidated their position the offensive swept forward and Ojinaga fell to Villa and film.

When the pictures reached New York they were found to contain too much Villa and not enough war. The films were shown in the Mutual Film Corporation's projection room to various officials. Francisco Madero, Sr., the aged father of the murdered president of Mexico, was in the audience that 22 January 1914 exiled from his home.

When the victorious Villa rode, close-up, through the streets of

Ojinaga, a handsome young officer was at his side. The elder Madero leaped to his feet and shouted his name, 'Raoul! Raoul!' The motion picture had discovered for him his missing son. Raoul Madero was now riding to vengeance for family, in the rebel army.

Down through Mexico with Villa the Mutual's special camera cars travelled on the military trains, bearing to the peons the trademark message, 'Mutual Movies Make Time Fly.' Villa became one of the worst of that genus described in camera vernacular as a 'lens louse'. He had to be photographed riding at the head of a column every little while whether he needed it or not. Villa was not one of those controlled souls who can take it or leave it alone. This waste of film annoyed one photographer into an expedient of cranking an empty machine. 'I fooled the greaser that time – there's no film in the old box,' he remarked to his assistant. He was overheard by a Mexican who understood Americanese. The cameraman was put over the border with a blessing and advice that afternoon.

It probably would have been pleasanter to Villa to have shot the cameraman, but Villa was interested in the film business now. Business forces many good men into compromises like that.

For the benefit of the films Villa staged an excellent shelling scene with a battery of light field guns. The picture went from close-ups of the guns to telephoto long shots of the hillside under fire, with the bodies of men flying in the air after the shell bursts. The ugly rumor got about that the hills had been planted with otherwise useless prisoners as properties.

But the evidence of the films is not to be accepted entirely for that. After the battle of Torreon it became apparent that the war needed a director and a scenario writer. H.E. Aitken discovered then what others have spent a great deal to learn since, that the best place to make war pictures is on the studio lot. Aitken went south, and on 10 March returned from Juarez with a new contract for the making of *The Life of Villa*, as per a good snappy New York scenario.

Source: Terry Ramsaye, *A Million And One Nights: A History of the Motion Picture*, Simon and Schuster, New York, 1926.

The Worst Location in The World: Herbert G. Ponting in the
Antarctic
DENNIS LYNCH

Herbert G. Ponting's life (1870–1935) was never the same again after he
answered the advertisement for a photographer and cinematographer to
accompany Captain Scott on his fatal expedition to the South Pole. Until
his dying day, this mild-mannered man was driven by a peculiar cocktail

3 *Herbert Ponting's photograph of Captain Scott's ship,* The Endeavour *(1911).*

of obsession, duty and bitterness to keep Scott's memory alive, editing
and re-editing the remarkable footage he had shot during his two years
in the Antarctic into at least three major films between 1912 and 1933.

Although a seasoned still photographer and travel writer, Ponting had
absolutely no experience with moving pictures before he joined Scott.
Nevertheless, and despite the often difficult conditions in which he had
to work, his material is technically immaculate and frequently breath-

**takingly beautiful. No other expeditionary film-maker of the period
came close to matching Ponting's camerawork.**

The expedition sailed to Antarctica. Ponting did not get off to a good
start. He was seasick on the way out. Scott wrote that Ponting 'posed
several groups before the cinematograph, though obliged repeatedly to
retire to the ship's side. Yesterday he was developing plates with the
developing dish in one hand and an ordinary basin in the other.' He
made many shots of the ship, the crew, and the scenery. The angles from
which they were taken showed that Ponting continued to risk life and
limb for an expressive picture.

The most thrilling and commented-on film scene was taken from an
elaborate perch rigged over the side of the ship, where Ponting cranked
with one hand and held on for dear life with the other, and which
showed the bow of the *Terra Nova* breaking through the pack-ice. The
shot has been copied in many other films. One story must illustrate the
zeal and panache Ponting – this British clubman honed in the far
western United States – brought to his art. In sticky situations, when it
seemed to be a matter of saving himself or his kit, Ponting reflected,
significantly, that 'without my cameras I was helpless' and managed to
save both. One of Ponting's serious close calls in the Antarctic was with
a pack of killer whales. Ponting narrated the story. (Fantastic as it is, it is
corroborated by Scott.):

'The whales dived under the ice, so, hastily estimating where they
would be likely to rise again, I ran to the spot . . . I had got to within
six feet of the edge of the ice . . . when, to my consternation, it
suddenly heaved up under my feet and split into fragments around me;
whilst . . . the eight whales . . . burst from under the ice and 'spouted'
. . . They made a tremendous commotion, setting the floe in which I
was now isolated rocking furiously . . . Then they turned about with
the deliberate intention of attacking me . . . I wondered whether I
should be able to reach safety before the whales reached me; and I
recollect distinctly thinking, if they did get me, how very unpleasant the
first bite would feel, but that it would not matter much about the
second.'

Even Ponting thought he sometimes went too far. 'Several times I fell
through [the ice] up to my middle,' he wrote, and he felt that swift tidal
current pulling at him. 'In looking backwards I sometimes shudder at
the risks I took so recklessly in those early days, not knowing the

imminence of the dangers, which a year in those regions taught me to hold in greater respect.'

Whales aside, the technical difficulties of photography in the Antarctic are formidable today and were more so in 1910. The low temperatures – 100 degrees of frost – meant that film was so brittle it broke, that equipment had to be operated with thick gloves, and that if you took off your gloves, your skin froze to the metal.

'To so much as breathe upon a lens in the open air was to render that lens useless, for it instantly became covered with a film of ice which could not be removed. It had to be brought into warm air, and thawed off, then wiped dry.'

Source: 'H.G. Ponting in the Antarctic, 1910–1912' by Dennis Lynch, in *Film History*, 1989, Vol. 3.

Genuine War Films
W. STEPHEN BUSH AND CAPTAIN F.E. KLEINSCHMIDT

Captain F.E. Kleinschmidt was a professional explorer and adventurer who made his first film while leading the 1909–11 Carnegie Museum expedition to Alaska and Siberia.

In 1914 Kleinschmidt set out for Europe to film the Great War, obtaining some spectacular footage, mostly of the German side, which he eventually edited into *War on Three Fronts* (1916). When America entered the war the film was condemned as enemy propaganda and withdrawn from circulation. D.W. Griffith then bought the material for $60,000, planning to incorporate it into his semi-documentary feature *Hearts of the War*. But very little of it was ever used and Kleinschmidt's original film has vanished without trace.

The following letter from Kleinschmidt was sent to the journalist W. Stephen Bush of *The Moving Picture World* in August 1914. The explanatory comments are Bush's.

The Captain writes: 'Upon my arrival at the Great Headquarters of the Austrian Army I was invited by the Crown Prince to give a lecture on my last Arctic expedition and show my moving pictures to the officers of the general staff. The Archduke, Field Marshal Frederick, highest commanding officer, his wife, daughters and all generals and officers were present. This lecture gave me the magic key that unlocked all doors and gave me privileges and opportunities to accomplish things.'

Hardly ever before in the history of filmdom has a cameraman travelled in the *style de luxe* enjoyed by the captain. He was provided with a high officer who acted as his guide, then he was fitted with two military servants, who attended all the personal comforts of the captain and who soon learned to pack and set up the camera.

That the captain is in the best of spirits and making full use of his opportunities may be taken for granted. He speaks of 'Austrian hospitality and the Austrian readiness to help and favor you', and compares them to the aid and the hospitality he found 'on our own frontiers and the prospectors in their cabins and on the trail in Alaska.' They have not fought any battles for the special benefit of his camera, but they were willing to go to great lengths in order to oblige. 'Last week,' the captain writes, 'while I was in the foremost trenches and took pictures of the Russian trenches only three hundred yards away, a whole battery was ordered to cover the Russian trenches with shrapnel to enable me to take the pictures of the exploding bombs. Troops of cavalry have been alarmed for me, flyers have taken me up to take pictures from above: in fact everything has been done for me that could possibly be done, even the huge siege mortars that destroyed the forts of Antwerp, Liege and Namur were ordered to be set in motion for me, although even one single shot costs a pretty sum of money. One might think that I have taken pictures of about everything that could possibly happen, but every day a new feature comes up and I believe I can stay with the work during the entire war and not duplicate much.'

With ample facilities afforded to him, Captain Kleinschmidt feels that he can put a good deal of order and system into his war films. He believes in showing every stage of movement in the three great arms: infantry, cavalry and artillery. 'The great siege mortars,' he says, 'I have from the caves where the ammunition is stored to the loading, sighting and firing of the gun; then the ascension of the captive balloon and the observation of the hitting and exploding of the projectile from the basket or by pictures taken from above in flying machines. The cavalry I have taken from saddling to the charge, and the infantry from where they emerge from their underground dwellings, jump to their arms and run to the trenches opposite. I have stood on an eminence and taken panoramic views of a battlefield and a battle in progress, that will be highly interesting, especially to the American public. A modern battle-field really shows little or nothing, and the real scenes are diametrically opposed to the usual 'posed battle' scenes with which our public has been regaled so much. In real life a man who has been hit by a bullet does not throw up his hands and rifle and then fall in a theatrical fashion and roll a few times over. When he lies in the trenches and is hit, he barely lurches a few inches forward or quietly turns over on his side. The real picture is not as dramatic as the fake picture, but I believe the realization of the grimness of the genuine will grip the beholder far more than the fake, just as you can see far better animal pictures that were taken in the Zoo or in animal parks than mine taken in the wilderness, but the public appreciated the difference . . .'

Source: *The Moving Picture World*, 14 August 1915.

Filming Death
BÉLA BALÁZS

Béla Balázs (1884–1949) the Hungarian-born screenwriter, librettist and director, wrote the following piece on the development of war documentaries in his ground-breaking critical study *The Theory of Film*(1945).

What concerns us here are not open-air photographs of thousands of guns, flying armadas or bursting bombs and shells but what is at the root of it all, the human face, which only the film camera can approach so intimately.

In general war films are as primitive and brutal as is war itself. For this reason only one war film is to be mentioned here. Its artistic and moral message is such that it is worthy of being preserved forever in some Pantheon of greatest human documents.

This film was made after the First World War and its title was *Pour La Paix du Monde*. It was produced by the French organization of the most grievously injured of all war-wounded, the name of which was '*Les Gueules Cassés*'. The director who compiled the film from the strips in the archives of the armed forces was Colonel Piquard, chairman of the organization of the 'Faceless Ones', the men who lived like lepers in an isolated, secret community of their own, because the sight of them would have been unbearable for their fellow-men. The film begins by showing these faceless ones in close-up, their mutilations covered by masks. Then they take off their silken masks and with it they tear the mask off the face of war.

Those whom the war has robbed of their faces show the true face of war to those who know nothing of it. And this physiognomy of war is of an emotional power, a force of pathos no artistic feature film about the war had ever attained. For here war is presented by its victims, horror is presented by the horrified, torture by the tortured, deadly peril by those endangered – and it is they who see these things in their true colours. A panning shot glides over a quiet, a now quietened battlefield. The desolation of a lunar landscape. Nowhere a single blade of grass. On the mountainside gunfire has peeled the earth from the naked rock. Shell craters, trenches without end. The camera pans slowly round without stopping. Trenches full of dead bodies, more trenches and more and more and more. An immense space in which nothing moves. Corpses, corpses, only corpses. Panorama. This stolid monotony which takes hold of you and will not let go is like a long-drawn, desperate howling.

Here is another shot: a whole regiment blinded by poison gas is being driven through the streets of burning Bruges. Yes, the herd of blind men is being driven like a herd of sheep, herded with bayonet and butt to keep them from running into the burning ruins in their path. A picture for another Dante.

But there are worse things, although no human beings appear. The gardens of the Champagne after the German retreat. (It was not in the Second World War that the Germans invented some of their methods.) We see a charnel-house of an ancient and lovely orchard culture. Thousands of precious, noble fruit-trees neatly sawed off by power-saw, all exactly at the same height. The creation of centuries of skill and industry destroyed with machine-like accuracy. These pictures, too, have a physiognomy; the distorted faces of the tree-corpses are no less terrible than those of the human dead. But the caption to this, of course silent, shot was not: 'Behold the German barbarian!' It said *'C'est la guerre!'* The noble faith of French peace-lovers did not blame the Germans even here, it blamed war. Nevertheless, under the Weimar Republic the showing of this film was banned in Germany.

This French documentary of the First World War was dedicated to the six cameramen who had been killed on active service while shooting it.

The Soviet war film showing the conquest of Berlin names in its credits fourteen cameramen killed while shooting it. This fate of the creative artist is also a new phenomenon in cultural history and is specific to film art. Artists in olden days rarely died of their dangerous creative work And this has not merely a moral or political significance, but is of importance for the psychology of art as well.

This presentation of reality by means of motion pictures differs essentially from all other modes of presentation in that the reality being presented is not yet completed; it is itself still in the making while the presentation is being prepared. The creative artist does not need to dip into his memory and recall what has happened – he is present at the happening itself and participates in it.

When someone tells about past battles, these battles are already over and the greatest perils are no longer perils, once they are past and can be told by word of mouth or print.

The camera image is different. It is not made after the event. The cameraman is himself in the dangerous situation we see in his shot and it is by no means certain that he will survive the birth of his picture. Until the strip has been run to its end we cannot know whether it will be completed at all. It is this tangible being-present that gives the documentary the peculiar tension no other art can produce.

Whoever has listened to a report given over a field telephone, when the noise of battle, the rattle of shots and the screams of the wounded can be heard together with the words spoken into the microphone, will have experienced this tension in the acoustic sphere. Such telephone reports sometimes break off in the middle of a sentence and the silence that follows is as eloquent as a scream of mortal agony.

In the French war film just discussed, a sequence suddenly breaks off. It darkens and the camera wobbles. It is like an eye glazing in death. The director did not cut out this 'spoilt' bit – it shows where the camera was overturned and the cameraman killed, while the automatic mechanism ran on. In another picture we see the cameraman dying for the sake of his picture.

The significance of such shots lies not in the death-despising courage to which they bear witness. We have often heard of men who could look death in the eye. We may even have seen them. What is new and different here is that these cameramen look death in the face through the lens of a movie picture camera. This happens not only on battlefields.

Who could forget Captain Scott's film, which is almost as if he had shot his own death and breathed his last sigh into a microphone.

Who could forget Sir Ernest Shackleton's magnificent pictures of his Antarctic journey or the film taken by the Soviet Polar explorers camping beside the wreck of the ice-breaker *Chelyuskin*?

Yes, it is a new form of human consciousness that was born out of the union of man and camera. For as long as these men do not lose consciousness, their eye looks through the lens and reports and renders conscious their situation. The ice crushes their ship and with it their last hope? They shoot. The ice-floe melts under their feet? They shoot. They shoot the fact that there is scarcely room left for them to set up the camera.

Like the captain on his bridge, like the wireless operator at his set, the cameraman remains at his post to the last instant. The internal processes of presence of mind and observation are here projected outwards into the bodily action of operating the camera. The operator sees clearly and calmly as long as he is shooting in this way; it is this that helps him mechanically to preserve his consciousness, which in other circumstances consists of a sequence of images in the mind. But now it is projected outwards and runs in the camera as a strip of film, which is of advantage because the camera has no nerves and therefore is not easily perturbed. The psychological process is inverted – the cameraman does not shoot as long as he is conscious – he is conscious as long as he is shooting.

Source: Béla Balázs, *Theory of the Film*, Dennis Dobson Ltd., London, 1952. Originally published in Moscow in 1945.

Lowell Thomas and 'Lawrence of Arabia'
KEVIN BROWNLOW

T. E. Lawrence was probably the first public figure made famous by motion pictures. His Arabian exploits were unknown to the general public until the American journalist, broadcaster and academic Lowell Thomas released his lecture film *With Lawrence in Arabia* (1919). Overnight – much to his annoyance – Lawrence became a celebrity.

This piece is excerpted from Kevin Brownlow's seminal book on early non-fiction cinema, *The War, The West and The Wilderness*.

T. E. Lawrence was the most enigmatic figure of his time, and his exploits are clouded by romance. This handsome, twenty-nine-year-old colonel dressed in Arab robes and swept through the desert on a camel at the head of an Arab army, dynamiting Turkish troop trains. Recommended for almost every award the Allies had to offer, including the Victoria Cross, Lawrence shrank into the background. He was petrified by publicity. 'We saw considerable of Colonel Lawrence in Arabia,' explained Thomas, 'and although he arranged for us to get both still and motion pictures of Emir Feisal, Auda Abu Tayi and other Arab leaders, he would turn away when he saw the lens pointing in his direction. We got more pictures of the back of his kuffieh than of his face. But after much strategy, and using all the artifices that I had learned as a reporter on a Chicago newspaper, where it was worth one's job to fail to bring back a photograph of the fair lady involved in the latest scandal, I finally manoeuvred Lawrence into allowing Chase to take a 'sitting shot' on two different occasions. Then, while I kept Colonel Lawrence's attention away from Mr Chase by keeping up a rapid fire of questioning regarding our projected trip to the 'lost city' of Petra, which he believed to be the primary object of our visit to Arabia, Mr Chase hurriedly took a dozen pictures from as many different angles.'

. . . 'Shortly after Christmas 1919, I returned to America. But when a war ends people are searching for escape, and they want entertainment. They are not at all interested in hearing about the tragic days through which they have so recently lived. But I had a vast mass of material; what was I to do with it? Being young and somewhat naïve, I went ahead and launched myself in New York at what was then the largest theater in Manhattan. Theater managers and owners were not a bit interested; nor were the heads of the motion picture companies. To them I was neither fish nor fowl. Therefore, I had to raise enough capital to rent a theater, and go it alone. All of which turned out to be quite an adventure.

'I had a series of five film productions; one of the American army in Europe, one on the Italian campaign, another entitled *With Allenby in Palestine*, one that I called *With Lawrence in Arabia*, and *The German Revolution*. I soon discovered the public wasn't interested in the first two, but when I put on either my Allenby or my Lawrence show, I had packed houses. There were several reasons for this; Americans have always been interested in the Holy Land, and they had heard almost nothing about Allenby's campaign. Also, those productions included biblical places, camels, veiled women, palm trees, Jerusalem, Bethlehem, deserts, Arabs, cavalry charges – and the story of a mysterious young hero named T. E. Lawrence, of whom no one had heard a word until I came back from the Near East.

'I had such a surprising success with these two shows that we finally moved from the huge Century Theater to the even more vast Madison Square Garden, one of the largest places of entertainment in America. On my final night, a famous British impresario, Percy Burton, dropped in. He had managed such famous stars as Sarah Bernhardt, Sir Johnston Forbes-Robertson, and Sir Herbert Beerbohm Tree. Impresario Burton just happened to hear me on my final night at Madison Square Garden. If he hadn't done so, who knows what my future might have been? He was stunned at what he saw and heard. Here I, an American, was telling a story about a great British hero, Lawrence of Arabia, of whose name he hadn't even heard. Right away he saw possibilities, and determined to lure me to London. However, I said that was impossible. Because of my New York success, by then I had booked myself on a tour of the USA from coast to coast, with deposits made on a series of dates.

'But as we talked it over, I jokingly said that maybe I could make a quick trip to London just for part of July and August. In those days, there was no air-conditioning in auditoriums, and theaters in American cities closed down during the hot weather. For those few weeks, if he wanted me to do so, why I could go to London – but only if he would put me on in the most famous theater in the English speaking world. Also if he would get an invitation from the King. I was just pulling his leg.

'Burton hurried over to London, and soon wired me he had succeeded in getting the invitation from the King. As for Drury Lane, it was booked, but he could get Covent Garden.

'When I left New York, I figured it would be impossible for either of us to make any money. I wouldn't be in London long enough. So I decided to do some experimenting. First, I combined my two productions, the one on Allenby and the one of Lawrence, and made them one show with an interval between. I also cabled Burton to line up the finest musical organization in the British Isles, which he did in style. He hired the Band of the Royal Welsh Guards. In their bright scarlet uniforms, we put them on the stage for twenty minutes, while the audience was coming in. Then they were shifted to the pit, where for another ten minutes they played atmospheric eastern music that my wife had arranged. When the lights went out something else happened that had never been done before. You remember a spectacular film called *The Covered Wagon*? They copied the thing we did with our Allenby-Lawrence show, when we launched it at the Royal Opera House, Covent Garden, and for some time after that, many feature pictures copied our 'live prologue' idea.

'When I made my entrance, it was not in the usual way. There was no chairman saying, as was usual in lectures, "Ladies and Gentlemen, we have with us tonight . . . " I merely stepped out into the spotlight and said, "Come with me to lands of history, mystery, and romance." These words were spoken as the first scene appeared on the screen. I told the story of the Palestine and Arabian campaigns with each sentence beginning just a split second before each scene came on – so the sound of my voice would reach the audience simultaneously with the picture. The Guardsmen played softly in the background, but whenever there was a scene that needed something special they would produce it – charging cavalry, grunting of camels, and so on.

'For our opening night Burton had filled the boxes and the main floor with the most distinguished audience that had been assembled in London since before World War One.

'The following day, the London newspapers reviewed it in an unprecedented way by publishing their reviews on the first page. It finally dawned on me that we were enjoying an unexpected and fabulous success. In the days that followed, I would occasionally walk down to Covent Garden around nine a.m. to have a chat with Burton, pick up the mail, and so on. There I would find hundreds of people sitting on camp stools, where they sat until evening, just to get the less expensive seats. Members of the Royal Family paid us a visit – separately. One night David Lloyd George sent word that he was coming, accompanied by several members of his cabinet, one of whom turned out to be a rather cherubic-looking dignitary by the name of Winston Churchill. Parliament was sitting at night; as a consequence, the Commons actually gave the Prime Minister a vote of 'no confidence', on the grounds that he should have been in Parliament and not at Covent Garden listening to me. So, as a result of the Prime Minister's visit, you can imagine all the publicity.'

One unpublicized visit was that of Lawrence himself. He had

disappeared from public view, but a note was received in character-istically cryptic style:

> My dear Lowell Thomas:
>
> I saw your show last night. And thank God the lights were out!
>
> T. E. Lawrence

Lawrence wrote to his mother: 'We went to a Covent Garden entertainment yesterday. Lowell Thomas had asked us to accept a box. I had a very enthusiastic reception, and was often vociferously cheered by the entire house.'

A few days later, Lawrence came to tea and implored Lowell Thomas to stop glorifying his exploits. The Covent Garden show had wrecked his life, and he was hounded by women, reporters, and autograph-hunters. When Lawrence learned that the lectures were being extended, he fled from London.

Source: Kevin Brownlow, *The War, The West and The Wilderness*, Knopfler, New York, 1979.

Robert Flaherty Talking

There are many reasons for *Nanook of the North*'s power and originality: it depicts human beings and their relations with an honesty never seen before on the screen; it records those human beings in their own natural surroundings; there is no acting – at least none that would have been recognizable as such then. Most of all, the triumph of *Nanook* is that it found drama in the seemingly domestic, and synthesized the travelogue/expeditionary film with the narrative techniques of the fiction film.

This piece is from an interview Flaherty gave in 1950.

You ask me how I came to use movie at all. Well, I first used it on one of my expeditions in the North, the purpose of which was exploration – mining exploration. It was suggested by my principal that I take with me a motion picture camera. I was eager to do this, but the only thought I had in connection with the use of the motion picture camera was to

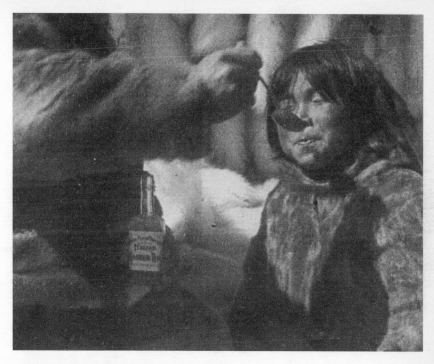

4 Nanook of the North (1922).

compile visual notes of the exploration, that is, notes about the people, who happened to be Eskimos, their life and habits as I saw them, and also scenes of the country and of the kind of territory we were exploring.

Some time after this expedition returned to civilization – we were away for a year and a half – I took up the matter of the film I had shot. I was getting it together in Toronto to ship to New York when carelessly, amateur that I was, I dropped a cigarette off the table in the little room where the film happened to be. It caught fire and some 70,000 feet of negative went up in a flash of flame.

However, there was an edited print of the negative that escaped the fire. I took this to New York in the forlorn hope that we might be able to dupe it, but in those days duping was almost impossible. I showed it to the American Geographical Society and then realized just how bad it was. It was utterly inept, simply a scene of this and a scene of that, no relation, no thread of a story or continuity what ever, and it must have bored the audience to distraction. Certainly it bored me.

My wife and I thought it over for a long time. At last we realized why the film was bad, and we began to get a glimmer that perhaps if I went back to the North, where I had lived for ten years and knew the people intimately, I could make a film that this time would go. Why not take, we said to each other, a typical Eskimo and his family and make a biography of their lives through a year. What biography of any man could be more interesting? Here is a man who has less resources than any other man in the world. He lives in a desolation that no other race could possibly survive. His life is a constant fight against starvation. Nothing grows; he must depend utterly on what he can kill; and all this against the most terrifying of tyrants – the bitter climate of the North, the bitterest climate in the world. Surely this story could be interesting.

It took several years before I could persuade anyone to finance such a film, for none of the picture people would listen to our idea. Who wanted to see a picture of people so utterly crude as the Eskimo? But finally Revillon Frères, the great fur company of Paris, who then were extending their trade in the far North, said they would finance it. I could go up to one of their posts on the eastern coast of Hudson Bay, take a camera with me, live there for a year and make the film.

It took two months by canoe and schooner to get to my destination, Revillon Frères' little post called Port Harrison, on north-east Hudson Bay. I took with me two Akeley motion picture cameras. The Akeley then was the best camera to operate in extreme cold, since it required the minimum of grease and oil for lubrication. These cameras fascinated me because they were the first cameras ever made to have a gyro movement in the tripod head whereby one could pan and tilt the camera without the slightest distracting jar or jerk or vibration. I have used this gyro type of tripod ever since in all my pictures. I think I was, perhaps, the pioneer in its use. I know that if at that time in Hollywood the cameraman panned his camera the studio would more often than not throw out the scene, because the pans being jerky would be too distracting on the screen.

I also took with me the materials and chemicals to develop the film, and equipment to print and project it. My lighting equipment had to be extremely light because I had to go by canoe nearly two hundred miles down river before I got to Hudson Bay. This meant portages, and portages meant packing the equipment on my back and on those of the Indians I took along for the river trip. And God knows there were some long portages on that route – one of them took us two days to pack across.

The Eastman Kodak Company arranged my developing equipment for me and, in fact, showed me how to develop film. I spent some several weeks with them for that purpose and they spared no effort to start me off in the right way. My printing machine was an old English Williamson Printer that screwed to the wall. I soon found when printing the film by the printer that the light from my little electric plant fluctuated too much; so I abandoned electric light and used daylight instead by letting in an inlet of light just the size of a motion picture frame through the window, and I controlled this daylight by adding or taking away pieces of muslin from before the printing aperture of the printer.

The greatest problem was not, however, printing the film or developing it, but washing it and drying it. I had to build an annex to the hut in which I wintered to make a drying room, and the only heating I could secure for this drying room was a stove that burned soft coal! Not only that, but I found that I ran short of lumber and didn't have enough to complete the drying reel that I set up in the room. So my Eskimos had to scour the sea-coast and finally pick up enough driftwood to complete its construction.

The washing of the film was the worst of all. My Eskimos had to keep a hole chiselled through six feet of ice all through the winter and then haul the water in barrels on a sledge with an Eskimo dog-team up to my hut, and there we all with our hands cleared out the ice from the water and poured it for the necessary washes over the film. I remember the deer hair falling off the Eskimos' clothing bothered me almost as much as the ice did.

It has always been most important for me to see my rushes – it is the only way I can make a film. But another reason for developing the film in the North was to project it to the Eskimos so that they would accept and understand what I was doing and work together with me as partners.

They were amazed when I first came with all this equipment, and they would ask me what I was going to do. When I told them that I had come to spend a year amongst them to make a film of them – pictures in which they moved – they roared with laughter. To begin with, some of my Eskimos could not even read a still photograph. I made stills of several of them as preliminary tests. When I showed them the photograph as often as not they would look at it upside down. I'd have to take the photograph out of their hands and lead them to the mirror in my hut, then have them look at themselves and the photograph beside their heads before, suddenly with a smile that spread from ear to ear, they would understand.

As luck would have it the first scene we shot for the film was of a tug-of-war with walrus. When I developed and printed the scenes and was ready to project them I wondered if the Eskimos would be able to understand them. What would these flickering scenes projected on a Hudson Bay blanket hung up on the wall of the hut mean to them? When at last I told them I was ready to begin the show, they crammed my little fifteen by twenty hut to the point of suffocation. I started up the little electric light plant, turned out the lights in the room, turned on the switch on the projector. A beam of light shot out, filled the blanket, and the show began. At first they kept looking back at the source of the light in the projector as much as they did at the screen. I was sure the show would flop, when suddenly someone shouted, 'Iviuk! (Walrus!)' There they were – a school of them – lying basking on the beach. In the foreground could be seen Nanook and his crew, harpoon in hand, stalking on their bellies toward them. Suddenly the walrus take alarm; they begin to tumble into the water. There was one agonizing shriek from the audience, until Nanook leaping to his feet thrust his harpoon. In the tug-of-war that ensued between the walrus now in the water and Nanook and his men holding desperately to the harpoon line, pandemonium broke loose; every last man, woman and child in the room was fighting that walrus, no surer than Nanook was at the time that the walrus would not get away. 'Hold him!' they would yell, 'Hold him! – Hold him!'

From that day on there was nothing Nanook and the crew would not do for me; Nanook was constantly thinking up new hunting scenes for the film. There was one scene in particular that became an obsession with him. There was a place far in the North, he said, that he knew about, where the she-bear dens in the winter while she gives birth to her cubs. 'That would make a picture,' said he. 'You know it is not hard to find the den of a she-bear which is deep under big drifts of snow, for there is always a vent from which a little steam which is the body heat of the bear rises out into the cold air. The dogs will smell this, and while you are getting your camera ready I'll crawl up to it on hands and knees with my harpoon and with my snow knife I will begin to cut the snow away. Of course, when I have made a hole big enough the she-bear will rush out, and she will be very angry when I do this. But then one of my men will have unleashed the dogs and they will make a circle around her, and then when you signal I will launch my harpoon. There will be lots of fighting,' Nanook went on to say, 'between the dogs and the she-bear as they run in on her. Sometimes she will throw the dogs high up in the air and they will turn around many times in the air before they land on their feet again. Now do you think that will make a good scene?' he would ask. Well, to make a long story short, that bear hunt took fifty-five days of travelling in the dead of winter and covered 600 miles over the sea-ice going and coming. And not an inch of film! For the conditions of the ice were so bad that Nanook couldn't kill seal. After losing two dogs by starvation we did finally get back, but we were lucky to get back alive.

When I got back to New York it took the better part of a winter to edit the film. When it was ready to be shown I started to make the rounds of the distributors in New York with the hope that one of them would be kind and give it distribution. Naturally I took it to the biggest of the distributors first. This was Paramount. The projection room was filled with their staff and it was blue with smoke before the film was over. When the film ended they all pulled themselves together and got up in a rather dull way, I thought, and silently left the room. The manager came up to me and very kindly put his arm around my shoulders and told me that he was terribly sorry, but it was a film that just couldn't be shown to the public. He said he had tried to do such things before and they had always ended in failure. He was very sorry indeed that I had gone through all that hardship in the North only to come to such an end, but that he felt he had to tell me, and that was that.

So then I went to the next biggest company in order of its importance, and they didn't even answer the phone to me after seeing the film. I had to go humbly to the projecting room and ask to be allowed to take the film away.

One day I showed it to Pathé Frères who were then much larger distributors of film than they are today. Like Revillon Frères, Pathé were a French firm, and blood being thicker than water, thought I, here might be a chance to do something. Pathé looked at the film; they thought it was interesting but that it could never run as a feature – it should be broken up into a series of educational shorts. But a few days later I had occasion to run the film again at the Pathé projection rooms. Mme Brunet, the wife of the president of the company was there, and also an old friend of mine, a journalist, who was with the company, the only one of the company who wanted to see it again. Well, they caught fire! And gradually the enthusiasm of the Pathé people built up until finally they decided to take the film on and do their best to distribute it as a feature.

The problem then was to get one of the big theatres to show it. Now the biggest theatre in New York then was the Capitol, run by a great film exhibitor, Roxy. But we knew very well that to show it to Roxy cold was to invite failure. Said Pathé, 'We'll have to 'salt' it.' The sister of the publicity head of Pathé was a great friend of Roxy's. So it was arranged to show it first to her and some of her friends and tell them where to applaud through the picture, and then they would come along to the showing to Roxy in his very elaborate projection room at the Capitol. We also told them never to talk directly to Roxy about the film but to talk to each other across him as if he were not in the room. Well, by the time the film was over, Roxy was tearing his hair. He used such words as 'epic', 'masterpiece' and the like. He booked it. But even then Pathé were not too trusting, and they decided to tin-can it – that is to tie it to *Grandma's Boy*, – Harold Lloyd's first big feature film which every theatre in New York was scrambling for. Roxy could have *Grandma's Boy*, but he'd have to take *Nanook* too!

A few days later when Major Bowes, the managing director of the Capitol, saw the film he threatened to throw Roxy out. His rage knew no bounds. Desperately, poor Roxy tried to get out of the contract, but no – No *Nanook*, no *Grandma's Boy*!

Nanook came out at the Capitol Theatre. The notices were mixed. One critic damned it with faint praise, but then wrote a better review a few weeks later. It wasn't until the film appeared in London and ran for six months at the New Gallery, and for six months at the Gaumont in Paris, and then ran even more sensationally in Berlin and Rome, that the repercussions came back to America and it was really accepted in America. This has been true of all our films – by the way, they have all done better in Europe, and particularly on the Continent.

You ask me what I think the film can do to make large audiences feel intimate with these distant peoples. Well, *Nanook* is an instance of this. People who read books on the North are, after all, not many, but millions of people have seen this film in the last twenty-six years – it has gone round the world. And what they have seen is not a freak, but a real person after all, facing the perils of a desperate life and yet always happy. When Nanook died of starvation, two years later, the news of his death came out in the press all over the world – even as far away as China.

The urge that I had to make *Nanook* came from the way I felt about these people, my admiration for them; I wanted to tell others about them. This was my whole reason for making the film. In so many travelogues you see, the film-maker looks down on and never up to his subject. He is always the big man from New York or from London. But I had been dependent on these people, alone with them for months at a time, travelling with them and living with them. They had warmed my feet when they were cold, lit my cigarette when my hands were too numb to do it myself; they had taken care of me on three or four different expeditions over a period of ten years. My work had been built up along with them; I couldn't have done anything without them. In the end it is all a question of human relationships.

Source: *The Cinema*, 1950, ed Roger Manvell, Penguin, London, 1950.

Grass: A Nation's Battle for Life
MERIAN C. COOPER

Nanook's relative financial success spawned a series of imitations. Most were of poor quality; few film-makers had Flaherty's patience, skill or understanding. The exception was *Grass*, by Merian C. Cooper (1893–1973) and Ernest B. Schoedsack (1893–1979), a record of the annual migration of the Bakhtiari tribe over the precipitous Zardeh Kuh mountains in what is now Iran.

Like *Nanook*, *Grass* is a story of human ingenuity and stamina in an inhospitable environment. Unlike Flaherty's film, however, in *Grass* no individual is singled out; the protagonist is the tribe itself. Nevertheless, the film is engaging, largely thanks to two extraordinarily dramatic set pieces, the first of which shows 50,000 people, together with all their livestock, crossing a dangerous river on inflated animal skins, and the second of which follows their barefoot ascent up the snow-covered mountains on the last leg of their journey to high summer pasture land.

Cooper and Schoedsack were accompanied on their adventure by a mysterious lady called Marguerite Harrison, a one-time journalist and spy who had saved Cooper's life in Revolutionary Russia. It is Harrison who appears on screen throughout *Grass*.

After *Grass*, Cooper and Schoedsack made the semi-documentary *Chang* and then, in 1933, the box office phenomenon, *King Kong*, which parodies their own attitudes as 'white explorers'. Cooper went on to run RKO studios and produce some of John Ford's best films. In the 1950s he and Schoedsack teamed up again to make documentaries for the Cinerama process.

This piece is extracted from Cooper's published diary.

25th Camp of the Migration, May 29th [1924].
. . . Schoedsack and I are camped halfway up Zardeh Kuh. It is blowing like the devil, and cold. Our muleteers have gone Bolshevist; even Mohamet is ready to quit. We are about out of grub. We've had nothing to eat but a little native bread once a day for two days; and we are going to sleep a bit chilly here tonight almost at the top of Persia. Schoedsack is clothed only in a light suit, and his lips are cracked and bleeding. But both of us are at the peak of happiness. We've done it. There's no doubt about it. We've seen as great a struggle for existence as there is. And we have it for the screen! Somewhere, somehow, there may be a battle of man against nature that equals this for epic sweep and dramatic intensity, but I don't believe it.

Here's what we have seen. Here it is. Here are a whole people with all they own camped high up in the mountains, but still far higher above them towers a great stretch of snow mountain peaks. And that snow range is directly in the path of the tribes. It bars the way to Grass – the Grass that means Life to this migratory people living on their herds.

Now remember that these people have been on the march for over a month, that they have already swum an icy torrent in a seven day fight, that for week after week they have come across mountain country of the roughest, that they have slept unsheltered many nights in rain and storm, for only a comparatively few of the tribes have had adequate tent covering, as practically all have left their regular tents behind, carrying only makeshifts to be used in case of emergency. Therefore, both the people and their animals are feeling the strain of the trip, despite frequent rests in valleys. And let me repeat once more that these are no cold climate people; they have no fur coats, no warm socks; no shoes which can stand the snow. Remember, too, that this is spring, and that everywhere among the tribes are baby sheep, baby cows, baby horses, baby goats, baby donkeys, not to speak of any quantity of honest-to-God human babies. Then, remember, that the tribes are carrying with them everything they own.

Remember all these things – but remember first and last and all the time that, despite everything, they must go over that snow mountain. Ahead is Grass and Life. They must go on!

Well, here is what we saw of that crossing . . .

Three afternoons ago, when Schoedsack and I had been down bathing in the snow stream that ran by our camp, and, feeling like young fighting-cocks, were running up toward the trail, we saw that it was lined with people who were moving straight for the snow gorge. What was this? No one had told us that the tribes would move today. In an hour it would be dark! It wasn't possible that anyone would try to climb Zardeh Kuh in the night. We hurried back. We ran.

Seeing them set out was enough for Schoedsack and me. We gathered together our men and mules and followed. Mrs Harrison, though still weak from her recent illness, gallantly agreed to go on over the mountain and camp alone with Haidar and his people in order that Schoedsack and I may remain on Zardeh Kuh to film the crossing of the tribes.

Darkness had come on by the time Schoedsack and I struck the glacial ice and moved out into the snow gorge. Carefully we picked our way along, every man alert for those deep holes which we had seen when out with the trail makers. We could not afford to lose any animals in that way. We worked slowly up the gorge, near the end of which we saw little camp-fires burning. Here we found our people, and, throwing our blankets on the rock above the snow, we slept.

We were off before dawn, leaving our mules and mule-man behind and taking only a camera donkey. On foot we climbed higher and higher up Zardeh Kuh, zigzagging through the snow trails. Three-quarters of the way up we unslung the camera equipment. It was impossible to operate the camera on the trail itself because there was only room for a single person to pass between the snow walls; so we climbed gingerly out on the surface of the slope.

It was still early morning, and the snow crust was as hard and smooth as glass. The pitch was terrifically steep. I hesitate to venture a guess on how steep it really was. On the off-side, where we crawled, if anybody slipped, there was nothing to stop him from rolling breathless thousands of feet far down into a mountain gorge.

Mohamet and I perched quite safely on the edge of the trail, hanging our feet down in it, but Schoedsack had to set up his motion picture camera well outside the trail. With cool courage he started out, thrusting the ends of his tripod deep into the snow for support. Once he began to slide, and I thought it was all over except the shouting. But the very weight of the heavy apparatus saved him. The steel points of the legs of the tripods dug deep into the snow and gave him the necessary second to get his balance and hold on.

Now came the horde. Like a great twisting snake, black against the white snow surface, up it came. Closer! And now the head of the column was directly beneath us – men, women, children, and most of them barefoot – barefoot in the snow.

It will be long before I forget the sight. Close-ups of it now come flashing across my mind like great dramatic paintings. The background for them is the great mass moving up and up; the strong and hardy, defiant and apparently unmindful of snow and wind, shouting lustily as they drive on the weary stumbling beasts. And against this background now appears an old gray–bearded man with a child of three perched on his shoulders, and both he and the child crying with pain and cold as he stumbles on, leaning heavily on two sticks. An old woman, her gray hair straggling about her wrinkled face, beats onward a line of loaded cows. A sick boy, his face drawn so that his teeth seem almost to stick out through his upper lip, is fastened sprawling across the back of a donkey. A little girl carries on her back a calf almost as big as herself. Mrs Harrison struggles gamely on, a white woman here among the tribes, escorted by Haidar and Lufta. And always women, women, old and young, nearly all carrying babies. The biting wind tears through their cotton dresses at their bare feet and legs and throats.

On came the thousands upon thousands. And so slowly they climbed.

On account of a shoulder of rock the snow wall, at one place just above us, was only a few inches high. A scream behind me made me pause and look back at this spot. I saw a heavily loaded donkey stumbling just outside the trail. For one precarious second it stood balanced above eternity. Then it began to slide. It lost its footing and fell.

Rolling over and over, gathering speed as it went, it spun downward. Now it was going with the swiftness of an airplane in a nose-dive, falling, falling, falling, until far below it became only a tiny black dot. The woman in charge of it shrieked and, tearing her face with her nails, hysterically leaped outside the snow lane. There was a mighty howl all down the line of climbers as she squatted on her bare feet and began to slide. It seemed that nothing in this world could save her; but when she had shot along fifty yards with gathering speed, she struck the outside end of a turn in the trail below and went shooting in to safety between its high snow walls.

But howls below kept up; for, when the woman had jumped outside the path, she had dislodged a few small pieces of the rock, which now fell faster and faster. From them came one of the dangers of the climb. Every year many are injured by dislodged rock despite rigid attempts at protection. One must stay in the trail, or, if one went outside it, one must keep well clear, as did Schoedsack, of the climbers' line of march.

On and on mounted the endless black, twisting line of the tribes. As the sun grew hotter, it began to soften the snow. When the snow had been hard crusted in the early morning some had worn their cotton shoes, but now that the snow was soft and wet nearly all were barefoot. Soon the dogs were leaping safely outside the limits of the trail, though often causing great excitement by dislodging stones. Schoedsack, too, now worked with more ease. And ever the thousands came on. When the sun began to sink behind the mountain, the trail was still full.

For three days thus the tribes have been crossing. Every morning we have climbed to a new place on the mountain for pictures. Every evening we have camped somewhere down near its foot. But tonight we are lying under the stars on a rock high up in the snow itself; and we are done with our work on this side of Zardeh Kuh. Tomorrow for the summit!

Source: *Grass* by Merian C. Cooper, Putnam's, New York, 1925.

3 Kino Eyes and Agit Trains

INTRODUCTION

In spite the continuing civil war, severe shortages and material discomfort, the years after the 1917 Revolution were ones of intense, almost euphoric, artistic creativity in the newly created Soviet Union. The overthrow of the old order gave licence to iconoclasm, experimentation and re–evaluation in all the arts, but particularly in cinema, which for the first time in its short life was taken *seriously* by intellectuals, politicians and artists.

The Soviets considered film the most 'modern' and 'objective' art form and the least encumbered with bourgeoisie associations. 'Of all the arts, for us the cinema is the most important,' Lenin asserted in 1919. As if in response, Sergei Eisenstein, Dziga Vertov and Alexander Dovzhenko (amongst many others) turned from the traditional arts of theatre, poetry and painting respectively, to work with celluloid.

Lenin's statement was not primarily an aesthetic judgement – would he even have recognized such a thing? – but a measure of the significance he attached to cinema as a tool for communication and propaganda. The Soviet Union was a vast, heterogeneous country, peopled by predominantly illiterate peasants who spoke dozens of different dialects and languages. Educating them in the basic tenets of communism, and setting in motion the enormous socio-political changes of the Revolution was a massive job – for which cinema was ideally suited. The flourishing, state-sponsored Soviet cinema of the 1920s and 1930s should be viewed in this light: as essentially a cinema of propaganda.

From the outset film-makers debated whether factual or fiction films were best suited to this task of re-education and 'agitation'. Some believed that fiction could carry a message most effectively, because an often bitter pill could be coated in a sugary coating of entertainment. Others, influenced by constructivists like Mayakovsky and Rodchenko, espoused an 'art of facts', believing that fiction films were merely

5 *A poster for Dziga Vertov's* Kino-Glaz *(Cinema Eye, 1924)*

another opiate of the masses and should be banned from the Soviet
Union. To resolve the argument Lenin instituted the so-called 'Leninist
Film Proportion' which specified that a certain percentage of all film
production should be factual.

In the two decades immediately after the Revolution Soviet non-fiction film received unprecedented government support. The result was a gloriously fecund period of technical and formal experimentation that opened up a whole new area of possibilities for the documentary. At the forefront of these new ideas was a remarkable individual called Dziga Vertov.

Dziga Vertov: The Man with the Camera

Dziga Vertov was born Denis Kaufman in Bialystock (now Poland, then Russia) in January 1896, the eldest of three brothers who all left their mark on world cinema. The middle brother, Mikhail (1897–1981), became a renowned Soviet documentary director in his own right and was cameraman on most of Vertov's films, including the celebrated *Man With A Movie Camera*. The youngest of the three, Boris (1906–1980), was separated from his siblings during the Revolution and educated in Paris. There he photographed all of Jean Vigo's films before emigrating to America and becoming the cinematographer of choice for both Elia Kazan and Sidney Lumet.

Of the brothers, however, it was Vertov[1] who has had the most notable and lasting influence on cinema history.

Emerging from the Constructivist *mêlée* around Mayakovsky, Vertov began editing revolutionary newsreels during and after the Civil War, including *Kino-Pravda* ('Film-Truth'), a film equivalent to the Communist party newspaper, *Pravda*. Throughout his career, thereafter, he never strayed from an absolute belief in the revelatory capacity of unscripted documentary footage. What did develop were his complex ideas on montage and filming technique which were most fully expressed in a series of 'documentaries' in the late 1920s and early 1930s: *The Eleventh Year* (1928), *Man with a Movie Camera* (1929), *Enthusiasm* (1931) and *Three Songs of Lenin* (1934). For all their experimental form, Vertov insisted that his films had a clear purpose. 'The important thing,' he said, 'is not [to] separate form from content. The secret lies in unity of form and content.'

Vertov theorized relentlessly, and wrote numerous articles and

1 Denis Kaufman adopted the psuedonym Dziga Vertov after the Revolution. It has constructivist associations and translates roughly as 'spinning at great speed'.

6 *Members of the Red Army holding aloft a banner which reads: 'We go to the cinema film* Three Songs about Lenin' *(1934)*.

manifestos expounding his ideas. For all the complexity of their appearance (not helped by the peculiar layouts and typefaces he characteristically adopted), they are relatively straightforward. He and his associates (whom he dubbed '*The Kinoks*') believed that fiction cinema was an irrevocably bourgeois art form and should be abandoned. In its place they posited a cinema of facts, made up of documentary footage of real people in real situations, if possible filmed unawares. Central to his theories is a kind of idolization of the camera. Vertov believed that the camera (which, in combination with the editing process, he called the 'kino-eye') was in many respects superior to the human eye, able as it was to see at long distances, to film in slow or fast motion, etc. Moreover, in the editing process, scenes from different times and places could be cut together, the same scene viewed from several different angles, impressions of speed and energy given by fast cutting . . . The *kino-eye* was liberated from the confines of time, space and normal causation. A *kino-eye* film was able, Vertov believed, to reveal a deeper level of truth in the world than was normally perceived by the 'imperfect human eye'.

Watching Vertov's films today what is most impressive is their no-holds-barred willingness to explore every technical capability the cinema has at its disposal. Vertov and his kinoks did everything and anything: used freeze frames, multiple frames, animation, telescopic and microscopic lenses, multiple-exposures, 'subliminal' cuts of one or two frames, slow motion, fast motion, cameras in planes, cameras hand-held and cameras in cars.

Vertov's ideas on sound film were also prescient and were expounded several years before the process became technically feasible. He believed in using a combination of 'direct sound', music and effects. He did *not* think sound should be used naturalistically, but wanted it to create a tension with the image, by turns counterpointing and underscoring it. His own first sound film, *Enthusiasm* (including probably the first use of 'direct sound' in a documentary) was a masterpiece. Charlie Chaplin, who at the time was similarly preoccupied with how to use sound anti-naturalistically in *his* films, wrote: 'I regard the film *Enthusiasm* as one of the most moving symphonies I have ever heard. Dziga Vertov is a musician. Professors should learn from him instead of arguing with him.'

Not surprisingly, Vertov's radical ideas about the superiority of factual film were unpopular with the Soviet Union's fiction directors, particularly Sergei Eisenstein, who publicly lambasted them (although he had started his film career working for Vertov). Perhaps it was inevitable that as the renown of the fiction directors increased in the 1930s, Vertov's influence would wane. Even more problematic was the increasingly hostile interference of Stalin's bureaucratic régime, which insisted that all films should have a detailed script for perusal prior to shooting. Vertov, whose films rested on the very idea of spontaneity and the rejection of scripts, was crippled. He refused to compromise and fell under ideological suspicion. His position was not helped by an insistence that it was the documentary film-makers duty to show 'life-as-it-is' – not to show the ideal the aparatchiks wanted to see. He got into particular trouble for filming the great Soviet famines of the early 1920s and 1930s.

Vertov was largely forgotten in the West and reviled in Russia by the time of his death in 1954. However, his influence revived in the early 1960s with the rise of *cinéma vérité* – the very term being a French translation of his Kino-Pravda (see p. 249).

The first of these extracts is from Vertov's manifesto *The Council of*

Three (1923) and the second from *Provisional Instructions to Kino-eye Groups* (1927).

The Council of Three

1. Upon observing the films that have arrived from America and the West and taking into account available information on work and artistic experimentation at home and abroad, I arrive at the following conclusion:

> The death sentence passed in 1919 by the *kinoks* [the name given by Vertov to his collaborators] on all films, with no exceptions, holds for the present as well. The most scrupulous examination does not reveal a single film, a single artistic experiment, properly directed to the emancipation of the camera, which is reduced to a state of pitiable slavery, of subordination to the imperfections and the short-sightedness of the human eye.

We do not object to cinema's undermining of literature and the theatre; we wholly approve of the use of cinema in every branch of knowledge, but we define these functions as accessory, as secondary offshoots of cinema.

The main and essential thing is:

The sensory exploration of the world through film.

We therefore take as the point of departure the use of the camera as a kino-eye, more perfect than the human eye, for the exploration of the chaos of visual phenomena that fills space.

The kino-eye lives and moves in time and space; it gathers and records impressions in a manner wholly different from that of the human eye. The position of our bodies while observing or our perception of a certain number of features of a visual phenomenon in a given instant are by no means obligatory limitations for the camera which, since it is perfected, perceives more and better.

We cannot improve the making of our eyes, but we can endlessly perfect the camera.

Until now many a cameraman has been criticised for having filmed a running horse moving with unnatural slowness on the screen (rapid cranking of the camera) – or for the opposite, a tractor ploughing a field too swiftly (slow cranking of the camera), and the like.

These are chance occurrences, of course, but we are preparing a system, a deliberate system of such occurrences, a system of seeming irregularities to investigate and organize phenomena.

Until now, we have violated the movie camera and forced it to copy the work of our eye. And the better the copy, the better the shooting was thought to be. Starting today we are liberating the camera and making it work in the opposite direction – away from copying.

The weakness of the human eye is manifest. We affirm the kino-eye, discovering within the chaos of movement the result of the kino-eye's own movement; we affirm the kino-eye with its own dimensions of time and space, growing in strength and potential to the point of self–affirmation.

2. I make the viewer see in the manner best suited to my presentation of this or that visual phenomenon. The eye submits to the will of the camera and is directed by it to those successive points of the action that, most succinctly and vividly, bring the film phrase to the height or depth of resolution.

Example: shooting a boxing match, not from the point of view of a spectator present, but shooting the successive movements (the blows) of the contenders.

Example: the filming of a group of dancers, not from the point of view of a spectator sitting in the auditorium with a ballet on the stage before him.

After all, the spectator at a ballet follows, in confusion, now the combined group of dancers, now random individual figures, now someone's legs – a series of scattered perceptions, different for each spectator.

One can't present this to the film viewer. A system of successive movements requires the filming of dancers or boxers in the order of their actions, one after another . . . by forceful transfer of the viewer's eye to the successive details that must be seen.

The camera 'carries' the film viewer's eyes from arms to legs, from legs to eyes and so on, in the most advantageous sequence, and organizes the details into an orderly montage study.

3. . . . . I am kino-eye.
From one person I take the hands, the strongest and most dextrous;

from another I take the legs, the swiftest and most shapely; from a third, the most beautiful and expressive head – and through montage I create a new, perfect man.

I am kino-eye, I am a mechanical eye. I, a machine, show you the world as only I can see it.

Now and forever, I free myself from human immobility, I am in constant motion, I draw near, then away from objects, I crawl under, I climb on to them. I move apace with the muzzle of a galloping horse, I plunge full speed into a crowd, I outstrip running soldiers, I fall on my back, I ascend with an aeroplane, I plunge and soar together with plunging and soaring bodies. Now I, a camera, fling myself along their resultant, manoeuvring in the chaos of movement, recording movement, starting with movements composed of the most complex combinations.

Free of the limits of time and space, I put together any given points in

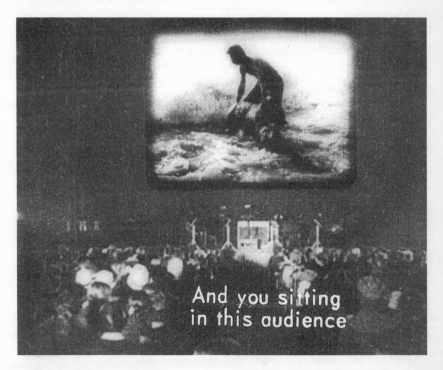

7 The Eleventh Year (1928).

the universe, no matter where I've recorded them.

My path leads to the creation of a fresh perception of the world. I decipher in a new way a world unknown to you.

Source: *Kino-Eye: The Writings of Dziga Vertov*, edited by Annette Michelson, University of California Press, Berkley, 1984.

Esther Shub and the Art of Compilation
JAY LEYDA

'It is amazing how many unexpected solutions come up when you hold film stock in your hands. Just like letters: they are born on the top of the pen.'

Esther (or Esfir) Shub (1899–1959) was perhaps the most outstanding woman film-maker of the silent period. Bringing her genius as an editor to bear on old news and home movie footage, which no one before her had bothered to give a second thought to, let alone looked after, she constructed a series of brilliant compilation films which told the story of Russia from the turn of the century to her own time: *The Fall of The Romanov Dynasty,The Great Road* (both 1927) and *The Russia of Nicholas II and Leo Tolstoy* (1928). Almost incidentally, Shub single-handedly brought about a world-wide awareness of the cultural and material value of 'archive footage', setting in motion the principles which would lead to the establishment of the first film archives.

Compilation films like Charles Urban's *The Battle of The Somme* (1916) and Vertov's *Anniversary of The Revolution* (1919) had, of course, been made before, but they were little more than a series of (more or less) evocative shots strung together with titles. What Shub did was bring a firm narrative sense and the creative montage techniques which she had learned from Vertov and Eisenstein, to bear on the material. Shub had an enormous talent for expressing her own viewpoint without distorting the authentic impact of the selected footage. Her films are fascinating cinematic essays, which for all their radical political purpose, are suffused with a sense of sympathy and humanity.

Although Shub was essentially a disciple of Vertov – believing like him in the pre-eminent value of filmed facts – she managed to stay friends with Vertov's arch rival, Eisenstein. As mentioned in the following extract she gave Eisenstein his first film job, as her editing assistant. Their influence on one another did not stop there. She was inspired by Eisenstein's montage in *Potemkin* (1926), while he in turn admitted that his staging of the events of the July revolt in *October* (1927) – one of that film's most effective sequences – was based on the impressions he had gained of the same event watching it unfold in factual footage on Shub's editing bench.

In addition to her early historical films, Shub edited or compiled numerous documentaries, including the powerful testament to the Spanish Civil War, *Spain* (1939). Unfortunately one of her most intriguing projects, *Women*, a history of Russian women from 1914 through to the mid 1930s, remained unrealized.

This piece is from Jay Leyda's history of the compilation film, *Films Beget Films*.

In 1922, as the Civil War and intervention ended and as NEP began[2], Esther Shub entered the distribution office of Goskino [the main Soviet film company], her work to be editing and titling foreign and pre-revolutionary Russian films for Soviet audiences. A friend of Maya-kovsky and Eisenstein in the Meyerhold group, she brought intelligence, taste and a sense of social responsibility into this generally despised employment. The first jobs given her were to adapt American serials – with Eddie Polo, Ruth Roland, Pearl White. When she discovered that the faithful Russian audiences did not need the usual swift résumés given at the start of each new chapter of a serial thriller, Shub took these discards to the cutting table she kept in her home, and evenings were spent with film friends there making film jokes with the scraps. (One of her friends was Lev Kuleshov [theoritician of montage and mentor to Eisenstein and Pudovkin], who had experienced a serious variant of this pastime when he edited newsreels of the Civil War.) Sometimes she would be handed such scraps – without title, subtitles, or any indication of order – to be transformed into a film that could be released; thus Chaplin's *Carmen* landed on her table in the form of a hundred confused little rolls. It was clearly intended as a parody on Bizet's opera,

2 NEP was Lenin's New Economic Policy which permitted limited private enterprise – an emergency step to prevent total economic collapse after the civil war.

so she supplied it with titles in the same spirit, and she remembered its reception (it may have been Chaplin's introduction to Russian audiences) as gratifyingly hilarious.

More difficult was the transformation of the two-part German thriller, *Doctor Mabuse*, with its lengthy time-and-metre consuming titles and an involved tangle of plots, into a single film that could be followed with less dependence on titles. This required a study of each shot's content and composition, a close examination of each actor's movements and expressions, unattached to the old titles. Rhythm and tempo – of each shot and in relation one to another – became vital factors that could not be ignored, as its director, Fritz Lang, had seemed to ignore them in his original cutting. Shub learned the power of scissors and cement in relation to meaning, and Eisenstein, whose assistance on this job was his first film work, learned too.

When Russian directors saw Shub's value to their own productions, she was transferred to the Third Studio of Goskino to advise and cut new films by Tarich, Ivanov-Barkov, Froelich, Roshal, Mikhin and Molchanov. There were also two months of work with Eisenstein, at her home, on the shooting script of *Strike*.

Shub writes that it was the impression made upon her early in 1926 by *Potemkin* that induced her to seek in newsreel material another film way to show the revolutionary past. She found lists of newsreels filmed in 1917, she learned that the Tsar had maintained his own court cameraman – and she felt sure that she could find enough footage to work with. But the Goskino director, Trainin, answered her every proposal and enthusiasm with 'No', and 'told me to go on editing fictional films – I might even get an opportunity to make my own film with actors.' She turned to the Sovkino Studio, where the livelier minds of Bliakhin and Shklovsky had some say in policy, and after several conferences they said 'Yes'.

At the end of summer, 1926, I went to Leningrad. It was even tougher there. All the valuable negatives and positives of wartime and pre-revolutionary newsreels were kept in a damp cellar on Sergievsky Street. The cans were coated with rust. In many places the dampness had caused the emulsion to come away from the celluloid base. Many shots that appeared on the lists had disappeared altogether. Not one metre of negative or positive on the February Revolution had been preserved, and I was even shown a document that declared that no film of that event could be found in Leningrad.

In spite of such assurances Shub persisted and some of that footage *did* come to light. An old newsreel worker, Khmelnitsky, who had helped her restore some of the damaged footage, brought her small cans of 'counter-revolutionary' film that turned out to be the private 'home movies' of Nikolai II that she had hoped would turn up some day. In her two months in Leningrad, Shub inspected 60,000 metres of film, from which she chose 5,200 metres to take back to work on in Moscow. She spent all her free time in wandering about Leningrad, a new city for her, to feel at home with its geography and appearance in the 1917 shots. Before leaving she supervised the filming of various documents, newspapers and items associated with the events she was reconstructing.

> In the montage I tried to avoid looking at the newsreel material for its own sake, and to maintain the principle of its documentary quality. All was subordinated to the theme. This gave me the possibility, in spite of the known limitations of the photographed events and facts, to link the meanings of the material so that it evoked the pre-revolutionary period and the February days.

After the first private screening (where the section on 'World War' was particularly admired) the release title was decided: *The Fall of the Romanov Dynasty*. The only credit on the posters was 'Work by E. I. Shub'. In March 1927, as her first 'work' was released, Shub began her second. *The Great Road* was to use all Soviet newsreels for the ten years since the October Revolution, beginning (hopefully) with whatever could be found of the Revolution itself. She learned that newsreels of the recent past had been kept just as carelessly, if not more so, than had the oldest Russian newsreels unearthed for her first film. Identification of place and time of shooting was an unforeseen obstacle, but the several living cameramen of the Civil War helped her here. She had more to inspect (250,000 metres) than for the older film, but after 1921–22 the material grew thinner:

> From that date newsreels were shot without much plan and quickly put aside with little comprehension of their historic value, which of

course increased with each passing year. Even worse is their change of tone after the Civil War; suddenly the concentration was on parades, meetings, arrivals, departures, delegates, and such – and almost no record was kept of how we transformed the country to a new political economy – or of the resulting construction.

Some precious footage had been sold abroad, without any master copies or negatives having been kept at home – too little raw film in those years to think of such niceties, or of the future. A quantity of early reels had been sent to the United States, as thanks for the work of the American Relief Association during the months of famine. This had fallen into private hands, yet Shub traced this footage and arranged through Amtorg (the Soviet trade office in the United States) for its purchase, for $6,000. (It was cannily copied before the sale, for a future interesting use against the Soviet Union!)

In this lot I found material of the imperalist war, of the funeral of victims of the February Revolution, and six completely unfamiliar shots of Lenin [filmed in 1920 by an American cameraman]. Soviet audiences saw these intimate scenes of Lenin for the first time in *The Great Road*.

The new film was intended for the celebrations of the tenth anniversary of the October Revolution – in early November. But the new film form discovered and perfected by Shub was not yet on secure ground. Her right as an 'author' of these films was challenged, and it was Mayakovsky who publicly ridiculed those who tried in any way to belittle the value of this extremely important work.

The Fall of the Romanov Dynasty had used newsreel material of 1912–17; *The Great Road* continued through the archives of 1917. In her searches Shub had found a tempting lot of Russian newsreel from 1896 through 1912, and the Tolstoy centenary to come in 1928 offered her an opportunity to employ it. Her first Tolstoy hope was to depend on the considerable footage that had been filmed of him, but she found only about 200 feet of this – a fifth as much as the footage of his funeral! She decided to place her actual Tolstoy footage in a larger frame of Russia since the turn of the century. The result was *The Russia of Nicholas II and Leo Tolstoy*:

This montage must serve as an eloquent illustration of the fact that any available acting method for the historical film, no matter how good or talented, has only an ephemeral value in comparison with the chronicle film, which possesses a conviction that can never pale and can never age.

. . . In Shub's first three precedent-forming films her cutting ideas usually combined a forcefully simple logic with a minute study of the formal elements in the available footage; the ideas were often built on contrasts that may seem obvious now – but it took imagination to dig them from her raw material. Here is an example, in *The Fall of the Romanov Dynasty*, of one of her direct poster juxtapositions:

A crowd of elegant idlers are dancing
[a mazurka on the awninged deck of a yacht].
The dancing tires some of them. They drink wine.
TITLE: 'It made me sweat.'
And again they dance.
TITLE: ' . . . sweat.'
A peasant, exhausted by his work, ploughs a furrow.

Source: *Films Beget Films* by Jay Leyda, Allen and Unwin, London, 1964.

Agit Trains and Mobile Laboratories
ROMAN KARMEN

Agit or Kine Trains (and sometimes boats) were a peculiarly Soviet invention: trains which travelled the country disseminating propaganda and 'agitating' the populace. Brightly painted with revolutionary slogans and scenes, on board they had a printing press that produced pamphlets, posters and newspapers, a theatre company, a cinema, film processing laboratory and cameramen. The first Agit Train was sent to the Eastern Front of the Civil War in 1918 – with Vertov on board, acting as an editor – but they were at their most popular in the 1920s.

This piece was written by Roman Karmen (1906–1978), who was a renowned documentary cameraman specializing in combat footage. His work includes *Moscow* (1933), *Spain* (1937), *China Defends Herself* (1938) and numerous films on Vietnam and Cuba.

Among the most noteworthy innovations in our work were the travelling film editorial laboratories sent to each of the major construction enterprises in various parts of our country. This is how it was done: units of documentary film workers – several cameramen, the director, the editor, the cutter and the laboratory assistant – went to an important construction, established themselves there, having organized a small laboratory, cutting room and printing machine for the titles. The task of these mobile laboratories was to give the workers on the construction active help by issuing film magazines regularly. These films were devoted to the most vital interests of the construction itself. They propagandized the latest methods of building, laying concrete, assembling equipment. They showed the achievements of individual pioneers,

8 *Exterior of agit-train.*

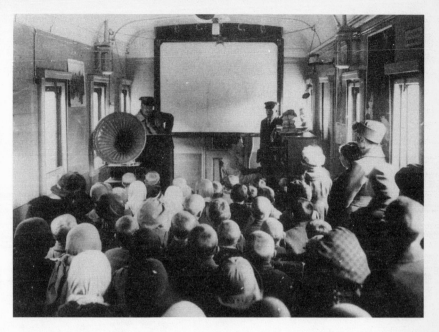

9 *Interior of agit-train.*

and mercilessly exposed the failures and delays observed in one or other of the departments. In these magazines you could see film reporting of the most different kinds: the feuilleton, brief notice, leading article, character study, portrait, satire. By adopting this new method the newsreel-makers were putting into practice Lenin's famous words about newspapers. He said: 'The newspaper is not only a collective propagandist and agitator, it is also a collective organizer.' The mobile cutting rooms had a great influence on the history of our actuality film. While performing the role of 'collective organizer', they played another important part – that of systematically recording all the stages of the country's construction. This was the beginning of organized historical recording in film. The record now consists of millions of metres of film. In this history, arranged on shelves in film vaults, are the 'biographies' of such giants as the Magnitogorsk metallurgical combine and the Dnieper hydroelectric station. These are biographies in the real meaning of the word – from the day of the giant's birth, from the first explosions of ammonite on the barren shores of the Dnieper to the exciting moment when the grandiose turbines were first set in motion and the meter indicator recorded its first tremor – from the first prospecting parties, camping in a tent at the foot of Magnitny Mountain, and the people digging the first excavations in frost and snowstorms to the first piece of metal obtained and the aerial panorama showing the greatest metallurgical combine in the world, surrounded by a town which, only a few years ago, was not marked on any map.

The mobile laboratories, fully justified in practice, served as a stimulus for a new experimental enterprise – the kine-train. This was a film studio on wheels. The coaches were equipped with film laboratories, cutting tables, projection room, a typography and a photographic laboratory. Two of the coaches had compartments which were the living-quarters of the directors, laboratory assistants and cameramen. There were also a kitchen and dining room. For several years, this original documentary film studio made expeditions all over the country. The train would arrive on the scene of a major construction, stay there for a long period and perform the same task

10 *Mikhail Kaufman filming* The Man with a Movie Camera *(1928).*

as the travelling newsreel laboratories. In addition to film magazines, the unit issued a newspaper and an illustrated gazette. The workers from the construction would come to the projection room to see the documentaries produced in the train. After completing an important job of cultural propaganda in one district, the train would go on to do the same work at the other end of the country. The material filmed by this kine-train, its various shorts and magazines, now have exceptional historical value.

Source: *Soviet Documentary* by Roman Karmen in *Experiment in the Film*, ed. Roger Manvell, Grey Walls Press, London, 1949.

A Kinok Speaks
MIKHAIL KAUFMAN IN INTERVIEW

In Dziga Vertov's most famous film, *The Man with a Movie Camera*, the actual man with the camera was his brother, Mikhail Kaufman – whose idea the film originally was.

Kaufman's practical nature was vital to the success of his more theoretical brother. An energetic innovator, he invented many new pieces of apparatus for his camera and developed several novel special-effects processes. Vertov's theories about 'capturing life unawares' were a response to Kaufman's experiences on location.

As a cameraman Kaufman's abilities were not just technical, he also had a remarkable facility for capturing striking, often poetic, images. Both Eisenstein and Dovzhenko, the two greatest Soviet fiction directors of the period, tried to get him photograph their films but he turned them down, declaring that he was committed to the documentary.

As a director Kaufman made several notable films of his own, including *Moscow* (1926), acknowledged as the first in the genre of *City Symphonies* and the little seen but greatly admired *Spring* (1929).

This rare interview appeared in the magazine *October* in 1979.

KAUFMAN: You could say that all of my work consisted in learning to film life in such a way that it could impress and influence one emotionally without the mediation of the artist or actor. To simply film, photograph life is to produce a chronicle. We actually went beyond the limits of the chronicle and began to create works of art – using the image, working on the image through every possible means: through camera angles, through photography. If you take someone's picture, you should make it an image, not simply a photograph. This doesn't mean that I have to compose the person into an image. Rather I catch the moment when reality becomes an image.

Ever since childhood Vertov had the ability to perceive things through images and to communicate them in poetic form. It's interesting, by the way, that even as a child I was attracted to different forms of representation than he. I studied photographs, I drew and since we're discussing the early stages of our collaboration, we can say that it began when our beloved Aunt Masha graduated from medical school. Vertov wrote a poem for her, and I drew a sort of congratulation picture of a dove in flight. There was already a certain . . .

OCTOBER: *Division of labour.*

KAUFMAN: Division of labour, and a form of collaboration – even though I did not always feel that Vertov perceived the material I shot quite as I did, even when something was missing. He was perceptive, however, and he had a way of communicating the emotional impact of life in very simple and effective ways, in both *A Sixth of the World* (1926) and *Kino-Glaz* (1924), where the material had the most immediate role. I feel that he collected footage for *A Sixth of the World* very well, very effectively. The sense of collaboration was also very strong in *Kino-Glaz*. It was not distorted in his diaries or by later theoretical interpretations.

Today it appears as though scenarios had always existed for *Forward, Soviet!* (1926) and *Man with a Movie Camera* (1929). Vertov wrote in his diaries that he would have liked to have created films based totally upon documentary footage. Having gone through the archives, he acquired the skill and the desire to work solely with documentary footage. He used found archival footage, probably shot by cameramen at the front, or footage that had been preserved in the archive for long periods of time. He made a wonderful film that was not, however, from my point of view, a poetic achievement, since it was made primarily from dry material, descriptive photographs of the civil war. Here there was a synthesized image of the army and of military heroism, of an army that had been victorious in this kind of warfare. I still remember this film, and I recall with great pleasure each frame of the civil war, shot by cameramen chosen at random and used without regard for chronology, but for the expressiveness which lay within each frame. Even though that expressiveness was primitive, since the shooting had been very standard, it had been extracted from the facts. They were found facts – not like what you get in Esfir Shub's work, where you have things like Tolstoy on a stroll . . .

OCTOBER: *In* The Great Way, *however, it's no longer so simple.*

KAUFMAN: Something special does happen in *The Great Way*. Until then Shub had tried to tell things in a poetic manner . . . By the way, I have Vertov's review of *The Romanov Dynasty*. In it he describes with revulsion this method of using footage – and to a certain extent he's right. From the point of view of historical context, however, it is extremely interesting, even if in terms of interpretation, the way in which images and emotions are presented, it leaves a great deal to be desired. The footage can speak for itself; it doesn't need the author's interpretation . . .

OCTOBER: *In* The Great Way *Shub uses much of the footage of Lenin's burial that is used in* Leninist Kino-Pravda *(1924) and in* Three Songs of Lenin *(1934). Would you say that the different editing styles are grounded in totally different conceptions of documentary cinema?*

KAUFMAN: Absolutely. With Shub, you somehow still have a connected plot, an accessible story which develops gradually. Her work is closer to Pudovkin's. We felt that when working with documentary material one shouldn't follow a standard narrative; it was extremely important to piece facts together and to unite everything in a single thrust. Actually, we felt that the point of editing, in the full sense of the word, was not only to have an image in every frame, but to produce . . .

OCTOBER: *A collision of images?*

KAUFMAN: No, an interpretation of images.

OCTOBER: *Do you feel this was more closely related to Eisenstein's principle?*

KAUFMAN: Not at all, although Eisenstein felt that he learned a lot from us. He came from the theatre; in the theatre one directs dramas, one strings beads. But he immediately realized, like an intelligent man with a good eye, that in cinema one needs a fresh outlook.

I want to clarify the basis for our impulse to seek a new film language, and the way in which I fulfilled my task and tried to improve the film camera. At the very beginning there were no telephoto lenses whatsoever, to film people unawares, let's say. It's harder to film straight on; it's much better to observe from afar. We had to work out a system of possibilities, independently of what we wanted or needed to film. The special problem was filming people. After an argument between us, Vertov decided to publish a sort of ban ruling out the 'kinokina' and temporarily ruling out the subject as an object of filming because of his inability to behave in front of a camera. As if a subject absolutely has to know how to behave! At that time I put it as follows: in the narrative feature one has to know how to act; in the documentary cinema one has to know how not to act. To be able not to act – one will have to wait a long time until the subject is educated in such a way that he won't pay any attention to the fact that he is being filmed. There's no school like that yet, is there? So instead of waiting, I said to him: 'You've just reminded me of the first photographs I took as a child.' I shot all sorts of interesting occurrences – the neighbours, and in school. There was an incident when I was expelled from school because I had snapped a picture of a pupil passing an answer to someone. And I said to Vertov, 'There's a whole system to be worked out. We have to find this system.'

Following that line of thought I constructed a sort of tent, something like a telephone booth, for *Man with a Movie Camera*. There has to be an observation point somewhere. So I made myself up as a telephone repairman. There weren't any special lenses, so I went out and bought a regular camera and removed the deep-focus lens. Standing off to the side I could still get things very close up, and that's why you saw those wonderful faces of the children and of the Chinese magician in *Man with a Movie Camera*. This method supplied us with material which was much more expressive. For instance, when I filmed 'the rescue,' the attempt to save the asphyxiated guard, the first-aid team left. Standing off to the side, I observed the display of emotions, and totally new and fresh material appeared.

Gradually all these methods were perfected, and the whole system as well. The shooting process for 'life as it is' required that people's attention be distracted. But there was more to it than just the shooting. We had to organize an environment in which we could work comfortably, one in which we could bathe as one would in oil. For example, when I filmed a threshing competition, nobody knew what was going to happen. I just promised that the one who could thresh the most would have his picture taken. At that time a photo was still worth a lot. They worked as hard as they could, and I observed from off to the side and filmed something that was reckless, wonderful fun, and an interesting work process. A wonderfully interesting episode came out of the threshing incident.

I also want to describe a series of devices which we succeeded in working out and which Vertov included in his memoirs. We worked on them daily. Every day we thought of something new in the way of shooting methods: for example, shooting while in motion, which finally led to the motorcycle and the racing car. I would take part in races – not for the prize, but simply to observe, which didn't bother anybody. It worked splendidly; the steering wheel was used to keep the objects in front of one all the time. One didn't even have to look through the camera. Everything was set automatically. Before it was automatic I had to crank the camera by hand. Those were the devices which then became the crane. At that time even narrative feature films didn't have cranes, the magnetic crane to cover a wide range. We had to use high look-out points, when these existed. There weren't any helicopters. One should really have climbed out on top of a chimney, because then one gets a sense of the whole layout, as well as a very unusual view of life. And I climbed on to the crane in front of millions of people.

Source: *October* Winter 1979, No.11.

4 Documentary and the Avant-Garde

INTRODUCTION

In the teens and twenties of the century, under the influence of cubism and futurism, visual artists of the western avant-garde were fascinated by the modern, the mechanical and the rhythmic. Naturally, the cinema, the most mechanical, modern and rhythmic of the arts, seemed an exciting area for experimentation. Among the well-known artists who worked in celluloid during this period were Man Ray (*Emak Bakia*,1927), Fernand Léger (*Ballet Mécanique*, 1925), Salvador Dali (*Un Chien Andalou*, 1928) and Laszlo Moholy-Nagy (*Dynamics of a Metropolis*, 1922).

Even if few of these artists did more than dabble in film, their efforts fostered a new attitude towards 'non-professional' cinema and encouraged many young film-makers to produce highly aesthetic, formally experimental work. Most looked to the world around them – particularly the automized environment of cities and factories – for their subject matter. Among the most prominent were Walter Ruttmann, whose *Berlin – Die Symphonie einer Grosstadt* (1928) was widely imitated; Alberto Cavalcanti, who made *Rien que les Heures* (1927) and later joined the British documentary movement; and Paul Strand and Charles Sheeler, whose *Manahatta* (1921) – a near abstract hymn in praise of Manhattan – was screened in Paris as part of a Dadaist programme with poems by Guillaume Apollinaire and music by Erik Satie.

These films were apolitical; only occasionally, as in the case of *Rien que les Heures*, did they contain even an implicit social critique. But as the 1930s arrived, and the friction between left and right became more pronounced, film-makers began to move from innovation to involvement and by the middle of the century the 'avant-garde documentary' had all but disappeared.

Haxan/Witchcraft through the Ages
TOM MILNE

Blending the straightforward tone of an academic lecture with spectacular historical reconstruction, outrageous fantasy and psychological interpretation, Benjamin Christensen's hugely expensive 1921 film

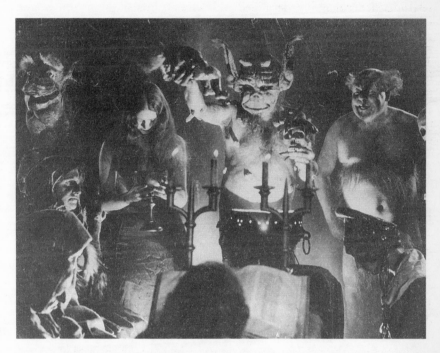

11 Haxan: Witchcraft through the Ages *in which the director Benjamin Christensen himself plays the devil (1922).*

Haxan/Witchcraft Through the Ages, defies categorization. It is what biologists would call a 'sport' and its influence on the subsequent development of the documentary was negligible.

This is a review of the film's re-release in 1968.

A history and examination of witchcraft, comprising: (1) A prologue describing, through documents and engravings, early astronomical and religious systems and beliefs, as well as graphic representations of demons and witches. (2) Medieval times: superstitions, potions and philtres; the persecution of old crones, how a witch-hunt leads not only to the destruction of an entire family, but to general hysteria; how witches are made to confess by religious and physical 'persuasion': what they confess to, demonic possession, the Black Sabbath; religion, flagellation and sexuality. (3) Modern times (1920): the old crones once burned at the stake as witches are now simply the physically deformed or mentally deranged old women one finds in homes and institutions; demonic possession is now recognized as a form of hysteria, and treated as such.

Despite a certain underground reputation and respectful (if inadequate) references in the history books, Benjamin Christensen (1879–1959) has never really won the recognition he deserves as one of the cinema's earliest and greatest stylists. The reason is probably mainly the inaccessibility of his films, for anyone who has seen *The Mysterious X* (1913) or *Night of Revenge* (1915) can hardly fail to have been left open-mouthed in astonishment by an extraordinary subtlety in direction which yielded nothing to Griffith or Feuillade, and a sophistication in lighting which made these two great precursors look like beginners. There may well be another reason for this neglect, however: the quirkish sense of humour which invades all his work, and seems to prevent people from accepting him as entirely serious. It is present in both the early Danish films, as well as in the brilliant Hollywood horror spoof, *Seven Footprints to Satan*, and very much so in *Witchcraft Through the Ages* not least in his own appearance as a stoutly leering, sneering Devil given to popping up nude in ladies' bedrooms with lubriciously wagging tongue. Christensen would probably have been delighted by the spoken commentary which has been added to the present version of his film: culled largely from the original titles (the rest are retained as silent film titles), and spoken by William Burroughs in the orotund and slightly absurd tones used in the days of Fitzpatrick travelogues, it maintains exactly the right distantiation, never allowing the audience to become more involved in these mysteries and manifestations of witchcraft than Christensen is himself. And Christensen, of course, is sceptical, arguing through the film that 'witches' are simply what the twentieth century would call hysterics, suffering from delusions. Hence the consciously absurd, pantomime ribaldry of much of the imagery: witches riding off to the Sabbath on their broomsticks, giving birth to fantastic monsters after copulation with the Devil, giving the ritual kiss to Satan's arse etc. etc. What makes the film genuinely chilling is that these excesses are staged (again with superb lighting which turns much of the film into a chiaroscuro equivalent of Bosch and Breughel) amid an astonishingly real imaginative evocation of the medieval landscape in all its filth and squalor, its repressions, perversions, intolerances and cruelties: old crones tortured on the rack, young monks suffering the ecstasy of flagellation, old ones prancing the witches' sabbath in obscenely naked corpulence; young girls burned to save their souls by a self-righteous, monstrous Inquisition. Although time and familiarity with even greater horrors on the screen have undoubtedly blunted the shock effect much of the imagery must have had fifty years ago (babies dropped into boiling cauldrons, and so on), the film has lost little of its essential charge, especially in the modern sequence with its sudden, arresting analogies between past and present. To some *Haxan* may seem little more than a bizarre period curiosity, to others, a remarkable attempt to analyse the mythologies and mysteries of witchcraft. Either way, if one remembers the date it was made, it is a remarkable piece of film history . . .

Source: *Monthly Film Bulletin*, December 1968.

Ruttman's Berlin

Walter Ruttman (1887–1941) started life as an architect and painter and in the early 1920s, under the influence of Viking Eggeling – a Dadaist who created several landmark abstract films, most notably *Diagonalsymphonien* (Diagonal Symphony, 1924) – he made experimental films of geometric shapes in motion. Combining these techniques with some of Vertov's ideas, in 1928 Ruttman made his landmark documentary *Berlin – Die Symphonie einer Grosstadt* (*Berlin – Symphony of a Great City*), an ingenious, rhythmically cut portrait of Weimar Berlin which started a vogue around the world for similar dawn-to-dusk, poetic 'City Symphonies'.

After the enormous success of *Berlin*, Ruttman made several other 'symphonies' including *Melodie der Welt* (Melody of the World, 1929) before lending his talents to the Nazis, and advising Leni Riefenstahl on her infamous *Triumph of the Will*. He died of wounds acquired while filming a newsreel on the eastern front.

Since I began in the cinema, I had the idea of making something out of life, of creating a symphonic film out of the millions of energies that comprise the life of a big city. The possibility of such a film arose the day I met Karl Freund [cameraman on numerous important German productions of the 1920s, including *The Last Laugh*, *Variety* and *Metropolis*], who had the same ideas. During several weeks, as early as 4 a.m., he and I had to photograph the dead city. It is strange that Berlin tried to escape my efforts to capture its life and rhythm with my lens. We were constantly tormented by the hunter's fever, but the most difficult parts were those of the sleeping city. It is easier to work with moving things than to give the impression of absolute repose and the calm of death. For the night scenes, the chief cameraman, Reimar Kuntze, developed a hypersensitive film stock so that we could avoid using artificial light.

Source: Walter Ruttmann, quoted in Sadoul-Morris, *Dictionary of Films*, Berkeley, California, 1972.

12 Berlin: The Symphony of a Great City *(1927)*.

The Failings of *Berlin*
SIEGFRIED KRACAUER

This piece by the celebrated German cultural commentator and film critic Siegfried Kracauer (1889–1966) is from his essay 'Film 1928'.

There has hardly been any artistic experimentation of the sort that pushes film into new territory. The abstract films cultivated primarily in Paris are an eccentric breed that is not at issue here. Ruttmann's interesting film symphony *Berlin* is worth mentioning as the only significant attempt to break away from the common production fare. A film without a real plot, it attempts to allow the metropolis to arise out of a sequence of microscopic individual traits. But does it convey the reality of Berlin? No: it is just as blind to reality as any other feature film, and this is due to its lack of a political stance. Instead of penetrating its enormous object in a way that would betray a true understanding of its social, economic, and political structure, and instead of observing it with human concern or even tackling it from a particular vantage point in order to resolutely take it apart, Ruttmann leaves the thousands of details unconnected, one next to the other, inserting at most some arbitrarily conceived transitions that are meaningless. At best, the film is based on the idea that Berlin is the city of speed and work – a formal idea that in no way leads to any content and that perhaps for this reason intoxicates the German petit bourgeois when it appears in society and literature. There is nothing to see in this symphony, because it has not exposed a single meaningful relationship. In his book *Film Technique* Pudovkin reproaches the film for its lack of internal organization. In what is obviously a jab at Ruttmann, he writes: 'Quite a number of film technicians maintain that montage should be the only organizing process of film. They hold that the pieces can be shot in any way and anywhere, just so long as the images are interesting; afterward, by simply joining them according to their form and kind, a way will be found to assemble them into a film.'

Source: 'Film 1928' in *The Mass Ornament*, Harvard University Press, 1995. Translated and edited by Thomas Y. Levin.

Making *Rain*
JORIS IVENS

Among the numerous young film-makers influenced by *Berlin* was the
Dutchman Joris Ivens (1898–1989). His first films – *The Bridge* (1928),
Breakers (1929) and *Rain* (1929) – were aesthetic excercises in the use
of montage and, like *Berlin,* used their documentary material in an
almost abstract way. Subsequent to an extended stay in the Soviet Union
in 1930, however, Ivens came to feel dissatisfied by his work's lack of
'social content' and all his future films were of a highly political nature.
For more than fifty years he travelled the world making films for leftist
political régimes, often attracting criticism and accusations of hypocrisy
for his seeming disregard for his paymasters' human rights records.

This description of the genesis of *Rain* is from Ivens' autobiography,
The Camera and I.

My next film started from a far more trivial motive. While on location
for *Breakers* we needed the sun, instead we got rain – those long days of
rain that you have in Holland. The idea – let's make a film about the
damn rain – came quite naturally.

Although this idea arose almost as a joke, when I returned to
Amsterdam I talked it over with Mannus Franken who sketched an
outline. We discussed and revised the outline many times until it became
a film for both of us. Unfortunately, Mannus Franken lived in Paris, so
the shooting in Amsterdam was done by me alone. Franken, however,
came to Amsterdam for a short time to assist in the editing.

In making such a film of atmosphere, I found that you couldn't stick
to the script and that the script should not get too detailed. In this case,
the rain itself dictated its own literature and guided the camera into
secret wet paths we had never dreamed of when we outlined the film. It
was an unexpectedly difficult subject to tackle. Many artistic problems
were actually technical problems and vice versa. Film experience in
photographing rain was extremely limited because a normal cameraman stops filming when it begins to rain. When *Rain* was finished and
shown in Paris the French critics called it a cine poem and its structure is
actually more that of a poem than the prose of *The Bridge* [Ivens' first
short film]. Its object is to show the changing face of a city, Amsterdam,
during a shower.

The film opens with clear sunshine on houses, canals and people in the streets. A slight wind rises and the first drops of rain splash into the canals. The shower comes down harder and the people hasten about their business under the protection of capes and umbrellas. The shower ends. The last drops fall and the city's life returns to normal. The only continuity in *Rain* is the beginning, progress and end of this shower. There are neither titles nor dialogue. Its effects were intended as purely visual. The actors are the rain, the raindrops, wet people, dark clouds, glistening reflections moving over wet asphalt, and so forth. The diffused light on the dark houses along the black canals produced an effect that I never expected. And the whole film gives the spectator a very personal and subjective vision. As in the lines of Verlaine:

Il pleure dans mon coeur
Comme il pleut sur la ville.

At that time I lived with and for the rain. I tried to imagine how everything I saw would look in the rain and on the screen. It was part game, part obsession, part action. I had decided upon the several places in the city I wanted to film and I organized a system of rain watchers, friends who would telephone me from certain sections of town when the rain effects I wanted appeared. I never moved without my camera – it was with me in the office, laboratory, street, train. I lived with it and when I slept it was on my bedside table so that if it was raining when I woke I could film the studio window over my bed. Some of the best shots of raindrops along the slanted studio windows were actually taken from my bed when I woke up. All the new problems in this film sharpened my observation and also forced me to relax the rigid and over-analytical method of filming that I had used in *The Bridge*.

With the swiftly shifting rhythm and light of the rain, sometimes changing within a few seconds, my filming had to be defter and more spontaneous. For example, on the big central square of Amsterdam I saw three little girls under a cape and the skipping movements of their legs had the rhythm of raindrops. There had been a time when I thought that such good things could be shot tomorrow as well as today; but you soon learn that this is never true. I filmed those girls without a second's hesitation. They would probably never again walk at that hour on the square, or when they did it wouldn't be raining, and if it was raining they wouldn't have a cape, or skip in just that way, or it would be too dark – or something. So you film it immediately. With these dozens of interrelated factors you get the feeling of shooting – now or never . . .

It took me about four months to get the footage I needed for *Rain.* To achieve the effect of the beginning of the shower as you now see it in the film I had to photograph at least ten beginnings and out of these ten make the one film beginning. The rain itself was a moody actress who had to be humoured and who refused any thing but a natural make-up. I found that none of the new colour-corrective film emulsions on the market were suitable for my rain problems. The old extra-rapid Agfa film with no colour correction at all, and used without a filter, gave the best results. All lenses were used with a fully opened diaphragm because most of the work was done with a minimum of light.

It's remarkable how easy it is to forget the most basic elements of your subject and how important those basic elements are to your work. In *Rain* I had to remind myself constantly that rain is wet – so you must keep the screen dripping with wetness – make the audience feel damp and not just dampness. When they think they can't get any wetter, double the wetness, show the raindrops falling in the water of the canal – make it super-wet. I was so happy when I noticed at one of the first screenings of the finished film that the audience looked around for their raincoats and were surprised to find the weather dry and clear when they came out of the theatre.

To give the rain its fullest, richest quality I had to make sure that the sunlight that began and ended the film showed its typical differences. You have to catch the distinction between sunlight before rain and sunlight after rain; the distinction between the rich strong enveloping sunlight before the rain and the strange dreamy yellow light afterwards. I know that this sounds oversubtle but it is important and you have to be aware of it and remember to catch these subtleties with your camera.

In addition to careful photography, these nuances in light quality can be emphasized in movement. For example, I heightened the sharp quality of the sunlight that precedes the rain by keenly defined movements of light and shadow. The sharp dark shadow of a footbridge rips across the wide deck of a boat passing swiftly underneath. This movement is cut off by immediate contact with a close–up of another boat moving in an opposite diagonal across the entire screen. As the rain begins I added to the changes in light, a change in these movements emphasizing the leisurely movement of barges, wet puffs of smoke and waving reflections in the water. When cutting these shots I was careful to avoid abrupt contrasts, letting them build up leisurely on the screen.

Another interesting thing I learned about the values of shots and movements was their relation to humour. In editing I guided the eyes of the audience to the right of the screen by a close shot of water gushing out of a drainpipe, following this immediately by a shot of a dripping wet dog running along. My intention was merely to pick up the movement and rhythm in the pipe shot with the shot of the dog and my simple movement continuity always got a laugh. If I had been a more skilful editor at that time I would have made a more conscious use of such an effect, but I was still learning. I was still too preoccupied with movement and rhythm to be sufficiently aware of the special capacity film has for communicating the humorous movements around us.

However, *Rain* did teach me a great deal about film emotion – much more than the emotional story of the *Breakers*. In editing *The Bridge* I had discovered the sad effect achieved by the rhythmic repetition of slow heavy movements. In *Rain* I consciously used heavy dark drops dripping in big pear-shaped forms at long intervals across the glass of the studio window to produce the melancholy feeling of a rainy day. The opposite effect of happiness or gaiety in a spring shower could be produced by many bright small round drops pounding against many surfaces in a variety of shots.

To strengthen the continuity of *Rain* I used the repetition of a second visual motif – birds flying in the sunlight and then as the rain starts, a flock moving against the gray sky (continuing a rhythm indicated in the previous shot by leaves rustling in the wind). During the storm I showed one or two birds flying restlessly about. After the rain has stopped there is a shot of some birds sitting quietly on the wet railing of a bridge.

I shot the whole film with my old Kinamo and an American De Vry hand camera. My assistant was a young Chinese sailor, Chang Fai, whom I had met as a waiter in a Chinese restaurant on the Zeedyk. Chang Fai had jumped a large Indies liner in order to stay in Holland and learn a profession before going back to Asia. His main job as my assistant was to hold an umbrella over my camera.

. . . Made almost entirely as a cameraman's film, *Rain* proved to be successful with audiences. It followed the same distribution channels *The Bridge* had experienced, and was shown in avant-garde movie theatres throughout Europe and in many cine clubs. One thing that spectators always commented on was the film's identity with the simple things of daily life – revealing the beauty in these things. It was, I think, a new field for the close-up which until then had been used only for passionate or dramatic emphasis. These close-ups of everyday objects made *Rain* an important step in my development.

The most serious criticism against the film was its lack of 'content'. In a certain sense this was an exact criticism. I failed to emphasize sufficiently human beings' reactions to rain in a big city. Everything was subordinated to the aesthetic approach. In a way I am glad that I laid a foundation of technical and creative perfection before working on other more important elements. I have since seen too many films so exclusively dependent on content that the available means for film-making have been neglected with injury to the content itself.

Source: Joris Ivens, *The Camera and I*, Seven Seas Books, 1969.

Jean Painlevé
RAYMOND DURGNAT

This outline of the work of Jean Painlevé (1902–89) is from *Film Dope*.

Son of a mathematician turned War Minister and then Prime Minister, and whose government was deeply embroiled in both the 'Paths of glory' and the 'Mata Hari' stories, Jean Painlevé became a Communist, a Surrealist, a biologist, an underwater diver, a motor-racing champion and a jewellery designer. Film historians, while acknowledging his contribution to the specialized scientific and medical *genre*, cherish in particular his 'popular' documentaries, whose rigorous scientific materialism leads straight into Surreality. Their recurrent subjects – vampire-bat, sea-urchin, sea-horse – are weirder than science fiction, but, being nature-fact, more disturbing. He not only omits the reassuring spin that gets put on nature-documentaries (from Mary Field at Gaumont–Instructional to Oxford Scientific films), but his deceptively simple filming is appropriately 'brutalist'.

In *Les Assassins d'eau Douce* ('Freshwater assassins'), pond and river insects grip, grapple, sting, stab, and semi-transparently suck each other's innards out; but their throes and spasms occur to background music by the Ellington and Lunceford bands. It's not funny; on the contrary; their spasms and palpitations somehow permeate the 'jungle'-music's rhythms, vibratos, and growls, until even good-time jazz acquires carnivore tensions. This is *not* the Surrealism of fancies and fantasies made safe by 'art', and cosy by Freudian emphasis on 'love'. It mixes the more virulent Surrealist strains: the disciplined self-alienation of 'the Surrealist laboratory'; the anti-humanism of the 'acephalics'; and some Dada humour (e.g. jokey end-titles).

Not that poetry is lacking. In *Les Oursins*, the physiology of the sea-urchin, in close-up and colour, and lovingly explained in voice-over, becomes a mad metaphor for the female genitalia. That's not this writer's purely personal neurosis speaking. At an American University a feminist colleague claimed that this film degraded women, and tried to have it banned from campus showings. Meanwhile a post-graduate student thought it must be a message from remote and benevolent mind controllers trying to encourage her sexuality.

Working to the limits of his 'early' technology, Painlevé exploits film form's strange power to involve our minds with the physicalities it depicts. Hence those freshwater insects, and human organs behaving just as weirdly, anticipate the nightmare visions of Burroughs, Cronenberg, and *The Naked Lunch*. But whereas, in 'Art' writing, everything dwindles into metaphors for human fantasies, Painlevé's factual life-forms seduce, tease, stretch our human imagination to breaking point. In *L'Hippocampe*, the sea-horse's perky face attracts a happy anthropomorphism which its mind-boggling biology progressively confounds. Darius Milhaud contributed a mournful, witty score.

Painlevé's micro-masterpieces reconcile attitudes usually kept stiffly apart (Surrealism + science, modernism + ultra-realism). They belong with a French documentary spirit, or movement (Epstein, Storck, Vigo, Franju, Resnais . . .) which, compared to the English, was less directly sociable, more open to material structures. It also explored 'indifferent nature' as Vertov's kino-eye never did. Perhaps Painlevé was a founding father of a scientific cine-culture whose day is overdue to dawn.

Source: *Film Dope* April 1994, Vol. 50.

A Propos de Nice
BORIS KAUFMAN

The radical and imaginative French director Jean Vigo (1905–1934) made two experimental short documentaries *A Propos de Nice* (1930)

and *Taris* (1931), before he turned to fiction with *Zéro de Conduite* (1932) and *L'Atalante* (1934), the films for which he is now largely remembered. All of Vigo's films were photographed by Boris Kaufman, the younger brother of Dziga Vertov and Mikhail Kaufman (see Chapter 3) who, by his own account, had learnt cinematography by letter from his celebrated siblings.

A Propos de Nice, his first collaboration with Vigo, was heavily influenced by Vertov's ideas, and used a full range of kino-eye devices including slow-motion, freeze-frames and hidden cameras.

Kaufman wrote this piece for the *Cine Club* magazine in 1949.

A documentary about the French Riviera. It has been described as 'one of the most unconventional documentaries ever made – with a bitterness and irony comparable to Von Stroheim's, the camera explores this centre of middle-class decadence, the monstrous hotels with their armies of servants, the baroque casinos, the amorous elderly women with their ruthless gigolos, the stinking alleys and grimy bistros filled with tramps, ponces, fences: a scathing contrast of the idle poor and the idle rich' (George Morrison in *Sequence 6*).

. . . *Point de vue documenté* was the phrase used by Vigo to describe his first film.

On 14 June 1930, *A Propos de Nice* was shown at the Vieux Colombier, to a special audience composed of the *Groupement des spectateurs d'avant-garde*. Vigo gave an introductory talk, called *Vers un cinéma social*, in which he paid tribute to the work of Luis Buñuel and outlined some of his own ideas:

'I would like to talk about a more defined form of social cinema, something to which I am closest: the social documentary – or, more precisely, *point de vue documenté*.

'In this area of endeavor, I affirm, the camera is King – or at least President of the Republic.

'I don't know whether the result will be a work of art, but I am sure it will be cinema. Cinema, in the sense that no other art, no science, can take its place.

'The maker of social documentaries is a man thin enough to squeeze through a Rumanian keyhole and shoot Prince Carol getting up in his nightshirt – assuming that were a spectacle worthy of interest. He is a fellow small enough to squat under the chair of the croupier – the Great

God of the casino at Monte Carlo – and that, as you may well imagine, is no easy thing.

'Social documentary is distinct from the ordinary short film and the weekly newsreel in that its creator will establish his own point of view: he will dot his own 'i's.

'If it doesn't involve an artist, it at least involves a man . . . Conscious behaviour cannot be tolerated, character must be surprised by the camera if the whole 'documentary' value of this kind of cinema is to be achieved.

'We shall achieve our end if we can reveal the hidden reason for a gesture, if we can extract from an ordinary person his interior beauty – or a caricature of him – quite by chance, if we can reveal his complete inner spirit through his purely external manifestations.

'A Propos de Nice is only a rough draft . . . In this film, the description of a whole town begging from sheer laziness, we are spectators at the trial of a particular world. After indicating this life and

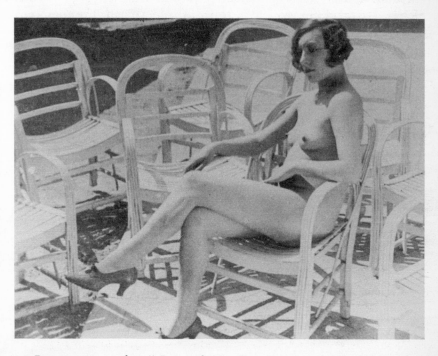

13 Fantasy sequence from A Propos de Nice (1930).

atmosphere of Nice – and, alas, elsewhere – the film proceeds to a generalized impression of gross pleasures, to different signs of a grotesque existence, of flesh and of death. These are the last twitchings of a society that neglects its own responsibilities to the point of giving you nausea and making you an accomplice in a revolutionary solution.'

He seemed both to love and to hate the town in which, for reasons of health, he and his wife had been obliged to live for two years.

Nice was getting ready for the Carnival . . . The focal point was the Promenade des Anglais, centre of action (or inaction) for the internationally lazy.

The method was to take by surprise facts, actions, attitudes, expressions, and to stop shooting as soon as the subject became conscious of being photographed.

Le point de vue documenté.
Old Nice, its narrow streets, washing hung between the houses, the baroque Italian cemetery. Pleasures. Regattas. Warships at anchor. Hotels. Arrival of tourists . . . Factories. An old woman. The young girl changing her dress in the middle of the Promenade (trick shot) and finally appearing nude. A burial service . . . Crocodiles. Sun. The female ostrich. The Carnival, the Battle of Flowers, the gradually slackening dances.

Above all this absurd gaiety, the ominous vistas of chimneys.

All this may look naïve now, but we were sincere. We rejected out of hand anything that was picturesque without significance, any facile contrasts. The story had to be understood without commentary or subtitles. We shot the film relying on the evocation of ideas by purely visual means. Which is why, in the cutting, we were able to juxtapose the Promenade des Anglais with the Nice cemetery, where marble figures (baroque style) had the same ridiculous features as the human beings on the Promenade.

Working with Vigo – his unfailing taste, his integrity, his depth and his lightness, his nonconformism, the absence of any kind of routine – took me into a kind of film-maker's paradise. It was ideal!

Source: *Cine Club*, February 1949.

Luis Buñuel Discusses *Las Hurdes*

Luis Buñuel (1900–1983) directed his only documentary *Las Hurdes* (*Land Without Bread*, 1932), immediately after his two most extreme surrealist films, *Un Chien Andalou* (1928) and *L'Age d'Or* (1930), both made in collaboration with Salvador Dali. Critics have long wondered whether *Las Hurdes*, a kind of perverse travel film detailing the appalling living conditions of the peasants in one of Spain's poorest regions, should be interpreted as a continuation of the Surrealist urge.

This interview was conducted with Buñuel in Mexico towards the end of his life.

COLINA: *How did the project for* Las Hurdes *come about?*

BUÑUEL: It came about because I had read the doctoral thesis of Legendre, director of the French Institute of Madrid. An admirable book, I still have it in my library. For twenty years Legendre spent every summer in Las Hurdes to conduct a complete study of the region: botanical, zoological, climatological, social, etc. A marvel! Later, I read some articles about the place that the Madrid magazine *Estampa* published when the king visited there.

COLINA: *There is also an essay by Unamuno, in which he says, more or less, that within the Hurdanos' extreme need you can see the Spaniards' soul and dignity naked . . .*

BUÑUEL: I was able to film *Las Hurdes* thanks to Ramón Acín, an anarchist from Huesca, a drawing teacher, who one day at a café in Zaragoza told me, 'Luis, if I ever won the lottery, I would put up the money for you to make a film.' He won a hundred thousand pesetas in the lottery and gave me twenty thousand to make the film. With four thousand I bought a Fiat; Pierre Unik came, under contract from Vogue to write an article; and Eli Lotar arrived with a camera loaned by [Marc] Allegret.

COLINA: *Acín gave you twenty thousand pesetas without making any demands about the film?*

BUÑUEL: No, none of that. He told me, 'If you return some of the money, so much the better . . .' Of course the film didn't make any money. Later, during Franco's 1936 uprising, he and his wife were shot by the rebels. First they took his wife prisoner and announced that they would shoot her if he did not turn himself in to the authorities. Acín presented himself. The next day he and his wife were both executed.

COLINA: *How was the filming of* Las Hurdes?

BUÑUEL: Eli Lotar, Pierre Unik, and Sanchez Ventura helped me. Las Hurdes was four hours by car from Madrid. It was a desert, but I found some Hurdanos who spoke French.

COLINA: *Where did you stay?*

BUÑUEL: At Las Batuecas. It is a paradise valley. Only one kilometre away, the Hurdano hell begins. We stayed at an inn that had been a convent managed by a Carmelite brother, who had stayed on as a layman. We slept there and left very early in the morning to film.

COLINA: *In one scene the text reads, 'At times, a goat falls from the rocks', but in the bottom corner of the image we see smoke from a gun shot. In other words, the goat didn't fall by accident.*

BUÑUEL: Since we couldn't wait for the event to happen, I provoked it by firing a revolver. Later, we saw that the smoke from the gunshot appeared in the frame, but we couldn't repeat the scene because it would have angered the Hurdanos and they would have attacked us. (They don't kill goats. They only eat those that fall by accident.) Since the Hurdanos didn't have any firearms, I used a revolver because I couldn't find a rifle.

COLINA: *The contradictions of cinema: to show the Hurdanos' poverty, you add to it by killing a goat.*

BUÑUEL: It's true, but we were trying to show an image of life among the Hurdanos and we had to show everything. It's a very different thing to say, 'At times a goat falls', than to show it as it really happens.

TURRENT: *And have you been back there more recently?*

BUÑUEL: Yes, some years ago I went to Las Hurdes. It had changed somewhat because it had become part of Franco's favorite region. There was electricity in some towns and they made bread everywhere.

COLINA: *You film people were outsiders to the Hurdanos; they didn't receive you badly in 1932?*

BUÑUEL: No, I brought a recommendation from Pascua, the Health secretary, and from Don Ricardo Urueta, the Fine Arts director, who were Republicans and very good friends of mine; they had given me permission to make an 'artistic' film about Salamanca and a 'picturesque' documentary about Las Hurdes.

COLINA: *But how were your relations with the Hurdanos . . . ?*

BUÑUEL: They were good.

COLINA: *What was the reaction to the film?*

BUÑUEL: It was banned . . . Later, during the war, Franco's rebels had a file on me which stated that I had made a film that was defamatory to Spain and that if I were arrested, I was to be taken to the Generalisimo's headquarters at Salamanca. The file was found at a Civil Guard barracks that the Republican troops took.

TURRENT: *Did you use a script for* Las Hurdes?

BUÑUEL: No. I visited the region ten days before the filming started and brought my notebook. I would jot down: 'goats', 'a child sick with malaria', 'anopheles mosquitoes', 'there are no songs, there is no bread', and I shot the film pretty much in agreement with those notes. I edited the film without using a moviola, on a kitchen table with a magnifying glass and, since I still didn't understand much about cinema, I eliminated many of Lotar's good images because the photograms looked blurred. I didn't know that movement can somehow reconstruct the image. So, by not having a moviola, I lost some good shots.

TURRENT: *Did you feel that the film was very different from* Un Chien Andalou *and* L'Age d'Or?

BUÑUEL: It was very different and yet, nevertheless, it was a twin. To me, it seemed very much like my other films. Of course, the difference was that this film was based on a concrete reality. But it was an exceptional reality, one that stimulated the imagination. Furthermore, the film coincided with the social concerns of the Surrealist movement, which were very intense at that time.

COLINA: *Why did you use music by Brahms?*

TURRENT: *The Fourth Symphony. It drew a lot of attention because it's very romantic music.*

BUÑUEL: There are only a handful of musical works that are etched in my brain in an obsessive way, and I've always searched for a way to use them in my films (even though I very rarely use music). They showed *Las Hurdes* in New York at a documentary makers' association, and this accompaniment caused a sensation. To me, it seems to go very well with the film. Why did I use it? It's something irrational, something I cannot explain.

TURRENT: *Did you use it as a counterpoint or to create a distance?*

BUÑUEL: I don't know. I heard it mentally while I was editing the film and felt it would go well with it.

TURRENT: *Don't you think the fact that the commentary is in French and spoken by a Frenchman makes the film very neutral?*

BUÑUEL: Yes. But also because the text itself is already very neutral. Pay attention to the end: 'After so much time in Las Hurdes, let's now return to Madrid.' That's how the commentary is, very dry, very documentary-like, without literary effects.

COLINA: *I understand the sound was added much later.*

BUÑUEL: Yes, since the film was banned during the so-called Black Biennium, it was not given a sound track . . .

COLINA: *The Black Biennium: the two years of the Republic when the right wing won the elections.*

BUÑUEL: Yes, with Lerroux and Gil Robles. Later, in 1936, the war broke out, and then the Republican government gave me money to add a sound track. The ban was only during the Republic's reactionary phase.

TURRENT: *Many people have said, and I agree, that* Las Hurdes *is like a response to* Un Chien Andalou *and* L'Age d'Or.

BUÑUEL: It's in the same line. The first two are imaginative, the other is taken from reality, but I feel it shares the same outlook.

TURRENT: *But while the first two are films of revolt,* Las Hurdes *explains the reason for the revolt. You also changed genres and made a documentary. What were your ideas about documentary film-making?*

BUÑUEL: I had no preconceived idea. I visited the region, read the book by Legendre, and since cinema is my means of expression, I made the film without *parti pris* of any sort.

TURRENT: *Don Luis, by filming reality as you see it, do you believe you faithfully follow the Surrealist spirit?*

BUÑUEL: Yes, yes, yes, of course. We're talking about a tendentious film. Such poverty doesn't exist in Las Hurdes Bajas. Of the fifty-two communities, or *alquerías*, as they call them, there are around thirty that have neither bread, nor chimneys, nor songs. I photographed Las Hurdes Bajas in passing, but almost the entire film occurs in Las Hurdes Altas, which are mountains like infernos, a series of arid gulches, a bit like the desert landscape of Chihuahua, but much smaller.

TURRENT: *I read one critic who said that the film is a declaration in favour of euthanasia.*

BUÑUEL: Of euthanasia? (He laughs.)

COLINA: *Did the Surrealists see the film?*

BUÑUEL: I don't remember. Perhaps when it was shown in France. I was already outside the group.

COLINA: *Did you leave the group voluntarily?*

BUÑUEL: Completely voluntarily. Aragon, Sadoul, Unik, Maxime Alexandre, and I all left at the same time.

COLINA: *Aragon and Sadoul had parted from the group because they were already in the Communist Party, but as far as I know you never became a militant Communist.*

BUÑUEL: No. I was a sympathizer, no more. Especially during the Spanish Civil War.

TURRENT: *Returning to* Las Hurdes, *did the documentary footage on the mosquito have the same intention as that of the scorpions in* L'Age d'Or?

BUÑUEL: No. I put it in as one more element of information, to demonstrate that malaria was a component of Hurdano poverty.

COLINA: *So, this bug isn't gratuitous the way the scorpions were in* L'Age d'Or.

BUÑUEL: No. Nothing is gratuitous in *Las Hurdes*. It is perhaps the least gratuitous film I have made.

Source: *Conversations with Luis Buñuel* by José de La Colina and Tomás Pérez Turrent. Originally published in Mexico as *Luis Buñuel: Prohibido Asomarse al Interior*. Translation Copyright, 1992 Marsilio Publishers, New York, 1992.

14 Las Hurdes: Land without Bread *(1932)*.

Part 2

5 The British Movement

The British documentary movement of the 1930s was the self-conscious creation of a single determined individual: John Grierson. Combining strong theoretical convictions with practical and political know-how, he obtained Government backing for the creation of a film unit based initially, in 1928, at the Empire Marketing Board (EMB) and from 1933 until the war at the General Post Office (GPO). A proselytizer, a theorist and a shrewd politician, Grierson gathered around himself a group of young, tremendously enthusiastic, but almost completely inexperienced, film-makers, whom he trained and shaped into a movement – a movement which produced a handful of documentary classics and continues to exert an influence today that can be both inspiring and limiting.

Grierson famously defined the documentary film as 'the creative use of actuality', a phrase so broad it is almost meaningless. In fact, his own ideas on what the documentary should and shouldn't be were much more specific and the key to them is a distrust of play-acting and entertainment instilled in him by his Scottish Calvinist upbringing. In one of his essays he recalls that the first film he ever saw was part of a Lumière programme and showed a boy eating an apple. 'The significant thing for me now,' he wrote, 'is that our elders accepted this cinema as essentially different from the theatre. Sin was somehow still attached to play-acting, but in this fresh new art of observation and reality, they saw no evil. I was confirmed in cinema at six because it had nothing to do with theatre, and I have remained so confirmed. But cinema has not. It was not quite so innocent as our Calvinist elders supposed. Hardly were the workmen out of the factory and the apple digested than it was a trip to the moon and, only a year or two later, a trip in full colour to the devil.' Elsewhere in his writings he even goes so far as to suggest that documentary can give us a glimpse of some pre-lapsarian paradise: 'The camera is in a measure both the discoverer of an unknown world and the rediscoverer of a lost one.'

Combined with a non-dogmatic Marxist concern for the community in precedence to the individual, Grierson's Calvinist background led him to believe that the only worthwhile type of cinema was factual and useful – of educational or material benefit to society. If a film served its utilitarian function well, he believed, it would also be of artistic merit. If it was entertaining, so much the better – but that was of secondary concern. He wanted his films to do good. 'I look on cinema as a pulpit,' he said, 'and use it as a propagandist.'

Grierson's two great cinematic influences were Flaherty – for his determination to find the drama in the seemingly mundane, and take his story from his subject, not impose it from without – and the Russians, who had been using cinema for propaganda for a decade before he set up his unit at the EMB. Vertov he disapproved of, accusing him of

15 A surreal image from Victor Turin's Turksib (1929), a film which greatly influenced John Grierson.

tricksy formalism, of forgetting the purpose of his films. More to his taste was Victor Turin's *Turksib* (1929) about the construction of a railway in Soviet Asia as part of a five year plan. Indeed, Grierson re-edited and titled the film for its English language release.

Grierson prided himself on 'putting the working classes on the screen' and giving them a voice, but in fact it is something he singularly failed to do. The working classes in his films are praised for their craftsmanship and hard work, but they are rarely humanized or allowed to speak for themselves. Another anomaly of his films is the extensive use of actors, sets, continuity scripts and dialogues. Few, if any, of the acknowledged classics of the documentary movement would be classified as documentaries by today's purists. Films like *Night Mail* (1936) and *The Voice of Britain* (1935) place no value on what Vertov called 'catching life unawares'.

Grierson's influence on the subsequent development of the documentary cannot be overestimated (adopting his model countries as far apart as Canada, India and Australia created state-sponsored 'film divisions'). But it is an influence which has its down side. So pervasive have Greirson's ideas been on the documentary as a tool for social betterment, that there has been a tendency ever since to underestimate the diverse imaginative possibilities of the form. Moreover, Grierson's disapproval of entertainment and personal expression has too frequently made the word 'documentary' a byword for tedium.

Grierson's Background and the Origins of his Ideas

This piece, in which Grierson discusses his early life and aims, is from what was, in all likelihood, the last interview he gave before his death in 1972.

I grew up in the Clydeside movement [the Scottish Socialist movement centred around the Clyde shipyards]. I've been in politics all my life. Nobody who ever grew up in the Clydeside movement forgets. Under no circumstances do we forget. But whether I went into politics in the ordinary sense was another matter. I was offered a couple of constituencies before I left the university, and the thing that interested me – not that I'd have got in, but I was offered the chance to stand for them – they were by two different parties. That tickles me – two different parties!

No, I thought I'd do a better political job the way I did, and I was very interested in this question of putting the working class on the screen, of bringing the working-class thing alive in another form than we were getting on the soapboxes of Glasgow Green. That wasn't good enough for me, the soapbox. You see, I worked in a factory down the Clyde, and I didn't think that we could live off platforms, platform relationships. And I think I saw early the possibility of other forms. Of course I was interested in the journalistic form first of all, that is the yellow newspaper form. I've always been interested in the yellow newspaper. But then of course Flaherty was a turning point. *Nanook* hit Glasgow round about 1922, I think. I was on to it by 1924, that film could be turned into an instrument of the working class.

From then on, there was no question of where one's duty lay. But it was an idea that didn't develop in Glasgow or in England. It was an idea that developed in America. I spent three years, 1924 to 1927, based in Chicago, and I was very concerned then with what was happening to the immigrants. There was no question that it started out in a political conception, a political social conception.

Now, if you think of the cinema, the motion picture, round about the twenties, you have a tradition of it's being used for theatrical purposes and developing quite a big tradition in comedy and also in theatrical shapes, through people like De Mille and D.W. Griffith and so on. You get the use of the film extending into musical comedy when sound comes along. But apart from entertainment, dramatic entertainment, you have very little use of the cinema's native and natural powers – for example, in the matter of getting around. There's nothing like the camera for getting around. That's what makes it unique, the fact that it can travel from place to place. It can see round corners, more or less. It can see upways, downways, all the way round. It can put a telescope at the end of a lens. It can, of course, look through a microscope. In other words, it's capable of an infinite variety of observations. But in taking the picture of the twenties, it had not greatly invaded the field of its possibilities.

There was a whole world undiscovered, a whole area of cinematic possibility undiscovered. All we did in documentary was we occupied Oklahoma. I saw this thing. I saw here was a territory completely unoccupied. I thought I was going in for newspapers, but obviously newspapers were very expensive and I couldn't see myself buying up a few newspapers. But here were newspapers – as it were, the whole power of newspapers – going for nothing. The only thing was to find a way of financing it. And, of course, the great event in the history of documentary was that we didn't go to Hollywood for money. We went to governments for money and thereby tied documentary, the use of the realistic cinema, to purposes.

Source: Elizabeth Sussex, *The Rise and Fall of British Documentary: The Story of the Film Movement Founded by John Grierson*, Berkeley, University of California Press, 1975.

First Principles of Documentary
JOHN GRIERSON

In this characteristic essay from 1934–6, Grierson, who never liked to be pinned down, comes as close as he ever did to setting forth the aims and methods of the British documentary movement.

First principles. (1) We believe that the cinema's capacity for getting around, for observing and selecting from life itself, can be exploited in a new and vital art form. The studio films largely ignore this possibility of opening up the screen on the real world. They photograph acted stories against artificial backgrounds. Documentary would photograph the living scene and the living story. (2) We believe that the original (or native) actor, and the original (or native) scene, are better guides to a screen interpretation of the modern world. They give cinema a greater fund of material. They give it power over a million and one images. They give it power of interpretation over more complex and astonishing happenings in the real world than the studio mind can conjure up or the studio mechanician recreate. (3) We believe that the materials and the stories thus taken from the raw can be finer (more real in the philosophic sense) than the acted article. Spontaneous gesture has a special value on the screen. Cinema has a sensational capacity for enhancing the movement which tradition has formed or time worn smooth. Its arbitrary rectangle specially reveals movement; it gives it maximum pattern in space and time. Add to this that documentary can achieve an intimacy of knowledge and effect impossible to the shim-sham mechanics of the studio, and the lily-fingered interpretations of the metropolitan actor.

I do not mean in this minor manifesto of beliefs to suggest that the studios cannot in their own manner produce works of art to astonish the world. There is nothing (except the Woolworth intentions of the people who run them) to prevent the studios going really high in the manner of theatre or the manner of fairy tale. My separate claim for documentary is simply that in its use of the living article, there is also an opportunity to perform creative work. I mean, too, that the choice of the documentary medium is as gravely distinct a choice as the choice of poetry instead of fiction. Dealing with different material, it is, or should be, dealing with it to different aesthetic issues from those of the studio. I make this distinction to the point of asserting that the young director cannot, in nature, go documentary and go studio both.

. . . With Flaherty it became an absolute principle that the story must be taken from the location, and that it should be (what he considers) the essential story of the location. His drama, therefore, is a drama of days and nights, of the round of the year's seasons, of the fundamental fights which give his people sustenance, or make their community life possible, or build up the dignity of the tribe.

Such an interpretation of subject-matter reflects, of course, Flaherty's particular philosophy of things. A succeeding documentary exponent is in no way obliged to chase off to the ends of the earth in search of old-time simplicity, and the ancient dignities of man against the sky. Indeed, if I may for the moment represent the opposition, I hope the Neo-Rousseauism implicit in Flaherty's work dies with his own exceptional self. Theory of naturals apart, it represents an escapism, a wan and distant eye, which tends in lesser hands to sentimentalism. However it be shot through with vigour of Lawrentian poetry, it must always fail to develop a form adequate to the more immediate material of the modern world. For it is not only the fool that has his eyes on the ends of the earth. It is sometimes the poet: sometimes even the great poet, as Cabell in his *Beyond Life* will brightly inform you. This, however, is the very poet who on every classic theory of society from Plato to Trotsky should be removed bodily from the Republic. Loving every Time but his own, and every Life but his own, he avoids coming to grips with the creative job insofar as it concerns society. In the business of ordering most present chaos, he does not use his powers.

Question of theory and practice apart, Flaherty illustrates better than anyone the first principles of documentary. (1) It must master its material on the spot, and come in intimacy to ordering it. Flaherty digs himself in for a year, or two maybe. He lives with his people till the story is told 'out of himself'. (2) It must follow him in his distinction between description and drama. I think we shall find that there are other forms of drama or, more accurately, other forms of film, than the one he chooses; but it is important to make the primary distinction between a method which describes only the surface values of a subject, and the method which more explosively reveals the reality of it. You photograph the natural life, but you also, by your juxtaposition of detail, create an interpretation of it.

This final creative intention established, several methods are possible. You may, like Flaherty, go for a story form, passing in the ancient manner from the individual to the environment, to the environment transcended or not transcended, to the consequent honours of heroism. Or you may not be so interested in the individual. You may think that the individual life is no longer capable of cross-sectioning reality. You may believe that its particular bellyaches are of no consequence in a world which complex and impersonal forces command, and conclude that the individual as a self-sufficient dramatic figure is outmoded. When Flaherty tells you that it is a devilish noble thing to fight for food in a wilderness, you may, with some justice, observe that you are more concerned with the problem of people fighting for food in the midst of plenty. When he draws your attention to the fact that Nanook's spear is grave in its upheld angle, and finely rigid in its down-pointing bravery, you may, with some justice, observe that no spear, held however bravely by the individual, will master the crazy walrus of international finance. Indeed you may feel that in individualism is a yahoo tradition largely responsible for our present anarchy, and deny at once both the hero of decent heroics (Flaherty) and the hero of indecent ones (studio). In this case, you will feel that you want your drama in terms of some cross-section of reality which will reveal the essentially co-operative or mass nature of society: leaving the individual to find his honours in the swoop of creative social forces. In other words, you are liable to abandon the story form, and seek, like the modern exponent of poetry and painting and prose, a matter and method more satisfactory to the mind and spirit of the time.

Berlin or the Symphony of a City initiated the more modern fashion of finding documentary material on one's doorstep: in events which have no novelty of the unknown, or romance of noble savage on exotic landscape, to recommend them. It represented, slimly, the return from romance to reality.

Berlin was variously reported as made by Ruttmann, or begun by Ruttmann and finished by Freund: certainly it was begun by Ruttmann. In smooth and finely tempo'd visuals, a train swung through suburban mornings into Berlin. Wheels, rails, details of engines, telegraph wires, landscapes and other simple images flowed along in procession, with similar abstracts passing occasionally in and out of the general movement. There followed a sequence of such movements which, in their total effect, created very imposingly the story of a Berlin day. The day began with a processional of workers, the factories got under way, the streets filled: the city's forenoon became a hurly burly of tangled pedestrians and street cars. There was respite for food: a various respite with contrast of rich and poor. The city started work again, and a shower of rain in the afternoon became a considerable event. The city stopped work and, in a further more hectic processional of pubs and cabarets and dancing legs and illuminated sky-signs, finished its day.

Insofar as the film was principally concerned with movements and the building of separate images into movements, Ruttmann was justified in calling it a symphony. It meant a break away from the story borrowed from literature, and from the play borrowed from the stage. In *Berlin* cinema swung along according to its own more natural powers: creating dramatic effect from the tempo'd accumulation of its single observations. Cavalcanti's *Rien que les Heures* and Leger's *Ballet Mécanique* came before *Berlin*, each with a similar attempt to combine images in an emotionally satisfactory sequence of movements. They were too scrappy and had not mastered the art of cutting sufficiently well to create the sense of 'march' necessary to the genre. The symphony of Berlin City was both larger in its movements and larger in its vision.

There was one criticism of *Berlin* which, out of appreciation for a fine film and a new and arresting form, the critics failed to make; and time has not justified the omission. For all its ado of workmen and factories and swirl and swing of a great city, *Berlin* created nothing. Or rather if it created something, it was that shower of rain in the afternoon. The people of the city got up splendidly, they tumbled through their five million hoops impressively, they turned in; and no other issue of God or man emerged than that sudden besmattering spilling of wet on people and pavements.

I urge the criticism because *Berlin* still excites the mind of the young, and the symphony form is still their most popular persuasion. In fifty

scenarios presented by the tyros, forty-five are symphonies of Edinburgh or of Ecclefechan or of Paris or of Prague. Day breaks – the
people come to work – the factories start – the street cars rattle – lunch
hour and the streets again – sport if it is Saturday afternoon – certainly
evening and the local dance hall. And so, nothing having happened and
nothing positively said about anything, to bed; though Edinburgh is the
capital of a country and Ecclefechan, by some power inside itself, was
the birthplace of Carlyle, in some ways one of the greatest exponents of
this documentary idea.

The little daily doings, however finely symphonized, are not enough.
One must pile up beyond doing or process to creation itself, before one
hits the higher reaches of art. In this distinction, creation indicates not
the making of things but the making of virtues.

And there's the rub for tyros. Critical appreciation of movement they
can build easily from their power to observe, and power to observe they
can build from their own good taste, but the real job only begins as they
apply ends to their observation and their movements. The artist need
not posit the ends – for that is the work of the critic – but the ends must
be there, informing his description and giving finality (beyond space and
time) to the slice of life he has chosen. For that larger effect there must
be power of poetry or of prophecy. Failing either or both in the highest
degree, there must be at least the sociological sense implicit in poetry
and prophecy.

The best of the tyros know this. They believe that beauty will come in
good time to inhabit the statement which is honest and lucid and deeply
felt and which fulfils the best ends of citizenship. They are sensible
enough to conceive of art as the by-product of a job of work done. The
opposite effort to capture the by-product first (the self-conscious pursuit
of beauty, the pursuit of art for art's sake to the exclusion of jobs of
work and other pedestrian beginnings), was always a reflection of
selfish wealth, selfish leisure and aesthetic decadence.

This sense of social responsibility makes our realist documentary a
troubled and difficult art, and particularly in a time like ours. The job of
romantic documentary is easy in comparison: easy in the sense that the
noble savage is already a figure of romance and the seasons of the year
have already been articulated in poetry. Their essential virtues have been
declared and can more easily be declared again, and no one will deny
them. But realist documentary, with its streets and cities and slums and
markets and exchanges and factories, has given itself the job of making

poetry where no poet has gone before it, and where no ends, sufficient
for the purposes of art, are easily observed. It requires not only taste but
also inspiration, which is to say a very laborious, deep-seeing, deep-
sympathizing creative effort indeed.

Source: *Grierson on Documentary*, ed Forsyth Hardy, Faber and Faber, London,
1946. The article originally appeared in *Cinema Quarterly* in three parts between
1932 amd 1934.

Song of Ceylon
AN INTERVIEW WITH BASIL WRIGHT BY CECILE STARR

Basil Wright's *Song of Ceylon* (1934) was the first of a handful of
masterpieces produced by Grierson's documentary movement. Technically very sophisticated for the period, with a multi-layered sound track
and intricate cross-cutting, it was commissioned by the Ceylon Tea
Propaganda Board to encourage a favourable image of Ceylon and its
major export. Not that one would guess its commercial intention from
watching it. Wright's film is an ambiguous, lyrical piece that bears none
of the marks of strident imperialism one might expect.

Basil Wright (1907–1987) was one of the first young film-makers to
join Grierson at the Empire Marketing Board in 1929. After *Song of
Ceylon* he co-directed *Night Mail* with Harry Watt, which took a
similarly poetic approach to a mundane subject, and experimented even
more adventurously with sound and narrative structure. He continued
to make sponsored documentaries into the 1970s. This interview was
conducted in 1975.

CECILE STARR: *How did you happen to go to Ceylon to make a film,
any film, about Ceylon?*

BASIL WRIGHT: While I was working for Grierson, he was asked if he
could send a unit to Ceylon to make some travel films about the
country. They thought that by doing this the British public might
become conscious of this beautiful island and therefore buy the tea
which was its principal product. The negotiations went through, and I
was sent off to Ceylon with one assistant to make four one–reel
travelogues.

cs: *At what point did you know you were not going to make travelogues but were on the road to something else?*

bw: There are two answers to that question. The first answer is that I did know while I was in Ceylon, but only in my subconscious. In practical terms I didn't know I was making this film until I was back in England and had the material on a cutting bench.

During the shooting in Ceylon, I'd split the material into areas of activity purely for convenience: I had it in mind to make one travelogue about fisheries, another travelogue about harvesting, and so on. It was to this scheme I was shooting. It's awfully difficult to explain this, but all the time I was doing this, some inner impulse kept making me shoot certain other things. I couldn't for the life of me realize why, particularly as they were often very inconvenient.

Like the little birds that fly up in the first reel. We'd been working tremendously hard all day, from early morning until the light had practically gone. The cameras were all packed and put away, and we were exhausted. Then I saw this bird sitting on the branch of the tree silhouetted against the lake and something told me, 'I've got to shoot quite a lot of birds – I must do it at once.' So I said to my colleague, John Taylor: 'Unpack the case. Put up the camera. Put on the telephoto lens.' And he said, 'You must be mad.' I said, 'I don't care; you've got to do it.' So he did it, and we went on and on and eventually got those shots. We even flung stones at the birds because they wouldn't fly when we wanted them to.

I'd no idea what the shots were for until I began cutting the film. Then I realized they were to go with some other shots which I subsequently took, in which the camera moves very rapidly from one end to the other of some huge granite statues. That's what they were there for. This was done by curious instinct, and in fact a lot of the film got built that way. My inner consciousness had been set off by the fact that although an irreligious person, I was tremendously moved and impressed by Buddhist religion which I had encountered and seen for the very first time in Ceylon.

cs: *Did you script anything, or was all of your shooting just taking what you could find as you found it?*

bw: After we got to Ceylon (we arrived on New Year's Day, so it's quite easy to calculate one's time factors) I decided to spend at least four

weeks simply driving around the island looking at everything, so I could
build up in my mind's eye the sort of pictures I wanted to take through
the camera. That took a month, and then there was another ten days in
sort of preparing.

But it was worth doing. We eventually got ourselves sorted out and
travelled and shot continuously for six weeks. Then we had three days
to pause and lick our wounds and look around and see what we'd done.
Remember, we couldn't see the dailies because there was no air-travel in
those days. The film was shipped back to England, but it would be at
least a month or more before you got a report on whether your material
was any good or not; so we were shooting in the dark, as it were.

When we were in these locations, the shooting script was something I
cooked up on a bit of paper in my hand once we had the set-up. I had a
big sort of sketchbook which I scribbled in all the time and sketched out
little pictures of the different angles from which we had to shoot.

For example, in the last reel, when the little man comes with his

16 Song of Ceylon (1934).

basket of rice and flowers and gives them to God. When we were on our first investigation, soon after we got there, I had been to this shrine and had been terribly impressed by the religious atmosphere there. I was sitting there by myself (the other people had gone off to look at something else) and I saw a little man come and make his offering. I made inquiries and was told: 'Yes, this is what they do. This is one of the most sacred places in Ceylon. Anyone passing this way is bound to make an offering.'

So I thought, 'Right. Well, we'll do it.' But it took us a whole day to do it, from 7:30 in the morning until the light went. And this poor little man, to whom I could never apologize enough, had to do it over and over again. You must remember, the set-up was this huge outcrop of rock with all the carvings in it which gave us an opportunity to shoot from every angle. We could even get up on top of the heads of the statues and shoot down. And everything had to come from these different angles simply because you had to have them looking at each other and confronting each other from the correct angles – gods from up looking down, and man from down looking up, and so on. So it took a whole day.

But there was no shooting script which said 'Song of Ceylon' and then all the shots. There was only a post-shooting script, which was for the cutting room when we put it together.

cs: *And there were just the two of you?*

bw: We collected willing helpers. We had a great caravan and a motor car and a lot of very nice Sinhalese people. But they weren't film people – there weren't any film people in Ceylon – they were simply people who helped us, carried the apparatus, kept us cheerful, and so on.

cs: *And you did most of the photography?*

bw: Yes. When we had two cameras, John Taylor took the other one; but basically I did the photography. We couldn't afford luxuries like cameramen in those days.

cs: *What cameras did you have with you?*

bw: A Newman Sinclair, similar to that used by Flaherty on *Man of Aran* (1934). The lenses were 1.5", 2", 3", 6" and 12". As a spare we had a small Eyemo, and as a further standby (which we hardly ever used) a 1912 model Newman Sinclair alleged to have been used by

Ponting in filming Scott's last expedition to Antarctica. We had an ordinary gyro tripod and another with a very finely balanced free head which was very tricky to use, but once mastered, was capable of very delicate movements.

It was a huge tripod – one of the heaviest I've ever in my life seen – with a completely fluid gyrohead, as though it was just floating in oil. You could literally move the camera as though you were holding it in your hand. It was awfully difficult to operate, of course, because the slightest jerk made it shoot around. But for smoothness, I've never had anything like it. It was like a gyro, but it didn't have any of the resistance you get in a gyro. We used tripods ninety-nine per cent of the time.

cs: *Had you used panning, moving a camera to this extent, before* Song of Ceylon?

bw: My besetting sin is that I pan too much. But it's better than using a zoom lens. Thank God there weren't any in those days. I think people should have a licence for zoom lenses and be allowed to use them only twice a year.

cs: *What about tracking shots? Did you have a dolly?*

bw: The important dolly shots at the end of the first reel were done from the back of a train. The train from Colombo, which goes right through this beautiful hilly country, had an observation platform at the end and we shot from that. And if there seem to be any others in the film, they were probably taken from a motorcar or something. At any rate, we didn't have a dolly.

cs: *At the end of the film, the images and statues are almost like double images. Were they done in the camera?*

bw: They were very long dissolves. There are two or three in the film in which the centre of the dissolve is held – that is, the point at which the two images (the one fading out and the one fading in) have both arrived at the centre point and instead of letting the normal process continue, which is for the dissolve to make its way out, I held that centre point for an appreciable time, maybe a couple of feet.

This certainly happens on the dissolve to the head of the great statue behind which you see the little man walking up as you hear a very faint echo of the radio Morse code from the previous reel. That was an incredibly and unduly elongated dissolve which I wouldn't recommend except under very exceptional circumstances. I thought it pretty naughty of me at the time, but I think it comes off.

Of course, it's easier to do dissolves now than it used to be. Ours all had to be done in a laboratory because time was too short to wind back your camera and start again.

cs: *And you did all the editing yourself?*

bw: Yes. Although with me in the cutting room was Walter Leigh, who not only wrote the music but did the whole sound track. Every sound of that film, except for the words of the commentary which were done separately, was his orchestral score. If there's a snatch of birdsong, or a dog barking, or the noise of saws, or that sort of thing, they were all on the score with the musical instruments as well. It was a music-plus-sound score, done down to split seconds. And Walter, as composer, lived with me in the cutting room, so he followed every change in the cutting of the film.

cs: *I've read about the various sound experiments, like running the gong backwards and so forth. Exactly how were these handled?*

bw: We had two days of one big recording session for the whole film. We had a number of elements: an orchestra, all sorts of metal objects to be banged to sound like oriental bells because we didn't want them to sound like church bells; the choir from the local school, because there was singing in some of the music; and the choir from the local church which also did the noise of the little boys learning to dance. They were trained by the two dancers we brought over from Ceylon to England, who did all the Sinhalese singing and drumming. We did no sound recording in Ceylon at all; everything was silent. So all the sound was put on in England with the instruments we brought back.

cs: *How were the sound tracks laid in?*

bw: It was very complicated because we had a rather primitive sound recording system and only three channels (or four at a pinch, if we used the projector). It wasn't very satisfactory.

The number of sound tracks that had to be combined went up to eight, which was a great problem because we had to re-record three together, and then two others together, and then try to find the right balance between all of those when you put them all together. And as the sound system was, as I said, rather primitive and rather noisy, it really was done with considerable difficulty. I think we spent over a week mixing because we didn't have instant playback. Sound at that time was developed just like a photograph in the laboratories. It came back the next day, you listened to it, and then you found out whether you'd been right or wrong. And if you were wrong and had to get your orchestra back, it would cost you another 100 pounds.

I sometimes wonder what sort of film it would have been if we'd gone to Ceylon with a nice selection of Nagras and different mikes. But you work within the limitations of your medium.

cs: *How did you happen to choose the narration and the narrator?*

bw: I was wondering about narration while I was editing the film, and I had no idea what I would use. Then one day I was walking near the British Museum and happened to glance into the window of a bookshop and saw this book on Ceylon by Robert Knox. As soon as I read it, I realized its 'period' flavour was just what I needed .

The voice was that of Lionel Wendt, our assistant and mentor while we were shooting. Wendt came from a racial group called Burghers – descendants of intermarriages between the Dutch colonists and the Sinhalese. He was a lawyer, a brilliant pianist, and one of the world's best photographers at the time.

He came back to England to help with the editing and look after the two dancers we had brought over for the sound track. Quite by chance, I tried him out reading passages from Knox and the result was perfect. This was two days before he was due to return to Ceylon, so we had quite a job completing the recording.

cs: *What about the rhythms in the film? There's a constant movement, a kind of dance in itself. Did it come from a musical rhythm you may have unconsciously assimilated, or was it a more deliberate effort?*

bw: We brought back a lot of ten-inch gramophone records. Walter Leigh listened to them and to a lot of oriental music. He was an incredibly gifted composer (he had studied under Hindemith in Germany for a long time), and had this marvellous gift for sort of soaking up the feeling of everything.

For instance, the clanking noises I mentioned we used for the bells ringing. Well, in that sequence in reel one when all the bells are ringing and the birds flying, he was determined that there must not be a single sound which resembled a European bell. So he armed himself with a soft hammer and a hard hammer and went off to the part of Covent Garden which is full of metal workers and went into their shops and said, 'Would you mind if I banged some of the things in your shop?' So he found all those sounds of the different sorts of metal and bought them and brought them back. The whole studio was draped with a great clothes-line on which were hung all these misshapen bits of metal which gave the sort of sounds he needed.

As for the visual rhythms, there was what I would call a bit of Flaherty shooting: you anticipate a movement and start moving your camera a moment before the movement you want is going to take place. I don't know how that happens; it's just an instinct. But it's very difficult to determine which came first. I think the basic rhythm of the film came from the pictures but as we started to shape the film and as I had Walter Leigh in the cutting room all the time, his ideas as to how the music might develop would echo back on to the cutting bench and I might make certain alterations in the cutting.

If you mean the rhythm of montage, all this came, I suppose, through experience and through having been very strongly influenced by Eisenstein. The three people, apart from Grierson, who influenced me were Robert Flaherty, Alexander Dovzhenko, and Eisenstein – and Eisenstein because of his dialectical montage and all his theories, which I still find extremely valid.

CS: *Song of Ceylon is often associated with the work of Robert Flaherty. Do you feel he greatly influenced you?*

BW: Very much so. I'd been tremendously impressed with *Nanook of The North* and *Moana*. And we had had the very good fortune at the EMB Film Unit to persuade Flaherty to come and work with us for a time.

He was kind enough to come on location with me on the first film I ever directed, *The Country Comes to Town* – which was about what you would find if you thought about what was behind the milk bottle on your doorstep or the piece of meat at the butcher's: what has happened, who's produced it, where it comes from, and all that. And it was marvellous having him on location with us. He never made criticisms; he just remarked on things. His wonderful eyes were seeing and taught you how to see particularly camera-wise, in a different way.

CS: *Can you explain what you mean by 'camera-wise, in a different way'?*

BW: When you look at something with your own eyes, you've got binocular vision: your vision goes out quite a long way to the side. If you look at something through the eye of the camera, it's a narrow vision. Another point about it is that the eye of the camera has no brain behind it – it's just a piece of machinery; when you're looking through your own eyes you have a brain which is taking in a lot of extraneous material which you might not, in fact, want. The camera narrows it down, but the great problem is to translate what you see with your eyes into the correct range of vision which you can make the camera give you. This was Flaherty's great genius, and this is what I learned a little bit of from him.

CS: *I know Grierson was an enormously dynamic person to have as a boss and a friend, and I know he was enormously fond of this film. What was his specific role, other than sending you off and handing you your expense money?*

BW: Grierson was a very great man, and maybe the greatest friend I ever had. As a producer, he was absolutely murderous. He was so tough, I remember when I was first working for him I was in dread. When you were shooting a film for him, he had to see your dailies every day. You'd come back into the studio and the dailies would be processed overnight, and Grierson would come in to see them. The worst sign would be if he didn't say anything and just spat on the floor. You knew you had to go back and shoot absolutely everything over again. If he just cursed you, you only had to re-shoot some of it. He was a perfectionist!

But I can give you an example of his genius as a producer: we got to the stage at which I said to him 'Here is the final cut for the film, it's ready to go to the lab to be processed – it's negative cut,' and I showed it to him. The lights went up and he said, 'You must be mad.' I said, 'What do you mean?' And he said, 'In the last reel, you committed an aesthetic blunder which you will never forgive yourself for unless you put it right.' I said, 'What do you mean?' And he said (and note this, because this was how the film was at the time), 'When that little man goes away from praying to the Buddha, you cut straight to those people in their head-dresses and so on dancing away like mad. Bang! Like that. Well, you're throwing away the drama of the dance.'

Well, I was pretty exhausted by that time (I'd been working on the film for about a year) and we had a most appalling row, screaming and shouting, and I finally slammed off and got in my car and went home. I sat in my flat drinking whiskey for three days and not speaking to anybody. But then on the third day a thought crept into my mind. If I took some of those sentences which were spoken on the mountain at the end of the film and illustrated them with a sequence I hadn't used of the men getting ready for the dance and other shots of people coming and getting ready to watch the dance, it would be a marvellous anti-climax to the end of the film! So I rushed back to the studio in the middle of the night and worked all night. When Grierson came in the next morning, I showed him the last reel again and he said, 'There you are.'

But the point is this: *he* didn't do it, he forced me to find something I didn't know I had. He didn't tell me what to do; he just said I'd made an absolute blazing mess of the thing and I had to put it right. And he was correct. But that's what I call the work of a great producer, and that's what a director wants from a great producer.

Source: *Film-Maker's Newsletter*, November 1975,Vol. 9, No.1.

BBC: *The Voice of Britain*
GRAHAM GREENE

The novelist Graham Greene served intermittently as the film critic of the *Spectator* between 1935 and 1940, and was one of the documentary movement's most ardent and perceptive supporters.

In this review of Stuart Legg's *BBC: The Voice of Britain*, Greene perhaps read more satire into the film than the makers intended.

The superb complacency of the BBC was never more delightfully parodied than in the title of the official film made by Mr John Grierson and the GPO Film Unit: *The Voice of Britain*. It is certainly the film of the month, if not the year; but I doubt if the BBC realize the devastating nature of Mr Grierson's amusing and sometimes beautiful film, the satirical background to these acres of dynamos, the tall steel towers, the conferences and contracts, the enormous staff and the rigid technique of a Kremlin which should be sufficient to govern a nation and all is directed to this end: Miss Nina Mae McKinney singing 'Dinah', Henry Hall's Dance Orchestra playing 'Piccadilly Riot', a spot of dubious education, and a spot, just a spot, of culture when Mr Adrian Boult conducts the Fifth Symphony.

This was the most cynical moment of a witty film: Mr Adrian Boult agonizing above his baton, and then his audience – a man turning the pages of his book beside the loud-speaker, a man eating his dinner, nobody giving more than his unconscious mind to Beethoven's music. The picture too of the cramped suburban parlour, the man with his paper, the woman with her sewing, the child at his homework, while 'Piccadilly Riot' reverberates noisily back and forth across the potted plant between flowered wallpaper and flowered wallpaper is even more memorable than the lovely shots of sea and sky and such lyric passages as Mr Chesterton driving gently like a sea-lion through the little tank-like studios. For this is the BBC's chief contribution to man's life: noise while he eats and reads and talks. I wish Mr Grierson had included a few shots from the damper tropics where the noise of the Empire programmes is not disguised at all as entertainment or education, but is just plain wails and windy blasts from instruments hopelessly beaten by atmospherics. At enormous expense from its steel pylon at Daventry the BBC supplies din with the drinks at sundown.

Source: The *Spectator*, 2 August 1935.

The Role of Aberto Cavalcanti
ELIZABETH SUSSEX

The British documentary movement was not entirely British. One of its key members was the Brazilian Alberto Cavalcanti (1897–1982), who, as the director of *Rien que les Heures* (1926) and *En Rade* (Sea Fever, 1927), represented a direct continuity with the continental avant-garde of the 1920s.

Cavalcanti joined the GPO film unit in 1934 bringing not only a taste for formal experimentation and social engagement, but a technical know-how that was sorely lacking in Grierson and his 'tyros'. A great inspirer, he was the force behind such original, non-literal films as *Pett and Pott*, *Coal Face*, *Night Mail* and, indirectly, the masterful wartime work of Humphrey Jennings (see chapter 6). But as this piece by Elizabeth Sussex, from her article 'Cavalcanti in England', shows, he and Grierson did not always see eye to eye.

It is . . . easy to find evidence which suggests that Cavalcanti's primarily aesthetic contribution to British documentary has always been a little underplayed by comparison with that of the social propagandists who took their lead directly from Grierson. Yet Cavalcanti's contribution is acknowledged to have been a large one. To understand it properly, I think we have to go back to the beginning which for Cavalcanti was earlier than it was for most of the others.

When Cavalcanti came to England to join the GPO film unit in 1934, he was thirty-seven years old and had a whole career behind him. Born in Brazil, he seems to have been a lot brainier and at least a little more argumentative than average from the beginning. He began law studies at the age of fifteen and remembers being the youngest student in the university, but he was 'expelled because of a quarrel with an old professor'. His father sent him to Geneva on condition that he steer clear of both law and politics, and he trained as an architect. At eighteen he was working in an architect's *atelier* in Paris. From there he

17 *The Cavalcanti influence: a whimsical image from* Pett and Pott *(1934).*

switched to interior decoration and then to the art department of the film studios. He did set designs from 1922 for Marcel L'Herbier, Louis Delluc and others, and he became a member of the avant-garde, which he describes as a movement of inward as well as outward dissent and strife.

. . . Cavalcanti came to England after several years in which, due to the arrival of synchronized sound, no avant-garde work had been possible. He had even had a period of exile from the studios 'because the French like the Americans thought the silent film directors couldn't do sound pictures', but he came back to make French and Portuguese versions of American films for Paramount. These were followed by a series of French comedies of his own which he claims were 'terrifically successful commercially' but 'very primitive' in their use of sound. 'I had learned sound the hard way,' he says, 'the know-how to record dialogue, but I thought dialogue was one small part of sound and not the sound film.' The moment Grierson's unit got its own recording equipment, he broke a contract to come over to England.

Grierson was happy. 'My boys don't know anything about sound,' he said, inviting him by all means to amuse himself for a while at the unit's newly acquired studios in Blackheath. Grierson's boys knew about Cavalcanti, of course. He was one of the names that had impressed them at Film Society screenings. Grierson was lucky or, perhaps more accurately, knew how to use his luck. First Flaherty, now Cavalcanti. Apart from any other considerations, the reputation of the fledgling school of British documentary was obviously much enhanced by its ability to attract international names like these.

Cavalcanti settled in contentedly: 'I was so happy I stayed seven years there, and I think the result was very good. But the atmosphere in Blackheath was wonderful, you know . . .' With the exception of Grierson, who worked mainly from the unit's offices at 21 Soho Square, Cavalcanti found himself 'the only sort of middle-aged person there'. Budding directors like Harry Watt, Basil Wright and Humphrey Jennings, then still in their twenties, naturally looked up to him as a film-maker of stature as well as someone with all the technical knowledge they still lacked.

'I was enormously grateful to him and always shall be, apart from his friendship which I managed to obtain, for all the things he did on films I was working on like *Song of Ceylon* and *Night Mail*. His ideas about the use of sound were so liberating that they would liberate in you about a thousand other ideas,' says Basil Wright. He remembers having both Grierson and Cavalcanti in the same set-up as 'absolutely magical . . . worth a million pounds to any young man to be there.' Harry Watt goes further. 'I believe fundamentally that the arrival of Cavalcanti in the GPO film unit was the turning point of British documentary,' he says. 'If I've had any success in films I put it down to my training from Cavalcanti, and I think a lot of other people should say the same thing.'

Grierson's relationship with Cavalcanti was always a little difficult. 'He only came to the studios to upset my work,' Cavalcanti claims now. 'He used to shift everybody all the time, which upset me a lot . . . Indeed everybody knew this well in Blackheath.'[1] People knew it and, like Cavalcanti himself perhaps, chose mostly to make a joke of it.

'It must have been very difficult for Grierson when we technicians more and more turned to Cavalcanti with our problems,' wrote Watt in his recent autobiography [Don't Look at the Camera], 'but he (Grierson) was honest and shrewd enough to realize how much more polished and professional our films were becoming under Cav.' In fairness it must be added that Harry Watt was never quite on Grierson's wavelength as far as work was concerned. For some people, Grierson was still the dominant influence. For instance, despite his warm appreciation of Cavalcanti, it is Grierson's artistic contribution to Song of Ceylon that Basil Wright has almost total recall of, and indeed describes in every detail with undiminished gratitude to this day.

In any case, arriving as he did at such a crucial moment in the GPO film unit's story, Cavalcanti's influence as a teacher and adviser really goes without saying. More than that, however, the story of Grierson's movement is one from which Cavalcanti, at least in spirit, had never been entirely absent. Himself a pioneer in the making of avant-garde films virtually indistinguishable from what Grierson labelled 'documentary', his example was there from the beginning, and indeed the influence on British documentarists of Cavalcanti's Rien que les Heures (1926), which was shown in London earlier than the famous Film Society programme introducing Drifters along with Battleship Potemkin, is put

---

1 Cavalcanti is refering to Grierson's habit of moving his staff around from one job to another all the time, in an attempt to train them all in every aspect of the film-making process. Editors would suddenly find themselves as projectionists, cameramen as producers.

on record by the movement's own historian Paul Rotha.

. . . *Rien que les Heures* is an odd mixture of images of a Paris not frequented by tourists. A kind of theme suggests itself in the recurrent shots of a lame and wretched woman dragging herself at a snail's pace along alleys and byways, but these shots seem to be presented quite without comment. They are bizarre, incongruous, even comical – especially in juxtaposition with the light Parisian songs that Cavalcanti himself selected to accompany a recent screening at the National Film Theatre. Perhaps it is because these shots, in their sad hopelessness, come so near to provoking laughter that they remain so strongly in the memory. Cavalcanti has been accused of a certain lack of warmth in this film, and a certain lack of feeling in general. I think it is not fully understood that his vision is surrealist rather than realist, and always therefore had the virtue of avoiding sentimentality. Apart from that, it was to be another eight years before British documentary attempted any comparable social document, in the sense of showing conditions during the Depression.

One of Cavalcanti's earliest experiments at the GPO was a fantasy called *Pett and Pott* which cannot be counted among his best work. According to Basil Wright the idea of recording the sound track first and putting on the picture afterwards was Grierson's as well as Cavalcanti's; it was a way of getting the unit accustomed to using its newly acquired sound-recording equipment. The idea of making it a grotesque comedy Wright thinks must have been Cavalcanti's, because it stemmed from the kind of films he had been making earlier in France. Certainly Paul Rotha has strayed far from the point when he describes it in *Documentary Diary* as showing 'Cavalcanti's influence at its most mischievous'. This attitude, however, is not unique. John Taylor, for instance, remembers *Pett and Pott* as 'the beginning of the division . . . I mean, looking back on it, it was a great mistake to have Cavalcanti really, because he didn't understand what documentary was supposed to be doing.'

Was Cavalcanti in some way undermining Grierson's work? What exactly was the difference of opinion between them? 'The only fundamental difference was that I maintained that "documentary" was a silly denomination,' says Cavalcanti. 'I thought films are the same, either fictional or otherwise, and I thought that films ought to go into cinemas. Grierson little by little started creating the theory that they should be put in a different, what he called non-theatrical circuit, and I thought it was as silly as calling those films 'documentary'. I say, if films are good, they should and could be shown anywhere. There is no reason why they should be destined only for the parsons and for the church halls etc.

'I had a very serious conversation in the early, rosy days with Grierson about this label "documentary" because I insisted that it should be called, funnily enough (it's only coincidence, but it made a fortune in Italy), "neo-realism". The Grierson argument – and I remember it exceedingly well – was just to laugh and say, "You are really a very innocent character. I have to deal with the Government, and the word documentary impresses them as something serious, as something . . ." I said, "Yes, as something dusty and something annoying." But that was his argument, that documentary was a kind of name that pleased the Government . . .'

Of course this is much more than an argument about labels. Cavalcanti is attacking the whole basis on which Grierson decreed that documentary should develop. Cavalcanti's whole approach to life is so very different from Grierson's that it is possible he never realized the increasing gravity of his offence.

In 1937 Grierson left the GPO film unit and set up Film Centre in order to extend documentary into a wider field. Sir Stephen Tallents who, as secretary of the Empire Marketing Board and public relations officer at the GPO, had always given him such invaluable support, had left the GPO in 1935 to become controller of public relations in the BBC Overseas Services and was now an active member of the Imperial Relations Trust set up in 1937 by the Government. It was this Trust which first sent Grierson as film consultant to Canada, New Zealand and Australia.

After Grierson's departure the GPO film unit continued as creatively as ever under Cavalcanti. Humphrey Jennings made *Spare Time* and Harry Watt made *North Sea* – the former being attacked by the Grierson school when it came out, and the latter receiving slightly grudging praise. It was said that Cavalcanti lacked Grierson's ability to deal with the higher civil servants at the Post Office, and certainly there is evidence that Cavalcanti was no political operator. He could inspire creative people whom he approached on a personal basis, but he never really sought power and was never able to make the most of it when he had it. Both Grierson and Cavalcanti were dedicated to their work, but Cavalcanti was the more vulnerable in being, by comparison, politically naïve.

When war broke out in 1939, Grierson had gone to Canada to set up the National Film Board – an exceedingly impressive operation that in itself demonstrates the difference between his kind of ambition and that of the unaggressive Cavalcantis of this world. There seemed to be a situation of considerable confusion at the newly created Ministry of Information, which took over the GPO film unit. According to Harry Watt, there was a longish spell when nothing at all happened because no instruction came through: 'Then Cavalcanti took upon himself to send us out. This is where Cavalcanti was great. He said, "History is being made. We can't sit here."' All the members of the unit, which included Watt and Jennings, went out and shot everything that looked interesting, and a film was quickly put together. Called *The First Days* it was quite a promising start to the unit's wartime activities particularly in the area that would be cultivated by Humphrey Jennings. Before Cavalcanti left the GPO film unit which became the Crown Film Unit when it was taken over by Ian Dalrymple in 1940, Harry Watt made *Squadron 992* and *Dover Front Line*, Jennings made *Spring Offensive*, Jack Holmes had begun *Merchant Seamen* and ideas for *London Can Take It* and *Target for Tonight* were being discussed. In fact, the unit was fairly well set on the course that it would follow throughout the war.

Cavalcanti was forced to leave the unit because of his status as a foreigner – he refused to adopt the British citizenship. He went on to work for Michael Balcon, first on documentaries then directing several notable features, including *Went The Day Well?* (1942) and *Dead of Night* (1945).

Source: Elizabeth Sussex, 'Cavalcanti in England' in *Sight and Sound*, Autumn 1975.

Night Mail
DAI VAUGHAN

Coal Face (1935) and *Night Mail* (1936) were the GPO's two most successful experiments in 'poetic documentary', combining the talents of the film-makers, the poet W. H. Auden and the composer Benjamin Britten.

This piece is from Dai Vaughan's study of the documentary editor Stewart McAllister, *Portrait of an Invisible Man*.

If there is one film which would be generally recognized as embodying the essence of British documentary, it is *Night Mail* (edited by R. Q. McNaughton, with [Harry] Watt and [Basil] Wright sharing the directing credit, in 1936, the year before McAllister joined the Unit). The very title seems to encapsulate a philosophy. It was, of course, no scriptwriter's contrivance that the 'down postal to Edinburgh' should run at night; but it is difficult to believe that a film *Day Mail* would have entered the public consciousness in that peculiarly compulsive way which establishes a work as a classic, even to those who have not seen it.

The shots have an air of irrefutability, as of objects fixed for ever in the representations proper to them – the greasy iron connecting rods and pistons, the gleam of sunset on the flanks of passing coaches, the sinuous trundling of linked trolleys through the multiplex shadows of a platform at night, a grimy face relaxing at dawn – which both contributes to and derives from our sense of the fitness of the totality. But what is of particular interest is the handling of the mail train itself: throughout the first third of the film, the train is the focus of a network of communications and organization, of telegraph wires, points and signals. It is the object of admiring glances, of conversation and of comment. Its whistle, approaching, announces it. Mailbags are hung from it and newspapers thrown from it. It is followed from the air; it passes us closely in a hurried impact; and we see from its viewpoint the skimming countryside and the racing shadow of its own smoke on the banks of a cutting. But never once do we see the people inside it. The image is of something massive, swift yet benign – a visored knight upon a mysterious errand. This section reaches its climax on Crewe station, with a montage of activity as mailbags accumulate from all over the country. The great train pulls in, the driver's hand leaves the controls and the carriage doors are swung open to reveal at last the sorters, who emerge to help with the loading and to change shift.

When the train leaves Crewe, we remain inside it; and the film enters upon its expository section. The burden of explanation, initially carried by commentary, is soon taken over by the action itself as a man receives advice from the supervisor about a poorly addressed envelope and an older man shows a new recruit how to strap up a pouch which will be deposited by the speeding train into a railside net. Asked whether it is

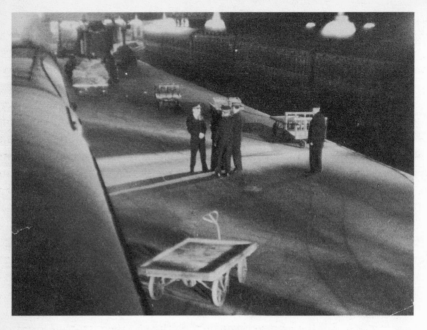

18 Night Mail *(1936)*.

time to swing out the arm carrying the pouch, the older man replies, 'Two bridges and forty-five beats.' The bridges pass, and the two men count the beats silently together. It has become a sequence about the camaraderie of work and the passing on of the tricks of a specialized trade. Other elements contribute to this feeling. The badinage between the changing shifts, about there being no water left for the tea, is gently rounded off when later we see the supervisor drinking a small cup of milk. He too, despite his position, is one of the boys. It is a vital paradox of *Night Mail* that people and objects to whom such qualitative attributions as 'mysterious' or 'valorous' are systematically denied should be reinvested with mystery and chivalry by the simple device of concealment – a concealment which corresponds reasonably with our experience of ordinary yet important social activities as out of sight and by the pervasive imagery of the steam locomotive, heroic in the battle against its own thermal inefficiency, which alone is granted the rhetoric of symbolism. It is a treatment which avoids the pitfalls of socialist realism in the exaltation of labour by positing a distinction between the external and internal views – though no doubt those on the inside are encouraged to lay some claim to the external perception in the form of pride. We may recall that Father Brown's 'mentally invisible man' was a postman.

Furthermore, if we look carefully at the constituents of *Night Mail* we will find, I think, the elements of what may fairly be described as the central myth of British documentary: the tight-knit group, the journey through the night, perhaps the control over fire; the physical isolation amid a sustaining and succouring network of communications; the task accomplished for the benefit of a still more diffuse community whom the group, even through this network, never meets. (The representation of this wider community is again archetypal in *Night Mail*. As we mix to a high-shot of the train reaching its terminus, Auden's accompanying poem, which has spoken of the thousands who are still asleep dreaming of monsters, adds, 'They continue their dreams . . .') All these elements are present in *Target for Tonight*, and all are present in *Fires Were Started*; and they occur again and again, individually and in various clusters, throughout British documentary *oeuvre*.

The myth articulates a meaning of 'work': the work of people, enclosed in windowless carriages, whose efforts, dedicated yet routine, sustain a civilization where the sleep of reason may be safe from its progeny of terror. And of course, the most obvious point to be made about this is that the comradeship of the small group, rattling through the night and against the clock, with its levelling of social ranks in the higher interest of the job's completion, may have more in common with the experience of film technicians – including those who made *Night Mail* – than with that of the majority of the population. (Annette Kuhn has argued, with some justice, that the GPO Unit aspired towards a pre-capitalist mode of production.) Yet assent to the film does entail, at least as one of its possibilities, commitment to an ideal of the status of work in a humane society; and to reject it out of mistrust for the paternal liberalism of which we may suspect it to have been an expression would be to deny a legitimate reflection of our experience. *Night Mail* does, if nothing else, give form to a myth oppositional to that of the Great Artist in a way that the verbal literature of film has so conspicuously failed to do.

Source: Dai Vaughan, *Portrait of an Invisible Man*, BFI 1983

Tackling Social Problems

Concurrent with their experiments in 'poetic documentary', the GPO unit also made its most radical and socially engaged films, *Housing Problems* (1935) and *Nutrition* (a.k.a. *Enough to Eat*, 1936).

Housing Problems was particularly innovative. Instead of using actors or scripted amateurs, and post-recording a voice-over, as was their normal method, the film-makers took their bulky equipment to the slums and had the inhabitants tell their own story in their own words.

Although she is only credited as an assistant on the film, Ruby Grierson, John's younger sister, was largely responsible for this change in attitude. According to fellow documentarian Paul Rotha, her contribution to *Housing Problems* was really that of a director, '[Her] ability to win people's confidence, gave a spontaneity and an honesty to the "interviews" that contrasted sharply with the previous, romantic method of handling people.' Grierson himself recalled how Ruby had accused him of looking at the world as though he were in a goldfish bowl and declared that she was going to break it. She told the slum-dwellers: 'The camera is yours. The microphone is yours. Now tell the bastards exactly what it's like to live in slums.'

It was a great loss to British documentary when, having directed her first few films, Ruby died in the second year of the war while making a film about the evacuation of British children to Canada. Her ship was torpedoed.

John Taylor (1914–92), Grierson's brother-in-law, joined the EMB film unit in 1929 as an assistant at the age of sixteen. Edgar Anstey (1907–1987) and Arthur Elton (1906–73) were part of a group of Cambridge University contemporaries – which also included Stuart Legg (1910–92) and Humphrey Jennings (1907–1950) – who joined the unit in its early years.

Arthur Elton: [By 1935] Grierson was determined that we should apply the knowledge we had acquired in government service in the GPO Film Unit, to industry. Though I'm not sure that I particularly appreciated it at the time, I was thrown out to the cold world and made to apply our knowledge to industry. I worked with the gas industry, both the Gas, Light and Coke Company and the British Commercial Gas Association, jointly with Edgar Anstey, and we made a whole series of films, of which the famous one is *Housing Problems*.

Housing Problems was like a television presentation, only long before television. It pioneered the interview. It pioneered all that kind of thing.

Edgar Anstey: This [i.e. *Housing Problems*] was a sort of political thing coming out which had been suppressed a bit, because we were all in a way politicians, but we were operating very indirectly. We were trying to show things as they were, people as they were, and there was a lot of indignation about unemployment, about malnutrition, about the bad housing at that time.

Arthur Elton and I succeeded in persuading the gas industry, who, after all, had a liberal tradition, a nonconformist tradition, that what you could do with film was to identify a big organization with social purpose, to the advantage of both. Perhaps this was the Grierson notion passed on by Elton and myself; that, in a way, no great corporation can dissociate itself from whatever the national social issues are at any given time – particularly if, like gas, you're in the field of housing, basically. You're providing a public service.

Anyway, we argued with them about this, and they agreed to do a film on slums and slum clearance and rehousing. We seized on this, because everybody had been told about the slums, but there was no direct communication about them. I mean, you could make still pictures and write articles in the press, but nobody had thought of the idea which we had of letting slum-dwellers simply talk for themselves, make their own film.

[Paul] Rotha often criticized *Housing Problems* because he thought there wasn't enough directorial intervention and guidance and shaping of the material. Well, Arthur and I talked a lot about this, and we felt that the camera must remain sort of four feet above the ground and dead on, because it wasn't our film.

Basil Wright: When Ruby Grierson and John Taylor and Anstey went down into the slums with their great, enormous sound truck and their microphone, they did *cinéma-vérité* interviews with the people who lived there. The circumstances were terribly difficult, but that's what they were doing.

John Taylor: There was a British camera called a Vinton, which was a very cumbersome thing. The early models of it were very cumbersome. Most of it was shot on the Vinton. Some of it was shot on a Mitchell, which is an American camera and a very good one. We could shoot

1,000 feet (ten minutes) before reloading. We had to have a car full of
batteries – twelve-volt car batteries – to do the lighting, and even then
we could only have two 500-watt lamps, or something like that, and the
stock was slow in those days. We had a vast sound truck outside, full of
batteries and a big sound camera. It was terribly cumbersome
equipment to try and do that stuff with.

Edgar Anstey: Nobody had been able to bring these poor, suffering
characters to an audience before, and the woman in *Housing Problems*,
the woman who jabs at the rat with a broom, was absolutely
astonished. I got her to the Stepney Town Hall (I think it was) to see
the film. They were all there, the people who appeared in the film, and
you couldn't hear a word because of the roars and shouts as soon as a
neighbour came on the screen. So we had to run it again, and this
woman who killed the rat was absolutely astonished. I don't think she'd
ever seen a photograph of herself before. She didn't recognize herself,

19 *Giving voice to the people*: Housing Problems *(1935)*.

didn't identify. She had to be told, and she gradually accepted it the second time through. But she had never been to the centre of London. She was a woman of, I suppose, forty-five or fifty, and she had never been further than this two and a half miles from her slum house . . .

[After *Housing Problems* Edgar Anstey directed *Enough To Eat?*, also for the Gas, Light and Coke Company. The subject was malnutrition.]

Edgar Anstey: We had people suffering from malnutrition, and mothers who couldn't feed their children, talking. It was very much like the contemporary television programme – but again, no attempt to dress it up, although I did start at that point to introduce animated diagrams to show what is meant by the importance of vitamins and proteins and so on. There was a bit of that kind of production value in it. Later on Rotha started doing films of this type, much more elaborately and with much more production finesse. *Enough to Eat?* was half-way between *Housing Problems* and these much more elaborate things which Rotha did, where you would introduce artists, as well, to play out scenes. It came also from the Living Newspaper technique, which developed in America, where you had these documentary things played out on the stage during the Depression . . .

Those films [i.e. *Housing Problems* and *Enough to Eat?*] seemed so remarkable at the time to the press that they probably achieved more by the influence they had on journalists and public men, politicians and so on, than in their actual showings. Both *Enough to Eat?* and *Housing Problems* had whole pages in the *Daily Herald* and, I think, the *Daily News* as it then was. Ritchie Calder wrote the page in the *Herald*. I think the influence of those films through the press was much much greater than through the cinema screen, rather curiously. Suddenly a new thing had happened in the possibility of communication.

Source: Elizabeth Sussex, *The Rise and Fall of British Documentary: The Story of the Film Movement Founded by John Grierson*, Berkeley: University of California Press, 1975.

6 Battling for Minds

INTRODUCTION

Throughout continental Europe and beyond, the 1930s were a time of political extremism, when, to many people's eyes the stark choice between communism and fascism was the only one on offer. In the resultant struggle for ideological (and, ultimately, military) dominance, the mass media played a more crucial role than at any previous period in history, and documentary films became almost exclusively a medium for propaganda, used to persuade, manipulate and control.

The Nazi régime was the first of the 1930s extremist governments to fully recognize the power that could be wielded through the use of effective propaganda. In March 1933 Hitler appointed the film-obsessed Joseph Goebbels as Reich Minister for Popular Entertainment and Propaganda. For the next twelve years Goebbels, with his genius for mass psychology, had almost total personal control over German cinema. Influenced by the success of Soviet film propaganda, he paid particular attention to newsreels and documentary, distorting or ignoring the facts if he wished; propaganda, he declared, has 'nothing to do with the truth'.

Pre-war Nazi documentaries like Leni Riefenstahl's *Triumph of the Will* (1934) and *Olympia* (1938), and the unattributed *Blood and Soil: Foundation of the New Germany* (1933), masterfully fed the German population an image of themselves, their history and their destiny, that reinforced the power of the state and the idolization of the Führer. With hindsight, these films, seem alternately ridiculous – bronzed Nazi bodies engaging in callisthenics reminiscent of a Busby Berkley number – and chilling – the equation by montage of Jews with rats in *The Everlasting Jew* – but their effectiveness at the time cannot be disputed.

In 1936 the international struggle between left and right crystallized in the Spanish Civil War. Neither Franco's fascist Nationalists nor the loyalist Republicans made much use of documentary themselves, but a number of foreign films about the conflict were produced from the left's perspective. The most notable were Esther Shub and Roman Karmen's Soviet-made *Spain* (1939), Joris Ivens' *The Spanish Earth* (1936) and Herbert Kline's *Heart of Pain* and *Return to Life*. Kline and Ivens' films were produced to help Republican fundraising in the United States.

With the outbreak of the Second World War, democratic and totalitarian régimes alike relied on documentary propaganda to communicate their ideas. Of the hundreds of films made by the Germans, Americans and British, some were straightforward training films, others provided psychological preparation for troops going into battle, explaining who they were fighting and why. Others were used to sustain civilian morale, inciting fear, courage and more abstract notions like honour, patriotism and duty.

It is tempting, if harder than one would imagine, to generalize about how British and American films differ from those of the Germans – except in extreme cases like *The Everlasting Jew*. It is largely true that while the allies appealed to their troops and citizens as *individuals*, the Germans tended to stress efficiency, cleanliness and the pre-eminence of the state over the individual, cramming their films with Wagnerian echoes of the 'great German past'. But British films like those of Humphrey Jennings were not beyond appealing to a near-mystical notion of 'Englishness', loaded down with references to King Arthur, Agincourt and the rest.

News Films
BÉLA BALÁZS

Béla Balázs (1884–1949) the Hungarian-born screenwriter, librettist and director, was a refugee from German fascism, living in Moscow when he wrote the following.

We are accustomed to seeing them at the beginning of film shows, just before the main feature comes on. To all appearances they are an innocent form of pictorial reporting. In fact they are the most dangerous instruments of propaganda. They are not put together with poetic, artistic subjectivity, as are the reality fragments of the *Ciné-Eye* – they express the intentions of the interests and power groups who pay for them. They lie even more boldly than the lying, distorting newspapers, for they appear to be objective and authentic photographic records, a sort of pictorial diary of the age. They are really interesting and instructive only if we have the opportunity of seeing side by side, or rather face to face, news films made of the same events by groups hostile to one another. They show no similarity at all, although they purport to show the same things and what is truly characteristic of them and expressive in them is what they do not show.

One need only edit them a little, however, and they are completely transformed. Before Hitler's seizure of power, but when the Weimar republic was already on its last legs, a workers' film society was formed in Berlin. It arranged film shows and would have shown newsreels of its own, but the censors banned them. So they bought old UFA newsreels, which had long finished their run and had been approved by the censors in their time. From these they cut new reels. For instance, in the 'Dogs' beauty contest', overwhelmingly glamorous ladies held expensive lap-dogs in their arms. Next to this was 'One who did not take part in the contest': a blind beggar and his guide dog, watching over his miserable master in the cold of winter. Then 'St Moritz': skating rinks and the guests on the terrace of a luxury hotel. 'This, too, is St Moritz': a melancholy procession of ragged, hungry snow-shovellers and rink-sweepers. 'Brilliant military parade' followed by 'Disabled ex-service-men begging in the streets'. There were no other captions. The police were itching to ban these newsreels but could not do so, as they were all respectable UFA newsreels, every one of them approved by the censors. Only the order of showing had been altered a little.

Single pictures are mere reality. Only the montage turns them into either truths or falsehoods. Herein lies the immense responsibility devolving on the newsreels. Their convincing power is in the fact that the spectator feels that he is an eye witness. The shot is accepted as a fact, a presentation of conclusive proof, although of course it is not by accident that the camera comes to a halt in front of one particular object and not of another.

Source: From Béla Balázs, *Theory of the Film*; Dennis Dobson Ltd, London, 1952. First published Moscow, 1945.

20 Olympia *(1937)*.

Leni Riefenstahl, Art and Propaganda
MANOHLA DARGIS

Leni Riefenstahl (born 1902) was the athletic heroine of a whole series of German 'mountain films' of the late 1920s and early 1930s, before turning to direction in 1931 with *Das Blaue Licht* (co-written with Béla Balázs) which was much admired by Adolph Hitler. Under his patronage she subsequently made documentaries on the Nuremberg Nazi Party rallies of 1933 (*Sieg des Glaubens*/Victory of Faith) and 1934 (*Triumph des Willens*/Triumph of the Will); one of the German military (*Tag der Freiheit – unsere Wehrmacht*/ Day of Freedom) and *Olympia*, the official film of the 1936 Berlin Olympics. They are still considered among the most 'potent' propaganda films ever made.

At the time of writing Riefenstahl, aged ninety-four, is completing a documentary on scuba-diving. Her energy for film-making remains outstanding, although ethical and aesthetic controversy still rages around her career. This piece is taken from a review of her 1993 memoir, *The Sieve of Time*, in which she claims that political ignorance, not sympathy, led her to collaborate with the Nazi party.

During her years as a Reich director, Riefenstahl enjoyed critical acclaim – *Triumph of the Will* was awarded Germany's National Film Prize, the gold medal at the Venice Biennalle, and the gold medal at the Paris World's Fair – but she didn't have all that much competition. By 1933, the year the propaganda ministry seized complete control of the film industry, most of Germany's greatest screen talents had either already gone to Hollywood (Murnau, Lubitsch) or fled into exile (Lang, Wilder, Ophüls). In 1936, criticism of the arts, including film, was abolished; hissing Reich movies was a punishable offence. By 1941, theatre doors were locked to keep patrons inside during newsreels.

To this day, Riefenstahl insists *Triumph of the Will* is 'a factual documentary,' not propaganda. 'Nor were the shots posed for the camera.' In actuality, with a crew of 172 under her command, Riefenstahl bent reality to her will from *mise-en-scène* to montage. A soldier turns his head at the exact moment a panning camera stops to frame his image; spectacular troop formations are shot from an elevator towering above, an elevator ordered expressly for the film. As Susan Sontag has pointed out, it's not for nothing that Hitler's favourite architect, Albert Speer, had a film credit. Still, for all this, Riefenstahl's film rarely suffers the sort of ontological agonies visited on the documentary genre as a matter of course. Film-maker and writer Richard Meran Barsam argues:

> Riefenstahl's task was to make a film of the Party rally, not a documentary of prevailing social conditions . . . [M]ore than a mere record of events, it is a cinematic expression of the Nazi mystique . . . Riefenstahl transcends the genre limitations of either the documentary or the propaganda film . . . Riefenstahl presents Hitler, a figure of national importance, as a leader of great historical significance to the destiny of Germany. In this sense, of course, she is only recording history.

Barsam is not the first, last, or worst Riefenstahl admirer to make this aestheticist move, one in which the film's 'art' allows it a truth beyond that of routine documentation. 'Of course, one cannot argue that Riefenstahl's propaganda is acceptable,' Anthony Slide, editor of Scarecrow Press's film-makers series, gushes in his introduction to David B. Hinton's 1991 volume on the director's *oeuvre*. 'But any student or scholar of the cinema must try and separate the propaganda from the art. And Leni Riefenstahl is a supreme artist of the cinema.' Goebbels would approve. In 1935, the minister of propaganda wrote of *Triumph of the Will*: 'This film has successfully avoided the danger of being merely a politically slanted film. It has translated the strong rhythm of these great times into convincing artistic terms; it is an epic, beating the tempo of marching formations, steel-like in its conviction, fired by a passionate artistry.'

When describing Riefenstahl's work, critics have tended to concentrate on her montage, her dramatic framing, the contrasting shots between Hitler and his swooning multitudes, the familiar Expressionist play of light and shadow. Less examined is Riefenstahl's use of dissolves, fades and superimpositions, though they are among her more conspicuous signatures. Consider the initial sequence of *Triumph of the Will*, one of the most famous in cinema history. After a brief preliminary text with its own revisionist spin ('Twenty years after the outbreak of the war, sixteen years after Germany's crucifixion . . .'), the film begins: images of clouds, a plane, aerial views of Nuremberg, the plane landing, Hitler disembarking, the welcoming public, Hitler's ride through the thronging masses.

It usually goes without mention that this infamous opener is virtually identical to that of *Olympia*, which also opens with images of clouds, a bird's-eye descent from the sky, a sweep over buildings (here, classical ruins), and a heroic, solitary figure. This character, dressed like a Greek youth, is transformed into a Reich athlete (who will also make his way through the multitudes) by means of an arresting superimposition in which the athlete emerges from flames, Olympic torch in hand. Likewise, in *Triumph of the Will* the ideological light is passed from one declaiming Reich official to another through a series of dramatic fades. From Hess to Rosenberg to Goebbels ('May the shining flame of our enthusiasm never be extinguished'), an inviolability develops that is ultimately, irrevocably, fulfilled by the image of the Führer.

A logic of wholeness builds throughout *Triumph of the Will* – Nuremberg's church spires dissolve into the pitched tents of the Hitler Youth, much as in *Olympia*, an intimate group of gymnasts gives way to a massive field of German women in formation. Unlike the montage techniques of either Vertov or Eisenstein, Riefenstahl's melting edits are strategically anti-dialectic. As Eisenstein held that montage is a 'collision . . . from the collision of two given factors arises a concept', so her editing strategy erases discord and dissonance. As she shuffles the images – Hitler, children, gaping women, the militia, the Volk – an oceanic effect swells to an apotheosis in which each edit and fade is also a denial of difference.

In *Male Fantasies*, his study of German protofascist military groups known as the *Freikorps*, literary theorist Klaus Theweleit writes, 'What we witness in *Triumph of the Will* is the liberation of massive forces through a process of internal amalgamation. The men in the film submit to orders and connect into sites that promise to eliminate what they experience as lack. The word they repeatedly scream is "whole" – heil, heil, heil, heil – and this is precisely what the party makes them.' Hitler is at once slightly ridiculous (human) and awesome (godlike). Under his gaze (the camera always frames him from below) the German mass becomes the *Volk*, the *Reich*, the Führer. 'The party is Hitler,' shouts Hess, 'but Hitler is Germany, just as Germany is Hitler.'

Blind allegiance to art rather than the Reich has been the *locus classicus* of Riefenstahl revisionists for some fifty years, a historical dodge her admirers have eagerly advanced. That she attained her highest 'artistic' success during the Third Reich hasn't deterred apologists . . .

What does it mean to call a film like *Triumph of the Will* a masterpiece? To name Leni Riefenstahl the greatest woman director in cinema history, as many have done in the past and continue to do? Critic David B. Hinton insists that 'understanding the historical background of the film is necessary when approaching the film as a document, but it reveals nothing of the nature of Leni Riefenstahl, the film-maker. For that, the film must be studied apart from its historical background.' Why? What on earth can be gained from looking at *Triumph of the Will*, or even *Olympia*, outside history? Innocence, for one thing. Sontag was right to see the attraction of Riefenstahl's work as symptomatic of 'fascist longings', but she mistook cause for effect. Certainly in the wake of punk and mainstream sado-masochistic imagery, the enduring 'fascination' with fascism seems to have less to do with 'rituals of domination and enslavement', a thrusting sexual

21 Olympia (1937).

envelope, as it were, than a desire to eliminate the boundaries – of taste, politics, moral reason – that might otherwise separate subject from object, film-maker from film, viewer from view.

The debates about Riefenstahl's films can't be reduced to spurious formalist hedges. Apologists like Hinton believe that by ripping *Triumph of the Will* from its context, scraping away at the accumulated odds and ends of the past, the 'truth' about its director becomes manifest. It's an approach, he explains, that ensures the film's 'true political implications will be underscored and not dismissed,' specifically the 'mass, symbolic manipulation' of the participants. Except that the manipulation was real, not symbolic. And those 'true political implications' were inflicted less on the bodies who cheered wildly for Hitler than on bodies who imagined 'impurities' banished them first from the rally, then the Reich, then lastly, from life itself.

Truly, the only way to see *Triumph of the Will* as simply a terrific-looking movie, to find *Olympia* a splendid, if overlong, idyll on human athleticism, is to ignore history and all its casualties. In an age in which appeals to universal truth inspire panic and paralysis – think of Bosnia – it is essential to raise questions about moral choice. Riefenstahl and her defenders would rescue the director and her films from the very history and aesthetics of hate she helped create. 'Politics too is an art,' wrote Goebbels, 'perhaps the highest and most comprehensive there is, and we who shape modern German policy feel ourselves in this to be artists who have been given the responsible task of forming, out of the raw material of the mass, the firm concrete structure of the people.' Like Speer, sculptor Arno Becker, and Hitler, who along with building the gas chambers also designed the Party's swastika standard, Riefenstahl bent art to fascist ends. Those who refuse to recognize the blood debt of her films and her life are complicit in that debt. They look at her films from the vantage point of the oppressors, but where they see beauty there is only, finally barbarism.

Source: A review of Leni Riefenstahl's *A Memoir* (St. Martin's Press, 1994) by Manohla Dargis in the *Village Voice*, literary supplement, March 1994.

The Spanish Earth
JORIS IVENS

In 1936 Dutch born Joris Ivens (1898–1989, see p. 76) obtained backing from the American Leftist group Contemporary Historians, Inc. and the help of Ernest Hemingway to make *The Spanish Earth*, a film about the Spanish Civil War from the Republican perspective.

This account of the film's production is from Ivens' autobiography, *The Camera and I.*

Hemingway was a great help to John [Ferno – the cameraman] and me. In consulting and talking over how to film the battle, he helped us with what you might call the general strategy of the film. He showed a quick comprehension and understanding of the documentary film and a very helpful humility towards this new profession. A lot of writers imagine that because they have worked in the field as correspondents, they can pick up the documentary medium in an afternoon. Hemingway went everywhere with us. He felt that if he was participating in the making of

a documentary film, he had to stay with the crew no matter where they
they went or how dull it might be at times.

He expected, and rightly, that out of the daily hard repetitious work
would come a real knowledge of what the documentary film is. He
stuck to the job and never played visitor or guest. As a writer he was
interested in how such a crew is able to become so involved in actual life
– more involved than a writer who comes to a foreign village and looks
and looks and doesn't bother writing when he doesn't feel like it. In us
he saw hard-working craftsmen of a motion picture unit, a team, doing
intricate and delicate work of camera and direction, simultaneously
thinking and composing the subject in the same broad terms as those
used in a considered writing job. I don't think he had ever met people
like us before.

We watched and filmed the constant fighting in the outskirts of
Madrid, particularly the Loyalist efforts to liquidate the fascist forces
lodged in University City. Ten minutes by streetcar and then a short
walk and you were at the front-line. But the first full-scale battle we
went to was on the Morata de Tajuna front – and later the Jarama front.

As we drove into a little valley village on our way there, we suddenly
saw hundreds of people with their hands up, like birds, running towards
the hills. We were not yet experienced or we would have stopped
immediately. In a closed car you do not see the planes coming over, nor
do you hear them. I didn't know what was happening. My first thought
was that the Franco troops were approaching from the other side. We
went on for a half mile and when our motor stopped we heard the
motors of heavy bombers. These villagers had no air-raid shelters. Their
only hope was to flee into the hills – hundreds of distraught people with
their hands in the air. We had the sense to pull our car into the shadow.
The village was empty. We thought we had better stay there a while.
John took our cameras and entered a small courtyard, just a roofed-
over shady place. In a war anything looks like protection, anything –
particularly if it has some sort of a roof.

Then we saw three bombs being released from the four Caproni
planes. They were the first bombs we had ever seen coming in our
direction and John and I went flat on the ground. They were such
shining bombs. As soon as the sun hit them, they were like matches
being struck. They fell about half a block from our courtyard – five
hundred pounders, we decided later. After the explosions there was
complete silence in the village. We thought the people would come back

now. Then we realized that they were listening to see if the planes would return and bomb again. Silence between two people may be dramatic, but you should hear the silence of five hundred people after the crash of bombs. Then the wounded in the village began to yell – maybe a baby, or an old man who couldn't get to the hills in time. Still the people didn't dare to come back.

We took the cameras out into the street to photograph the first thing that appeared in front of the lenses. We didn't know or care whether the shots were good or bad; we didn't even know whether they were in focus. We just shot. The bravest began to come back and John filmed those first women wandering through the dust of the explosions still hanging over the streets. The women looked bewildered, their hands over their bellies in the agony of shock – not yet knowing what had happened. We filmed them not realizing that we were being brutal, but

22 *Moments after an air attack.* The Spanish Earth *(1937).*

feeling we had to get those pictures. Nobody paid any attention to us – until the first tensions had been relieved. Then the town became more openly dramatic – we shot scenes of running people; and then I began to think, how do I cover this completely? There must be more to shoot. Let's go around. Let's look. We found two women picking up a baby. We saw other women unconscious of their movements, simply holding handkerchiefs over their eyes. We filmed some dead. Women looking from a window. Little kids playing with parts of a rifle. Now I was thinking more calmly and I began quietly stalking material that was to complete this sequence someday on a cutting table.

I did not have so much the feeling of 'let me get as much out of life as I can' which I had previously experienced just before going to the front, but more a feeling of meditation. This had the special effect of sharpening you for the actual work at the front, increasing efficiency and alertness in action – meaning you have less chance of being killed or wounded, and so keep the men with you from being endangered by your carelessness.

In war photography you have to know when you should take a chance, risking your life and that of the cameraman, and when you should not take that risk. Each member of your unit has to know all about the day's work and the importance of the action and of the shots you are going to take of that action. It has to be worthwhile – there is no sense, otherwise, in risking a life, an arm or a leg for a shot that will later land on the cutting room floor. Every member of your unit has the same right as every man of a machine-gun crew to know where and when to go forward, who is on his flank, what support he can expect from them, what there is to be known about the enemy's position and the enemy's strength.

In filming the fighting in Madrid we used much the same tactics, except that we rarely got carried away as could have happened in the excitement of a battle. This too was a battle, a battle between German artillery and the people of Madrid, but you didn't have to go looking for the significant human detail – it was always staring you in the face.

The way we looked at and filmed the shelling of Madrid must have been the right way, the human way, because six years later John Steinbeck, in gathering Londoners' memories of their blitz, found that 'in all of the little stories it is the ordinary, the commonplace thing or incident against the background of the bombing that leaves the indelible picture.'

This observation might well be a documentary film-maker's guide to

camera observation of a tragedy. In *The Spanish Earth* I use the sound
of broken glass in the sound track, and the slight crunching of it, around
two dead Madrid victims – two kids. This found its echo in one
Londoner's memory of his own experience: 'It's the glass, the sound in
the morning of the broken glass being swept up, the vicious, flat tinkle.
That is the thing I remember more than anything else, that constant
sound of broken glass being swept up on the pavements. My dog broke
a window the other day and my wife swept up the glass and a cold
shiver went over me. It was a moment before I could trace the reason for
it.'

. . . There were more than tragedies to film in Madrid. There were
also events. We filmed the meeting at which the People's Army was
officially founded. All the different regiments fighting in their own way
on the Loyalist side – the communist, socialist, anarchist regiments were
fused into one Republican Army at a meeting attended by delegates
from all fronts. We didn't realize it at that time, but we were recording a
vital historical document.

Besides keeping a strong central theme during the making of a
documentary film, you have to keep on the lookout for events that will
illuminate that theme. These passing events are sometimes too precious
to your theme to ignore them. You have to be something of a newsreel
cameraman, too. But you can't afford to judge events by 'news value'.
Events of apparently limited news value may prove later to be focus
points for your entire structure. They have to be weighed almost solely
on their importance to your film and theme. We could easily have said
of this People's Army meeting, it's just another meeting – but this
particular meeting helped us draw together the two main lines of our
film.

. . . I was often asked, why hadn't we gone to the other side, too, and
made an objective film? My only answer was that a documentary film-
maker has to have an opinion on such vital issues as fascism or anti-
fascism – he has to have feelings about these issues, if his work is to have
any dramatic or emotional or art value. And too, there is the very simple
fact to consider, that when you are in a war and you get to the other
side, you are shot or put into a prison camp – you cannot be on both
sides, neither as a soldier nor as a film-maker. If anyone wanted that
objectivity of 'both sides of the question' he would have to show two
films, *The Spanish Earth* and a film by a fascist film-maker, if he could
find one.

23 The Four Hundred Million *(1939)*.

This was actually done once: The London Film Society showed two films of the Ethiopian war, side by side – one made by a crew of Soviet cameramen, and the other by an Italian crew. You were given the evidence against any possible 'objectivity' when you saw, in the Italian film, the decorative, flower-like effects of the exploding bombs as seen from the bombing planes, and, in the other, the death, the maiming, the bleeding, and the blinding caused by those same bombs.

I was surprised to find that many people automatically assumed that any documentary film would inevitably be objective. Perhaps the term is unsatisfactory, but for me the distinction between the words document and documentary is quite clear. Do we demand objectivity in the evidence presented at a trial? No, the only demand is that each piece of evidence be as full a subjective, truthful, honest presentation of the witness's attitude as an oath on the Bible can produce from him.

I think that Ernest Hemingway, speaking at the Writer's Congress shortly after our return from Spain, defined the documentary film's job completely satisfactorily in his definition of the writer's job:

> 'A writer's problem does not change. He himself changes, but his problem remains the same. It is always how to write truly and having found what is true, to project it in such a way that it becomes a part of the experience of the person who reads it.'[1]

I would like to add that a militant documentary film has to reach further. After informing and moving audiences, it should agitate – mobilize them to become active in connection with the problems shown in the film.

I continue to make documentary films because I know there is unity between what I believe and what I do. If I felt I had lost that unity, I would change my profession. A documentary film-maker has the sense of participating directly in the world's most fundamental issues – a sense that is difficult for even the most conscious film-maker working in a studio to feel.

Source: Joris Ivens, *The Camera and I*, Seven Seas Books, 1969.

---

1 *The Writer in a Changing World*, edited by Henry Hart, 1937.

The Wandering Jew
ERWIN LEISER

Film-makers of the Third Reich demonstrated the extent to which seemingly 'factual' footage can be warped to serve a political pupose. In this extract from his book on Nazi cinema, Erwin Leiser discusses Franz Hippler's notorious *Der Ewige Jude* and other anti-semitic 'documentaries'.

There were several versions of the 'documentary film' produced by the Reich Propaganda Department of the National Socialist Party under the title *The Wandering Jew* [*Der Ewige Jude*, also known as *The Eternal Jew*]. 'Sensitive souls' were advised to see the shorter version, from which the Jewish ritual slaughter sequences were omitted. The commentary by Eberhard Taubert was dropped in the foreign language versions of the film; its demagogic tone, aimed at German audiences, might have damaged the credibility of the 'document'. The effect of this was to give more prominence to the music, which here, as in other anti-Jewish propaganda films, took on a turgid oriental flavour the moment Jews appeared on the screen. Shots of Nordic people, on the other hand, were accompanied by Bach. The film was mostly shot in the Jewish areas of Poland, though the commentary omits to mention that it was the Nazis themselves who were responsible for the dingy, cramped conditions of these ghettos. The opening sentence immediately sets the tone: 'The civilized Jews such as those we know in Germany provide an incomplete picture of their racial characteristics. This film shows original material shot in the Polish ghettos, shows us the Jews as they really looked before they concealed themselves behind the mask of civilized Europeans.'

The ghetto was 'a breeding ground of epidemics . . . endangering the health of the Aryan people.' The implication is that here was a menace which must be 'resisted'. A montage sequence of rats, calculated to leave an indelible impression on the minds of any audience, is accompanied by a commentary informing us that rats 'have followed men like parasites from the very beginning', destroying the country and spreading disease. 'They are cunning, cowardly and fierce, and usually appear in large packs. In the animal world they represent the element of insidious subterranean destruction.' 'Not dissimilar from the place Jews have among men,' the commentary continues, as the rats are followed

24 *A face from* The Eternal Jew *(1940)*.

by shots of Jews crowded together in the ghetto. It could hardly be
stated more clearly: the killing of one or of many Jews was not a crime
but a necessity. Jews, the film implies, are not human beings but pests
which have to be exterminated.

This montage was duly applauded by the critics. The correspondent from the *Deutsche Allgemeine Zeitung* 'heaved a sigh of relief when the film ended with pictures of Germans and things German.' Apart from *The Wandering Jew*, distorted documentary material included several short exercises which in similar vein compared Jews with cockroaches.

. . . Emmanuel Ringelblum, the historian of the Warsaw ghetto, has described how the German film cameramen went about their work in the summer of 1942. Jews were herded together and then the Jewish security police were ordered to disperse them. Scenes showing very Jewish-looking men locked together in the ritual baths with young women were manufactured to create the impression that the Jews bathed together in the nude. A restaurant owner was forced to lay his tables to suggest to the audience an abundance of delicacies and champagne; then Jews were indiscriminately rounded up on the streets and filmed eating and drinking. Grocery shop windows were filled with rare delicacies before being filmed. These shots were supposed to convey to German audiences that the Jews in the ghettos were far too prosperous. The banquet was meant to incite envy and resentment among those who could not afford such expensive food. At the same time film of the miserable conditions in the ghetto was juxtaposed with doctored images of a fictitious prosperity; some of this material was used in a series of articles in the *Berliner Illustrierter* entitled 'Jews at home'. Jews were said to be cruel to each other, while the rich Jews of the ghetto were indifferent to the poor; and scenes were shot to prove this cruelty. A member of the Jewish security police is about to strike a Jew when a German runs up to stop him. A boy is made to steal a loaf of bread and run off with it to his friends, who are supposed to be hiding him and his loot. In reality there was hardly any bread in the ghetto, and the guards at the walls stopped any food being taken in. But in the film the little thief is protected from the baker and the police by a German. Beating children is wrong.

According to the commentary of *The Wandering Jew*, the ghetto's poor were not poor at all, but 'through decades of trading had hoarded enough money to make clean and comfortable homes for themselves and their families. Yet they continue to live for generations in the same dirty, flea-ridden holes.' In reality, according to Governor General Frank, the one consolation the Poles themselves had was that 'the Jews are even worse off.' While one of Himmler's aides was proposing that the Poles should be forced to practise birth control and should be

allowed only four years of primary school education, the ghettos which
the SS set up all over the East were being designated as the first phase in
the physical annihilation of all Jews. They were deliberately located
near railway lines; it would thus be no trouble to deport those who
hadn't died on the spot to one of the extermination camps.

Nazi cameramen recorded every stage in the demoralization process,
filming starving people begging on the streets or lying outside their
houses too weak to move; children who grew up in the shadow of
death, plagued by vermin and disease, unsmiling and with no toys to
play with, their eyes already old and accustomed to misery and death;
epidemics raging in the ghetto – though there was of course no
mention of the fact that these very epidemics were spread by the Nazis
under the pretence of fighting them. There is also no reference in these
filmed records to the fact that immediately after the defeat of Poland
an area of ten square kilometres in Warsaw was transformed into a
ghetto. This district had previously housed a population of 240,000
Jews and 80,000 non-Jews. Now the non-Jews had to move out to
make room for hundreds of thousands of Jews forcibly transported to
the ghetto. There were initially six people to every room in the ghetto,
but this soon rose to thirteen to a room. People who only a few weeks
before had been living a normal life found themselves forced to live
and die like rats in the ghetto. Herein lies the cynicism of a 'document'
like The Wandering Jew: people confined in a world of dirt like
animals in overcrowded cages, and their subsequent degradation
presented as though it were completely normal, an existence which
these victims of the Nazi terror had supposedly chosen for themselves,
a simple demonstration of the theory that Jews are not people like you
and me.

The most harrowing sequences from these Nazi films on the hell
devised in the Polish ghettos for the victims of the 'final solution' were
never used. It was by no means certain that the material would actually
induce loathing and resentment in the general public. Preview audiences
had in fact been sympathetic. And it was precisely the most vicious of
the doctored sequences which produced this unintended effect. Pairs of
Jewish men and women had been put in front of the camera to
demonstrate social differences which had been contrived for these very
shots, but the eyes of those filmed expressed something altogether
different from what the cameramen had been trying to register. What
was communicated was the silent despair of these humiliated people,

who knew that what awaited them after the filming was an unknown and degrading death.

In 1945 representatives of the International Red Cross visited the Jewish 'model camp' at Theresienstadt (Terezin) in Czechoslovakia and were shown part of a film made there in the summer of 1944. Kurt Gerron, a once prominent actor who had emigrated to Holland in 1933, had fallen into the hands of the Gestapo there and was now a prisoner at the camp, was given the responsibility for writing and directing a film called *The Führer Gives the Jews a Town*, which was designed to reveal Theresienstadt as a 'paradise for Jews'. Like all other investigators, when I questioned survivors of Theresienstadt, I found some dispute about Gerron's contribution to the film and his motives for collaborating on it. When the film was completed, Gerron and most of the other leading collaborators were deported to Poland and gassed. At the very moment when the transports to the extermination camps were being got under way, thousands of Theresienstadt inmates were recruited as extras in a film designed to camouflage what was really happening in the camp. The film included a number of scenes with children designed to create the impression that Theresienstadt was a particularly pleasant place for children to be. Since in the autumn of 1944 an estimated 1,600 children were deported from Theresienstadt, and in the Auschwitz selection-process no child who looked under fourteen escaped the gas chamber, most of the children in the film must have been murdered soon after it was completed. There were shops in the film which were specially constructed for the cameras and in which there was nothing to buy. A stage was built for an open-air cabaret show at a spot which was normally out of bounds to prisoners. In the film's Theresienstadt, people are happily playing football, well-fed men stand under showers, coquettish girls are busy putting on make-up. In his book *The Hidden Truth*, H. G. Adler quotes as an example of the way in which the Nazis were planning to use film – but which to a large extent was by this time no longer feasible – a newsreel from the autumn of 1944 which juxtaposes a coffee-house scene shot in Theresienstadt with a montage of scenes from the front lines. The commentator remarks: 'While Jews in Theresienstadt sit enjoying coffee and cakes and dance around, our soldiers are bearing the brunt of this terrible war, the suffering and the hardship, to defend their homeland.'

Source: *Nazi Cinema* by Erwin Leiser, Macmillan, New York, 1975.

John Huston at War
SCOTT HAMMEN

During the Second World War numerous prominent American fiction directors – including Frank Capra, John Ford, William Wyler and George Stevens – made government-sponsored documentaries. John Huston (1906–1987) made three such documentaries. The first, *Report from the Aleutians* (1943), was a detached examination of Air Force activities on the remote Aleutian islands North of Alaska. This was followed by *The Battle of San Pietro* (1945) and *Let There Be Light* (1946), two of the most realistic and affecting of all war films.

. . . *The Battle of San Pietro* begins, as did *Report from the Aleutians*, with the careful delineation of the geographic areas involved. But this time, the film is in black and white, the location is the opposite side of the globe, and combat no longer consists of the bloodless strategic problems of aerial bombardment. It has come down to earth. Little time is spent establishing viewer empathy with the film's subjects; the attention is squarely on the brutal facts of infantry warfare.

The village of San Pietro sits in the commanding position of a valley in the south of Italy. Like the Aleutian Islands, the place has no unique significance in the outcome of the war, but does typify the conditions encountered throughout the campaign of which it was a part.

Huston's narration is spare and objective, only occasionally sounding a note of bitter irony or strong emotion. 'St. Peter's,' he remarks with mock pedantry, as his camera pans across the already scarred face of the town. 'Note interesting treatment of the chancel.' The church in the centre of the frame is completely in ruins.

It is 6:20 a.m., December 8, 1943. The faces of weary American soldiers are glimpsed singly and in groups. They differ not at all from those who were seen passing the time performing mundane chores on the Aleutians, but they are clearly not in the most ebullient of spirits. Their expressions convey what the narration describes accurately as 'the expectation of mortal punishment and bloodshed'.

The War Department had commissioned the film to explain to the public at home why the American forces had advanced through Italy so much more slowly than had been predicted. Huston's response to the assignment not only makes it amply clear why the Italian campaign hadn't gone smoothly, it inspires a good deal of amazement as to how

Allied forces had managed to prevail at all. For the unsavoury truth about the battle for San Pietro – as well as those launched in hundreds of similar locations throughout Italy – was that there was simply no way to fight it without a heavy loss of life. Huston chose to convey an impression of what it was like to enter an arena with so slight a chance of survival.

The danger was as great for Huston and the Signal Corps cameramen under his command. Shot after shot depicts the ferocity of the fighting. At one point, the camera loses sight of one soldier in a cloud of smoke and then pans to the right just in time to witness another falling to the ground riddled by machine-gun fire. 'Volunteer patrols made desperate attempts to reach enemy positions and reduce strong-points,' Huston says in his flat voice. 'Not a single member of any such patrol ever came back alive.' The price paid for the Allied advance frequently exceeded one death per yard.

How Huston was able to function as an artist in the situation is difficult to fathom. He reportedly moved continuously in the face of enemy small arms and mortar fire from one cameraman to the next, explaining to each exactly what he wanted from their footage. The scenario was developed and revised in the quiet moments between attacks; the narration was written in his tent at night while enemy shells continued to explode nearby. And he was unable to review the film he and his men had shot until he returned to America: all of his raw footage was sent back to Washington for processing and printing. That Huston not only survived the Battle of San Pietro but managed to create a powerful and coherent film out of it makes the usual film-making obstacles – the struggles with budgets, actors, and producers – seem negligible by comparison.

Yet Huston was to have to fight this more common film-maker's battle as well to preserve the integrity of San Pietro. The series of military engagements that the film recorded had resulted in the loss of over 1,100 men to the 143rd Infantry – and Huston had focused unflinchingly on the wholesale slaughter, documenting it in the same straight forward style with which he had recorded the building of an airfield in the Aleutians. When the military hierarchy first saw San Pietro, they were shocked and immediately ordered substantial changes made – particularly in the juxtaposition of the voices of men talking and joking with scenes of the same men's bodies being dumped into sacks for burial. His Pentagon overseers condemned the film as pacifistic and, even after many cuts had been made, delayed the work's release almost until the end of the war.

In retrospect, it's not hard to see why *The Battle of San Pietro* so frightened those who had commissioned it. Not only did it fail to encourage its viewers to exult in the American victory – directing their attention instead to what that victory had meant in terms of the deaths of individuals – it refused to accord a grand significance to the sacrifice made by those who had perished. Most War Department sponsored documentaries, when they acknowledged individual suffering and loss of life at all, at least invested the occasion with a special importance in the larger scheme of things. John Ford's *The Battle of Midway*, for example, labels its subject as nothing less than the 'Grandest Naval Victory of the world to date.' The closing scene of *San Pietro* makes no such boast. Over scenes of soldiers at work digging graves for their comrades, the narration only tells us that there were to be 'many more San Pietros, a thousand more, and many of those you see here alive will die.'

Huston does allow a meagre note of hope to creep in at the film's end: he notes that the land scarred by the battle retains a regenerative power, and that the children among those who inhabit it may live to forget the bloodshed. (And the Mormon Tabernacle Choir is heard singing an elegy – a saccharine note one suspects was imposed by the film's sponsors.) But this brief note of faith in the power of human endurance in no way allays the horror of the killing that has occurred. The camera has the last word: a pan over the rubble that was once the village of San Pietro.

They might have been the survivors of San Pietro, shovelling the corpses of their comrades into body bags. Now they are 'home'. As narrator Walter Huston explains, 'Every man has his breaking point. And these, in the fulfilment of their duties as soldiers, were forced beyond the limits of human endurance.' It is a theme central to almost all of John Huston's work, but he never found so apt a medium for its expression as in his final war documentary, *Let There Be Light*.

The Army wanted a film that would deliver an encouraging message to prospective employers of veterans, to convince them that the men who had been psychologically injured were as capable of recovery as those whose wounds had been solely physical. The very acknowledgement that grave nervous and emotional casualties had occurred at all seemed unusually enlightened; it was a side of warfare never before touched on by the War Department films.

Huston brought his cameras to the Mason General Hospital in Brentwood, Long Island. He had never before been in a psychiatric hospital. He spent three months there, and shot 375,000 feet of film. Cameras, concealed in the hospital wards, recorded the patients' individual encounters with staff psychiatrists as well as group therapy sessions. The subjects, as the narration says, do not 'wear badges of their pain, the crutches, the bandages, the splints . . . They show no outward signs, yet they too are wounded.' The cases shown do not appear to have been scientifically selected as a cross-section of different combat-induced neuroses. The sense is that the disorders involved are routine and quite susceptible to appropriate therapy. And yet the images evoked by these troubled men are so immediate and devastating that they seem at times to be almost literal descriptions of scenes from *The Battle of San Pietro*.

One soldier attempts to come to terms with his own survival after a close friend's death. 'I lost my last buddy up there. They were shelling us. He was the second scout. I was the first scout and I should have been in front of him . . . After he got killed, I was all right when I was moving forward, but when I stopped, I thought about him lying back there. I don't care if I live.'

Another suffers from amnesia. A psychiatrist puts him under hypnosis and begins to draw fragmentary recollections from him. 'We were forced to take cover, five of us. One of the boys got hurt.' Suddenly the patient's face flinches as if in great pain, then he continues, 'An explosion, they're carrying me across the field, they're putting me on a stretcher . . .'

The film's most extraordinary sequence concerns a young man who has lost the capacity for intelligible speech. Through the prompting of a psychiatrist, the reason is unearthed. It had started with the sound of the letter 'S', the sound of explosive shells approaching, the sound of death in combat. Slowly, carefully, the doctor probes, reassuring the young man. And then, suddenly, a breakthrough: 'I can talk, I can talk! Oh God, listen I can talk!'

If the intent of *Let There Be Light* was to establish the fact that neurotic problems could be successfully treated, that those suffering from them deserve as much honour and respect from civilian society as those who had been wounded in other ways, then it clearly was an unqualified success. But the Army was unhappy. The brass seemed to think not that the film failed in its official purpose, but that it succeeded in too many other unofficial ways. No mention is made, for example, of the American victory in World War Two. The only victory seen as worth celebrating is the healing of individual wounds – and even that celebration is subdued by an awareness of the many whose wounds were mortal.

The one false note in the work is its implausibly optimistic ending. It's implied that every case shown under treatment has resulted in a completely successful cure. And, evidently for the sake of dramatic effect, every patient is presented being discharged into civilian life at the same time, as if they were all graduating in a class from school. The presumption appears to be that they will now all face life without the burden of any war-time scars – that the wounds of war, whether psychological or physical, have all healed. Yet the sense of all that Huston has captured earlier leads the viewer to just the opposite impression.

Perhaps it was precisely this clash between the wrenching early sequences and the suspect happy ending that provoked the Army's objections. None of Huston's three war assignments had been completed without disagreements between the film-maker and his employers; the premières of the first two works had been substantially delayed. But *Let There Be Light* met much more serious resistance: it was withheld entirely from public view.

The War department made three public objections to the film. It contended that the men who had appeared would bring suit against the government if the scenes of their treatment were ever publicly exhibited. Huston had anticipated this objection and had been careful to secure written releases from everyone who had appeared in the film; the Army then argued that the signed releases might not stand up in court because they had all been given by men in a mentally unstable condition! In other words, the project had been doomed from the start.

The second objection was even more unfathomable: that there would be an adverse reaction on the part of the families of those for whom the psychiatric rehabilitation had not been successful. These families would complain, said the War Department, that the film's impression was misleading and would encourage the reduction of the already inadequate resources being devoted to those whose problems had not proved so easily soluble. This argument is particularly suspect in view of the fact it was only at the War Department's insistence that the film's ending had been made as optimistic as it was.

The final announced objection probably comes closest to the Department's true feelings. They admitted that they had never intended for a film like *Let There Be Light* to be made at all, and that Huston had, in their words, 'pulled a fast one'. What exactly they did have in mind has never been made clear. Whatever it was, it apparently in no way resembled the disturbing work of art that John Huston had created.

Despite the weaknesses of the reasons cited, the prohibition on the showing of *Let There Be Light* remains in effect today . . .

Let There Be Light left a mark both on its subjects and on its creator. The ward of Mason General Hospital in which Huston filmed reportedly showed a better record of recovery than all others in the hospital. Far from objecting to the camera's presence the patients were fascinated by the mechanics of movie-making and excited about their own participation. Their enthusiasm appears to have extended to the plastering of movie posters on to the walls of their ward and to the designation of its location as 'Hollywood and Vine.'

Huston too was affected. He called the experience 'the most hopeful and optimistic and even joyous thing I ever had a hand in. I felt as though I were going to church every day out in that hospital.' And the impression was deep: in *Key Largo* Humphrey Bogart's bitter reminiscences of his war-time experiences – pinned down by enemy fire in a small town in Italy – echo the images of San Pietro and the words of *Let There Be Light*. And surely his 1950 adaptation of Stephen Crane's *The Red Badge of Courage*, which starred World War Two hero Audie Murphy as a soldier traumatized by combat, owes much to Huston's own conviction, as expressed in *Let There Be Light*, that war injuries to the mind are no more shameful than those to the body. In fact, Huston's treatment of the later film's entire story can be seen as an analogue of the efforts of the patients at Mason General Hospital to recover and persevere.

Source: *Film Comment*, April 1980.

Only Connect: Some Aspects of the Work of Humphrey Jennings
LINDSAY ANDERSON

Humphrey Jennings' films have aged well. They have none of what – to modern ears – is the crass, hectoring quality of most propaganda. They

25 *Humphrey Jennings directs his actors in* Fires Were Started *(1943).*

are quiet, affectionate, poignant and human, though made with a patriotic purpose in mind.

Jennings (1907–1950) read English at Cambridge, but abandoned his post-graduate studies to become a painter and in 1936 he helped organize the first exhibition of Surrealist art in Britain. In need of money, he joined the GPO film unit in 1934, though he was never really an 'insider'. Grierson, practical and literal in his attitude towards film, mistrusted Jennings' aestheticism and conscious artistry, accusing him of a patronising élitism. Even in later years, when Jennings was widely regarded as the most notable film-maker to have been associated with the British documentary movement, Grierson was dismissive.

Jennings' films were all tightly scripted, and blend *vérité* footage with 'reconstruction', often blurring the line between documentary and fiction. What is remarkable is that a film like *Fires Were Started*, which uses sets, actors (both professional and amateur) and scripted dialogue retains the spontaneity and human honesty that we associate with documentary.

This famous essay was written by director and critic Lindsay Anderson (1923–1994) in 1957, when he himself was making documentaries (see p. 211)

It is difficult to write anything but personally about the films of Humphrey Jennings. This is not of course to say that a full and documented account of his work in the cinema would not be of the greatest interest: anyone who undertook such a study would certainly merit our gratitude. But the sources are diffuse. Friends and colleagues would have to be sought out and questioned; poems and paintings tracked down; and, above all, the close texture of the films themselves would have to be exhaustively examined. My aim must be more modest, merely hoping to stimulate by offering some quite personal reactions, and by trying to explain why I think these pictures are so good.

Jennings's films are all documentaries, all made firmly within the framework of the British documentary movement. This fact ought not to strike a chill, for surely 'the creative interpretation of actuality' should suggest an exciting, endlessly intriguing use of the cinema; and yet it must be admitted that the overtones of the term are not immediately attractive. Indeed, it comes as something of a surprise to learn that this unique and fascinating artist was from the beginning of his career in films an inside member of Grierson's GPO unit (with which he first worked in 1934), and made all his best films as official, sponsored propaganda during World War Two. His subjects were thus, at least on the surface, the common ones; yet his manner of expression was always individual, and became more and more so. It was a style that bore the closest possible relationship to his theme – to that aspect of his subjects which his particular vision caused him consistently to stress. It was, that is to say, a poetic style. In fact, it might reasonably be contended that Humphrey Jennings is the only real poet the British cinema has yet produced.

He started directing films in 1939 (we may leave out of account an insignificant experiment in 1935; in collaboration with Len Lye); and the date is significant, for it was the war that fertilized his talent and created the conditions in which his best work was produced. Watching one of Jennings's early pictures, *Speaking from America*, which was made to explain the workings of the transatlantic radio telephone system, one would hardly suspect the personal qualities that characterize the pictures he was making only a short while later. There seems to have been more evidence of these in *Spare Time*, a film on the use of leisure among industrial workers: a mordant sequence of a carnival procession, drab and shoddy, in a northern city, aroused the wrath of more orthodox documentarians, and Basil Wright has mentioned other scenes, more sympathetically shot – 'the pigeon-fancier', the 'lurcher-loving collier', and the choir rehearsal – are all important clues to Humphrey's development. Certainly such an affectionate response to simple pleasures is more characteristic of Jennings's later work than any emphasis of satire.

If there had been no war, though, could that development ever have taken place? Humphrey Jennings was never happy with narrowly propagandist subjects, any more than he was with the technical exposition of *Speaking from America*. But in wartime people become important, and observation of them is regarded in itself as a justifiable subject for filming, without any more specific 'selling angle' than their sturdiness of spirit. Happily, this was the right subject for Jennings. With Cavalcanti, Harry Watt, and Pat Jackson he made *The First Days*, a picture of life on the home front in the early months of the war. On his own, he then directed *Spring Offensive*, about farming and the new development of agricultural land in the eastern counties; in 1940 he worked again with Harry Watt on *London Can Take It*, another picture of the home front; and in 1941, with *Heart of Britain*, he showed something of the way in which the people of Northern industrial Britain were meeting the challenge of war.

These films did their jobs well, and social historians of the future will find in them much that makes vivid the atmosphere and manners of their period. Ordinary people are sharply glimpsed in them, and the ordinary sounds that were part of the fabric of their lives reinforce the glimpses and sometimes comment on them: a lorry-load of youthful conscripts speeds down the road in blessed ignorance of the future, as a jaunty singer gives out 'We're going to hang out our washing on the Siegfried Line.' In the films which Jennings made in collaboration, it is risky, of course, to draw attention too certainly to any particular feature as being his: yet here and there are images and effects which unmistakably betray his sensibility. Immense women knitting furiously for the troops; a couple of cockney mothers commenting to each other on the quietness of the streets now that the children have gone; the King and Queen unostentatiously shown inspecting the air-raid damage in their own back garden. *Spring Offensive* is less sure in its touch, rather awkward in its staged conversations and rather over-elaborate in its images; *Heart of Britain* plainly offered a subject that Jennings found more congenial. Again the sense of human contact is direct: a steelworker discussing his ARP duty with his mate, a sturdy matron of the WVS looking straight at us through the camera as she touchingly describes her pride at being able to help the rescue workers, if only by serving cups of tea. And along with these plain, spontaneous encounters come telling shots of landscape and background, amplifying and reinforcing. A style, in fact, is being hammered out in these films; a style based on a peculiar intimacy of observation, a fascination with the commonplace thing or person that is significant, precisely because it is commonplace, and with the whole pattern that can emerge when such commonplace, significant things and people are fitted together in the right order.

Although it is evident that the imagination at work in all these early pictures is instinctively a cinematic one, in none of them does one feel that the imagination is working with absolute freedom. All the films are accompanied by commentaries, in some cases crudely propagandist, in others serviceable and decent enough; but almost consistently these off-screen words clog and impede the progress of the picture. The images are so justly chosen, and so explicitly assembled, that there is nothing for the commentator to say. The effect – particularly if we have Jenning's later achievements in mind – is cramped. The material is there, the elements are assembled; but the fusion does not take place that alone can create the poetic whole that is greater than the sum of its parts. And then comes the last sequence of *Heart of Britain*. The Huddersfield Choral Society rises before Malcolm Sargent, and the homely, buxom housewives, the black-coated workers, and the men from the mills burst into the Hallelujah Chorus. The sound of their singing continues, and we see landscapes and noble buildings, and then a factory where bombers are being built. Back and forth go these contrasting, conjunctive images, until the music broadens out to its conclusion. The roar of engines joins in, and the bombers take off. The sequence is not a long one, and there are unfortunate intrusions from the commentator, but the effect is extraordinary, and the implications obvious. Jennings has found his style.

Words for Battle, Listen to Britain, Fires Were Started, A Diary for Timothy. To the enthusiast for Jennings these titles have a ring which makes it a pleasure simply to speak them, or to set them down in writing; for these are the films in which, between 1941 and 1945, we can see that completely individual style developing from tentative discovery and experiment to mature certainty. They are all films of Britain at war, and yet their feeling is never, or almost never, warlike. They are committed to the war – for all his sensibility there does not seem to have been anything of the pacifist about Jennings – but their real inspiration is pride, and unaggressive pride in the courage and doggedness of ordinary British people. Kathleen Raine, a friend of Jennings and his contemporary at Cambridge, has written: 'What counted for Humphrey was the expression, by certain people, of the ever-growing spirit of man; and, in particular, of the spirit of England.'

It is easy to see how the atmosphere of the country at war could stimulate and inspire an artist so bent. For it is at such a time that the spirit of a country becomes manifest, the sense of tradition and community sharpened as (alas) it rarely is in time of peace. 'He sought therefore for a public imagery, a public poetry.' In a country at war we are all members one of another, in a sense that is obvious to the least spiritually-minded.

'Only connect.' It is surely no coincidence that Jennings chose for his writer on A Diary for Timothy the wise and kindly humanist who had placed that epigraph on the title page of his best novel. The phrase at any rate is apt to describe not merely the film on which Jennings worked with E. M. Forster, but this whole series of pictures which he made during the war. He had a mind that delighted in simile and the unexpected relationship. 'It was he,' wrote Grierson, 'who discovered the Louis Quinze properties of a Lyons' swiss roll.' On a deeper level, he loved to link one event with an other, the past with the present, person to person. Thus the theme of Words for Battle is the interpretation of great poems of the past through events of the present – a somewhat artificial idea, though brilliantly executed. It is perhaps significant, though, that the film springs to a new kind of life altogether in its last sequence, as the words of Lincoln at Gettysburg are followed by the clatter of tanks driving into Parliament Square past the Lincoln statue: the sound of the tanks merges in turn into the grand music of Handel, and suddenly the camera is following a succession of men and women in uniform, striding along the pavement cheery and casual, endowed by the music, by the urgent rhythm of the cutting, and by the solemnity of what has gone before (to which we feel they are heirs) with an astonishing and breathtaking dignity, a mortal splendor.

As if taking its cue from the success of this wonderful passage, *Listen to Britain* dispenses with commentary altogether. Here the subject is simply the sights and sounds of wartime Britain over a period of some twenty-four hours. To people who have not seen the film it is difficult to describe its fascination – something quite apart from its purely nostalgic appeal to anyone who lived through those years in this country. The picture is a stylistic triumph (Jennings shared the credit with his editor, Stewart McAllister), a succession of marvellously evocative images freely linked by contrasting and complementary sounds; and yet it is not for its quality of form that one remembers it most warmly, but for the continuous sensitivity of its human regard. It is a fresh and loving eye that Jennings turns on to those Canadian soldiers, singing to an accordion to while away a long train journey; or on to that jolly factory girl singing 'Yes, My Darling Daughter' at her machine; or on to the crowded floor of the Blackpool Tower Ballroom; or the beautiful, sad-faced woman who is singing 'The Ash Grove' at an ambulance-station piano. Emotion, in fact (it is something one often forgets), can be conveyed as unmistakably through the working of a film camera as by the manipulation of pen or paintbrush. To Jennings this was a transfigured landscape, and he recorded its transfiguration on film.

The latter two of these four films, *Fires Were Started* and *A Diary for Timothy*, are more ambitious in conception: the second runs for about forty minutes and the first is a full-length 'feature documentary'. One's opinion as to which of them is Jennings's masterpiece is likely to vary according to which of them one has most recently seen. *Fires Were Started* (made in 1943) is a story of one particular unit of the National Fire Service during one particular day and night in the middle of the London blitz: in the morning the men leave their homes and civil occupations, their taxicabs, newspaper shops, advertising agencies, to start their tour of duty; a new recruit arrives and is shown the ropes; warning comes in that a heavy attack is expected; night falls and the alarms begin to wail; the unit is called out to action at a riverside warehouse, where fire threatens an ammunition ship drawn up at the wharf; the fire is mastered; a man is lost; the ship sails with the morning tide. In outline it is the simplest of pictures; in treatment it is of the greatest subtlety, richly poetic in feeling, intense with tenderness and admiration for the unassuming heroes whom it honors. Yet it is not merely the members of the unit who are given this depth and dignity of treatment. Somehow every character we see, however briefly, is made to stand out sharply and memorably in his or her own right: the brisk and cheery girl who arrives with the dawn on the site of the fire to serve tea to the men from her mobile canteen; a girl in the control room forced under her desk by a near-miss, and apologizing down the telephone which she still holds in her hand as she picks herself up; two isolated aircraft-spotters watching the flames of London miles away through the darkness. No other British film made during the war, documentary or feature, achieved such a continuous and poignant truthfulness, or treated the subject of men at war with such a sense of its incidental glories and its essential tragedy.

The idea of connection, by contrast and juxtaposition, is always present in *Fires Were Started* – never more powerfully than in the beautiful closing sequence, where the fireman's sad little funeral is intercut against the ammunition ship moving off down the river – but its general movement necessarily conforms to the basis of narrative. *A Diary for Timothy*, on the other hand, is constructed entirely to a pattern of relationships and contrasts, endlessly varying, yet each one contributing to the rounded poetic statement of the whole. It is a picture of the last year of the war, as it was lived through by people in Britain; at the start a baby, Timothy, is born and it is to him that the film is addressed. Four representative characters are picked out (if we except Tim himself and his mother, to both of whom we periodically return): an engine driver, a farmer, a Welsh miner, and a wounded fighter pilot. But the story is by no means restricted to scenes involving these; with dazzling virtuosity, linking detail to detail by continuously striking associations of image, sound, music, and comment, the film ranges freely over the life of the nation, connecting and connecting. National tragedies and personal tragedies, individual happinesses and particular beauties are woven together in a design of the utmost complexity: the miner is injured in a fall at the coal face, the fighter pilot gets better and goes back to his unit, the Arnhem strike fails, Myra Hess plays Beethoven at the National Gallery, bombs fall over Germany, and Tim yawns in his cot.

Such an apparently haphazard selection of details could mean nothing or everything. Some idea of the poetic method by which Jennings gave the whole picture its continual sense of emotion and significance may perhaps be given by the sequence analysed and illustrated here, but of course only the film can really speak for itself.

The difficulty of writing about such a film, of disengaging in the memory the particular images and sounds (sounds moreover which are constantly overlapping and mixing with each other) from the overall design has been remarked on by Dilys Powell: 'It is the general impression which remains; only with an effort do you separate the part from the whole . . . the communication is always through a multitude of tiny impressions, none in isolation particularly memorable.' Only with the last point would one disagree. *A Diary for Timothy* is so tensely constructed, its progression is so swift and compulsive, its associations and implications so multifarious, that it is almost impossible, at least for the first few viewings, to catch and hold on to particular impressions. Yet the impressions themselves are rarely unmemorable, not merely for their splendid pictorial quality, but for the intimate and loving observation of people, the devoted concentration on the gestures and expressions, the details of dress or behaviour that distinguish each unique human being from another. Not least among the virtues that distinguish Jennings from almost all British filmmakers is his respect for personality, his freedom from the inhibitions of class-consciousness, his inability to patronize or merely to use the people in his films. Jennings's people are ends in themselves.

Other films were made by Jennings during the war, and more after it, up to his tragic death in 1950; but I have chosen to concentrate on what I feel to be his best work, most valuable to us. He had his theme, which was Britain; and nothing else could stir him to quite the same response. With more conventional subjects – *The Story of Lili Marlene*, *A Defeated People*, *The Cumberland Story* – he was obviously unhappy and despite his brilliance at capturing the drama of real life, the staged sequences in these films do not suggest that he would have been at ease in the direction of features. *The Silent Village* – his reconstruction of the story of Lidice in a Welsh mining village – bears this out; for all the fond simplicity with which he sets his scene, the necessary sense of conflict and suffering is missed in his over-refined, under-dramatized treatment of the essential situation. It may be maintained that Jennings's peacetime return to the theme of Britain (*The Dim Little Island* in 1949, and *Family Portrait* in 1950) produced work that can stand beside his wartime achievement, and certainly neither of these two beautifully finished films is to be dismissed. But they lack passion.

By temperament Jennings was an intellectual artist, perhaps too intellectual for the cinema. (It is interesting to find Miss Raine reporting that 'Julian Trevelyan used to say that Humphrey's intellect was too brilliant for a painter.') It needed the hot blast of war to warm him to passion, to quicken his symbols to emotional as well as intellectual significance. His symbols in *Family Portrait* – the Long Man of Wilmington, Beachy Head, the mythical horse of Newmarket – what do they really mean to us? Exquisitely presented though it is, the England of those films is nearer the 'This England' of the pre-war beer advertisements and Mr Castleton Knight's coronation film than to the murky and undecided realities of today. For reality, his wartime films stand alone; and they are sufficient achievement. They will last because they are true to their time, and because the depth of feeling in them can never fail to communicate itself. They will speak for us to posterity, saying: 'This is what it was like, this is what we were like – the best of us.'

Source: *Sight and Sound*, April–June 1954.

26 *A barrage baloon raised aloft in* The First Days *(1939).*

Interlude

7 Aspects of Asia

INTRODUCTION

Arguably, if cinema – the art form of the century – belongs to any single continent, it belongs to Asia. The great film industries of India, Japan, China and Hong Kong have given us more films than any other country.

Not that it is merely a matter of quantity. One could easily contend that Asian fiction directors have enriched the medium, given us more new ways of looking at the world than the directors of any other continent. The work of Satyajit Ray, Akira Kurosawa, Naruse Mikio, Chen Kaige, Zhang Yimou, Ozu Yasujiro, Shohei Imamura, Ritwik Ghatak and Kenji Mizoguchi, to name but a few, is surely the equal of anything that has been produced in either Europe or America.

But if Western audiences do not know Asia's fiction cinema as well as they ought, they know Asian documentary hardly at all.

Even the size of the audiences for which Asian factual films have been made is breathtaking: in 1988, the Chinese documentary *Heshang* was seen by a total audience of six hundred million people; from the sixties, government legislation guaranteed Indian documentary a daily audience of ten million. The scale and diversity of subjects with which Asian documentarists have been faced is similarly remarkable: the struggle for Indian independence and sub-continental partition, the rise of Chinese Communism, the Sino-Japanese war, Hiroshima and Nagasaki, the Vietnam War, mass poverty, genocide in East Timor, Japan's technological project, the struggle for democracy in China, and many others.

Asian film-makers have always been within firing range of politicians, and the region's tumultuous history in the twentieth century has seen the documentary form by turns encouraged, exploited, endangered and proscribed. It is a measure of the intensity of the relationship between Asian film and politics that Joris Iven's film camera is exhibited in Beijing's Museum of the Revolution.

Initially, Asia was almost exclusively filmed by outsiders: sympathetic

Western Griersonians on excursions to the Orient. Only gradually did authentic Asian voices emerge in the post-war era. These new indigenous films were not necessarily all distinguished, but the best emerged from Asian philosophies and aesthetic traditions and forged new forms and styles.

In order to do justice to the documentary industries of the Asian countries, we would need to present a book several times the present length. Instead, we have focused on Japan and reproduced some key pieces from India. Regrettably, China has been left to one side.

In post-Tiananmen China, documentary film-makers are more active than they have ever been before. The work is independently produced, often with non-Chinese production partners, and the impact of the June 1992 massacres has been such that the Tiananmen documentary can be seen as a growing genre in itself.

A Chinese non-fiction film, one of the biggest and most important in the history of the medium, contributed to the climate of political clampdown which led to Tiananmen. *Heshang* explored the history of ancient Chinese civilization by focusing on the culture and economics of the Yellow River. In six thematically arranged hour-long segments, the film-makers argued that the lesson learned by studying the Yellow River civilization is that China must modernize and westernize. *Heshang*'s first TV transmission, which took place over six consecutive nights, had a huge impact. Its thesis was widely discussed throughout China and newspapers carried its transcript. Subsequent transmissions have been interrupted and the film is now banned by the authorities.

Moments of Creation
ARUN KHOPAR

Mani Kaul is one of India's most distinguished documentarists.

Mani Kaul has been fascinated by the process of creation. His early feature film *Ashad Ka Ek Din* has a shot of a new-born infant with its wrinkles, its dazzled, closed eyes unable to bear the light of the world, clenched toes and fists and the agonized cry of being ejected from the paradise of the womb.

His documentary films are a search for such moments. In his

Siddheshwari Devi (1989) he looks for the specific form of angst that gives rise to her thumri. His mobile compositions of the winding lanes of Benares are his response to the graceful curves of thumri singing. He situates the majesty of *Dhrupad* (1982) in the colonnades and domes of the Gwalior palace. He looks for clues in the middle-class homes and tea shops of a small town for the genius of Gajanan Muktibodh – poet, writer and thinker (*Satah se Uthata Admi*, 1980). The hand that shapes clay into animated forms is held for a sufficiently long time for it to yield its secret to the screen (*Mah Manas*, 1985)

His is not a search for the meaningless, naturalistic detail forming a part of the environment of his artist subject. In fact, he assiduously avoids that myopic version of 'authentic historicity'. Like a palaeontologist, he is looking for a footprint that would give him the animal, like a sorcerer he looks for the part that would summon the whole. He picks up a feather and fashions a fluttering, swooping, gliding winged creature.

Mani Kaul is a superb craftsman. He treats his films like magic *mandalas*. For him a wrong lens brings the universe crumbling down.

His films are made with the same infinite love, patience, care and meticulous attention to detail that the master craftsman has for his creations. Even when he uses technicians whose work, otherwise, is quite ordinary, he seems to inspire them to give of their best (or perhaps a little more) to his films. But generally he chooses his tools and his crew with great care.

However, it would be a serious mistake to think of his preoccupation with technique as an end in itself. In fact, for someone who has an eye with such a fine resolution, and who is so flamboyant in speech and gesture, he is extremely austere with his images and sounds.

His search for a technical solution is motivated by wanting to pare down the image to its most essential elements. A director without imagination would choose a club to drive his point home. A rhetorical director would choose a sword for flourish. Mani would use a fine sliver of light to illuminate.

This austerity has made a number of people hostile to his work. They find his films boring. A member of parliament once said that Mani's *Uski Roti* was so boring that she would never forget it in all her life. Ironically, she was paying Mani a compliment. When a film is boring, you don't remember it all your life. But Mani's images have a staying power that goes beyond your liking or disliking his films.

Many times metaphor is the source of Mani Kaul's images. In his first documentary, *Nomad Puppeteers* (1974), he has a number of shots of these puppeteers in a bus. The movement of the bus rocks their bodies in the manner of the puppets they animate. Tossed around in the turbulence of modern India, his puppeteers are themselves moved by unseen forces.

Mani does not force his metaphors on us. He merely takes us to a point where the common denominator with the other phenomenon that gives rise to a metaphor becomes physical. *Chitrakathi* (1976) is about a narrative form of audio-visual presentation preserved in Pinguli, a village in Maharashtra. These artists exhibit a series of pictures, sing and narrate the incident depicted in the drawing. The pictures have been quickly drawn with a supple contour. The human figures are two-dimensional. The action in battle scenes is depicted with a great deal of vigour, with much scattering of limbs around. Mani's images of these artists when they are fishing and swimming have similar compositions. A raised arm, a torsoless head, a leg stretched skyward. Identity between the creator and his image? Creation in his own likeness and image? Take it whichever way you like. Some vital aspect of his theme comes to us through his metaphors. The metaphors truly change – transform – the viewer.

Some directors make films to state a thesis, to illustrate a statement. The abstractions of their statements or slogans seldom achieve a tangible quality. Mani takes an idea like 'food' in his film about the immigrant labourers in Bombay (*Arrival*, 1979). He brings to us a thousand concrete instances of food: types of food, ways of eating, the spaces for eating, for storing food. Each of these images takes us beyond the dictionary meaning of food. These images hit us, not only our sight, but our hearing, touch, smell. The smoke of burning oil enters your nostrils. The sounds made by people eating make concrete music as a hand-held camera rushes through eating places. With people looking at the lens, Mani makes no pretence at naturalism or at candid camera. But this look is not a simple Brechtian, Godardian alienating device. He allows the subjects' effervescence and aggression to pass. Then they begin to reveal themselves. Helplessness, the feeling of being trapped, the faked indifference, the suppressed excitement: it all comes through. Again you have a metaphor: those dozens of pigeons flying out of the places which stack thousands of gunny bags full of grain. A metaphor that does not take you to a predetermined place but just points the way.

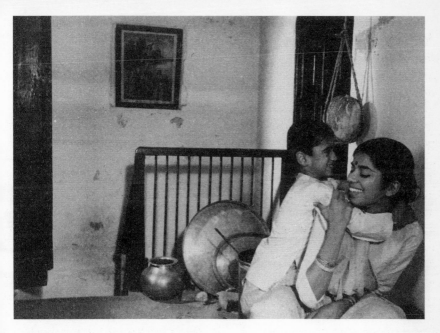

27 *Mani Kaul's* Siddeshwari Devi *(1989).*

The spectator is invited to Mani's films as a co-author.

His metaphor could be as extended as the colour blue in his *Siddheshwari Devi*, a film that blurs the distinction between documentary and fiction. The images of this film, which combines footage of Siddheshwari Devi's life with enactments using actors, are soaked in blue, lit in blue, emerge and merge in blue. The blue God, Krishna, is everywhere – in the water and the sky, on the walls and in the alleys. He holds quivering orange flames and shivering human bodies in his compassionate blue infinity. Centuries of Indian miniature painting, millennia of Indian music find their expansive space in the ninety minutes of this film. Time glides down the *meends* of Siddheshwari's voice, halts in her expressive pauses and is trapped in the *khatkas* of her tappa. Vivan Sundaram describes Siddheshwari as a film shot underwater (thanks to excellent colour grading by the cameraman Piyush Shah). *Siddheshwari* takes us to the depths of a world submerged in the waters of creation.

Mani's earlier films have passages that lift them to a plane experienced in the best poetry. The passage of the stampede of cattle in *Desert of a Thousand Lives* pushes us from a spectator's seat into the matador's shoes. Light as metaphor is as ancient as poetry. But when a floating tracking camera shows us hundreds of terracotta figurines gradually illuminated by glowing light, you have the feeling of life emerging, with Darkness being separated from Light (*Mati Manas*).

Mani uses the changing light in Nature as in *Dhrupad* to establish a relationship between a raga and the appropriate time at which it is sung. The ragas of Sandhikal (the zone of union of light with darkness) are rendered with the light just breaking out. The static shots stay. The music flows on in slow *nom-toms*. It is as if the notes caress the darkness to yield light.

Mani makes an interesting choice in *Dhrupad*. Many mediocre film-makers have been fascinated by the relationship between Nature and Indian musical modes. While making films on Indian music, they invariably show clouds, thunderstorms, peacocks and many other hoary clichés of the Indian miniaturists. But Mani relates the classical forms of music to architecture, folk forms to rituals and tribal forms to magic. His understanding is more profound because it recognizes the role of man's intervention in the world of sounds rather than think of it as mimesis pure and simple. The geometric intricacies of that master-piece of Indian architecture, the Jantar-Mantar, vying with modernist and post-modernist architecture in its complexities and contradictions, visually accompany the composition about an auspicious hour. These patterns make us experience the abstract nature of Indian music, its graceful curving forms, its geometric perfection. The only thing that I find fault with in *Dhrupad* is Mani's failure to deal with the mythical and the narrative aspect of Indian music.

It is precisely this aspect that makes *Mati Manas* go beyond *Dhrupad*. When Anita Kanwar places her hand in the place of the missing hand of a terracotta figurine, man's creation merges with Nature's. Myth merges with history. Fiction crystallizes into facts and facts dissolve back into the waters of imagination. Water, the contained and the container. The formally perfect stony structures of Mani's *Dhrupad* make way for the yielding clay of *Mati Manas* which dissolves in the blue fluidity of *Siddheshwari Devi*, Mani's finest film.

If *Dhrupad* plays with the annual and diurnal cycle in a limited way, *Before My Eyes* plays with it in a free way. Time lapse photography, speeded up action, critical exposures and exquisite aerial shots take us to realms which the eye cannot see. Imagination drives the camera motor to record what is beyond one's eyes.

Kashmir has been an obligatory location for Indian films. It has been shot *ad nauseam*. You feel you have seen it all whether it is flowers or snow. You have heard it all, birds or brooks. But *Before My Eyes* convinces you that seeing does not depend only on the object being out there. It is as much dependent upon the eye that beholds.

George Berkeley (1685–1720) in his *Essay Towards a New Theory of Vision* challenges the traditional view which accords depth and solidity to the physical properties of the eye. He emphasizes the active and symbolizing nature of perception. He goes to an extreme in stating that 'To exist is to perceive or to be perceived.' Some of the shots in *Before My Eyes* make you realize a nugget of truth contained in Berkeley's position.

Mani creates images that make you feel you are the privileged viewer, not only of Nature as it exists but as it is being born. You are physically close to the point from which water springs, swells into a stream, breaks against rocks. You witness light reflected in dark waters – that nameless light which could be the sun or the moon. Perhaps it is pre-sun, pre-moon – it is the new-born light being seen for the first time. It is yet to be named.

Source: *Cinema in India*, October–December 1989, Vol. 3, No. 4.

Worlds of Command
TOM WAUGH

In this, one of the most stimulating pieces of writing on Indian cinema, Tom Waugh isolates and analyses a distinctive stylistic trope characteristic of Indian documentary: 'the talking group'.

The discussion around Third (World) Cinema(s) as it has been proliferating in the Film Studies milieu, gives short shrift to documentary work despite the fact that many of the prototypes of this cinema, from *Hour of the Furnaces* to *The Battle of Chile*, are within the documentary tradition. At the same time, we still pay considerable attention to non-fiction images by Euro-American image-makers of Third World societies. All but swamped under the media flood of earthquakes, violence, deprivation, and indebtedness, 'Northern' independents making images of the 'South' tend to fall into three main camps: 1) The left solidarity advocates, following in the tradition of [Joris] Ivens and [Chris] Marker and showing no signs of slowing down in the 1990s; 2) The 'ethnographers', descendants of Flaherty, from the mystic Robert Gardner (*Forests of Bliss*) to the anti-ethnographic ethnographer Trinh T. Minh-ha; and 3) The occidental tourists, 'personal visions' of 'auteurs on tour' from Michael Rubbo to Louis Malle and Werner Schroeter, claiming as their ancestors Renoir, Pasolini and Rossellini. However progressive and useful these three groups of independents may sometimes be, they can't help being part of the unequal flow of images from North to South. Somehow Euro-American mediators still seem to be the required filters for images of our Third World Other.

The situation with India is a case in point. Despite the current Northern boom in interest in the Indian cinema, independent documentary film and video from that country have been unjustly neglected.

. . . This neglect is not only the result of careful orchestration on the part of the Indian state cultural bureaucracy, but unfortunately a reflection of Northern taste. Somehow Indian documentary seems less translatable than the exotic mysteries of Indian auteur fiction for First World audiences – at least for influential festival programmers, especially North American. With its frequent availability in domestically circulated English versions and despite its use of a largely familiar documentary vocabulary, this impermeability of taste is paradoxical to say the least. The cultural untranslatability of Indian documentary is perhaps *because of* (not *despite*) its familiar vocabulary. By this I mean that Indian documentary inherits the same dread Griersonian legacy as our own. Its insistently 'realist' mode, increasingly discredited in the North (even without the authoritative voice-overs that Indian practitioners are maintaining, for reasons I will elaborate later), rings just a little too close for comfort and is not quite either inscrutable or glitzy enough for our jaded post-modern and orientalist tastes.

The Griersonian legacy in India is heavy indeed: the Films Division of the Ministry of Information and Broadcasting was modelled after a colonial institution developed during the War – at the same time and with the same mission as [the National Film Board of Canada]. The Films Division held a virtual monopoly on the documentary film in India during the first four decades of Independence, fattened by a regimen of omnipresent and compulsory (but little-heeded) theatrical screenings. Only in the 1980s has its paralysing grip – aesthetic,

political, and economic – been eroded by upstart independents and
television documentarists. The Films Division has ensured at least one
consensus among its independent successors, and this in terms of
audience practice: Films Division fare has been so universally hated that
commercial theatres are the last place anyone will ever want to show a
documentary! Instead, richly diverse and resourceful distribution
strategies are being built up, based on settings as different as rural
educational networks, improvised urban slum screenings, hand-to-hand
videotape circulation and specialized or élite networks within the labour
or civil liberties movements. Some films have even made it on to
Doordarshan, the national TV network – not without occasional
litigation to pry open the airwaves.

Otherwise, after scarcely a decade of work, it is too soon for a distinct
Indian national school or style of documentary to have emerged – even
if a homogeneous school were likely or desirable in the face of proud
regional autonomies. Still, for all the variation in technique and cultural
positioning among the young independents, there are certain common-
alities beyond the inherited baggage of Films Divisions formats that
they all have simultaneously clung to and cast off. Something is to be
learned from looking at certain corners of this work as a corpus and
thinking about how the idiom of direct cinema is being inflected by the
cultural, political and economic imperatives of a post-colonial society.

One major inflection of direct cinema is apparent as soon as a generic
inventory of the films in question is undertaken, namely the conspicuous absence of important Euro-American documentary genres. Both
the compilation-interview genre ([Emil] de Antonio) and pure observational documentary ([Frederick] Wiseman) are very minor traditions
indeed (the limited development of the 16mm infrastructure is an
obvious material factor here). At most, observational and compilation
work are occasional components of a hybrid vocabulary (significantly,
two women's films that use observational strategies, Mira Nair's *Indian
Cabaret* and Nilita Vachani's new *Eyes of Stone*, were directed by
individuals trained or residing abroad and shot by Northern cinematographers). As for autobiographical, experimental or otherwise self-
reflexive strands, these are almost nonexistent in India. Virtually the
only exception is Mani Kaul, state-funded author of *Siddheshwari*,
Indian cinema's most visible presence on the major international art
cinema festival circuit this year (a first for documentary); however,
Kaul's astonishing *oeuvre* can be explained in part by the fact that his

ethno-musicological orientation falls within the Films Division's cultural vocation.

A far cry from Kaul's formally challenging exploration of traditional cultural forms, the didactic social documentary, the most favoured genre of the Indian independents, is in some ways a look-alike of its institutionalized Northern counterpart, and no less unquestioning of its 'realist' stance. Anchored in the interventionist mode of direct cinema consolidated in the North in the early seventies by the New Left and the Women's Movement, it deploys a similar mode of collaborative low-ratio *mise-en-scène*, and relies heavily on interviewing. This formula is nurtured by an oppositional political context and marginal economic basis not dissimilar to that in the North. However, what is specific and distinctive to the Indians within this general model are certain variations in direct cinema vocabulary and structure on a microcosmic level. These variations, related no doubt to the generic pattern observed above, are largely cultural, one suspects, but have distinct political ramifications.

Talking Groups
The ensemble of these Indian variations in the direct cinema lexicon crystallize, I would argue, in the trope that might be called the 'collective interview' or the 'talking group'. Though this trope is not statistically overwhelming, it is specific to and symbolically representative of the independent documentary current, as I will attempt to demonstrate through referring to three representative films made in the 1980s by different directors in various regions of India: *Voices From Baliapal, The Sacrifice of Babulal Bhuiya* and *Bombay City*.

In the key scenes described below, as in several more like them in each film, everyone is often talking at once. The speakers' address is direct, aimed at the film-maker who is standing or seated beside the camera (in fact the director is operating it in the case of *Voices*). The voices are fast and emotional, in unison, overlapping, yielding to each other and taking turns, or interrupting, seconding or disagreeing with each other. There are also natural pauses and moments of silence. The camera is mobile without being flamboyant, moving from medium to close range and back, either fluidly mounted or tightly hand-held. Together with the microphone, the apparatus has a finely tuned sensitivity to the shifting organic equilibrium of individual and collective voice. The pro-filmic event is set up in collaboration between subjects and film-maker, either at their advance suggestion or his/hers, or else, if more spontaneously, still based on a prior relationship and an instinctively agreed-upon format of the group interview/declaration. Trigger questions are sometimes retained by the editor, but seem hardly necessary.

One of the fascinating revelations of the 'talking group' is the social functioning and constitution of the group. Roles within a group are usually understood and prescribed through an unspoken consensus (or, sometimes, a spoken consensus signalled by a 'You tell it!' from offscreen, or else triggered by the film-maker's 'Let Mother speak.'). This process in which a spokesperson is designated to express a collective will, whether spontaneously or through deliberation, is of course dependent on which preconstituted group entity is present. In Bombay the scene I have described involves a large extended family, who are introduced one by one by the materfamilias and who provide the paternal grandmother with honorary space for her commentary. In other examples, the group is an occupational or economic community (e.g. the Baliapal fishermen), whose shared but unspoken pride in their catch and their tools bolsters their rhetoric of solidarity and defiance. Or else the group is composed of victims of a shared calamity, as in two Indian documentaries about the Bhopal industrial catastrophe, in which case panic and grief are closer to the surface, making consensus both easier and more difficult than with a preconstituted occupational or gender group.

The 'talking group' trope arises from a society where the group rather than the individual is the primary site of political discourse and of cultural expression . . .

. . . In Indian documentary, articulations of the 'talking group' often revolve around the private/public spatial dimensions of the individual/ collective dichotomy. For one thing, there are few interiors in Indian documentary. This is partly due to climate and technology – the small, dark but cool, living spaces of the poor are often unwired, though Datta managed a few inside shots, using available light through the door of the hut in question. (A more famous poet of doorways and available light, Trihn T. Minh-ha enters the West African dwellings of *Naked Space – Living is Round* to construct a sense of dwellings as dim and mysterious social corridors, Datta does so to get away from the police!).

In the talking group convention, allowing oneself to be filmed is not a private affair, but a participation in collective speech, in group identification and affirmation. As such being filmed takes place in public space. Talking groups are often shot in community meeting places, in *Sacrifice* almost ritualistically under a beneficent community shade tree. Or, very commonly, the setup is in semi-public courtyard space in front of dwellings, that space where food is prepared where sleeping cots are moved in the hot weather. In *Bombay*, interestingly, even when the dwelling is demolished by municipal bulldozers, the semi-public courtyard space continues to exist, and the talking group is filmed there, the matriarch fully in control of this her continuing domain. Otherwise communal working space is featured, as on the beach at Baliapal: here the busy backdrop of sea, equipment and catch constitutes a cinematic arena for the subjects' proud declarations. Thus this film about the defence of space integrates the talking group into a cinematic articulation of subject-controlled space.

. . . The presence of the 'talking group' engages, it goes without saying, a whole complex of cultural attitudes to the camera in the host community, including larger cultural attitudes to representation and self-representation itself. For example, when the peasant and working-class subjects of the Indian independents are isolated in close-up, they are usually awkward and inarticulate (unlike their Euro-American counterparts whom a skilled director can often get to blurt out their deepest feelings). But an Indian group confronting a camera is overtaken by a dynamic energy and an inspired gift of speech, even a pride in facing the camera together. At the same time, formal demonstration scenes, a staple of contestatory cinema in both North and South, are sometimes much stiffer in India, when participants become self-conscious about prescribed behaviours like unison chanting and synchronized gestures that contradict deeper-rooted and improvisatory group conventions.

. . . Is it possible to speculate about how our own social and cultural formation have inflected documentary discourse in the North? If the trope of the 'talking group' has a counterpart in Euro–American documentary, it is surely the solitary interview, the 'talking head'. If our 'talking head' is also reflective of social organization, it is surely that organization [Raymond] Williams called 'bourgeois':

'an idea of society as a neutral area within which each individual is free to pursue his own development and his own advantage as a natural right.'

The long-take intimate close-up declarations of subjects in direct-cinema works from *Golden Gloves* to *Roger and Me*, from *Chronique d'un Été* to *Shoah* are symptomatic of a social ideology organized around the individual, and, what is more, a religio-cultural tradition based on the confession. Politics is privatized and internalized, the self is fetishized and dramatized. The individual confronts trauma first and foremost in isolation. If our 'talking head' embodies the culminating point of what Brian Winston has called the Griersonian tradition of the victim, it is also the key trope of the hybrid interview format pioneered by Emile de Antonio. In this format, the 'talking head' belongs more often than not to an expert and hence becomes not confessional in its function, but sacerdotal, administering the sacrament of absolution to the conscience of the audience, bestowing the authority of scripture on the word of the author.

Groups are often seen but not heard in Northern documentary. Most often and typically the group appears a) in long shot, and/or b) silent, spied upon, or otherwise disenfranchised. If heard, groups are often constructed through the common newsgathering format of the crowd on the street, talking into a rotating, director-controlled microphone about something trivial ('How do you feel about the Expos' chances?') or, if about something serious, in the desired monosyllabic 'sound-bites', that tend to sentimentalize ('Did you all lose everything in the hurricane?') or ridicule ('What are the cultural advantages in Flint Michigan?').

. . . The clash between the cultural foundation of 'talking head' and 'talking group' becomes symptomatically visible when Northern cinematographers look at the Third World. One of the three Indian directors mentioned above told me about his/her tour of the National Film Board of Canada where s/he had been shown rushes shot by an eminent Canadian cinematographer for a film on popular music in a Third World society. Various scenes had unfolded before the camera according to the 'talking group' structure, but the rushes revealed that the Canadian cinematographer had consistently and unwittingly singled out speaking individuals within the frame, thereby distorting the social weave of the pro-filmic event.

. . . In the North, as I have intimated, the close-up has a kinship with the ritual of confession, with the film-maker (or expert witness) as confessor. An individual is isolated and constructed as victim and his/her confession is expressed through the codes of (illusory) intimacy. In

India and elsewhere in the South, where religious rituals are collective, not the solitary confession but the group darshan, the close-up 'talking head' is still present but has a specific and different function. Here, the 'talking head' is usually a marker of material status rather than of spiritual or ideological role. The one-shot subject is usually shown having control over space, more clearly articulated through greater camera range and frontal compositions than in Northern conventions. A characteristic Indian locale is the chair set out on the lawn, which is perhaps the ultimate marker of privilege with its occupation of unproductive and purely decorative land. Individual control over space is usually synonymous with middle-class authority, and other favourite conventions say it all: the bureaucrat seated behind a distancing desk, or the shopkeeper enthroned idly in front of his wares (both bureaucrat and merchant following the discursive conventions of public spatial power as well as of documentary shorthand). To be sure, one also encounters in Indian documentaries, somewhat atypically, the isolated victim in the western Griersonian sense (with a Northern trained film-maker as often as not behind the camera), but the testimony is usually stiff, unnatural, and unproductive.

Source: *Cine Action*, Winter 1990–91.

A Foreigner's View of the Japanese Documentary Scene
SCOTT SINKLER

The following article by award-winning American documentary film-maker Scott Sinkler is based on nine months he spent in Japan watching Japanese documentaries and talking to their directors.

Apart from a few visionaries, most documentary in Japan has been rather orthodox formally, and more or less predictable in terms of its ideology and approach. With some notable exceptions, Japanese documentaries seem to hug fairly closely to a notion of *kiroku eiga*, or educational or informational film, with less stylistic variation from film to film than one finds in the West . . .

In the West, since the birth of documentary in the 1920s, there has been a constant fertile exchange between genres and sensibilities, allowing for a diversity of styles and modes which could be considered documentary. This tendency has accelerated over the last decade to a point where the term 'documentary' has become in many cases almost useless. Personal, experimental, and fictional techniques have all found their way into the form and have been absorbed into mainstream TV production as well.

In Japan, however, it's the rare documentary that deviates from the prescribed form of the day (generally a more or less Griersonian model since the 1950s). Perhaps this has something to do with the several decades of militarism, wartime control, and finally occupation censorship to which film-makers in Japan had to adapt. It could be argued that Japanese society remains rather controlled in many ways, at least compared with the United States. Yet, when Japanese documentaries do stray from the beaten path, they are apt to wander quite far. The best and most interesting of these films seem to abandon many basic rules of film-making altogether – incessantly jump-cutting from shot to shot (Kazuo Hara's *The Emperor's Naked Army Marches On*, 1987), cutting shots extremely long (most of Ogawa's work), constructing films of epic length (Tsuchimoto's *Minamata Disease: A Trilogy*), or incorporating a grab bag of experimental tricks, like Toshio Matsumoto's *Security Treaty* (1959).

But overall, there seems to me a kind of starkness to Japanese documentaries, a seriousness and perhaps lack of playfulness. They also seem to rarely manipulate the image, space and time to any great degree, but to stick to a notion of 'reality' that ought not to be overly tampered with (even when it's downright boring). Producer Tetsujiro Yamagami told me that many Japanese documentarists feel morally bound to strictly observe actual chronology in editing, which I would think drastically limits their option at that stage. He said that as a result, many Japanese documentaries practically edit themselves, and the cutting is accomplished in no time. The documentaries may occasionally shoot themselves as well, if cameraman Masanori Sawahata's account is any indication. He said about the shooting of *I-Omante*, an acclaimed ethnographic film about an Ainu bear sacrifice festival, 'We had no editorial perspective; we just tried to be precise. We were trying to make a documentary without the style of the film-maker intruding.' This reminds me of things Richard Leacock has said about Direct Cinema, but even he wouldn't have been so self-effacing and denying of his own artistry.

At the same time, emotion plays a big role in many Japanese

documentaries. It has been said that Japanese psychology, and thus culture, places more emphasis on the emotional, whereas the West places more on the rational. Hiroo Fuseya, producer of most of Ogawa Shinsuke's films, told me that while he has had few chances to see them, he generally doesn't like western documentaries because they are too 'analytical': they focus too strongly around a central point and become in his opinion 'simplistic, propagandistic, and uninteresting'. He said that such films are always 'about some incident, political issue, problem'. He prefers films that 'explore the subtleties of day-to-day life'.

While engaging the emotions of viewers to make a message stick is crucial for any documentary, Japanese works often seem to go further than western ones. At their most effective, they use empathy to drive a point deeply home, as in Tsuchimoto's *The Shiranui Sea* (1975), which includes some of the most moving scenes in documentary film anywhere, about children afflicted with Minamata disease. But while Tsuchimoto somehow manages to stay above the threshold of sentimentality, the average documentary dealing with such issues in Japan seems to dwell on physical dysfunction in a fetishistic way. Perhaps a catharsis to the repression and taboo against confronting disability or difference in Japan, this tendency feeds a steady diet of mawkish reports on TV. One of Japan's most respected film critics, Sato Tadao, wrote about Tsuchimoto's *Minamata, Victims and Their World* (1971): 'many shots cause a wave of emotions in the viewer, which makes it into a masterpiece.' While I read this sentence out of context and in translation, I doubt a western critic would draw such a casual relationship between emotionalism and quality.

In all Japanese film genres, long shots are favored much more than in the West. While the most common framing in a western documentary is a medium shot, the more distant long shot forms the backbone of the Japanese documentary. This is most notable during conversations between two people. In a western documentary, the film-maker would tend to pan from person to person, using medium shots and close-ups to reveal emotional information. In Japan, there is a tendency to frame both people in a rather loose long shot and hold it for long periods of time without much camera movement. While this gives the viewer more choice about what or whom to look at, it requires that one read a lot more into the situation than if more detail were provided. This correlates, I think, with a tendency for western culture to generally be more explicit and Japanese to be more implicit, leaving more to the imagination. Unfortunately, this becomes an added problem for distribution in the West, where most documentaries are seen on a television screen, rendering the details even more indistinct.

An added effect is that the long shots make Japanese documentaries seem slow and long. Indeed, many are, which could be another reason why they are not shown abroad. While the American system will tolerate epic form when content merits (i.e., *Shoah*), films longer than ninety minutes are much more difficult to distribute. Tsuchimoto manages to get away with his long takes and long form most of the time because his interactions are enriched by letting them play out. In some of Ogawa's films, on the other hand, it's a little more difficult to sustain interest, in part because his characters – farmers and student activists fighting to keep their land – are more predictable in what they say or do, and perhaps because the details of their struggle are often somewhat arcane. In Mitsuo Yanagimachi's *Black Emperor* (1976), interminable long scenes of petty arguments between teenage motor-cycle gang members somehow seem justified because they force us to confront the bleakness and claustrophobia of the kids' lives. On the other hand, long-windedness is sometimes less excusable, such as in the recent 111-minute *Theatre of Mirage* (1992) by Nobuaki Sugimoto, which used most of that time to cover the building of a travelling theatre in such detail that a viewer could qualify for a degree in civil engineering after sitting through it.

In addition to being long, one major difference I've noticed in looking at works in all genres is that Japanese work seems much less concerned with structure and with what we call plot, at least as defined in Aristotle's *Poetics* or in any form recognizable to me (pardon my ethnocentricity). Transitions often seem abrupt and illogical. Films are not structured around the notion of climax, and often end suddenly, or at a weird juncture. But then, Japanese literature usually seems more devoted to evoking subtle emotional states or describing delicate gestures or unimportant events to be savoured for their atmosphere and nuance than to moving a story forward. Hiroo Fuseya told me that throughout his career Ogawa was increasingly trying to move away from structure in order to capture the reality of ordinary life.

The idea is fresh and fascinating to a western film-maker like me, and it is one of those things that make Japanese films interesting. But a westerner's expectation of a film is generally that it guide him or her from a beginning to a middle to an end. Without such a structure, many

Japanese films can feel vague, meandering, slow, long and lacking in the coherence and self-confidence by which I am used to judging western media. But yet again, if one chooses a good film, these very qualities can seem refreshing.

Generally speaking, Japanese documentaries seem to me more reluctant to take the point of view of a particular individual, and look at conflicts on a group level. Even in western documentaries that take on social and political issues, the concern for 'character' is often central in the film-maker's attempt to hook the audience into an issue. While individuals are used to illustrate larger issues in Japanese documentaries, there is rarely the kind of screen time devoted to character development in the West. Even when the whole film is about one person, such as Hara's *The Emperor's Naked Army Marches On*, the character is only utilized to the extent that he embodies the issue and is not illuminated in a way which allows us to really know him. Maybe Japanese rules of interaction limit how close the film-maker can get to the subject (unless he's sleeping with her, as in Hara's *An Extreme Private Eros* [1974], the main exception to this trend I saw). If so, that distance is passed on to the viewer. As a result, Japanese film-makers often seem excessively polite to their subjects.

A quality which film-makers like Tsuchimoto, Ogawa, and Sato have to a greater degree than most western film-makers is their dedication to a particular issue. Each has followed one situation for years, enriching each successive film (Sato has made one so far) through a deeper understanding, and closer connections with the subjects. While that's certainly positive, it unfortunately keeps these talented artists from addressing other neglected topics.

While perhaps the mainstream in Japanese documentary is proportionately a bit wider than it is in the West, and therefore the overall quality of Japanese work somewhat lower, in my opinion, the best Japanese film-makers are great innovators and great artists. Tsuchimoto uses a reflexive interviewing style that places him in the frame without becoming a personality himself. Casually calling attention to the film-making process, he reminds us of our personal obligation to confront and engage the injustice we see rather than accept it passively. He occasionally plays back films and audiotapes within his films, creating a multi-levelled reality. His shooting of interviews from another room to put subjects at ease, his running of conversations over related footage, are other techniques I found unique to his work. Unlike other social issue documentarists, Tsuchimoto's ideological openness allows room for interesting but difficult philosophical questions that don't always advance the cause of his film directly.

Ogawa's innovations mainly stem from his apparent desire to become his subjects. His earlier films about the Narita Airport struggle, like *Summer in Narita* (1968), seem to float over the battle scenes and organizing meetings with a passive eye. When titles appear trumpeting revolutionary slogans, one gets the sense that the director is merely passing them on from his subjects. His lengthy shots relinquish control of time to his subjects. Critic Tetsuro Hatano cited a shot in *Narita: Heta Village* (1973) in which an activist holds a candle in front of an air vent in an underground bunker to demonstrate his group's engineering prowess. While I did understand why it had to be so long, Hatano termed it an extremely moving shot, because its length brings us inside the world and the mindset of the besieged activists. Ogawa eventually moved himself and his crew to Yamagata and set up a dual life as an agriculturalist and film-maker. His intervention in the reality his films depicted increased in proportion to his participation in his subjects' lifestyle. In *Magino Village: A Tale* (1986), he eventually melded a kind of intensive science-film style with observational documentary and fictional recreations in further pursuit of the breakdown of the filmmaker–subject distinction.

Makoto Sato's first film, *Living on the River Agano*, suggests a new talent on the documentary scene. Aside from his beautiful cinematography and confident cutting, Sato plays with techniques that are relatively new to Japanese documentary. The most obvious is his use of reflexivity within an observational framework. He includes many comments by the subjects to the film-makers in an effort to make the film more casual and honest. But these are awkwardly employed at times, perhaps because Sato has not seen many western films that have explored this area with varying degrees of success over the last twenty years. In the final analysis, *Living on the River Agano* is long on atmosphere, but short on who these elderly subjects really are.

An earlier innovator was Fumio Kamei, who was pressed into service during the war to turn out propaganda. His reluctance led him to make several very interesting films, which in turn landed him in jail for a year. His *Shanghai* (1938) and *Fighting Soldiers* (1939) were remarkably soft and ambivalent as war documentaries. Both revealed Kamei's mastery of constructing atmosphere through smooth tracking shots that suggest a kind of omniscient eye, his focus on mundane and 'insignificant' details such as flies landing on a soldier's clothes, skilful editing, and the use of sound. In *Fighting Soldiers*, he let a stationary camera record in long shot an apparently real ten minutes of life in an Army command post at the front. Sitting on the edge of my seat for that length of time, I was convinced it was real, but Akira Shimizu of the Kawakita Memorial Film Institute informed me it had been staged. Kamei said in an interview that he had wanted to communicate in these works the wasteful reality of war. That he managed to do just that while under orders from the military government is an incredible accomplishment.

Source: *Documentary Box*, 1993, Vol. 3. Published by the Yamagata International Documentary Film Festival.

Iwasaki and the Occupied Screen
ERIK BARNOUW

Erik Barnouw is a distinguished non-fiction historian who befriended many of the major documentary figures he has written about, including Akira Iwasaki, the subject of this article from 1988.

The curious and meteoric career of my friend Akira Iwasaki (1903–1981), film historian, critic, and documentarist widely known in his native Japan, intersected in dramatic ways with American interests, yet his name remains almost unknown in the United States. This account will attempt in some measure to remedy that.

Iwasaki was executive producer of the earliest extant Hiroshima and Nagasaki disaster film, all of which was seized as war booty by the US military occupation and kept under lock and key for almost a quarter of a century. A few feet were extracted by the Pentagon for training and for propaganda films to reassure the public about atomic warfare, but the most revealing footage was kept impounded under a 'Secret' classification while its very existence remained unknown to most of the world. In 1970, twenty-five years after the bombings, key sequences were finally seen by audiences – first in the United States and then elsewhere. Since that time excerpts have appeared in documentaries throughout the world, providing many people with their principal images of the 1945 atomic holocaust.

Because I became involved in the surfacing of this historic material through its appearance in Columbia University's 1970 compilation film *Hiroshima – Nagasaki, August 1945*, the first use of the most carefully guarded footage, I entered into correspondence with Iwasaki, visited him twice in Japan, and recorded interviews with him. Our correspondence continued until the day of his death. During his final years he wrote tellingly about the impact of the US Occupation on the Japanese film world and on his own extraordinary career in a short memoir titled *Occupied Screen: My Postwar Story* (*Senyo Sareta Sukurin: waga sengo shi*, 1975). The present account is based on our conversations and correspondence, translated passages from *Occupied Screen*, and other sources as noted.

That Iwasaki, in the last weeks of World War Two, was commissioned by a Japanese government agency to document on film the destruction that ended the war, was in itself extraordinary, inasmuch as he had spent part of the war in prison condemned as a traitor for his public opposition to expansionist and militarist trends. This had begun in the late 1920s.

Prokino

Having graduated in 1927 from the University of Tokyo (then the Imperial University of Tokyo), where he studied literature while becoming a film devotee, he soon began to attract attention as a writer and film critic. In 1929 he joined others in forming 'Prokino' (short for Proletarian Film League), a counterpart to the leftist Workers Film and Photo Leagues in the United States and Britain and similar groups on the European continent – all products of the 'united front' against fascism, Nazism and, in Japan, militarist imperialism. Iwasaki became head of Prokino.

All these groups looked on the glossy newsreels of the time with contempt because of the newsreels' steady disregard of strikes, demonstrations, and hunger marches in favour of military parades and battleship launchings attended by beauty queens. The woes of the Depression were virtually taboo in the dominant newsreels. In answer, all the film and photo leagues started their own newsreels, showing them in labour unions, political meetings, and occasionally fringe theatres. In Japan, as elsewhere, they worked on a shoestring budget, generally using 16mm reversal film and projecting and circulating the originals. Iwasaki himself produced many such newsreel sequences in the early 1930s and meanwhile wrote books about film as well as a stream of articles of social criticism. His books during the 1930s included *History of Film* (Geibunshoin, 1930), *Film and Capitalism* (Ohraisha, 1931), *Film Art* (Kyowashoin, 1936), *Cinematography* (Mikasashobo, 1936), *Film Aesthetic* (Seibido, 1937), and *Film and Reality* (Shunyodo, 1939).

In the mid-1930s the government began a rapid series of moves to bring all media under tight control. All Japan's newsreels – which had originated as subsidiaries of the major Japanese studios – were consolidated into one government newsreel, *Nippon Eiga Sha*, popularly known as *Nichi-ei*. As the Japanese struck in various directions to create a Greater East Asia Co-Prosperity Sphere, *Nichi-ei* became a propaganda organ of Imperial Headquarters; theatres were required to book (and pay for) its releases, offered under such titles as *Rising Sun News* and *Banzai News*. Prokino was declared illegal and dissolved. A new cinema law, modeled on those of Joseph Goebbels in Germany, decreed that only government-licensed directors could make films and only government-licensed films could be shown. A government 'stop order' listed authors whose works it was 'imprudent to publish'; Iwasaki was on the list. Preventative detention of suspect individuals reinforced the system. Confronted by this avalanche of control measures few dared write or speak in protest, but Iwasaki did so. In 1939 he was arrested and taken to a place known as the 'pig box', the subterranean Ikebukuro police prison. Here a police officer assured him it was time for him to pay for his treasonous activities. After nine months of imprisonment, hearings, and conviction for violating the Peace Preservation Law, he was moved to Sugamo Prison, considered a place where Class A war criminals were kept, and in some cases executed. But here conditions were better. He was permitted to read prison-approved books, but was not allowed writing materials, not even pencil and paper. Iwasaki had developed a rare and mysterious eye ailment, which a doctor was permitted to examine. The doctor urged his release, and after almost two years of imprisonment Iwasaki was returned to his home in Setagaya-ku, a Tokyo suburb. An inspector came each week to check on his activities. His books had been confiscated. Enjoined from writing, he lived quietly with his wife Iku and their daughter Atsuko, tended his vegetable garden, and maintained cautious but friendly relations with his neighbours, even taking part in communal defence measures. He occasionally – again, cautiously – saw old friends from the film world, but assumed that that arena was now closed to him.

. . . In *Occupied Screen* Iwasaki described 14 August 1945 as a stiflingly hot day in Setagaya-ku. No breeze stirred; there was even a lull in the enemy air raids. It was Iwasaki's turn to head the neighbourhood association, so he had to go to the office of the town council to deal with rationing. Burdened with emergency gear including the helmet and puttees of his national civilian uniform, he needed strong determination to drag himself through the scorching heat. On the way he met the wife of his next door neighbour. The neighbour worked for Nippon Optics, a military contractor, so the family was rumoured to get extra supplies, yet her face was as sunk as his own, and her pants had holes at the knees. When she saw him she exclaimed, as he recalls in his memoir, 'Mr Iwasaki! Did you hear on the radio? It seems there will be a broadcast of highest importance, tomorrow at noon!'

'I heard.'

'What in the world can it be – this broadcast of highest importance?'

'I wonder. I don't know, but – ' After a moment Iwasaki was surprised to hear himself saying, 'It could mean the war will be over.'

At this her face lit up radiantly. Overflowing with joy she said, 'That must mean America has unconditionally surrendered!'

In answer to his neighbour's wife Iwasaki merely said they would soon know. He confided his opinion only to his wife. Next day he and his wife listened to the important broadcast. From the radio came 'the frailest, most subdued voice I had ever heard – the voice of the Emperor.'

After pondering deeply the general trends of the world and the conditions of our empire today, we have decided to effect a settlement of the present situation by resorting to an extraordinary measure.

The tone was so quiet that many passages were lost in the static, but they heard:

We have resolved to pave the way for a grand peace for all the generations to come by enduring the unendurable and suffering what is insufferable.

Had Japan lost? Had she surrendered? Those words were not there. Listeners were told to 'follow the direction of the Allied joint proclamation.' This apparently meant the Potsdam Declaration, issued late in July. But most Japanese had never heard of it.

Iwasaki thought he should be jubilant. But he suddenly found himself weeping uncontrollably; tears formed blotches on his lap.

The Benefactor

The family's survival to this point owed much to an old friend of Iwasaki, Kan'ichi Negishi, who before the war had headed the Nikkatsu studio's Tamagawa studio. In the 1930s Negishi had been sent to Manchukuo, the puppet state set up in Manchuria, to head the Manchu Film Corporation; he stayed there throughout the war. Worried about his friend Iwasaki, in the Manchu Film Corporation budget he provided for a part-time Tokyo liaison agent, with a small stipend. Throughout the war these payments were routed to the Iwasaki family. Whether this arrangement escaped official attention or was ignored is not clear from Iwasaki's account in *Occupied Screen*. But the payments kept the family from destitution, and Iwasaki refers to him gratefully as 'my benefactor'.

Soon after the war ended he heard again from his benefactor. An intermediary brought news that *Nichi-ei*, the government newsreel, was in total turmoil and Kan'ichi Negishi had been summoned from Manchuria to save it. He wanted Iwasaki as his production head, in charge of both newsreels and documentaries. Iwasaki was over-whelmed. He had ceased to think of himself as a film-maker, and doubted his capacity for this new task. But the historic nature of the moment, and his immense debt to his benefactor, swept him forward. He became production head of *Nichi-ei*, an organization in shambles. It was short of film stock and cash. Much of its equipment had been destroyed or was in disrepair. Fewer than half the nation's film theatres survived. With the military collapse, many of these felt freed of their obligation to book *Nichi-ei* newsreels; virtually no funds were coming in to *Nichi-ei*. Above all, no one knew what the US Occupation – which was expected to arrive within weeks or months – would mean to Japanese life. Amid these uncertainties, Iwasaki took office.

On one project a consensus had developed at *Nichi-ei*: a documentary must be made on the 'new style bomb' and what it had done at Hiroshima and Nagasaki. There was some difference of opinion as to what sort of film it should be – a protest film? a scientific study? a requiem? But it was agreed that the subject could not wait. As early as 8 September a *Nichi-ei* newsreel camaraman, Shihei Masaki, had reached the outskirts of Hiroshima and spent a few moments among the ruins and overwhelming stench. Living humans he encountered looked 'as if they had had their souls extracted from them' and none seemed able to answer when he spoke to them. In front of a blackened wall he noted a girl of seventeen or eighteen standing 'without a stitch of clothing'. At first he tried to film her from a hidden position but she seemed oblivious. So he went up to her and photographed her strange eyes in close-up. In Tokyo his footage was submitted to the military censor and vanished, presumably destroyed in the interest of maintaining morale. On the same day a cameraman from Osaka, Toshio Kashiwada, likewise made a brief entry into Hiroshima and later reported 'dead bodies floating in the river, swollen deep red', and streetcars hurled four feet from their tracks. His few feet of film, shown privately to members of the Japanese General Staff – perhaps their first look at evidence beyond imagination – likewise vanished without a trace. Surrender brought pressure for new action – not just a newsreel sequence but a full-length documentary. It was seen as an obligation to all posterity. It could not wait for the arrival of the Americans. (Would Americans want such a film? That was another question, which no one could answer.) But it seemed clearly a *Nichi-ei* mission. Help was now offered from various sources. Iwao Mori, head of the Toho studio, offered equipment and personnel. Minoru Yamanashi, director of Eiga Haikyusha, offered Y100,000 in cash. The Ministry of Education came forward to offer sponsorship of the project. This proved the final catalyst, and helped to determine the nature of the film: it would be a scientific report, guided by the ministry's consultants, on the impact of the bombs on soil, vegetation, metals, concrete, and living creatures. By September organizational planning was almost complete. The location budget provided for thirty-three people for a twenty-day period. Consultants had been designated for architecture, biology, botany, medicine, and nuclear physics. Cameramen and other technicians had been selected. None resisted, even though many assumed that the assignment might be a death warrant. Lives may have been saved by organizing delays. Signs of radiation sickness were not observed among crew members during the following months.

It was clear they must take equipment and provisions for the entire period. Each carried a knapsack. During September camera crews went into action in both Hiroshima and Nagasaki. As Iwasaki joined *Nichi-ei*, he became the executive supervising this historic venture. In charge of location work was Ryuichi Kano, well known to Iwasaki. As footage began arriving at *Nichi-ei* headquarters, Kano and Iwasaki together viewed and studied all rushes. Iwasaki writes: 'Every frame burned into my brain.'

The Occupation

On 22 September Occupation authorities gave film industry representatives a first briefing on what would be expected of them. Motion pictures were clearly considered a high-priority area. In accordance with the Potsdam Declaration, Japan was to be transformed into a democratic nation that would never again disturb the peace of the world. To this end feudalistic, militaristic, imperialistic tendencies would have to be uprooted. In the major media this would involve both personnel and content. During the following months Japanese films made during the war period were reviewed by 'GHQ' – the letters would become very familiar to all Japanese – and 236 of the films were condemned for feudal or anti-democratic content. They were ordered destroyed and a large burning took place.

GHQ also listed themes that were to be incorporated into films: Japanese people in every walk of life helping to create a peaceful nation; industry and farm groups resolving their post-war problems; the peaceful formation of labour unions; the replacing of arbitrary bureaucratic rule with a government responsible to the people; encouragement of free discussion of government problems; respect for individual rights. All this would be supervised by the Civil Information and Education-Section of the Occupation, which quickly became known as CIE.

It was late in October when GHQ first became aware that a documentary film was being made on the atomic bombs and their impact. Toshio Seki-guchi, assistant cameraman in the Nagasaki unit, was found photographing in the Urakami area near the epicentre of the Nagasaki bomb, and was promptly arrested. He was working alone while his unit director and chief cameraman were elsewhere amid the desolation, scouting other locations. Word of the arrest was promptly conveyed to GHQ in Tokyo. In *Occupied Screen* Iwasaki recalls a summons to GHQ and an abrupt questioning. 'Who authorized the filming of an atomic bomb documentary?'

Iwasaki explained that *Nichi-ei* had the task of recording and reporting significant events. The event here concerned was one of historic importance.

'Fine. From now on, in the name of the army occupying Japan, the filming is suspended.'

The matter was not so easily disposed of. While Iwasaki did not challenge the order, he kept asking questions. In view of the plans for re-educating Japan and establishing democratic principles and procedures, would it not be well to clarify the issue for him and his staff? If this was a subject *not* to be filmed, should he not have a written directive from GHQ – if only for the future guidance of him and his staff? In the interest of good procedure, he kept pressing for a written directive.

In November CIE suggested a compromise. The *Nichi-ei* units were to continue their photography under US supervision. They were also to proceed with cataloging and editing the accumulating thousands of feet of film – a task almost impossible for anyone not familiar with its content. This too would be done under US supervision. Iwasaki promptly accepted the compromise.

In these negotiations both sides avoided clarifying a basic issue: who would *own* the material? The GHQ personnel felt that they now had ultimate control over the film and the use to be made of it. Iwasaki and his colleagues had a different perspective. They were all aware that the film they would edit under US supervision might differ in many ways from the film they themselves would wish to make. But they also assumed that having completed an 'American version' they would be able to make a 'Japanese version'. For this purpose they had their laboratory during the following weeks make a duplicate set of all footage. The important thing was, the photography would now continue. In fact, the work planned for Hiroshima was virtually complete. In Nagasaki some essential shooting remained to be done.

In Production

Keeping watch over the atom-bomb project, planning and supervising weekly newsreels, Iwasaki also developed proposals for new documentary projects, the area closest to his heart. Every day ended in almost total exhaustion. Most Japanese were seriously undernourished. Going home by commuter railway, still in woeful disrepair, most felt they could not stand while awaiting their trains; they sat or slumped on the platform. At home Iwasaki could do little more than fall into bed. Yet each day he found himself approaching his tasks with exhilaration. He worked 'with eight faces and six arms'. It was as though the Prokino days had returned under miraculous new circumstances.

It was, in many ways, a high point in Iwasaki's *Nichi-ei* period. His life had a sense of direction. His domestic life was happy; his wife had given birth to a son, whom they named Hiroshi. The photography at Hiroshima and Nagasaki and the editing of the footage under US supervision were rapidly completed, and the Americans soon afterwards recorded the sound track for the two-hour, forty-minute compilation, which they titled *Effects of the Atomic Bomb*. *Nichi-ei* technicians assisted with this recording, though they were chilled by the sound track's detached survey of the military achievements of the new weapon in the US arsenal. The *Nichi-ei* leaders kept thinking about the version they themselves would make.

Conspiracies

At this juncture a devastating blow fell. Two US military personnel arrived at Iwasaki's office with an official document. As recounted by Iwasaki, they stood in front of him while he read it. He quickly realized what it was but read slowly, to give himself time to think and gather his composure. The document was an order to turn over to GHQ all footage relating to the atom-bomb film including negatives, rushes, prints, and out-takes – in short, every scrap of film. Iwasaki, finishing his reading, told the two Americans he would comply with the order. It would take a while to organize the material, he said, so he asked that he be given till the following day to comply. They agreed. Iwasaki conferred with Kano and two of their closest associates. The duplicate copy of the original negative footage was hurriedly packed and taken to a former *Nichi-ei* technician who had started his own developing laboratory. They would like him to store this for a while, they told him, asking that he say nothing about it. The technician, Shigeru Miki, agreed and concealed the material in a space over his laboratory. He did not ask what it was. They thought he might have guessed, but nothing was said.

Next day the soldiers returned to *Nichi-ei* in a jeep and received from Iwasaki a number of boxes of film. He was asked to sign a document affirming that every foot of the atom-bomb project had been handed over and nothing withheld. He signed 'without blinking'. The film, now classified 'Secret', was soon on its way to the United States.

The four conspirators joined in a solemn oath to tell no one, under any circumstances, about their action. They thought little, at this time, about its possible consequences for them. Later, as they read about the trial and execution of the Rosenbergs on charges of conveying atomic information to the Russians, they wondered what charges might be levelled against them. But at the time they were remembering the disappearance and apparent destruction of the first Hiroshima footage, and the bonfire in which 236 Japanese films had been consumed. They felt they were averting some act of irreparable vandalism. It was a duty to humanity.

For six years – until 1952, the end of the US Occupation – the four men breathed no word to anyone about the hidden footage. Its existence comforted them. Some day they would make their film.

Preview Time
The Tragedy of Japan was completed in the spring of 1946, and a preview for the CIE was immediately scheduled. Other previews would follow.

An early sequence of *The Tragedy of Japan* focused on the *Tanaka Memorial*, a memorandum that was supposed to have been submitted to Emperor Hirohito in 1927 by the Prime Minister of the time, Tanaka Giichi. If Japan wished to conquer China, the document reportedly advised, she must first conquer Manchuria and Mongolia; if she wished to conquer the world, she must first conquer China. The original document has never been produced, and the authenticity of the memorandum is questioned. On the other hand, Japan's moves during the following years – including the Kwantung Army Incident of 1928, the Manchuria Incident of 1931, the Marco Polo Bridge Incident near Peking in 1937, and other 'incidents' used to justify aggression – followed so well the pattern of the Tanaka Memorial as to lend it an air of validity. *The Tragedy of Japan*, chronicling the conquests with archive shots, threaded them with a series of maps in which region after region was seen impaled by a plunging Japanese sword, a graphically 'feudal' touch. At the end of the film Kamei had placed a sequence that Iwasaki especially liked: a long dissolve from the Emperor in the glittering splendour of his wartime uniform to the same Emperor in his post-war public garb, a business suit. Until then few Japanese had seen him in this guise, and it was still somewhat shocking. The dissolve symbolized historic transformations – from a god to a mortal, from an emperor to a constitutional figurehead. The CIE was enthusiastic. The next step, the censorship step, would involve the CCD, where Iwasaki anticipated some resistance. The CCD did ask for several cuts, but none seemed damaging to Iwasaki, and he accepted them. Thus, with only minor changes, the film was approved for theatrical exhibition and received its formal certificate. Iwasaki and Kamei were jubilant. They soon found that major distributors were fearful of the film's content but that provincial tryouts won a favourable reaction. *Nichi-ei* was hopeful of successful distribution.

In August, Iwasaki was summoned to CCD, and suspected that it might concern the distribution arrangements for *The Tragedy of Japan*. He was not worried, inasmuch as the exhibition licence was safely in hand. But a CCD officer abruptly informed him that the approval had been cancelled. Within a week all prints and negatives were to be turned over to CCD. He was given a written order.

Iwasaki was incredulous. How could a film approved by democratic procedures, in full accordance with regulations, be banned in such a manner? Iwasaki's usual contacts at CIE and CCD said they could do nothing to help him in this matter. It had been decided at higher levels.

By persistent inquiry, and with some help from Chicago *Sun* correspondent Mark Gayn, Iwasaki learned what the higher levels were. The Japanese Prime Minister, Shigeru Yoshida, liked movies and regularly arranged screenings at his residence, to which other dignitaries might be invited. On 2 August the films his staff had selected for him and his guests included *The Tragedy of Japan*. Among those present were high-ranking American military men including, Iwasaki was told, Major General Charles Willoughby, aide to General Douglas MacArthur.

The Prime Minister reportedly fumed during the film. At the end, when he saw the symbolic dissolve of imperial glory, he exploded in fury, and called it outrageous. The American military men promptly agreed with him, and said it was detrimental to Occupation policy; this time 'those reds in the CIE' had gone too far. Whether Major General Willoughby subsequently conferred with MacArthur or acted on his own, Iwasaki could not learn. The cancellation came from General Willoughby.

Museum Screening
The negative and prints of *The Tragedy of Japan* were to be delivered to CCD on 18 August, a week after the cancellation. For that week the

Nichi-ei staff rented the small auditorium (*c.* 250 seats) of the Transportation Museum near the Kanda Mansei bashi railroad station. By scheduling three screenings a day they arranged for twenty-one screenings. They were determined that as many Japanese as possible should see *The Tragedy of Japan* before its demise. Handmade bulletins were posted throughout the area. Throngs came; every screening was packed. There was no air-conditioning and all openings were covered for projection purposes, so the place in those August days was like a steambath. Yet people kept coming. Iwasaki estimated that at least five thousand people saw the film. The fact that the first anniversary of the end of the war fell within this week may have added to the impact. The posted bulletins announced:

> The controversial film *The Tragedy of Japan* banned for the general public for its overzealous search for truth. Membership tickets: 3 yen.

Response cards were distributed. The most frequent theme of the responses, according to Iwasaki, was surprise that the film had been banned. Many expressed indignation over the ban; some reportedly wrote protests to GHQ. But nothing was heard from GHQ. Iwasaki comforted himself that the basic footage of the film was archive material, and that the film could some day be reconstructed. He made the delivery to CCD, prelude to destruction, on schedule.

Transitions
During the next few years Iwasaki and many others were apparently on a semi-official blacklist to which units of the Occupation and the major film studios adhered. All artists who had begun their careers at Prokino were apparently included in the 'red purge'. With others, Iwasaki formed Shinsei Productions to make feature films and in 1952 produced *Sinku Chitai/Vacuum Zone*, one of the most successful of the independently produced films of this period, many on antiwar themes.

The year 1952 also brought an end to the US Occupation. Iwasaki had never stopped thinking about the atom-bomb film, and now conferred with Kano and others. Three of the conspirators survived, and felt it was now safe to talk about the hidden negative. How could the project be revived? They would need capital. Among their exploratory moves they paid a visit to Shigeru Miki's laboratory and found to their surprise that he no longer had the film. He told them the Toho studio had in recent days heard about the footage and as owner of *Nichi-ei* sent someone to claim and collect the material. Toho seemed entitled to it, so he had relinquished it. Iwasaki and his associates decided on a visit to Toho. Nobuyo Horiba, who had become general manager for *Nichi-ei Shinsa*, was not interested in a documentary on Hiroshima and Nagasaki. The company was unwilling to release the footage to others for such a project. Weeks and months of negotiations and pleas failed to budge this position. The company was adamant. It used a small amount of the footage for its newsreel, and seems to have made a few feet available to Alain Resnais for his *Hiroshima, Mon Amour* (Argos Films, 1959). But a documentary report on the Hiroshima–Nagasaki holocaust was out of the question. The studio recognized no such 'duty' to posterity.

Iwasaki and his friends were baffled. Some thought Toho's attitude stemmed from the fact that Japanese features, including Toho's, were beginning to win international distribution, sparked by the triumphs of Kinugasa's *Jigokumon/Gate of Hell* (Daiei, 1953) at various film festivals and its capture of the Academy Award for best foreign film. The United States and Europe suddenly loomed as important markets for Toho films. Perhaps Toho feared that the atom-bomb film would anger the Americans and bring retaliation. In any case, the decision remained firm.

In 1967 came another moment of transition. Japanese newspapers carried a report that the US government had agreed to return to the Japanese government the Hiroshima and Nagasaki film 'confiscated' in 1946. Iwasaki and friends were 'transfixed' by the news, but were alarmed at follow-up reports. According to a 26 January 1968 story in *Asahi Evening News*, the Japanese government was making plans for a public screening 'after certain scenes showing victims' disfiguring burns are deleted'. It also announced severe restrictions on distribution of the film.

What did it mean? Would this historic record, after decades of US suppression, be sabotaged by Japan's own government? If so, why? Surviving participants in the film's production now formed a Committee of Producers of the Atomic Bomb Movie. They protested the proposed cuts and asserted the producers' right to participate in further decisions. They were ready, as ever, to devote themselves to a Japanese version. The issue precipitated meetings, resolutions, and heated letters to the press. In the end the government did precisely what it had said it would. Its screening over NHK–TV, the non-commercial, government-controlled network, showed little more than ruins and rubble. Everything the government called 'medical footage' had been eliminated.

In terms of length, these cuts amounted to little. The impounded compilation had actually included only some fifteen minutes of human-effects footage. But to the producers it was the most precious and meaningful portion.

The showing touched off a new firestorm of protest in letters and editorials. Showing Hiroshima and Nagasaki ruins (not so different from Tokyo ruins) without showing the torment of the Hibakusha – the human victims of the atom bomb – was condemned as a cruel hoax, a suppression of the very meaning of the atomic attack.

Because the government said its deletions were in deference to the 'human rights' of the victims, the committee sought out surviving Hibakusha appearing in the film (its logs included all the names) and found twelve; all signed an appeal that the human-effects footage be included in a new showing. A number of the scientific consultants joined in the demand. But the government stood its ground.

What was its motive? Had the return of the film been hedged by secret understandings? Had it all been an international public relations gesture without meaning? Or did the policies represent a Japanese decision?

It was a time of intricate US–Japanese relations.

The Vietnam War was at its height. Airlifts of military material were flying to Vietnam continually via Japanese airfields. US supply ships stopped at Japanese ports. The co-operation was carried on with as little fanfare as possible. Was the government afraid the footage would focus new anger on the US, and on Japan's current assistance to it? The producers, while pondering such questions, continued to plead their case, but without success.

November 1969 brought a startling development from an unexpected source. Iwasaki received an airmail letter from the United States on stationery of the Columbia University Press, signed by Barbara Van Dyke. She explained that she was associate producer of a film being made at Columbia from previously 'Secret' Hiroshima and Nagasaki footage released to it by the Pentagon, and shot by a Japanese film unit. The Columbia group was disappointed at the paucity of footage showing effects on humans and had written to film historian Donald

Richie in Tokyo asking for names of people who might know of additional footage of this sort. He had suggested Iwasaki and several others. Could Iwasaki help them in any way? Did he know of any human-effects footage retained in Japan?

He scarcely knew how to reply. That he could do nothing for her was clear. And was she to be trusted? In the end he left the letter unanswered.

The year 1970 brought new developments in rapid order. In January the principal Japanese papers carried a United Press report that a preview of *Hiroshima–Nagasaki, August 1945* had been held at the Museum of Modern Art in New York and had left a packed audience stunned. Columbia was starting distribution of the sixteen-minute film, selling prints to anyone for $96 per 16mm print. The dispatch gave the address. Iwasaki at once sent an order for a print.

Meanwhile he was startled to learn that a representative of TBS, Tokyo, one of Japan's commercial television systems, had attended the Museum of Modern Art preview and purchased rights for two Japanese telecasts of the film. A few days later Iwasaki had the strange experience of seeing on prime time television the footage that had 'burned itself' into his brain a quarter-century earlier, and that he had struggled so long to make public. Stranger yet, he was asked by a major magazine to review the film's television debut.

The TBS telecast used the English-language narration written for the film by Paul Ronder and spoken by him and Kazuko Oshima. Nevertheless the film apparently won a wide audience and was at once rescheduled for a second telecast, again in prime time. According to Mainichi Shinbun, it 'caused a sensation throughout the country'. One paper thanked Columbia University for showing the Japanese people 'what our own government tried to withhold from us'. In Hiroshima 'the viewing rate soared to four times the normal rate.' The government made no comment. Plans for a Japanese-language version of *Hiroshima–Nagasaki, August 1945* were announced.

The magazine that had asked for a review by Iwasaki was *Asahi-Graph*, a large-format pictorial magazine similar to *Life*. It carried an extensive report including stills from the film. In his review Iwasaki described his feelings after watching the first telecast.

I was lost in thought for a long time, deeply moved by this film . . .
I was the producer of the original long film which offered the basic

material for this short film. That is, I knew every cut of it . . . yet I was speechless . . . It was not the kind of film the Japanese thought Americans would produce. The film is an appeal or warning from man to man for peaceful reflection – to prevent the use of the bomb ever again. I like the narration, in which the emotion is well controlled and the voice is never raised . . . That made me cry. In this part, the producers are no longer Americans. Their feelings are completely identical to our feelings.

Columbia's film included almost all the shots eliminated in the NHK showing.

Final Credits

Iwasaki wrote a long letter to our group at Columbia, expressing appreciation for the way we had handled the material. He apologized for his failure to answer Barbara Van Dyke's inquiry.

When I visited Tokyo two years later, we had long talks. I was there with my wife, collecting material for a history of the documentary film. Iwasaki was endlessly helpful, setting up meetings with major Japanese documentarists, arranging screenings, and reminiscing. My wife and I made a return visit in 1978 when the book appeared in a Japanese translation. I had meanwhile entered into correspondence with Iwasaki. He translated one of my books into Japanese. Meanwhile he wrote to say he had written a book titled *Occupied Screen: My Postwar Story*, and was sending me a copy. He felt portions of it would be of special interest to me, and hoped I might persuade a Japanese student at Columbia to translate them. In due time I did commission a translation.

He said he was writing a longer memoir on his life but making slow progress because of ill health. His New Year's greeting that year said: 'I had a heart attack, but getting better.' His last letter was dated 15 September 1981:

Dear Mr Barnouw!

Thank you very much for your new book, *The Magician and the Cinema*. It is most interesting – informative and instructive. The Japanese version is absolutely needed. If I were not ill, I would do the translation. But after the second heart attack I am weakened, spending better part of time in bed. It is quite regrettable.

Nevertheless, I am slowly getting better. It seems I can live on a few years more. I am looking forward to seeing you again in Japan. With best wishes for you and your family,

Akira Iwasaki.

The letter came to me with the following note from his son:

Dear Sir,

I send you the last letter of my father, found on his desk the day after his death – Akira Iwasaki died on the evening of the 16th September, as his disease had a sudden turn for the worse.

I herewith wish to express my deep thanks for your kindness and favours given him while in life.

Hiroshi Iwasaki

The note moved me deeply, but its last words were also troublesome. Years earlier, when we at Columbia University obtained the footage released to us by the Pentagon, we were informed that it had been shot by a Japanese unit named *Nippon Eiga Sha*, but no individual names were given. Thus the compilation *Hiroshima–Nagasaki, August 1945* appeared with a series of credits that included mine as its producer but made no mention of Iwasaki. He had never spoken of this, and we never discussed it. Yet I was very conscious of my debt to Iwasaki. Expressions of gratitude from him and his family made me uneasy.

Later, when I finally obtained a translation of *Occupied Screen*, I began to glimpse how they must have viewed his 'post-war story'. Iwasaki had written and published, according to *Japan Quarterly*, some fifty books, many of which had been substantial successes. But he had poured his life's blood into the documentaries of the post-war period, and his frustrations over them were deeply galling. In *Occupied Screen* I was astonished to read: '*Hiroshima–Nagasaki, August 1945* is all that I now possess.'

I discussed the situation with Barbara Van Dyke and others involved in our film, and we decided to add to all subsequent prints a final credit: 'Japanese footage shot by *Nippon Eiga Sha* under the supervision of Akira Iwasaki.'

Source: *Film History*, 1988, Vol. 2.

Conflict, Ogawa and Japanese Film-making
ANDRÉE TOURNÈS

Sinsuke Ogawa is a remarkable film-maker who takes to extremes
Flaherty's idea that documentarists should live among their subjects. He
spent more than a decade living with the peasant famers of the Narita
valley outside Tokyo while they campaigned against the construction of
a new airport. The resultant films are long, meditative, intimate and
highly partisan but unlike many similar western documentaries,
completely unvoyeuristic.

The following article on Ogawa was written in 1972 and is
accompanied by a short interview with the film-maker.

The contrast between fiction and documentary filming is starkly underlined in Ogawa's series of four *Narita* films. Telling of how a peasant
community defended its land against the proposed construction of an
airport, each film lasts two hours and took more than five years to make.

These are films about conflict, yet what is astounding is the gentleness
of manner and the unending patience of the peasants.

For over five years, the Sanrizuka peasants in the Narita province,
fifty kilometres from Tokyo, delayed the construction of the new
airport. Women chained themselves to fences against the assault of the
police.

. . . At the beginning of the second film, other women catch a coward
who had begun work for the airport property developers: rows of
people jostle, a handful of earth is tossed at him ritually as if he was a
corpse, a body lying prostrate, face in the ground: that's all. We also see
an old peasant defiantly talking of how precious is the earth, how
money cannot compensate for its loss, how 'President Sato himself will
find that out on his dying day'. Later we learn that the man has
committed suicide.

For Ogawa and the women who later berate the police, this suicide is
an unforgivable crime. The whole film is a extended meditation on the
sadness of the divisions in families between the quitters, and the fighters.
It also explores one man's reasons for giving in and the way in which the
struggle, especially for the younger people, has strengthened the
community and formed new bonds across families. Those scenes which
show how empathy is born of the struggle, how understanding grows
even in the face of the menace, are especially poignant. It is rare to see

such a tangible growth in polical awareness, almost like a law of nature, almost like a ripening fruit.

The student involvement in the peasants' struggle underlines the nature of the political growth which takes place. In the first film, *A Summer in Narita*, they attempt unsuccessfully to impress on the peasants the political dimension of their actions. In the second film, they are absent from the debate. In the third, *The Second Fortress*, they return, but only as the campaign broadens.

Peasant women are at the front of the most intense fighting, shouting at the police, 'We peasants produce your rice. When you eat, you should be ashamed!'

Ogawa on his work and the struggle of the Narita peasants:
'On the eve of the first day's shooting at Sanrizuka near to Narita, the crew members agreed on two principles:

Firstly, all our set ups would be on the side of the peasants engaged in the struggle . . . If the police hit the peasants, then our camera will also receive the blows, and power relationship would be transmitted to viewers through the screen.

Secondly, without becoming preoccupied with the difficulties of making this film, we must never try to hide the camera or use the telephoto lens. In place of filming people who do not know they are being filmed, our camera should be where it should be – that is to say, in the centre of the peasants' struggle.

These were effectively our points of departure, and the peasants began a 'dialogue' with us precisely from there, revealing themselves spontaneously to the camera . . .

What made me choose Sanrizuka?

It's easy to imagine that when I arrived there I did not know into what I was about to embark; at the beginning who would ever have thought that we would stay there so long? Something fascinated me about the smell of the ground, and I mean that very sincerely. Above all, I love seeing how something happens to lives sunk into the mud . . .

Let us imagine for a moment that the Sanrizuka airport was moved to the smart centre of Tokyo. I suspect that . . . these atrocities would not have happened. The government didn't consult the peasants. Japan is a fully developed industrialized society; what weight do these poor people have?

I have an enormous interest in everyday life. Until my *Narita* films, my work was very far removed from human problems; I made mostly advertising films and eventually I reacted against this kind of film-making.

I can't say that I arrived at Sanrizuka with a well-structured project plan, but I was obsessed by today's affluent society and its vast pile of accumulated prejudices . . . We should not lose sight of the fact that it was not long ago – in the time of Meiji to be precise – that the population was eighty per cent peasantry, and that the country has since shafted them. Our society is based on this 'indelicacy', with its stockpile of cars, toasters, ovens, colour TVs, hi-tech gadgetry and all that follows . . .

It was against rationalized despoilment in the purest modern style that the people of this land rose up to say 'no'. It is a no which I believe existed in me before I could shout it here at Sanrizuka.

Why did we continue to film when you could say that the struggle against the airport's construction was over?

Because I don't think it is over. No, the struggle has not reached its natural end. Certainly the runways have been finished, and even the ground installations: in that sense, one can say that in spite of everything, the airport has been built. But what have we done, or more exactly, what did the task we set ourselves consist of? . . . Yes, the airport is finished. But the people, the peasants who said no to this airport continue to do so and still value their refusal. So the airport is not finished. And as long as we live we will continue to witness, to develop for those who are still alive, the significance and the deep social, political, historic entreaty of this 'insubordination'. We will still continue to affirm that no, the airport is not finished . . .

Source: *Jeune Cinéma* magazine, 1972.

An Interview with Shohei Imamura
TOICHI NAKATA

Shohei Imamura is one of cinema's most under-appreciated directors. In early works such as *Pigs and Warships* (1961), *Insect Woman* (1963) and *Profound Desire of the Gods* (1968), he eschewed the grace and poise of his master Ozu for often violent studies of the sexual and social lives of working-class Japanese. He came belatedly to international attention with his remake of *The Ballad of Narayama* (1983) which won the Cannes' Palme d'Or.

In 1970 Imamura retired from drama to make a stunning series of television documentaries, portraits of barmaids, prostitutes and soldiers, which rank among the highest achievements of Japanese non-fiction film-making. Imamura has expressed his distaste at what he sees as the politeness of much documentary cinema. His credit as 'planner' on one of the least polite documentaries ever made, Hara's *The Emperor's Naked Army Marches On* (pp. 205), is highly appropriate.

This interview with Imamura was conducted[1] by Toichi Nakata, a young Japanese documentarist whose *Osaka Story* (1994) was one of the most exciting documentary debuts of recent years.

TOICHI NAKATA: *The first of your films to blur the line between fiction and fact was* A Man Vanishes *(Ningen Johatsu), which you made independently in 1967.*

SHOHEI IMAMURA: My original intention was to investigate twenty-six cases of men who had disappeared, but it soon became clear that one case alone would be quite complicated enough to deal with. I centred the film on the case of Tadashi Oshima, who disappeared in 1965 while on a business trip. I learned about him through meeting his fiancée Yoshie Hayakawa, and I soon guessed that Oshima had vanished because he wanted to get out of his obligation to marry her.

TN: *How did you go about researching it?*

SI: I always try to talk to people myself as much as I can. That can get boring, but sometimes I can sense that there's something that needs to be explored further behind what they're saying. While making *A Man Vanishes*, my crew and I stayed in the room next door to Yoshie Hayakawa for a whole year. She had every imaginable bad quality, and none of us could really stand her. And yet I wanted to understand why I found her so disturbing, and that was enough to keep me going.

TN: *Did you ever think twice about using hidden cameras and exposing her and other people's private feelings in public?*

---

1 At the Edinburgh Film Festival.

SI: Yoshie Hayakawa gave her explicit consent to being filmed. She took leave from her job to be in the film, and we paid her a salary. In other words, she approached the project as a job and she soon took on the role of an actress in front of the camera. She used the cameras as much as we used her as a subject. Of course, there are serious ethical questions involved. Hayakawa didn't know what the film's outcome would be, but we behind the camera didn't know where reality was going to lead us either. I'm not sure myself if the use of hidden cameras was justified, and I have to admit that the finished film did hurt Hayakawa's feelings. These are difficult areas, and I have no glib answers. As a film-maker, though, I did what I had to do to see the film through to completion. I put the needs of the film first. I had no other choice, really.

TN: *After A Man Vanishes*, you made one more fiction feature (*Profound Desire of the Gods*, 1968), and then switched to making documentaries for the next nine years. What happened?

SI: The filming of *Profound Desire of the Gods* took place on Ishigaki Island in the Okinawan archipelago, and it was originally scheduled to last for six months. But six months got dragged out to one year, and then eighteen months . . . I had a great time on this remote island and got on very well with the local people. I immersed myself in Okinawan folklore and tradition. But my actors and actresses couldn't stand the protracted filming and began to complain about being stuck on the island for so long. I'd never had any problem working with actors before, but on this occasion their complaints made me really fed up. Funnily enough, I was so fed up that I lost all desire to make fiction films for many years.

Also, I came out of *A Man Vanishes* with a feeling that fiction – no matter how close to reality – could never be as truthful as unmeditated documentary. And documentary seemed a better vehicle for my unending desire to get close to people's true natures. I started with *The History of Postwar Japan as Told by a Bar Hostess* in 1970, and devoted myself exclusively to documentaries for some nine years. No actors to worry about. I simply travelled around with a skeleton crew: often just one cameraman and one sound recordist.

In Search of Unreturned Soldiers (Mikikan-hei o Otte, 1971) was about former soldiers of the Japanese army who chose not to return to Japan after the war. I found several of them who had remained in Thailand. Two years later, I invited one of them to make his first return

28 History of Postwar Japan as Told by a Bar Hostess *(1970)*.

visit to Japan and documented it in *Private Fujita Comes Home*
(Muhomatsu Kokyo ni Kaeru, 1974). During the filming my subject
Fujita asked me to buy him a cleaver so that he could kill his 'vicious'
brother. I was shocked, and asked him to wait for a day so that I could
plan how to film the scene. By the next morning, to my relief, Fujita had
calmed down and changed his mind about killing his brother. But I
couldn't have had a sharper insight into the ethical questions provoked
by this kind of documentary film-making.

In 1975 I went to Malaysia to look for Japanese women who had
been sent to South-East Asia during the war to serve as prostitutes for
the Japanese troops. These women were known as *Karayuki-san*. While
researching the project, I met around twenty old ladies who had been
Karayuki-san, but none of them seemed right for the film. And then I
met Zendo Kikuvo, a gentle old lady of seventy, who came from the
family of a poor farmer in the Hiroshima area, and she became the
focus of *Karayuki-san, the Making of a Prostitute* (1975). She was very
open with us from the start, but I had to ask her a series of shockingly

direct questions: 'How many men did you have to sleep with every night?', 'Did you enjoy sex with your clients?' and so on. Despite everything, she remained astonishingly kind and tolerant towards us.

For my part, though, I was less and less sure that I could justify asking her such questions. I had to ask myself whether I was exploiting her, whether or not I really understood her feelings. I also found myself wondering whether documentary was really the best way to approach these matters. I came to realize that the presence of the camera could materially change people's lives. Did I have the right to affect such changes? Was I playing god in trying to control the lives of others? I'm in no way a sentimental humanist, but thoughts like these scared me and made me acutely aware of the limitations of documentary film-making.

Imamura returned to fiction film-making in 1979 with *Vengeance is Mine*.

Source: Toichi Nakata in *Projections 6*, Faber and Faber, 1995.

The Emperor's Naked Army Marches On
JILL FORBES

Like Imamura's documentaries, at first glance *The Emperor's Naked Army Marches On* appears to be a film almost without style: many scenes are under-lit and roughly shot. The film's real strength is not pictorial, but flows from its outstanding *impoliteness*, its doggedly amoral determination to record its subject's violent crusade.

As documentarists seldom set up scenes, they give their films shape by making moral and aesthetic choices about what is decent to film and when to switch off. Hara's film is so daring, some would say unethical, that it shows its protagonist actually planning to shoot one of the interviewees. Other films might indeed narrate such an event in the past, but for Hara the event was in the present, part of the action which comprises his story. Some would say this is collusive, that the director is encouraging the campaigning soldier to intimidate these old men. The result is profoundly 'unGriersonian'.

The seventy-year-old Kenzo Okuzaki is serving a sentence of twelve years hard labour for attempted murder. He does not chafe at the

29 The Emperor's Naked Army Marches On *(1986)*.

confinement but accepts it philosophically: 'Outside prison I would have to fend for myself.' But then, this is not his first brush with the law. Back in 1969 he made the headlines in Japan for having fired four pachinko balls at Emperor Hirohito as he stood on the palace balcony, accusing the Emperor of War Crimes as he did so.

Okuzaki is a bit of a maverick, the self-styled 'impartial soldier' of the 'Divine Crusade' or 'Shin-gun', a one-man campaigner who, when he is not doing time, tours Japan railing against the 'Showa', the reign of Hirohito who, he believes, must be held responsible for crimes committed during the Second World War. Hirohito's death has not altered Okuzaki's determination: 'Even if the Japanese nation were to praise Hirohito, the fact that he is a serious criminal will remain unchanged before God and God's law.'

Okuzaki served during the war with the 36th Independent Engineering Corps in New Guinea. This was a doomed expedition and one of the bloodier episodes in the Pacific campaign. Soldiers on the island scattered into the jungle and most of them died of malaria or starvation, or both. Of more than a thousand in Okuzaki's corps only about thirty survived, so Okuzaki can count himself lucky.

But he saw his fellow soldiers die and the experience has scarred him for life. He starts to visit the survivors of the campaign and the relatives of those who died. He is particularly moved by an encounter with the mother of a comrade whom he had buried himself. During these investigations he discovers that a bizarre and apparently illegal shooting incident took place when two soldiers were executed for desertion more than three weeks after the war had ended.

Okuzaki is determined to discover why they were really shot. He presses Sergeant Yamada, the only survivor from the squadron, who admits that the officers were told to shoot the soldiers, who were then reported killed in action. Yamada explains that privates were killed in order for officers to survive, and that lots were drawn at regimental HQ.

It becomes clear that cannibalism was carried out on quite a wide scale, with some witnesses alleging that private soldiers were killed and others that no Japanese soldiers were killed and that a distinction was maintained between 'white and black pork'. Not surprisingly, Okuzaki is extremely disturbed by this discovery. The horror of cannibalism and the revulsion he feels on religious grounds – 'forty years after the end of the war their souls are not sleeping, they return to visit us' – these emotions combine with his single-minded campaign against the criminal Emperor.

What gives *The Emperor's Naked Army Marches On* its impact is that it is the portrait of an individual who not only continues to be traumatized by his wartime experiences, but because of them is marginalized and criminalized. Okuzaki's experience is tantamount to a refusal to participate in the post-war consensus, so that it is not just the Emperor who is challenged but Japanese society itself.

This means that, in addition to the gruesome tale it has to tell, *The Emperor's Naked Army* becomes a film document as much of interest for its chequered production history as for the story it recounts. It was produced by Shisso films, a company which appears to specialize in physically shocking material (the 'self-liberation of a spastic person' or the filming of child birth in 'real time'). The line between their taboo-breaking practices and pornography is a fine one, but in *The Emperor's Naked Army* their willingness to transgress takes on a clear political dimension.

The film-makers Shohei Imamura and Kazuo Hara sought out Okuzaki and constructed the film to mirror his – and their – process of discovery and reconstruction. They also had considerable difficulties to surmount, with the confiscation of footage shot in New Guinea and Okuzaki's further imprisonment. The film was more than five years in the making and was refused by all mainstream Japanese distributors. It has nevertheless touched a chord in Japan where it ran to packed houses for over a year.

One reason for its success, beyond the alternative version of history that it proposes, is undoubtedly that Okuzaki comes across as a man of such evident sincerity and humility. He is a genuine enquirer after truth rather than a publicity-seeking sensationalist and thus helps to place the Japanese army in a quite different light from that in which we – and no doubt its members – have been accustomed to view it. It is the confusion and humanity of those involved which strikes the viewer. These were private soldiers or NCOS dumped in an alien environment in which the objectives of the war they were fighting entirely disappeared in their immediate struggle for survival.

Source: Jill Forbes in *Sight and Sound*, Winter 1989–1990.

Part 3

8 The Essayists

INTRODUCTION

In the 1950s a new generation of film-makers began to reject the restrictive notion that documentary was merely a medium for mass communication and 'social betterment'. Instead, they looked at documentary as a means to express strong personal opinions and points of view. Directors like Alain Resnais, Lindsay Anderson, Georges Franju and Chris Marker developed idiosyncratic personal styles, suited to their individual tastes and modes of expression. The often complex subjects which they chose to explore would, in a previous era, have been left to the literary essay. Unlike most earlier documentaries – which generally aspired to, but failed to find, a wide audience – these films tended towards intellectual élitism.

The 'essay film' continued to thrive into the late 1970s and beyond, particularly on continental Europe. Significantly, the British, who have frequently been regarded as the world leaders in documentary, never took to the form, always retaining a Griersonian distaste for 'personal expression' and a sense that film must be useful.

The category of 'essay film' is not a precise one and the pieces collected together in this chapter often share little except the film-makers strong personal perspective.

O Dreamland
GAVIN LAMBERT

Best known for feature films such as *If* and *This Sporting Life*, Lindsay Anderson (1923–1994) spent more than a decade at the start of his career making documentaries. *Thursday's Children* (1954) about the Royal School for the Deaf in Margate, won him an Oscar, but more representative are *Every Day Except Christmas* (1953), a celebration of the market traders in London's Covent Garden, and the satiric ten minute film *O Dreamland* (1953), about a tawdry working-class funfair.

In the mid 1950s Anderson was instrumental in founding the iconoclastic Free Cinema movement with Tony Richardson and Karel Reisz. Like the Nouvelle Vague in France, they were outspoken in their criticism of conventional, class-bound British cinema. Derisive of glossy stylistic perfection, they insisted on shooting real people in real locations, frequently with a hand-held camera, foreshadowing many of the techniques of *cinéma vérité*. Anderson was particularly scathing of Grierson's documentary movement, writing that 'the first duty of the artist is not to interpret, nor to propagandize but to create.' In nonfiction Anderson looked to the lyrical work of Humphrey Jennings (see p. 151) for inspiration.

This piece, by critic and screenwriter Gavin Lambert was part of an evaluation of the first Free Cinema programme in 1956.

The first time [one sees *O Dreamland*] it is like a blow in the face; the second, one approaches it with a kind of eager dread. For ten minutes it assaults eye and ear with a rough-edged but sharp-centred impression of this South Coast amusement park, in which the ugliness and degradation of most of the distractions offered are symbolized by the mocking mechanical laughter of a dummy sailor. There is a working model of the execution of the 'atom spies', the Rosenbergs, which reconstructs the ritual for sixpence at the door; equally, a hanging may be viewed as often as someone cares to put a penny in the slot, and a lifesize Joan of Arc, looking something like the heroine of a touring pantomime twenty years ago, is burnt at the stake; while 'Torture Through the Ages' dramatizes the ordeals of boiling oil, thumbscrews, etc. Yet, whether the rendezvous is with violent death or a smutty peepshow, with a fire-eater or a gambling machine, a listless caged animal or an old mug of tea, reactions appear the same. People stare – a child blinks suddenly, an enormous woman creaks forward to reveal one stocking rolled below the knee, a family stands to watch the firebrand entering the mouth as if waiting for a bus, and even the gaunt women at the gambling tables are like a factory line, mechanically engrossed in routine. Signs of real vitality are produced by greed – the man watching the crane, as it nearly scoops a trinket, with an expression of rigid lust – by the juke-box music of Frankie Laine and Muriel Smith to which the girls giggle, sway, get hep, link arms in cowboy hats, and by the thrill of physical motion – the great aerial contraptions that look like spaceships, shooting diagonally up and down past each other and provoking laughter, mock-terror and a feverish elation.

Everything is ugly. A papier-mâché façade with a swollen, grimacing gargoyle, an immense 'artistic' statue representing a coyly nude pseudo-classical figure, a 'Swiss beer garden' in which local music and yodelling emanate from twitching, squeaking puppets, the steaming, slippery, greasy trays of food labelled 'SAUSAGES' and 'ONIONS' in the Happy Family Restaurant; feet shuffle clumsily across ground fouled with all kinds of litter, buttocks encased in grey, shapeless material spread and crease over stools at counters; and all the time the sleek charabancs pour in. It is almost too much. The nightmare is redeemed by the point of view, which, for all the unsparing candid camerawork and the harsh, inelegant photography, is emphatically humane. Pity, sadness, even poetry is infused into this drearily tawdry, aimlessly hungry world. It is infused by imaginative comment – the counterpoint of sound and image, with Frankie Laine's passionately emetic 'I Believe' blaring over the shot of the imprisoned lion pacing its cage like a creature in an endless dream, with the drawling cry of Muriel Smith's 'Kiss Me – Thrill Me' rhythmically matching the spaceships as they cross in mid-air – but even more by the director's absolute fidelity to his subject.

The unexpected image tells. A haggard, elderly woman in a salad-bowl hat calmly, almost fatalistically drinks her tea; a plump, derisive one points at the 'artistic' statue and staggers with laughter; a derelict little row of tramps and nomads chew their lunchtime sandwiches; the trio of girls lights up with ecstatic vivacity as the juke-box plays their favourite tune – and protest at this anonymous, bedraggled search for happiness turns into compassion, into love. All these people, one realizes, are seeking something they will probably never find. The Rosenbergs die again and they bleakly, willingly stare – but there is nothing perverse about it, only a kind of uncertain passivity, an oppressive, sometimes intolerable sense of loss and deprivation. The pleasures are sad not because they are ugly but because there is nothing else. Where else should they go? At the end, the camera moves swiftly, vertiginously up to a panoramic view of Dreamland twinkling and blaring in the night – and it is like a plea for release.

Source: 'Free Cinema' by Gavin Lambert in *Sight and Sound*, Spring 1956.

30 O Dreamland *(1953).*

The Sunday Musicians
KRZYSZTOF KIEŚLOWSKI

To celebrate its 400th issue, the editors of the French film magazine *Positif* asked film-makers from around the world to write something 'about an actor, or a film, or a director who has had a special significance for them'. Here is Krzysztof Kieślowski's response.

In the name of the friendship I feel for you and *Positif,* I am answering your three questions. In all sincerity, though, I don't believe this type of enquiry can help us to grasp either the state of cinema or the state of mind of us film-makers. With the approaching centenary of cinema, many newspaper and television journalists have tried to make lists of the directors, actors or films which are the favourites of other directors, other actors or the public. This can often lead to amusing results. I was recently asked by the editors of *Sight and Sound* to make a list of the ten films which have most affected me. Here is my list – although the order is by no means significant (film number one could be number ten and vice versa):

La Strada by Fellini; *Kes* by Ken Loach; *Un Condamné a Mort s'est Echappé* by Robert Bresson; *The Pram* by Widerberg; *Intimate Lighting* by Ivan Passer; *The Sunday Musicians* by Karabasz; *Ivan's Childhood* by Tarkovsky; *Les Quatre Cents Coups* by Truffaut; *Citizen Kane* by Orson Welles; *The Kid* by Chaplin.

Nine of these films you know. So I shall speak about the one you don't know, which for me is as important as all the others.

The Sunday Musicians [Muzykanci, Polish documentary by Kazimierz Karabasz (1958) 10 minutes]

Twenty, perhaps thirty, men enter a small and dimly-lit hall. We recognize it to be in one of those places, so redolent of the period, that were called a 'medium-sized industrial unit'. The sort of place where all the chairs are broken, the tables are scratched, the walls are peeling, and the floor hasn't been cleaned for ages. Night has fallen. The men have the faces of workmen, their thick hands and fingers indelibly stained by labour. The director doesn't attempt to place them socially, but as we see them in close-up for ten minutes, we guess them to be men involved in hard physical labour.

Most of them are already in their forties or fifties.

They take musical instruments out of battered old cases. Horns, trumpets, trombones, mandolins, guitars, accordions. If I remember rightly, there are no violinists or pianists; all the instruments are rather crude. The conductor is even older: over sixty, with grey hair and moustache. They put their music on rickety stands. The only thing which evokes the grander world of the concert hall or opera house is the conductor's baton. It's a baton of good quality. It stands out. The men sit down.

Almost all of them solemnly put their spectacles on. The conductor too. Unlike the baton, the spectacles belong to their world – almost all are held together across the bridge of the nose or at the hinges by Elastoplast. Sellotape didn't yet exist, so people used Elastoplast bought in chemists. You can see this very well on the screen. A few of the spectacles, the conductor's for example, have cracked lenses.

Karabasz's *The Sunday Musicians* won the Grand Prix at the Oberhausen Short Film Festival in the late fifties. At the time, this was the most important documentary festival in the world. The film was then shown in several countries. A Dutch spectacle-maker saw it in Holland. He wrote to Karabasz, who then asked the heroes of his film what their sight defects were. A few months later, they all received brand-new spectacles from Holland. In those days, in Poland, such a gift had great value.

The men start playing. They play clumsily and, even though the music is as simple as their instruments, it's rather difficult to make out a melody. The conductor quickly interrupts them by tapping the table with his baton. It isn't the first time they've rehearsed the piece, and he's annoyed that the musicians seem to have forgotten everything they learnt at earlier rehearsals. He loses his temper and even starts shouting. But he comes from Vilnius (the city was part of Eastern Poland before the war) and his accent, so soft and pleasing to the Polish ear, gives even his most terrible outbursts a soft, lilting quality. They rehearse again and again. Gradually, and after many interruptions – during which the conductor takes various musicians to task and, humming, shows them how and when to play – the melody starts to appeal. By the sixth or seventh minute the music becomes recognizable.

For a couple of minutes we watch the men: we see their hands, their faces, we follow their fluid, uninterrupted playing. Then the camera leaves this dark place. A wide shot reveals a tram depot at dawn. We see men in overalls covered in grease-stains. They have hammers of various sizes, pincers, anvils. Sparks fly from soldering machines. The first trams leave the depot. In the maintenance pits, the men work on the trams that won't be running in town that day. During this little scene, the sound of the music mixes with the sounds of the depot. Final credits.

I know that Karabasz spent several months with his musicians and that he was with them during rehearsals. It's rare for a short film to express so much, in such a beautiful and simple manner, about the fundamental human need to create.

Because, apart from satisfying our elementary needs – survival, breakfast, lunch, supper, sleep – we all aspire to something more, something that can give a meaning to life and elevate it. The more difficult this is to achieve, the greater the joy when one succeeds. For two minutes of *The Sunday Musicians*, this is the joy one reads on the faces of a few dozen middle-aged men with broken spectacles who together play a simple melody in a 'medium-sized industrial unit'.

Source: *Positif* No. 400, 1994. This translation from *Projections* 4½, Faber and Faber, 1995.

Nuit et Brouillard
ANNETTE INSDORFF

The preoccupation with memory and time which permeates Alain Resnais's feature films such as *Last Year in Marienbad* (1961) and *Providence* (1977) was first displayed in the remarkable documentary *Nuit et Brouillard* (*Night and Fog*, 1956).

This piece is extracted from Annette Insdorff's seminal book on the cinema of the Holocaust, *Indelible Shadows*.

Night and Fog [is] still the most powerful film on the concentration camp experience. Directed by Alain Resnais in 1955, *Night and Fog* is a film whose very shape challenges existing visual language, mainly through an editing style that both reflects and elicits tension. Whether the counterpoint is between image and sound, past and present, stasis and movement, despair and hope, black-and-white and colour, or oblivion and memory, Resnais's film addresses the audience's intelligence – and moves beyond a facile stimulation of helpless tears. As François Truffaut pointed out,

> It is almost impossible to speak about this film in the vocabulary of cinematic criticism. It is not a documentary, or an indictment, or a poem, but a meditation on the most important phenomenon of the twentieth century . . . The power of this film . . . is rooted in its tone, the terrible gentleness . . . When we have looked at these strange, seventy-pound slave labourers, we understand that we're not going to 'feel better' after seeing *Nuit et Brouillard*; quite the opposite.

Night and Fog begins with a long tracking shot of a peaceful landscape in colour. As the camera glides across the grass, the narration, written by survivor Jean Cayrol, introduces the locale – Auschwitz – a façade whose present calm seems to deny its ineradicable ghosts. Simultaneously, the music of Hanns Eisler (a German composer who was himself driven from his country by Hitler's rise to power) laces the scene with a certain delicacy that will become increasingly contrapuntal as the images cut into the horrific past. Our auditory guides carry us into newsreel footage and documentary stills whose black-and-white graininess contrasts with the scenes in colour. Moreover, the serene landscape gives way to harsh images of sealed freight cars and barbed wire that signify the arrival of Auschwitz's victims. The camera moving inside the abandoned structures of the concentration camp often stops, acknowledging its own limitations with a cut to a black-and-white still; while confronting and investigating, this fluid camera suggests transience, or the licence of smooth mobility that can exist only after the fact. Opposing itself to the rigidity of death captured by the newsreels, Resnais's camera glides past the now-empty barracks and crematoria until it can go no further, arrested by haunting photographs.

At these moments, the voice (of actor Michel Bouquet) quietly recalls, probes, offers statistics, and bears witness – all with an admirable lack of emotionalism. (Contrast this with Richard Widmark's histrionic verbal accompaniment to some of the same archival footage in *Judgment at Nuremberg*'s courtroom.) The voice lets the images speak for themselves, illustrating the crucial lesson of restraint that Resnais might have learned from cinema master Jean Renoir: 'The more emotional the material, the less emotional the treatment.' Likewise, the music invites a more complex response because, according to Resnais, 'the more violent the images, the gentler the music.' Unlike the pounding dramatic orchestral scores exemplified by Carlo Rustichelli's music for Gillo Pontecorvo's *Kapo* (1960), 'Eisler wanted to show that hope always existed in the background,' claimed Resnais.

Among other things, the sound track enables us to look at unbearable newsreels, such as living skeletons being prepared for hospital experiments. Cayrol's commentary takes into account the audience's predictable difficulty at seeing such horror. For example, it breaks off from its presentation of the gas chamber ceiling clawed by victims' fingernails, insisting, 'but you have to know' . . .

Resnais's revelatory camera is restricted to surfaces, requiring testimony from the past to complete the picture. The vacant images of the ovens are brutally defined by black-and-white photos, and montage activates the silent railroad tracks covered with green grass into sputtering newsreels of transports. The 'picture postcard' becomes a stark nightmare, as *Night and Fog* assumes the function of an X-ray:

through the spine of documentary footage and Cayrol's calmly vigilant meditation, we are forced to see the deformities hidden from the unaided eye (and camera), and to struggle against the imperturbability of surfaces. 'Who is responsible?' asks the narrator, after a wordless presentation of soap and lampshades made from human skin.

The alternation of history and immediacy insists upon responsibility, whether for those during World War Two who were responsible for the Holocaust, or those today who are responsible to it. The quiet landscape of post-war Auschwitz is deceptive, as the narrator insists:

> War slumbers, with one eye always open . . . Who among us watches over this strange observatory to warn of the new executioner's arrival? Are their faces really different from ours? . . . We look at these ruins as if the old concentration camp monster were dead under the debris . . . we who pretend to believe that all this happened in one time and one place, and who do not think to look around us, or hear the endless cry.

Night and Fog fulfils what the critic and film-maker Eric Rohmer once said about Resnais – that he is a cubist because he reconstitutes reality after fragmenting it. The effect is not only opposition, but a deeper unity in which past and present blend into each other.

Source: Annette Insdorf, *Indelible Shadows*, Cambridge University Press, 1983.

Warhol's *Sleep*
JONAS MEKAS

Andy Warhol (1927–1986) started making films in 1963. His early productions were avant-garde exercises in minimalism and included the eight-hour film *Sleep* (1963) in which a man sleeps for eight hours, and *Empire* (1965) a similarly lengthy shot of the Empire state building in which the only action is the lights being turned on and then off. These films take *cinéma vérité* to its logical but ridiculous extreme.

This piece appeared in film-maker, archivist and writer Jonas Mekas's *Village Voice* column in 1964.

I received a letter from Mike Getz, manager of the Cinema Theatre in

Los Angeles, reporting on the screening of Andy Warhol's movie *Sleep*:

Amazing turnout. 500 people. Sleep started at 6:45. First shot, which lasts about 45 minutes, is close-up of man's abdomen. You can see him breathing. People started to walk out at 7, some complaining. People getting more and more restless. Shot finally changes to close-up of man's head. Someone runs up to screen and shouts in sleeping man's ear, 'WAKE UP!!' Audience getting bitter, strained. Movie is silent, runs at silent speed. A few more people ask for money back. Sign on box office says no refunds.

7:45. One man pulls me out into outer lobby, says he doesn't want to make a scene but asks for money back. I say no. He says, 'Be a gentleman.' I say, 'Look, you knew you were going to see something strange, unusual, daring, that lasted six hours.' I turn to walk back to lobby. Lobby full, one red-faced guy very agitated, says I have 30 seconds to give him his money back or he'll run into theatre and start a 'lynch riot'. 'We'll all come out here and lynch you, buddy!!' Nobody stopped him when 30 seconds were up; he ran back toward screen. In fact, the guy who had said he didn't want to make a scene now said, 'Come on, I'll go with you!!'

I finally yelled at him to wait a minute. Mario Casetta told crowd to give us a chance to discuss it. Mario and I moved into outer lobby. Thoughts of recent football riot in South America. People angry as hell, a mob on the verge of violence. Red-faced guy stomps toward me: 'Well, what are you going to do?'

'I'll give out passes for another show.' Over two hundred passes given out.

Decided to make an announcement. 'Ladies and gentlemen. I believe that *Sleep* was properly advertised. I said in my ads that it was an unusual six-hour movie. You came here knowing that you were going to see something unusual about sleep and I think you are. I don't know what else I could have said. However – [shout from audience: 'Don't cop out!! Don't cop out!!'] – however . . .'

Sleep continued on. Projectionist kept falling asleep. People are not able to take the consequences of their own curiosity. Woman calls at 11 'Are you still there?' 'Sure, why?' 'I was there earlier. Heard people in back of me saying this theatre's not going to have a screen very much longer so I left.' Fifty were left at the end. Some people really digging the movie.

Source: *Cinema Journal*, 2 July 1964.

Orson Welles's *F for Fake*
RICHARD COMBS

F for Fake (1975) was Orson Welles's second foray into the borderland between documentary and fiction. The first, *It's All True* (1942), an appreciation of Brazilian culture, was never completed.
   This piece originally appeared in *Monthly Film Bulletin*.

At a railway station, Orson Welles performs some simple feats of magic, greets Hungarian actress Oja Kodar alighting from a train, and promises to tell her story later to the camera crew, led by documentarist François Reichenbach, who are filming him. Stating that for the next sixty minutes he will tell the complete truth, Welles introduces two men, art forger Emyr de Hory and his biographer Clifford Irving, living on the island of Ibiza. In the next sequence, hidden cameras catch the reactions of men to Oja walking down a street. Welles is then seen performing more sleight of hand to help the stranded Oja leave an airport, before returning to Ibiza, where de Hory explains how he found refuge on the island in 1959 and where he was interviewed by Irving, sometime before the latter's involvement in the forgery of Howard Hughes' manuscript was exposed (which leads Welles to speculate that Irving's book on de Hory might be a fake about a fake faker, and to wonder at the part played by Irving's wife Edith in the affair). De Hory, Irving and Welles comment on the fallibility of art 'experts', and the market for fakes that this establishment creates. Some of the mysteries of the Hughes legend are exposed and after talking of his own early career in fakery (pretending to be a Broadway star at age sixteen; his *War of the Worlds* broadcast), Welles indicates where his own path crossed Hughes' (the latter was originally to be the subject of the film that became *Citizen Kane*). Welles meditates on the anonymous masterpiece of Chartres, then finally tells Oja's story. After a summer encounter with Pablo Picasso, Oja carried away twenty-two canvasses Picasso had painted of her; enraged when an unauthorized exhibition of his work subsequently opened in Paris, Picasso arrived there to discover not his original but twenty-two fakes, painted by Oja's grandfather, the world's greatest unsung forger, who had burned Picasso's originals. Welles concludes by announcing that his promise to tell the truth for an hour expired some seventeen minutes ago.
   Although it scarcely looks comparable to anything else in his career,

this quixotic essay in fictional documentary – conjured, it seems, out of nothing more substantial than an extraordinary dexterity at the editing table – may be Welles' most concerted, complete and certainly his wittiest attempt to exorcize the ghosts of *Kane*, Rosebud and his own 'failed' genius. A personal meditation on the art of fakery, and the fakery in art, *F for Fake* switches subjects and styles even faster than its ubiquitous presenter/narrator/director switches hats. But what unites the presences of master art-forger Elmyr de Hory, biographer and tyro faker Clifford Irving, and the Hungarian actress Oja Kodar – as well as a host of more putative personages, such as Picasso and Oja's own master-forger grandfather – is the domineering absence of Welles, since what his film proposes is that fiction-making in any form is a lie and a puzzle and a constantly repeated disappearing act for its creator. The 'key' is in the opening sequence, where Welles as a becloaked 'charlatan' takes such an object from a small boy, first to make it vanish and then to transform it into a coin. 'As for the key,' he concludes, 'it is not symbolic of anything. This isn't that kind of movie.' So, exit Rosebud; or fades, at least, into its rightful place in the pattern. In the words of the investigative journalist for *News on the March*: 'It wouldn't have explained anything . . . I guess Rosebud is just a piece in a jigsaw puzzle – a missing piece.' *F for Fake*, thus, is a puzzle fiendishly constructed to frustrate any single attempt to unlock it, or even to identify one ultimate and all-determining creator for the myriad of pieces that have gone into its making – despite the very recognizable flourishes with which Welles wraps himself in the cloak of his own montage, even doodling a signature at one point on the screen of a movieola. The origin of the film was apparently a 16mm essay on Elmyr de Hory, shot by François Reichenbach for a French TV series on forgers, from which Welles requested some footage for a separate programme he was putting together. With the amazing doubling (and punning) on the subject matter that occurred with the disclosures about the fake Howard Hughes manuscript put out by Clifford Irving, a different film evidently began to emerge from Welles' mind. Internal evidence suggests that Welles was already part of the close circle of de Hory, Irving and the 'beautiful people' on Ibiza before the latter scandal broke, and in an interview in *Ecran* with the film's French producer, it is claimed that Welles shot all the footage with Irving. But 'internal' evidence in this context has no great stamp of reliability: a shot of Welles strolling in straw hat and tropical shirt while talking of Ibiza is not proof positive of his presence in that spot, any more than is his shadowed profile briefly edging into an image of Chartres, or the editing effect that puts him outside Howard Hughes' eyrie in Las Vegas. Add to this the unrelated material shot for different purposes which is suddenly related once it emerges from the same hat: the girl-watching episode with Oja, the brief feat of legerdemain with Oja and Laurence Harvey at an airport, and the footage from a science-fiction film with a *War of the Worlds* theme. Given that the irony of these Byzantine permutations is largely directed at those 'experts' in the art world who 'speak to us with the absolute authority of the computer', and who have been extensively taken in by de Hory and Irving, it is hard to avoid the conclusion that Welles has created a maze in which his own commentators might lose themselves. *F for Fake* is truly a 'centreless labyrinth', in which the alleged credit-hogger, accused of doing down Herman Mankiewicz to claim *Citizen Kane* as totally his own creation, parodies the very notion of 'pure' creativity and autonomous (and attributable) authorship. The ribbing of the experts continues, even in those sections which seem like the most reliable autobiography: in a presumed excerpt from the original broadcast of *The War of the Worlds*, the commentator corrects himself on the invaders from outer space: 'Sorry, folks, that's what the experts are saying . . . they're Martians'; and a 'real' newsreel of Howard Hughes being given a tumultuous reception in New York is preceded by the *News on the March* insignia from *Kane*, before twisting itself into parody again as the newsreader refers to the opinion of 'commentators' on the subject of ticker-tape. 'The fake is as old as the Eden tree,' intones Welles; and clearly, in answer to the critics who have deduced the dissipation of his own genius from the undisguised element of sham in his work, he holds up men like de Hory and Irving as his ideal of the creator – jesters at the court of art, who have demonstrated that the practitioners are not entirely their own men, nor are their works definitively tested by the names attached to them. 'Maybe a man's name doesn't matter all that much,' muses Welles before the anonymous splendour of Chartres; 'The most important distinction when you're talking about a painting is not whether it's genuine or a fake, but whether it's a good fake or a bad fake,' says Irving of de Hory. 'If they hang there long enough they become real,' says de Hory of his many forgeries in the world's best galleries. Even more than the 'experts', finally, the authority at whom this splendid piece of trickery is aimed is the one Welles has been teasing and deceiving from first (*The Hearts of*

Age) to last (*The Immortal Story*). 'We are going to die,' he apostrophizes before Chartres; and at the end, more playfully and pertinently, while performing a bit of levitation and quoting Picasso to the effect that, 'Art is a lie, a lie that makes us realize the truth', he defines how little that truth has to do with the things we think of as real. 'Reality – it's the toothbrush waiting for you in a glass at home . . . a bus ticket . . . and the grave.'

Source: *Monthly Film Bulletin*, January 1976.

Marcel Ophüls
IAN BURUMA

'If you spend your life running after the public, all you will see is its ass'
– Marcel Ophüls

Marcel Ophüls is the son of Max Ophüls. Like Jew Süss,[1] Max Ophüls was originally named Oppenheimer. He was born in Germany, became a French citizen in 1938, moved to Hollywood (where Marcel went to school with Marilyn Monroe), returned to France, and made superb movies such as *La Ronde, The Earrings of Madame De . . .* and *Lola Montès*. He died in 1957.

It cannot be easy to be Marcel, the son of Max. In the beginning of his latest film, a documentary about the press coverage of Sarajevo, Marcel sits in a train bound for Munich. The French conductor inspects his ticket and says, 'Mmm, Ophüls, a famous name.' Ophüls tells him it must be his father he has in mind. On another occasion, Marcel was invited to a film festival in some distant country. A disagreement about money caused a row between him and the organizer of the festival. The organizer turned his back, and murmured: 'Ah yes, Ophüls, the real one, what a director!' Whereupon Marcel said: 'My friend, between his genius and your insignificance, there must be room for my talent.'

I think he was too modest. *The Sorrow and the Pity* (1969) changed the art of documentary film-making. Instead of the usual mixture of

---

1 Jew Süss was the eponymous hero of a satirical novel about the pointlessness of race distinctions, by the German-Jewish writer Lion Feuchtwanger, published in 1925. The notorious 1940 Nazi propaganda film of the same title was a deliberate travesty of Feuchtwanger's original.

documentary footage and the narrator's voice, Ophüls offers history as a set of often conflicting eyewitness accounts. He turns the talking head into an art form. And yet sometimes it is as though Marcel feels a little ashamed of making documentaries instead of feature films. His father did not take documentary cinema seriously as an art. And Marcel has written about his inner voice, which is always wondering whether 'I am seeking refuge in grand and noble documentary projects, out of fear that I lack the imagination to express things closer to home.' This voice, Marcel thinks, sounds oddly like 'papa's'. Papa's voice is much in evidence in *The Troubles We've Seen* (1995), whose reception at international film festivals has been mixed to say the least.

In fact, Marcel Ophüls has made a few feature films, including one with Jean-Paul Belmondo and one with Eddy Constantine, the star of French detective films. The flop of the latter led producers – if not Ophüls himself – to the conclusion that his talents lay elsewhere. As a result Ophüls carried the legacy of papa, like a box of family jewels, to his documentary films. This is one of the things that give his movies such a distinctive flavour. He renders homage to his father's work, not just by larding his documentaries with visual quotations from Max's movies, but by displaying the same spirit. It is a humorous, irreverent spirit, akin to that of Arthur Schnitzler, Billy Wilder, or Ernst Lubitsch, the wry humour of a clown dancing on the brink of catastrophe. As they used to say in Vienna: the situation is desperate, but not serious. Marcel Ophüls is the survivor of a cultural tradition that is virtually extinct, except, possibly, in pockets of New York.

You hear it in his voice, especially when he speaks German, in the ironic, slightly mocking manner of pre-war Berlin. You see it in the way he interviews people, often very unpleasant people: his head cocked, chin in his hand, his mouth curled in a sceptical smile, his eyes watchful, unwilling to believe anything at first sight. In *Hotel Terminus* (1988), about the trial of Klaus Barbie, the former Gestapo chief in Lyons, Ophüls interviews a former Waffen SS officer, who remembers Barbie as 'a fantastic guy'. The officer mentions his mother-in-law, whom he calls 'the finest horse in the stable'. After a short pause, Ophüls slowly repeats the phrase: 'The finest horse in the stable . . .' His tone is one of amused but also horrified wonder.

Ophüls's voice, questioning a recalcitrant French collaborator, a German neo-Nazi, a former communist official, a Latin American torturer, or a warmonger in Belgrade, reminds me of an essay by George Steiner, entitled 'A kind of survivor'. Steiner tries to define the particular role played by secular Jewish intellectuals before the war, as critics of romantic nationalism and other dangerous pieties. 'In its golden period,' he writes, 'from 1870 to 1914, then again in the 1920s, the Jewish leaven gave to Prague and Berlin, to Vienna and Paris a specific vitality of feeling and expression, an atmosphere both quintessentially European and "off-centre".' The nuance of spirit is delicately mocked and made memorable in the unquiet hedonism, in the erudite urbanity of Proust's Swann.

Marcel Ophüls was born in Germany in 1927. He holds two passports, US and French. He has lived and worked in Germany, France and the US. He lives in Paris, but describes his position in France as that of an outcast, a man on the margins, a 'wandering Jew'. Always on the move, he is the man who proves – to quote a well-known phrase, invoked by Steiner – that 'whereas trees have roots, men have legs and are each other's guests.' There is a moment in most of his films when his Jewish background is declared, usually to a ferocious anti-Semite. 'I had thought as much,' says the German neo-Nazi, interviewed in *November Days* (1990), a film about the fall of the Berlin wall. 'You fit the stereotype: your facility with languages, your diplomatic manner, your friendliness . . .' 'Oily friendliness?' asks Ophüls. 'Oh, no,' says that blackshirt, ever so politely, 'I wouldn't go that far.'

Far from being oily, Ophüls is the man in the rumpled raincoat who asks questions most of us would be too shy to ask. This is why Ophüls was the perfect Frenchman to make *The Sorrow and the Pity*. His approach to the carefully contrived mythology of the post-war French Republic was distinctly 'off-centre'. Ophüls himself has described his film as a 'love-song' to France. If so, it was a devastating love-song, which was not allowed to be shown on French television until 1981. It didn't suit the vision of France stage-managed by General de Gaulle, who, in his own mind at least, was the centre.

De Gaulle had united a demoralized France by creating a myth of universal and unified resistance to Nazi Germany. Eternal France was symbolized by De Gaulle himself and the resistance hero, Jean Moulin. The worship of Marshal Pétain, the French volunteers for the SS, the active participation of the French police in persecuting Jews, the role of the Communists in the Resistance and in the bloody post-war purges, these were matters better left alone: 'The past is finished,' declared De Gaulle in 1959, in Vichy. 'Long live Vichy! Long Live France! Long live the Republic!'

To be sure there are heroes in *The Sorrow and the Pity*. The farmer, for example, who fought in the Resistance since 1941, and was jailed in Buchenwald. Or Denis Rake, the British agent, who wanted to prove that a homosexual could be brave. Or Pierre Mendés-France. Or Colonel Gaspard, the Resistance leader. These are all splendid characters. But what sticks in the mind is the farmer's remark: '*On nous prenait pour des cons*' – 'People thought we were fools.' Like people everywhere else, most of them just tried to stay out of trouble. The Gaullist myth of a united France is vulnerable, not because the film is a cinematic '*J'accuse*', but because Ophüls shows that every person has his or her own version of history, that all memories play tricks, and that there was no question of French unity in adversity.

The Sorrow and the Pity is not a history lesson, but a film about memories. Its originality lies in the way Ophüls probes the past, and allows others to do so. He lets people talk, sometimes cutting from face to face, to show us how they contradict one another. He illustrates the words with film clips and music. Voice-over commentary is kept to a minimum. He uses music and images as ironic and sometimes affectionate comments. Nothing is so evocative, so nostalgic-making as a popular song. Many will remember *The Sorrow and The Pity* for Maurice Chevalier, whose war record, like that of many of his compatriots, was one of making do, turning a blind eye, and obeying the authorities whatever uniform they wore at the time. The movie ends with Chevalier, just after the war, sitting behind a piano, telling the victorious allies that 'your old friend Maurice Chevalier' had done nothing wrong. Then he sings, in English:

I don't care what's down below,
Let it rain, let it snow.
I'll be up on a rainbow,
Sweeping the clouds away . . .

It might be called an ironic love-song to France.

Ophüls once said in an interview that he made *The Sorrow and The Pity* because he was asked to. 'If somebody had told me that I could make a movie with Fred Astaire instead, there's no doubt about what I would have chosen.' He has also called the film 'optimistic, even a bit naïve.' As time and his career went on, his view of the world darkened. The curious thing is that the more pessimistic he became, the more love letters to Fred Astaire, Bing Crosby, Lubitsch, Wilder, and Max Ophüls appeared in his films. He also became more of a movie character himself, with more funny hats, and more play-acting in front of the camera. His personal despair – that nagging inner voice, telling him fiction is a higher art – and his attitude to the state of the world have a way of coming together. This is the strength but also, occasionally, the weakness of his work.

Ophüls uses fiction to explore non-fiction, which is not the same thing as telling lies. He is not like Oliver Stone, who uses non-fiction to make fiction look like the truth. In the *Rashomon* world of Ophüls' documentaries, Lubitsch's *To Be Or Not To Be* is truer, or at least truer to itself, than the speech of a politician, or the 'stories' on television news-shows. By confronting his non-fiction with the fiction, or at least the spirit, of his beloved directors, it is sometimes as though history were on trial, judged by Lubitsch, Wilder, and papa.

He has pushed this confrontation further and further, especially in the two films he made since *Hotel Terminus*. His idiosyncratic approach has caused legendary rows with producers. Ophüls has never been an easy man to work with. His films are long, expensive, and take time to make. But he has never insulted the intelligence of his audience. He despises producers who think they know what the public wants. He has always stuck to his vision.

In *Hotel Terminus*, he appears as a kind of detective, trying to make sense of a packet of lies, evasions and distortions, a role he has compared to that of Inspector Columbo, the Peter Falk character. In the Klaus Barbie story, he finds that almost everyone has something to hide: the former US intelligence agents who recruited the ex-Gestapo chief after the war, the Colombian officials who used him as a torture instructor, his former colleagues in the SS, Frenchmen caught up in Resistance politics, lawyers with axes to grind, and so on and so on. At one point, looking for a former SS man in a bleak German suburb, Ophüls is so exasperated that he searches through trash cans, calling out the names of his elusive prey.

Despite its length and its digressions, *Hotel Terminus* is a brilliant film, which deserved its Oscar. Barbie's trial is the occasion for a complex meditation about exile, nationhood, nostalgia, morality and politics. The use of German folksongs, sung by the Wiener Sängerknaben, adds a grotesque poignancy to the main charge against Barbie: the deportation of small Jewish children to Auschwitz. (He probably tortured Jean Moulin to death, too, but killing a member of the Resistance does not qualify as genocide, on which there is no time-limit for prosecution.) Barbie's wanderings, through Europe and South America, make him seem like a character in an intercontinental road movie. We hear Barbie speak Spanish, French and German. Like Ophüls, sleuthing in his footsteps, he is forever travelling. 'His is the diaspora of the torturers,' said Ophüls, 'mine is the other one.'

Then there is the trial itself. Jacques Vergès, Barbie's half-Vietnamese lawyer, tried to turn it into a multicultural show trial against French colonialism by asking Arab and African witnesses to state in Barbie's defence that French policemen had been as bad as the SS. Finally, there is the unforgettable ending of the film, when a Jewish woman returns to her childhood home, which can never be home again. It is the house where she was arrested with her parents by Barbie's police. She is a small woman: 'I forgot to grow at Auschwitz.' In the house, she meets a former neighbour who looked the other way when the SS men called. There had been another person living in the house, who had tried to rescue the girl. The film is dedicated to her, the good neighbour.

In the next film, *November Days*, made for BBC television, the mixture of document and fiction is taken several steps further. The fall of the Berlin Wall, in 1989, offered the opportunity to probe into the myths, lies and horrors of the German Democratic Republic, while the memories were still fresh. But Ophüls is not content just to listen to former party bosses, Communist writers, dissidents, and ordinary people caught up in the events. He complements their stories with clips from his favourite movies; he sings songs; he cuts away from a lying politician to a shot of a squawking parrot. When everything converges – Ophüls's personal life, his love for papa, the politics of the past, his humanism – the mixture works quite beautifully. He succeeds in putting on film a kind of stream of consciousness, in which one image or thought evokes another.

In an extraordinary scene, Ophüls interviews the former spy chief, Markus Wolf. Wolf, who headed one of the most ruthless operations behind the Iron Curtain, is charming, articulate, and utterly cynical.

Like Ophüls, he is from a German Jewish family. His father was an intellectual, who fled with his family to Moscow, to escape the Nazis. As we hear Wolf describe himself as a sweet, trusting man, too good for this world, we see Ophüls sunk in thought. An old film tune starts up, and we see photographs of Max Ophüls directing movies in Hollywood. And Marcel says to Markus: 'I cannot help thinking to myself: Marcel, how lucky you were. Our fathers had the same ideas in the 1920s and the 1930s. Who was not on the Left in the Weimar Republic? But how lucky I was that the film director Max Ophüls emigrated West, instead of East.' As in the case of Barbie's diaspora, Ophüls draws a parallel between his own life and Wolf's. In the same scene, Ophüls has inserted cuts from Lubitsch's film, *To Be Or Not To Be*, which is all about a man and his double. It sounds bizarre, it is a bit bizarre, but it all makes sense.

Ophüls's mélange of show and document works because *November Days*, like most of his films, is about the past, about memories, lies, stories. It is about the ways history is transformed into fiction. In his latest film, *The Troubles We've Seen*, he applies the same technique to events still taking place: the siege of Sarajevo. Of course the siege itself is not fiction but Ophüls sees the way it comes across on television as 'reality show', squeezed in between soft drink commercials and the sports results. In this movie there are more Hollywood quotations, and more clowning, than ever. It is also Ophüls's darkest film, and the one that has been most criticized.

Departing for Zagreb from the Gare de L'Est, Ophuls speaks into the camera, telling the audience that he will start the film 'like my friend Woody Allen'. We see him missing the Orient Express, rushing absurdly across the station like Monsieur Hulot. On the next train to Munich, his comments on Hitler, ethnic cleansing, and the war in Bosnia are mixed with references to the Marx Brothers. Somewhere along the way – in Vienna, or Zagreb? – Ophüls puts on a funny hat, 'like Fellini', and continues his journey towards the action in the Sarajevo Holiday Inn, which reminds him of the movie, with Bing Crosby singing Irving Berlin: 'If you're burdened down with troubles/If your nerves are wearing thin/Pack your load/Down the road/And come to the Holiday Inn . . .'

This is typical of Ophüls, but there is more showbiz to come. At the end of the first part of the movie, Ophüls has returned from the war zone, and exchanged the rigors of the Sarajevo Holiday Inn for a comfortable hotel room in Vienna. He calls his producer in Paris on the telephone. While he is talking, we see a naked call girl lying on his bed, waiting for his attention. Like the scenes of Ophüls in his Fellini hat, taking a break at the Venice Carnival, the naked girl in Vienna is caprice, a fantasy, a flight from reality. Ophüls is clowning, as he did when he looked for the old Nazi in those suburban German dustbins.

Joris Ivens, the famous Dutch film-maker, who expressed his lifelong enthusiasm for communist dictatorships in documentary movies, once gave a lecture in Peking. He was asked whether it was permissible to make things up in non-fiction movies. Ivens said it was, but only if the audience wouldn't notice. He likened these 'reconstructions' to 'theft for a good cause'. The difference between Ophüls and Ivens is the difference between a propagandist and an artist. Ophüls never hides his inventions. The naked girl is an invention, or, in Ivens's weasel phrase, a reconstruction. The idea was to show the lust for life, and comfort, and sex, after being exposed to violence, deprivation and death.

Sarajevo has made Ophüls more pessimistic than ever; the Bosnians for him are victims of a second Holocaust. The Serbian aggressors are presented as villains, whose grotesque provenance fits oddly well into Ophüls' theatrical presentation: a Serb Shakespeare scholar bombarding his own city, a poet and psychology professor, Karadzic himself, committing genocide. There is no complexity in Ophüls' view of the Bosnian conflict. The bad guys are very bad, the good guys are very innocent. The complexity of the Ophüls film lies not in the war itself, but in the way it is covered.

We see the carnage nightly on our television screens, yet the public, blunted and dazed by pop culture and the superficial and sensationalist style of TV reporting, is indifferent. Or so Ophüls believes. He is also disgusted by western politicians, especially John Major and François Mitterand, who refuse to intervene. There are still devoted reporters at the Holiday Inn who care about the truth, such as John Burns of the *New York Times*, but their message fails to get through. As Philippe Noiret, the French actor, remarks at the beginning of the film, even if they could have shown Auschwitz on television, it wouldn't have made any difference.

Ophüls sees something similar in John Burns and his fellow newspaper reporters, who still take their jobs seriously, and the best Hollywood craftsmen of his father's generation: they are true to their *métier*, they still have values, and refuse to pander to the lowest tastes of a mass audience. Ophüls presents Burns as a heroic survivor of a dying culture. Ophüls: 'I think the culture of television and rock are to a large extent responsible for the tragedy of Sarajevo.' The way Ophüls has chosen to fight back is to let Burns talk, to sing Irving Berlin songs, to enjoy Venice, and to show the films of Wilder, Lubitsch, and papa. In Sarajevo, he says, 'you discover death, but also that life is beautiful, and that we must fight to preserve it.' We must dance on the brink of catastrophe.

To project such a view onto the events in Sarajevo is bold, but, in my opinion, misguided. I can sympathize with Ophüls, who says that the more pessimistic he becomes, 'the more I want to make fun of myself, to avoid becoming cynical'. But if that was his aim, his imagination has failed him. He wanted 'to be playful, in the most serious way'. He wanted 'to play with cinema, to play with reality, not by making a reality show, but by coming out against the reality show'. But it is one thing to do as his father did and make sophisticated and entertaining movies in a spirit of defiance of the Nazi menace. It is another to walk about in funny hats, sing songs, and fool around with nude models, with a human disaster as a kind of backdrop. The effect is to trivialize the war in Bosnia, which can't have been Ophüls' intention. What works when dealing with memories does not work nearly so well when the killing is still going on.

Ophüls says he is 'less and less interested in content. If I have made a contribution to documentary film, it is by trying to give it narrative structures.' He is right, but Ophüls has always been more than an aesthete. He has brought to film-making a great humanist sensibility. Yet it is as though he wants to rebel against his image as 'a knight of virtue'. He also wants to be a great clown, a fine ambition, but not in Sarajevo, not now. His own agonized struggle with cinematic form – that inner voice again – has caused him to look at the war from a skewed aesthetic angle. Television and rock culture are not responsible for the tragedy of Sarajevo. People do not care less about the victims of today's conflicts than people did in the age of Bing Crosby and Billy Wilder. The cynicism of television news producers is not the reason why Major and Mitterand refuse to intervene with military force. There are political reasons for that, which may be wrong, even ignoble, but have very little to do with popular culture.

Nor is it true that conscientious reporting, of the kind exemplified by John Burns, or even shoddy journalism of the 'reality show' variety, makes no difference. In Somalia, Haiti, let alone Vietnam (think of Cronkite after the Tet offensive), journalism has certainly had an impact. The question is whether the impact is always good. Public emotions do not necessarily result in sensible policies. Nor are even the best reporters necessarily right. No matter how hard a reporter tries to winkle out the truth, his job is still one of interpretation, selection, telling a story. Indeed some of the most interesting scenes in Ophüls' movie concern that elusive border between fact and fiction.

There are many good things in his long, maddening, never boring film. Ophüls is still a brilliant interviewer. There are some wonderful lines, like the one from a French woman journalist who says that women don't like being on camera in war reports, whereas men are always 'fussing about their make-up'. We learn a great deal about the reporter's trade. We also get some heartbreaking glimpses of the suffering in Bosnia, as Ophüls follows camera teams, photographers, and newspaper reporters around. But sometimes Ophüls' own performance robs other characters of their dignity. This is true, I think, of the ending of the film. Ophüls and John Burns visit a Bosnian surgeon who has been operating on wounded people, without oxygen, without proper drugs, without electricity, often even without light – he has to use battery torches. The man is mentally and physically exhausted. He cannot express his horror in words, so Burns and Ophüls ask him to sing a song. In a tired, broken voice he sings: 'Nobody knows the troubles I've seen.' If only Ophüls had left it at that. But then he cuts to a picture of himself, singing the same song, wearing a mask at the Venice carnival.

The film is flawed, not because of timidity, or stupidity, or bad intentions, but because Ophüls has misdirected his private demons. Perhaps he should listen a little less to that inner voice which tells him to be more like Wilder, or Lubitsch, or Groucho Marx, or papa. It is more than enough to be Marcel Ophüls.

Source: An unpublished article commissioned in 1995 by the *New York Review of Books*.

Phantom India
LOUIS MALLE

At the age of twenty Louis Malle (1932–1996) left France's IDHEC film school to work with Jacques Cousteau on *Le Monde du Silence* (1956), a feature documentary about underwater exploration. Although the rest of his career was largely spent in the world of fiction, Malle returned intermittently to documentary, most notably with the seven-part series *L'Inde Fantome* (*Phantom India*, 1969), a highly personal response to the culture of the subcontinent.

The BBC recently recut the original footage into a single ninety-minute film.

This interview is from *Malle on Malle*, edited by Philip French.

LOUIS MALLE: In the autumn of 1967 I was asked by the French Ministry of Foreign Affairs to present in India a series of eight French films, including *Le Feu follet* – films more or less representative of the new French cinema. And I said yes. So I went to Delhi and Calcutta and Madras and Bombay presenting those films. I was supposed to stay two weeks but I ended up staying almost two months. I was so amazed by India – it was my first trip, but I had always been interested in Indian religions. I knew India would be a shock, but it was much more so than I expected. After those two months I realized that although India was impossible to understand for a foreigner – it was so opaque – yet I was so completely fascinated by it that I would have to come back. So I returned to France at the end of 1967, and in a couple of weeks I raised the money I needed, which was almost nothing, and went back in early January with two friends of mine – a cameraman and a sound man. My proposition was that we would start in Calcutta, look around and eventually shoot. No plans, no script, no lighting equipment, no distribution commitments of any kind . . . At this moment of crisis in my life, when I was trying to re-evaluate everything I had taken for granted so far, India was the perfect *tabula rasa*: it was just like starting from scratch.

So I decided to immerse myself in India, the real India, not the westernized one, and see what would happen – and do it with a camera. The result was like being brainwashed. When I came back,I said, 'After six months in India you're not even quite sure that two plus two is four.' Everything in India – their way of life, relationships, family structure, spiritual needs – is so opposed to what we in the West are used to and take for granted, that living there constantly provokes your mind, and your heart. So, instead of wasting my time trying to understand, I decided that we would just drift around India and let things happen. The climax of our trip was the two months we spent in South India. Nobody in Paris or Delhi knew where we were. We had a van and a driver who could speak the five languages that you have to speak in South India to find your way around. From Madras we started drifting from temple to temple, from village to village. Little by little, we acquired a different perception of time. For the first time in my life I found some kind of peace. I started letting go. I felt incredibly well in this environment, which was unknown to me and so different. There was something about the relationship of Indians to nature that I felt was so organic and so true. Of course, I knew there was no way one could become Indian or Hindu – that's ridiculous. A lot of westerners were trying to do that in those years . . . I never felt I would ever belong there, but as an observer I was fascinated. It was a permanent challenge to a lot of preconceived ideas that I had accumulated since childhood.

PHILIP FRENCH: *Also preconceived ideas you had about documentary. The major change from ten, twelve years before, between working with Cousteau on* Le Monde du Silence *and this, is the change both of the available equipment and also of the perception of what a documentary is through* cinéma vérité, *the way it is presented, the relationship between the film-maker and his subject matter and the people he observes.* L'Inde Fantome *begins the series with an essay, as it were, about documentary, or* La Caméra Impossible.

LM: The first two months I was in India alone. I had a 16mm camera with me, but I shot very little. And I had no sound. I went back with the skeleton of a crew, three of us . . . During those four months of shooting I had not the faintest idea what I was going to do with the material. I thought vaguely that at best I could make a feature-length, hour-and-a-half documentary about 'my trip to India'. But very quickly I forgot about that; we just kept filming when it seemed necessary or pleasurable or interesting. When I was shooting I was never thinking, 'Well where is it going to come, how does it relate to something I did yesterday?' No, we were just shooting at random.

When I first discussed my plans with Étienne and Jean-Claude [the cameraman and sound man respectively], I said, 'I just want to immerse myself in India, be there, and eventually shoot.' For about two weeks, before we went to Calcutta, we stayed in a village about 100 miles north of Delhi. I thought it was important to start in a village, because it is still the essential Indian social structure. After a couple of days, Étienne Becker rebelled. He said, 'I don't understand what you want, Louis. I cannot work that way. Tell me what you want.' I said, 'I don't know what I want.' And then we started shooting scenes in the village, around the wells. We found out that the wells defined the caste system, in the sense that women from the same caste or sub-caste always went to the same wells – I'd found the invisible borders of the Indian social system.

And Étienne said, 'But they're all looking at me, it's not right, tell them not to look.' I said, 'Why should I tell them not to look at us since we're intruders. First, I don't speak their language; just a few of them speak a little English. We're the intruders, disturbing them. They don't know what we're doing, so it's perfectly normal that they look at us. To tell them not to look at us, it's the beginning of *mise-en-scène*.' It's what I resent about so many documentaries where film-makers arrive from somewhere and start by telling the people, 'Pretend we are not here.' It is the basic lie of most documentaries, this naïve *mise-en-scène*, the beginning of distortion of the truth. Very quickly I realized that these looks at the camera were both disturbing and true, and we should never pretend we weren't intruders. So we kept working that way.

Then we went to Calcutta, and filming in Calcutta was very difficult. We were shooting in the streets, and sometimes twice a day we would be arrested because they would think we were Pakistani spies! There was a lot of tension in Calcutta about the neighbouring state, with what has become Bangladesh but then was Eastern Pakistan. Because there were border incidents, people were suspicious and so we always ran into trouble. Or else middle-class Indians would come to us and say, 'You're shooting in the street; of course you're westerners and you want to shoot the poverty in India.' Well, if you shoot in the street in Calcutta, every morning you do find people lying on the ground and they're dead; they died during the night.

The first few days we were walking around with cameras it took us a while to find – I don't know – the innocence, I suppose; to deal with the reality as it was, and not try to distort it or interpret it, but just be there, and film it. Little by little it became a way of life. And my two friends started enjoying it. I'm not saying it became a method, because it never was in any way systematic. But we would go into temples and we would shoot or we would not shoot – sometimes they didn't want us to shoot and then we would not. Or we would be in a religious festival, and there was something about it that pushed us to film. Some times we would film a lot of footage in a matter of hours, and then we would not work for several days. It was completely improvised. We were sort of witnesses, but we never pretended that we were part of it or even understood it. Very quickly we felt very good about being there; we thought it was really doing something to us. We could have continued filming for ever. There was no reason to stop. It's just that at a certain point – it was the beginning of the hot season and we were physically exhausted – we decided to stop.

I was not sure I wanted to go back to France. I stayed one week after my two friends left, and I thought of going back to France to look at the footage, because I had not seen one foot of what we had shot, which was also part of the experience. We had shot something like thirty hours of film. I wanted to look at it, and then eventually return to India. What happened was, I came back and it was the beginning of May 1968. The whole of France was on strike, including the film labs, so I had to wait for weeks before I could start looking at the footage with Suzanne Baron, my editor. It took us through the month of July. And we didn't know what to do with it. Suzanne suggested that we start trying to put together all the Calcutta footage. We'd shot it in three weeks, and at least it was all Calcutta. So we edited Calcutta into a feature documentary. We'd shot in 16mm, we blew it up to 35mm, and it was released theatrically in 1969.

As far as the rest of the footage was concerned, my attitude was that if I wanted to be completely honest with the material, what I had shot had to be shown. If I cut out a lot of stuff for this reason or that reason in the editing process, I would be abiding by conventional rules, and trying to build an artificial rhythm that was not the rhythm of the experience we had in India. Of course, out of the thirty hours, ten to fifteen hours, say, were repetitious, or something that we'd started and given up on, or the material was really not interesting. So we selected and came up with about half of what I had shot, and we started from that. After we'd made Calcutta, which was an hour and forty minutes, we decided to do a series, which of course was meant for television, because it was too long for the cinema. And we tried vaguely to structure it as a series of six (which eventually became seven) films. I had made an agreement with French television, and the standard length in those days was a little under an hour – fifty-two minutes or something like that. So I ended up editing more than eight hours out of my thirty hours of rushes, so the ratio was about three to one, which is very unusual in documentaries; it's sometimes a hundred to one, or at best ten to one.

I thought it was also part of the experience that we would more or less follow our itinerary – not our geographic itinerary – it would have been a simple travelogue – but the itinerary of our emotions. In the narration I kept constantly coming back to the fact that I had not understood a thing about India. Each time I thought I'd understood something I was proved wrong. A good example was a religious ceremony in a little temple near a village, and after the ceremony the faithful were giving money and food to the beggars. But when I talked to them afterwards I realized those beggars were not really beggars, they were Brahmins. They were members of the higher caste, the priest caste, and were, by Indian standards, quite well off, but it was part of the ritual to give money and food to the Brahmins.

We westerners thought we were filming beggars and actually it was something else. It was typical of what always happened to us in India; we thought we were filming a reality and behind this reality there was another one. The truth was always more complicated and devious. So, I never pretended, 'This is eight hours of India, I am going to explain it to you' – I did exactly the opposite.

PF: *But two premises are established, one by implication, one directly, in the first film. First, you're not much concerned with the British legacy, though where that does come up, it's handled very critically. The other is that, after an opening montage of highly articulate Indian intellectuals, you reject the idea of India being mediated to you by westernized Indians. Were they conscious decisions, or was that something that came out in the way you presented the material?*

LM: It was a conscious decision because I realized very early that there were two vastly different Indias. There was this élite: Anglicized middle class by definition – people who would speak English, many of them would send their children to schools in England or to universities there. These Indians – although they came from different castes – were the ruling class, the politicians, the bureaucrats, the people on top of the economy. What these people had to say was very ambiguous and somewhat insincere because they were caught between two cultures. What I immediately noticed was that they were extremely uncomfortable. Many of them, not all of them fortunately, but many of them, were aggressive or very dubious and sometimes made fun of what we were trying to do: 'You're going to come up with these stereotypes again. It's always the same story when westerners come to India, they just don't get it.' Which, of course, was true. But I realized that if I wanted to see the real India, then these people were not the people that I should be dealing with . . .

The interesting aspect of those documentaries for me was that I took one month just to examine the material, and then stayed in the cutting room for a year, until the end of 1969 practically. I was in Paris, I was going to the editing room every day and it was as if I was still in India. It was the continuation of my trip. Just looking at my images and remembering what happened, I discovered certain contradictions that I had not even noticed. I had a couple of Indian friends in Paris and I would show them a scene and they would give me their explanation. Sometimes two different friends would give me two different explanations – India, it's so complicated! So I was deepening my experience of India by just watching what I had shot, and trying to make sense of it. I can almost say that I spent six months in India, plus one year in the cutting room, so it's like almost two years of my life, completely immersed in India. Plus the fact that after that I had to present the films and talk about them, and I was involved in this controversy. It's been like a big chunk of my life. It was enormously important for me, and I'm still trying to make sense of it today.

PF: *There were different levels of response; there are, for example, sections which I think may have proved later to be controversial politically – the authoritative account of the situation of the Untouchables; the sections about the problems of tribal minorities and their treatment. There is another area, entirely personal, examining your own reaction. But there was a third area, which is a great problem in this kind of film, where you find and present things which may or may not be metaphors or representative, but because of their great power they are often the most impressive parts of the film. In this latter category there's the unforgettable scene of a dead buffalo being picked over by dogs and vultures, and you say, 'We see this as a tragedy in a number of acts.' Now, when you filmed this – it seemed to have some meaning which you later came to understand or could have interpreted in quite different ways, but it must have been just visually very striking at the time.*

LM: This is a very good example of our *démarche*, of how we proceeded. In India you know they don't kill animals, cows or buffaloes, because they are sacred – well, it's more complicated than that.

But, anyway, if you drive on Indian roads it's almost routine to see a dead cow or a dead buffalo on the side of the road and hundreds of vultures. I told my two friends, 'At some point we have to film it.' And it just happened that one day we stopped and we spent half an hour just filming what we'd seen many times before.

PF: *There's a savage beauty about it.*

LM: Of course, for us it was incredibly striking. My reaction was that what struck us would probably not strike Indians. It seems incredibly dramatic for us when for the Indians it is just the cycle of life and death – animals die and the vultures eat them. Everything is part of a whole. You see it in all aspects of life. So it's not so noticeable. But for us it was very striking because of the savage and dramatic beauty of it. Or was it our imagination? Was it the way we shot it? I don't know. For me as a film-maker it was an extraordinarily liberating experience shooting these documentaries. *Le Monde du Silence* was a very prepared kind of documentary. I don't want to say rehearsed, because there were real accidents like the death of the whale and the sharks, but essentially it was reconstituted documentary. When I was shooting in India, what I discovered was the incredible freedom of being there and finding myself in front of something happening that I was curious about and shooting it. And then we would try to understand what we had shot. We had no time to organize the shooting, or decide whether we would choose this angle rather than that, or how we were eventually going to structure the scene in the editing – this was a moment when I worked completely by instinct, by reflex. One of the interesting aspects of this editing period was for me to look at the material and say, 'Why did I shoot it that way?' The only thing I might do was to tell Étienne, 'To your left, the little girl to your left,' and he would pan to her – he's a remarkable cameraman.

I think this experience of relying on my instincts was quite decisive in my work. When I went back to fiction, I've always been unconsciously, and also very consciously, trying to reinvent those very privileged moments. I've always tried to rediscover the state of innocence that I found so extraordinary working in India. Of course, it doesn't always work that way, but since then I have made a number of films with children and adolescents, and have always tried to give them the freedom of expressing themselves, trying to let them loose, rather than trying to boss them around – seizing those moments when they were free, when they were themselves – for these privileged moments will always bring to the screen something completely different. I was able to accomplish that when I did documentaries in the following years. But even in my fiction work I think I've been enormously influenced by what I discovered in India.

Source: *Malle on Malle* edited by Philip French, Faber and Faber, London, 1993.

Chris Marker and *Sans Soleil*
TERRENCE RAFFERTY

Chris Marker (born 1921), the maker of *Letter From Siberia* (1958), *Cuba Si!* (1961), *Le Joli Mai* (1963), *The Koumiko Mystery* (1965), *Sans Soleil* (1982) and *The Last Bolshevik* (1993), amongst many others, is a true cinema essayist. As the critic David Thomson points out, his 'work makes no attempt to be cinematic or literary; it is based, instead, on the assumption that a cultivated man should express himself in words or in film.' He has made 'documentaries' (although he would not approve of the term) in a variety of cinematic styles, including *cinema vérité*, but usually makes use of any and every means of expression, including, stills, music, archive and interview and cannot properly be said to belong to any school or grouping. Watching a Marker film is like being engaged in a passionate, fascinating, if at times puzzling, conversation.

An elusive personality, who refuses interviews, Marker served in the Canadian Air Force during the war and fought with the French Resistance. His films are often political, but never dogmatically so. In his most recent work he has embraced video and computer technology, and shot much material on home video.

This essay on *Sans Soleil* first appeared in *Sight and Sound*.

31 Sans Soleil *(1980)*.

Trying to remember Chris Marker's *Sans Soleil* [*Sunless*] after seeing it for the first time, a viewer might recall nothing but how he feels at the end dazed and excited, overwhelmed by a smooth, rapid flow of images and ideas. Or he might recall only vivid, random moments: the face of an African woman and a porcelain cat with one paw raised; an emu on the Ile de France and sleeping passengers on a Japanese train; a carnival in Guinea-Bissau and a volcano erupting in Iceland. And if, as an aide-memoire, he has taken notes as the film unrolled, his impressions will be more concrete, but perhaps more confused. Did he really manage to take in, during the first ten minutes of the film, an epigraph from Eliot's 'Ash Wednesday', a shot of three children on a road in Iceland in 1965, a short sequence on a train in Hokkaido, shots of women on the Bissagos Islands off West Africa, a prayer for the soul of a lost cat in an animal cemetery outside Tokyo, a dog on a deserted beach, a bar in a rundown district of Tokyo? How did he assimilate, at the same time, the lyrical, aphoristic commentary – in the form of letters from a traveller we never see, read by a woman we don't see either – and how did he get his bearings in this no-man's-land of documentary images and oblique fiction? Finally, recalling the vertiginous speed of the film's transitions, he suspects that his notes are incomplete, inaccurate, a distorted memory. He'd have to see the film again.

The creation of the need, and the desire, to see things again is part of the method of *Sans Soleil*, and also, perhaps, its real subject. What Marker means to communicate to us is the solitude of the film editor at his machinery, his reverie over the footage he's shot (or that has been sent to him by friends), the scenes he watches over and over again. He wants to explain why he returns to Japan, the subject of his 1965 film *The Koumiko Mystery*; why the images of the emu, the porcelain cat (called *maniki neko*), the children in Iceland won't go away, why they keep bobbing up in the course of *Sans Soleil*; how it's possible to see *Vertigo* nineteen times; how images are replayed as memories, as obsessions, and as the troubled dreams of travellers.

This film has so many showpieces of montage, under such imaginative and varied pretexts – a visit to San Francisco intercut with scenes from *Vertigo*; a deserted island in the Atlantic where the narrator 'can't believe the images that crop up', shots of Tokyo crowds mixed with the lush Impressionist landscapes of the Ile de France; an imaginary science fiction movie in which images of poverty and desolation are linked by the consciousness of an investigator from the year 4001; a sequence on a Tokyo train in which the sleeping faces of commuters are cut with television images of samurai films, horror movies, erotic entertainment, all attributed to these exhausted travellers as their dreams – so much virtuosity, in fact, that *Sans Soleil* risks being seen as no more than an exercise in the art of editing, a highly conscious miming of the involuntary processes of memory.

In a sense, it is that. But there's something else in Marker's work, something which distances him even from his own models, like Dziga Vertov and Eisenstein. It's in those qualities that aren't easily transcribed as notes: not simply the juxtaposition of shots but the rhythms of their juxtaposition. The sequences in which disparate times and places are made to correspond have the speed and urgency of passionate argument. Other scenes, like a Tokyo festival with dancers whose hands seem to be telling a story we don't quite understand, are rapt and quiet, as if the editor and commentator were simply transfixed. *Sans Soleil* is an editor's film worthy of the Russian masters, but its undulating rhythms – rushing forward, stopping to gaze, following, corresponding across great distances, returning to the same places – are those of a melancholy, obsessed lover.

This tone isn't so difficult to identify, but its source – the real object of this love is more elusive. In Marker's earlier film about Japan the object was a face, the face of Koumiko Muraoka picked out of the crowd at the 1964 Tokyo Olympics. The film-maker follows her, interrogates her in the crowded streets, in the department stores, photographs her in a revolving bar high above Tokyo, the city moving in a slow circle behind her, as if she were merely the focal point of an investigation of Japanese culture. But in the last section of *The Koumiko Mystery*, the focus shifts. The film-maker has gone back to Paris, having left Koumiko a short questionnaire – he receives her answers on tape. The noises of Tokyo, the bits of radio transmission which have interrupted the sound track, have dropped away, leaving only the taped voice of Koumiko to evoke Japan for the distant interrogator.

Visually, the mix is as before: a combination of crowd shots with and without Koumiko, images (ads, samurai films) picked up from Japanese TV, footage of exotic ceremonies and a variety of close-ups, often stills, of Koumiko's face. What has changed is the relationship between the soundtrack and the images: Marker has exchanged the you-are-there documentary illusion he started with – the clipped, present-tense narration ('Koumiko Muraoka, secretary, more than twenty years old, less than thirty . . .'), the on-camera interviews – for a tone of retrospection, past-tense narration. The illusion in this last section is that what we see is what Marker is seeing as he listens to Koumiko's tape, the images summoned by her voice and the memory of her face, as if time and distance have turned a job of reporting, the investigation of a culture, into some thing more intimate and novelistic – the story of a relationship. Koumiko is never made to represent Japan, but she seems, in these passages, to replace it.

The shift from the present tense of documentary to the past tense of reverie isn't just a formal experiment in the relationship of sound and image. It's not playful, like the passage in *Letter from Siberia* in which a single montage of village life is played three times with three different narrations (communist, capitalist and 'objective'). In Koumiko the effect is haunting, because it embodies the chronic melancholy of the traveller, who's always leaving places and people behind, places which, from a distance, cannot be fully imagined distinct from the consciousness of those who remain. (How can Marker run a sequence of the Tokyo monorail on his moviola without thinking of Koumiko? How can he hear her voice without a picture of the Ginza owl flashing through his mind?) The traveller, better than anyone else, knows that isolation from others means not seeing the same things every day . . .

In conventional documentaries, the film-maker is primarily a reporter, answering a questionnaire: How do people live in Siberia? Is Castro's revolution working? How does Israel survive? Marker's earlier films, like *Letter From Siberia* (1957), *Description of a Struggle* (1960), and *Cuba Si!* (1961), may not have given conventional answers, but they remained within the framework of the understood questions. *Koumiko*, while it plays with a style of reportage only to abandon it, fools us for a while, but finally reveals itself: the question all along, was not 'What is Japan like?' but 'Who is Koumiko?' But *Sans Soleil* seems, rather, to be generating its own questions in the audience, like: Where are we now? Is this a film about Japan? About Guinea-Bissau?

Why does he bring up the children in Iceland here? Was there a project? Or several? Why *Vertigo*? Why the emu?

These stupid questions (which are also the sort we might ask of a bad, incoherent film), strangely, help pull us along through the movie: we keep following the subject, feeling that it's almost in our grasp if only the speeding images would slow down a bit, if only those passages that look and sound like summations would allow us to linger before they rush us on to new information, new syntheses. And the stupid questions turn out to be the right ones. *Sans Soleil* is the diary of a return, a return which induces – naturally – retrospection, reverie, the need to account for the distance travelled in coming back: a review of notes from other places, beginning with three children in Iceland in 1965 (the year after *Koumiko* was shot).

These notes – the odd shots saved from Marker's own travels, supplemented by footage sent by friends – are, like all notes, taken spontaneously, for their own sake, or perhaps for the sake of a vague sense that they might someday fit a pattern. Returning to Tokyo, Marker seems to feel as Koumiko did sixteen years earlier when she complained that her head was full of 'things, things, things – all mixed up, without any order' – and he must feel that way again when he's back home editing his footage, reviewing his notes, the cans of film all mixed up, as he tries to analyse and recreate that feeling, with no tape from Tokyo to listen to, just Marker the editor asking questions of Marker the photographer: Why do these shots exist? Where are we now?

This is the way I imagine Marker working on *Sans Soleil*. His method

invites this sort of attempt to evoke him: it's both profoundly personal
and utterly detached: the films have a distinctive voice, but it's the voice
of a ghost whispering in your ear. The far-flung documentary images of
Sans Soleil are assembled as an autobiography – the film has no subject
except the consciousness, the memory of the man who shot it – yet
Marker attributes this consciousness to the invented 'Sandor Krasna',
removes it from himself to a yet more spectral entity. And then he adds
further layers of mediation: 'Krasna' himself is often made to attribute
his thoughts to others (as, for instance, when he imagines the alien time
traveller from 4001 commenting on the twentieth century); and the
entire narration is read by another invention, the nameless woman
receiving Krasna's letters.

32 *Chris Marker (right).*

Marker has always had a fondness for complication, subterfuge, disguise: even his name is a pseudonym. For *Si J'avais Quatre Dromadaires* (1966), a feature length assembly of still photos taken all over the world between 1955 and 1965, he invented a commentary for three voices, a photographer and two friends. In *Le Fond de l'Air est Rouge* (1978), a four-hour history of the years 1967–1970 composed of newsreel footage and fragments edited out of Marker's earlier films, he submerges his own voice almost entirely. (In his introduction to the published text, Marker confesses to having 'abused' his function as commentator in earlier films, and says that his aim here is 'for once . . . to return to the spectator through montage', his commentary, that is to say, his power – as an extension, perhaps, of the *cinéma-vérité* method of his 1963 documentary on Paris, *Le Joli Mai*, although in that film Marker reserved for himself as commentator the first and the last words.)

In his 1982 book *Le Depays*, a photo and text record of the same trip to Japan which provided the material for *Sans Soleil*, Marker writes his impressions; not in the first person but in the second – because, he finally admits, he wants 'to establish a distance between the one who, from September 1979 to January 1981, took these photos of Japan and the one who is writing in Paris in February 1982 . . . One changes, one is never the same, it's necessary to address oneself in the second person for all one's life.' Most of Marker's works are, like *Sans Soleil*, mixtures of documentary and invention, intimacy and distance, self-revelation and disguise.

In 1962, when he shot *La Jetee*, Marker wasn't travelling. He was in his home city of Paris: in that year, he also shot (with Pierre L'homme) and edited *Le Joli Mai*, a documentary portrait of the city. This is one of his most straightforward films, composed primarily of on-camera interviews and coverage of current events, but it's also a film whose commentary (sparing though it is) seems to be reaching towards fiction, a more fantastic framework, an alien perspective on familiar landscapes. *Le Joli Mai*'s first half assumes a detached, lofty vantage point – this section is called 'A Prayer from the Eiffel Tower' – and its second-half narration imagines a city haunted by 'the return of Fantomas', the mysterious criminal of Louis Feuillade's silent serials, here transformed into a metaphor for Parisians' fears and uncertainties near the end of the Algerian war. And at the end of *Le Joli Mai*, Marker shows us a prison in the heart of Paris, and his commentary asks us to imagine a prisoner who has had no part in the daily life that the film has chronicled, and asks us, finally, to assume the prisoner's perspective upon his release, as he looks into the faces of ordinary Parisians and sees only their tense unhappiness, the features of another kind of prisoner.

Source: *Sight and Sound*, Autumn 1984

9 The Grain of Truth

At the very beginning of the 1960s a series of technical innovations in sound and camera equipment completely revolutionized the documentary film. Up until that time all documentaries had been shot using bulky, virtually immobile 35mm cameras, but now manufacturers began to improve their 16mm stock, making it acceptable as a professional format. Because 16mm cameras were much smaller, more manageable and mobile, cameramen were suddenly able to shoot with an ease of access and fluidity they could never have obtained before. Simultaneously, the increased speed of the new 16mm film stocks meant that less light was required in order to obtain an acceptable image, so film-lights could be dispensed with, and most situations filmed in natural light. This again gave rise to a new sense of spontaneity and freedom in filming.

The technical developments in sound recording were equally – if not more – important in this documentary revolution. The first step was the invention of the portable sound recorder, specifically the Swiss 'Nagra', which was as unobtrusive and mobile as the 16mm camera. Prior to the Nagra's introduction a recording machine was an enormous sofa-sized apparatus, and subjects had to be taken to it rather the other way round.

But the Nagra in itself was not enough. The key was to record sound that was synchronous with the picture, without having a cumbersome umbilical link between the camera and the recorder. When this hurdle was overcome in 1960 (as described in the first piece in this collection), it opened the flood-gates to what was variously known as Direct Cinema (in America and Canada), *cinéma vérité* (in France) and – slightly later – Observational Documentary (in Britain).

In many respects *cinéma vérité* and Direct Cinema were very different, but they did have vital features in common: they both valued immediacy, intimacy and 'the real'; they both rejected the glossy 'professional' aesthetic of traditional cinema, unconcerned if their images were grainy and wobbly and occasionally went out of focus – in fact, these 'flaws' in themselves seemed to guarantee authenticity and thus became desirable, eventually developing into an aesthetic in their own right.

Where *cinéma vérité* and Direct Cinema parted was over the question of film-maker intervention. The French, lead by sociologist Edgar Morin and anthropologist Jean Rouch, followed Dziga Vertov in thinking that the camera was able to reveal a deeper level of truth about the world than the 'imperfect human eye'. They interviewed their subjects and intervened constantly in the filming, using the camera as their tool and the film-making process as a means in itself to explore their subjects' preoccupations. They named their aesthetic *cinéma vérité*, a direct translation of Dziga Vertov's *Kino-Pravda*. The Americans, on the other hand, were lead by *Time-Life* journalist Robert Drew who saw Direct Cinema as a 'theatre without actors'. He was radically opposed to interviewing, and believed that his film crews were so unobtrusive and mobile that they could record 'reality' without influencing it. Drew and his followers, Richard Leacock, Don Pennebaker, the Mayseles Brothers et al. deliberately chose subjects who were so involved in what they were doing that they forgot all about the camera: John F. Kennedy running for office in *Primary* (1960), a man about to be executed in *The Chair* (1962) and politicians in a crisis in *Crisis* (1962).

The advocates of Direct Cinema were always quick to codify exactly what they thought was the 'right' way to make a documentary and what was the 'wrong' way, drawing up a kind of filmic ten commandments: thou shalt not rehearse, thou shalt not interview; thou shalt not use commentary; thou shalt not use film lights; thou shalt not stage events; thou shalt not dissolve. Paradoxically, the film-making movement which seemed to stand for iconoclasm and freedom became one of the most codified and puritanical.

In its original form, *cinéma vérité* was practised by few film-makers although its influence can still be seen in the work of contemporary film-makers like Molly Dineen and Nick Broomfield. Direct Cinema (which, confusingly, soon co-opted the term *cinéma vérité* for its own use) on the other hand, was *the* dominant documentary form up until the late 1970s. Today, however, apart from a few purists like Fred Wiseman and Don Pennebaker, there are few orthodox practitioners left. Gradually,

the use of interviews, lights and staged-events seeped in. The grand-
children of those original Direct Cinema films are the endless
'documentaries' about firemen, hospitals and vets which clog our
televisions.

These days *cinéma vérité* is a vague blanket term which is used to
describe the *look* of feature or documentary films – grainy, hand-held
camera, real locations – rather than any genuine aspirations the film-
makers may have. As so often, what started as a revolution, has ended
up a style choice.

Richard Leacock Remembers the Origins of 'Direct Cinema'

**In this piece, Richard Leacock (born 1921) describes how the key
technical development in sound camera synchronization came about
that made direct cinema possible.**

**Leacock, who had shot Robert Flaherty's last film, *Louisiana Story*,
went on to be one of Direct Cinema's most ardent advocates. His
numerous films include: *Primary* (1960), *The Chair* (1962), *A
Stravinsky Portrait* (1968) and *Monterey Pop* (1968). In recent years
he has been an outspoken supporter of the Video-8 cameras, which he
sees as ideal for unobtrusive documentary filming.**

Later that year [1954] Roger Tilton came to me with what seemed, at
that time, to be a wild idea. He wanted to make a short film, that could
run in theatres, of young people dancing to a Dixieland band. He
wanted the camera to be mobile, hand held, to be as joyful in its
movements as the dancers, but it should be 'synch' . . . I liked his
approach and we did it. We rented a hall and the band from Nicks with
Peewee Russell on clarinet. We lit the hall with the new high intensity
spot lamps, deciding that we would not bother to hide them . . . let
them be in the picture. I shot on the floor. I had two 35mm Eymo 'news'
cameras. Their maximum load was 100ft. (one minute of film) and the
spring motor would only shoot about twenty seconds till it had to be
wound up again. I had two so that Hugh Bell, a superb still
photographer and a graduate of the Harlem film school, could reload
while I shot. Bob Campbell, the other cameraman, filmed the band with
a rudimentary synch system attached to his camera and was therefore
less mobile. We spent a fabulous evening shooting to our hearts'

content. There were slow numbers, medium numbers and fast numbers . . . Roger and his editor sorted it all out and made up a mosaic that certainly looked to be in synch and was wild and free and wonderful . . .

Jazz Dance gave me a taste of freedom. I will never forget the sheer joy of shooting that night, the exhilaration of a small, utterly mobile camera in my hands, whirling, spinning, creating . . . but was this the only story we could make this way?

It seemed hopeless and I was losing patience. We were stuck! Hopelessly stuck!

. . . Around this time Morris Engle made a feature film, *Weddings and Babies* . . . Morris was accustomed to the mobility and ease of shooting with a Leica, he was a photographer of the *Life* magazine tradition and was horrified by the stupidity of sound filming. He had a 35mm hand camera adapted to work in synch with a small tape recorder using a tuning fork as a time control. His was a clumsy, cumbersome solution and noisy too. But it worked and he managed to create some wonderful scenes. I wrote an article on this work published in *Harpers*. We became friends. In the interim I had made a second film for Omnibus, which was all re-enactments of testing an F-100 fighter plane. Bob Drew, besides being a *Life* magazine editor was a former fighter pilot and a nut on flying. He visited again and talked about maybe getting *Life* magazine to fund some experiments in TV journalism, a kind of *Life* magazine of the air.

. . . I don't recall ever having thought to create equipment that would do what we knew had to be done. I thought more in terms of other people, the 'industry', doing it. We had ideas as to how our problems could be solved; I remember going, with Morris Engel, to see the head of research at NBC. We suggested solutions and he listened to us with courtesy and patience, then, glancing at his watch, he said that if, by chance, we came up with something, to let him know . . . I replied with some ambiguous platitude concerning the fate of dinosaurs.

. . . We were able to come up with solutions to various problems based on the development of magnetic reading machines, the discovery and use of the transistor which, for the first time, made it possible to build amplifiers and recorders which could run on batteries, and the development of mini-tuning-fork timing devices that were used as the control mechanism in the new Bulova watch. Their TV advertising went something like: 'Buzzzz . . . the sound of the future!! . . . Bulova watch time! . . .' Willard Van Dyke was making a TV commercial for Bulova and showed me one of the new watches. It occurred to me that we could build them into our cameras and tape recorders as a control system. We did and it worked. With funding and moral support from Bob Drew's *Time* connections we were able to solve our problems.

Far more was involved than the technology of portable equipment. The film industry had, with the exception of Robert Flaherty and few if any others, been divided up into craft categories. Directors were the 'creators', writers, editors and cameramen served them. As Jean Renoir had recently pointed out, the bulky camera and sound machine were the altars before which all was sacrificed . . . as far as I was concerned this system didn't work. I do not remember any discussions of what we did in fact do. I know that I was a rare bird in that I believed in writing, directing, photographing and editing my own work. D.A. Pennebaker, with whom I shared an office and some equipment in New York, also worked this way.

After several brief efforts to cover stories with Bob Drew, using equipment that was not yet right, Drew came up with the wild idea of filming a primary election in Wisconsin which pitted Senator John F. Kennedy against Senator Hubert Humphrey. What a motley crew we were! Spring 1960. We had only one Auricon camera with a cable connecting it to a portable tape recorder. Drew and I used this rig. The others, Pennebaker, Maysles and Terry MacCartney-Filgate, an acerbic Englishman brought up in British India, used noisy old Arriflex cameras and 'wild' recorders. Pennebaker was in charge of a crazy machine built for us by Lorren Ryder, a Hollywood sound 'expert' which was to put the non-synch sound in synch with the non-synch picture. We all worked out of a hotel room. What was remarkable was that we edited our own material with Bob Drew and his journalist yellow pads hovering over us. It worked! We made a film that captured the flavour, the guts of what was happening. No interviews. No re-enactments. No staged scenes and very little narration. When we returned to New York we showed our film to visiting British documentary film maker Paul Rotha, he was astounded and said, ' . . . my God! We have been trying to do this for the last forty years and you've done it . . .' He was in tears! We went out and got smashed!

Soon thereafter we had the equipment we had dreamed of, and sometimes it worked. The important thing is that we were experimenting. All the rules were new. We were in fact, developing a new grammar which was entirely different from that of silent film-making and of fiction film-making. We were acutely aware that by this emphasis on sound we might be losing the visual basis for our medium. Looking back at the results it is apparent to me that the visual strength remained largely because of the avoidance of the interview, which I still regard as the death knell of cinematic story telling.

During the next three years, from 1960–1963, I continued working with Bob Drew and his organization which became a kind of super film school where people got paid to be involved with the development of this new way of making films.

Source: From an unpublished memoir written in 1992.

Richard Leacock
INTERVIEWED BY MARK SHIVAS

In March 1963 Radio Television Française (RTF) organized a three–day conference on the new documentary film style which was being called *cinéma vérité* in France and Direct Cinema in America. Among the delgates were all the major practioners, including Robert Drew, Richard Leacock and Don Pennebaker from America and Jean Rouch and Edgar Morin from France.

This interview was conducted towards the end of the conference.

A: My dream had been reportage more or less of the kind of *Primary*, but Bob [Drew] had started to think of something more ambitious. I don't know whether he thought of it then, but what came out of Eddie was not just a report on what happened. We found that what happened to Eddie had the structure almost of a classical drama. We began to realize and this is to me particularly Bob's aspect – that just as the theatrical sense of drama stems from reality, people in real situations will produce drama if we're smart enough to be able to capture it, if we're smart enough and sensitive enough in our filming within the discipline that we have established and stick to – of never asking anybody to do anything.

There are only two people present: one a human being – not a technician – a human being who is also a photographer, with a camera that's silent, no tripods, no lights, no cables; the other, a human being who records the sound. These people work in a very, very intimate way, in a delicate relationship with the person whom they are filming, who is involved in doing something that is more important to him than the fact that we are filming him. Instead of worrying about what we're seeing or something, he has to do what he has to do because it's so damned important.

At the moment we can deal with intense situations, but we have greater difficulty dealing with less intense situations. As we get smarter and our equipment gets better, we shall be able to deal with situations of far less intensity, because it's our conviction that every aspect of life contains its own drama.

Q: *Some of the events that you go for may lack intensity, but they generally have a certain natural progression about them, don't they?*

A: And there's a certain structure. Now the strange thing is that in filming these, we find that there are two adventures. You have a sort of exploration: you go out and film, and all your acts are final. You can't go back. You can't say 'Please do that again.' If you missed someone coming through a door, you've missed him: that's it. Don't say a thing. You're making your judgements and each judgement is final . . .

We find that the editing is often a process of discovering that what we thought was the structure doesn't seem to work. It's hard to say exactly what I mean by that, but it just doesn't seem to be right. And so we go back . . . often we have to reconstitute the whole film after an attempt to cut it. It's my belief – and I think most of us would agree – that the extraordinary thing is that there is a structure in what you've shot that is not necessarily the structure that you thought you'd shot. Often we discover a new kind of drama that we were not really aware of when we shot it. This has been particularly true in the more difficult films that we've done. And so you've got two levels of discovering. It's hard to explain. You have to do it to get the idea.

Q: *It means that every cameraman has not only to be a cameraman, but a director in that he selects, and a sound recordist as well.*

A: I would put it differently and say that there will be no such thing as a cameraman; there'll be film-makers. There'll be no such thing as editors, there'll be film-makers. It'll become an integrated process . . .

33 *On the way to his death. The Chair (1962).*

Q: *There seems to be a difference in belief between you and Jean Rouch; he thinks that the presence of the camera modifies the action, and with your technique you say this doesn't happen.*

A: We find that the degree to which the camera changes the situation is mostly due to the nature of the person filming it. You can make your presence known, or you can act in such a way as not to affect them. Also, of course, it depends on the intensity of what's happening to them.

But we don't think that it affects people very much, at least I don't. Let me add that, of course, it affects them in Jean Rouch's films, since the only thing that's happening to them is the fact that they're being filmed. There's nothing else to think about. How can they ever forget it?

Q: *You've said that your relationship with your subject is a personal, equals, relationship. Do you think that this is ideal, rather than attempting to be invisible?*

A: You can't be invisible. You're either an equal or a subordinate, to put it bluntly. That's a grisly word.

Q: *Would you say that when you had to resort to the use of interviews you had to some extent failed ? At least in your sort of film.*

A: Bob said recently that it wasn't a question of being better or worse. We feel that if in a Rouch film you turned the picture off and listened to the sound track you would get the full contents of the film. If you turned the picture off in our case, though it's full of synch sound, then the thing would be absolutely incomprehensible. You wouldn't have the foggiest idea what's going on. Now this may not be a virtue, but I think it is.

Q: *You seem to studiously avoid comment in the old documentary sense. Would you say that your aim was limited to presenting evidence?*

A: Bob Drew pointed out at the meeting, if anything, the films of Rouch give carefully thought-out answers to problems, and that we, if anything, attempt to give evidence about which you can make up your own mind. That's what we hope we're doing anyway. Obviously we have our own bias and selection, obviously we're not presenting the Whole Truth. I'm not being pretentious and ridiculous: we're presenting the film-maker's perception of an aspect of what happened. That's about as crammed down as I can get it. Or there may be three film-makers involved, so we get three aspects. But within this, we're still trying to present, to try and convey the sense of what happened, what it was like to be there when it happened. You make up your own mind, and the strange thing about our films in general is that we get extremely varied reactions to them.

Q: *What would you say was your requirement for a subject? To begin with you seem to have had one particular subject, which was the contest.*

A: Let's see. The other day I tried to write out a definition of what we know we can make a film of relatively easily. That doesn't mean that if something doesn't fit all these conditions . . . Let's see if I can remember it. 'A film about a person who is interesting, who is involved in a situation which he cares about deeply, which comes to a conclusion within a limited period of time, where we have access to what goes on – we can be there, in other words' – yeah, that's about it. But funnily enough some of the most interesting films we've come out with this year have been where this definition didn't fit.

It certainly didn't fit *Nehru*. He wasn't involved in anything that came to a conclusion. He was just doing what he usually does day after day after day. I guess our feeling is that at the moment we're very young. We do need high-pressure situations. As we get smarter and as our equipment gets better, as we learn more about this kind of film-making, we will be able to go into situations that are less and less pressure situations.

The Maysles Brothers
INTERVIEWED BY JAMES BLUE

The following piece from 1964 is one of the best early interviews with the Maysles brothers, Albert and David (born 1926 and 1932 respectively; David died in 1987). The interviewer, James Blue, was himself a film-maker; in 1962 his feature on the Algerian War, *Les Oliviers de la Justice*, won the Society of Motion Picture and Television Writers prize at Cannes. Throughout their discussion, Blue presses the brothers on the issues of intentionality and creativity which were key elements of the early *vérité* ethos. At one point in the interview, not published here, Al Maysles quotes Bacon: 'The contemplation of things as they are without error or confusion, without substitution or imposure, is in itself a far nobler thing than a whole harvest of invention.' This was to be the Direct Cinema creed for more than a decade.

Subsequent to this interview the Mayseles went on to produce some of their best work, including: *Salesman* (1969), *Gimme Shelter* (1970 – see pp. 273) and *Grey Gardens* (1975).

New York commercial film-makers turn red and clutch their drinks when you talk about the Maysles. In Hollywood, the prestigious members of the lofty Motion Picture Academy saw ten minutes of *Showman* (1962) and stopped the projection. Old school documentarists call it 'anti–audience', 'anti-art'.

Al was first associated with Richard Leacock, Don Alan Pennebaker and Robert Drew. Together they shot the early classics of American *cinéma vérité*: the now famous *Primary* (1960) about the Kennedy-Humphrey battle in the 1960 Wisconsin primary election, and the controversial *Yanki No* (1961), which dealt with rising anti-Americanism in Latin America. Greg Shuker joined them at the end of 1960, and together they shot a two-part story on Kenya: *Land of the White Ghost* and *Land of the Black Ghost*. Al left the group in 1961 to set up his own company with his brother David ... Since leaving Drew Associates, Al, and his brother David, who records the sound and does the editing, have sought to make films about people in all walks of life. Rather than treat journalistic subjects as the Drew group had done, they have attempted to deepen their penetration into a person or a group of people, taken at certain moments in their lives. This quest has produced *Showman* – about [Producer] Joe Levine – and, recently, *What's Happening?* [about The Beatles]. Neither of these films has received public release; however, *Showman* has been seen in film festivals around the world, and it has provoked both ear-splitting protest and thunderous praise.

Because of Al's avowed purpose to catch a kind of 'subjective-objective' truth, his cinema is one in which ethics and aesthetics are interdependent, where beauty starts with honesty, where a cut or a

34 Joseph E. Levine and Sophia Loren in Showman *(1962).*

change in camera angle can become not only a possible aesthetic error but also a 'sin' against Truth. In things cinematic, Al Maysles is a religious zealot.

AL: When I went to Cuba to shoot part of *Yanki No*, I didn't know any more about Castro and Cuba than any other person. I don't think I would have done better if I had prepared myself. When I got off the plane, I went to a mass meeting where Castro was talking to the mothers, and my first shot was the big close-up of Castro. I could spend five years tracking him around the world and I never would have gotten a shot like that. The better you know somebody, the more you are at a disadvantage. You are no longer curious to put down things familiar to you. The essential you let go by, because you say to yourself: 'everybody knows that' . . .

JAMES: *The Chair (1961), by Drew Associates, was shot by several cameramen. Would another cameraman help you in any way?*

AL: We shoot everything with one camera. You, as a viewer, become the one camera. You are not two or three cameras that are impossibly in two situations at the same time. When you go to a reaction shot, it's false. You, as a person, could not have jumped across the room. In my films, you rarely see any shooting from positions that are not natural to an observer of the situation. The shots are either from a seated position in a chair or from a standing position and not from crazy angles. In *What's Happening?* there is this disc jockey in a room and The Beatles are there and the camera is moving from one to another. It's some of the best shooting I've ever done. It could have been done by waiting for the best moment to shoot each one of them and then editing it together. But if you are able to shoot them continuously, from one to the other, the interrelation is not editor-made, and that moment becomes much more convincing to the viewer. It's much more honest.

JAMES: *Ethics plays a great part in the way you shoot. By shooting with one camera and linking things, you feel you are assuring the spectator that what he sees is really taking place and has not been created for his benefit. In this way, you feel you have obtained Truth. Many people feel, however, that this is not Truth at all. They say you are filming trivia. Mere surface appearance.*

AL: Life is made of trivia. In a sense, [Joe] Levine is a trivial person.

JAMES: *They mean by this that you do not penetrate into the person.*

AL: Fiction film-makers and writers think that they are catching important things by creating them. I don't think they are. I'd like to know what you would have an actor say or do in the role of Levine that would reveal him more. I'd like to see the subject done better. I don't think it can be.

JAMES: *Why do you need so desperately to draw things out of Nature, out of the world around you? Why this need to know that what you are filming is authentic and not something that you have created?*

AL: My background has been more scientific than artistic. I taught Psychology at Boston University. I was going to spend my life doing research. Scientific method was my main interest. Apart from that, I just feel more comfortable as an acute observer. I admire people who have a humble attitude to the subject matter and to the world around them. There is another thing: if you take this humble attitude toward something outside yourself, the chances are that you are rewarded. It satisfies a selfish need. It means that your work is going to become more permanent.

JAMES: *Because it documents something?*

AL: Because it depends, in the final analysis, on something outside of you. I know damn well that people will see *Primary* one hundred years from now. In these last five years, people have come to see it all the more as a truthful film. If we had started out with some definite point of view, I am positive that film would be rubbish today . . .

I want to make a film called *Coup de Foudre*. I want to meet a girl and film the very moment I'm meeting her and stay with her for a while. An experience totally new for me, new for her, and be filming. I have tried it with two girls. The first one was . . . well, she said nothing at all. The other kept talking all the time.

JAMES: *They were playing for the camera?*

AL: They were. But when you meet someone for the first time they reveal more of themselves than at any other time.

JAMES: *This desire to 'have an experience' has led you into this long-run shooting technique, has it not?*

AL: Within that long run or long take of the camera, if it is continued, it works to the film-maker's advantage in that the person has to break down and reveal himself within that long run. Whereas, in a short take, the person can put on his mask.

(I followed my conversation with Al Maysles by a chat with his brother, David, who handles sound, editing, and business affairs for the pair.)

JAMES: *Your brother has talked about the need of being honest, of gaining the audience's confidence in the authenticity of what is shown. He feels that he does this by linking scenes rather than making separate shots, by keeping the camera rolling, by submitting himself to the life going on around him. I wonder what principles guide you in cutting Al's material. In Showman, there are many places where you relate shots, cut back and forth, use cut-aways. I even saw places where you profited from the fact that we couldn't see a person's mouth move to lay in dialogue from another shot. Does this pose for you an ethical problem?*

DAVID: There is no such thing as being strictly objective in anything that is at all artistic. The objectivity is just a personal integrity: being essentially true to the subject and capturing it essentially. One of the places you are referring to is where Levine is on the phone and says Kim Novak is coming. We have that in the out-takes where you can see his lips moving, but it just didn't work in combination with the shot preceding it. He did say it, maybe not at that time, but to preserve a certain continuity we changed it. We wouldn't distort his words and change them around to make him look bad. When you see the film you have an overall belief that you are seeing something real. You mentioned cut-aways – we used very few. There are mostly intercuts of different scenes. The vice-president giving a pep-talk, the salesman, then back to Levine on the phone . . .

JAMES: *What do you do once you have material on film? How do you proceed?*

DAVID: I line it up exactly as it is shot – chronologically. Then I look at it a couple of times and make notes and try to put a structure down very very roughly on paper. And the theme, too. Then, with a couple of people here, we chop it down roughly into that version. We try to go for broke in the first cut. We don't make any two hour assemblies when we know it's an hour picture.

JAMES: *You say you try to establish a theme. What thematic ideas occurred to you in making* What's Happening? *– on* The Beatles.

DAVID: I was trying to show how they typify a great part of American youth. I feel that there is a sort of restlessness. They want to find out what's happening in town. Where are we going to go? It's like *Marty*. They're always looking for something – for a 'beat'.

JAMES: *One of the criticisms made against your work – even by people who admire it – is that it lacks structure. What do you do to make us want to see more?*

DAVID: Ideally, we'd like to have a story that has a beginning, a middle and an end – a logical development. I tried in *Showman* to get a structure that gave it direction. The guy that gets fired – you see him at work and you finally see him fired. The build-up to the night when Levine gets the Oscar. The sequence about Joe's visit to Boston – wheeling and dealing and finally a very humble moment at home in Boston. I think you come out of the film feeling that you have been involved in something you didn't know about before. I think there is structure. We have learned one thing from hard experience: the quicker you shoot a film, the easier it is to edit it. There is a continuity in time.

JAMES: *What is the role of narration in your films?*

DAVID: Ideally, part of our whole purpose is to make the viewers their own commentators. Not to tell anything, but to show. Narration is only a leg that you use for support if you need it. It picks up something that isn't in the picture that you missed. I want to make a film that doesn't need narration, that stands together as a film. I feel that the same criteria that apply to a Hollywood film should apply to ours as well. You shouldn't have to say 'Well, that's a documentary so you can have narration.' I don't want any of these allowances or apologies . . .

JAMES: *Did you see* Pather Panchali?

DAVID: Terrific film.

JAMES: *But these are actors. Ray has directed them in a 'down' style where they do not enlarge upon life, but their effects are simplified and highly controlled. Let us compare a scene as it might happen in reality and as Ray staged it – when at the end of the film the father comes back with the shawl for the daughter who has died. He has been away in Calcutta and is not aware of his daughter's death. He says 'I brought this shawl for Duga.' The mother takes it suddenly, bites into it, falls down crying, and at that moment the father without a word of explanation understands what has happened. He falls down accusing himself. He is in terrible pain. Now, in reality this scene might have been a wordy exchange over a period of time. It would not have had the poetry of this kind of selection. The scene, then, might have been less powerful or poetic if you had filmed it as it happened.*

DAVID: All film people are after the same thing: an emotional response. As you say, it might be a wordy thing, but I think we could cut that wordy thing so that it might be even more convincing and even more exciting. Essentially we are allowing things to happen rather than controlling them. We feel that things that really happen are much more exciting.

Source: *Film Comment*, Autumn 1964, Vol. 2, No. 4.

Jean Rouch
INTERVIEWED BY G. ROY-LEVEN

This interview from 1969 illustrates just how much classic *cinéma vérité* differed from Direct Cinema. Unlike the Americans, Jean Rouch (born 1917) felt that a film-maker ought to present an argued point of view in his or her films.

Rouch's films have mostly been anthropological and include: *Les Magiciens Noirs* (1949), *Moi Un Noir* (1958, one of Rouch's few forays into drama) *Chronique d'un Été* (1961), *The Lion Hunters* (1965) and *Dionysos* (1984).

G. ROY-LEVEN: *Let me begin by asking why you began to make films. Was it because you really liked films?*

JEAN ROUCH: No. There are two reasons. Before the war, when I was a student in a school for engineers, I used to go to the Cinémathèque Française, which was run by Henri Langlois. So I was passionately interested in film even when I was a student. The second reason is that I studied ethnology. I became a film-maker because I discovered that you have to have a camera to do research. So right after the war I bought an old 16mm Bell & Howell, and I was very lucky, because it was then that 16mm first started to be used professionally.

. . . The last piece of good luck I had was when I made my first films about Nigeria. I left with an amateur cameraman's manual, and I had the good luck to lose my tripod at the end of a week, and was forced to work without a tripod. That was in 1945, and to work without a tripod was absolutely forbidden! But I realized that it really wasn't important. So again I had great luck. If you like, that was the beginning.

GRL: *There are film-makers in the United States who make what are called* cinéma-vérité *films, and some of them feel that this is the only way to tell the truth, because it's objective.*

JR: That's false. Essentially you have to make a choice: if I look at you, I look here and there; what's behind me is perhaps important because of the woman making noise, and perhaps my attention will be drawn to her, and from the moment that I've chosen to look in one direction or another, I've made a choice – which is a subjective process. All editing is subjective. In brief, I'm one of the people responsible for this phrase [*cinema vérité*] and it's really in homage to Dziga Vertov, who completely invented the kind of film we do today. It was a cinema of lies, but he believed simply – and I agree with him – that the camera eye is more perspicacious and more accurate than the human eye. The camera eye has an infallible memory, and the film-maker's eye is a multiple one, divided . . .

The one thing I want to say about *cinéma vérité* is that it would be better to call it cinema–sincerity, if you like. That is, that you ask the audience to have confidence in the evidence, to say to the audience, 'This is what I saw. I didn't fake it, this is what happened. I didn't pay anyone to fight, I didn't change anyone's behaviour. I looked at what happened with my subjective eye and this is what I believe took place.' . . .

GRL: *When you go to Africa to make films, do you get to know the people well, as, say, Flaherty did?*

JR: Yes. Perhaps even better. These are people I've known for twenty years, they're old friends whom I've always known. And I've always presented my films as Flaherty. The great lesson of Flaherty and *Nanook* is always to show your film to the people who were in it. That's the exact opposite of the ideas of the Maysles and Leacock.

GRL: *In* Moana, *Flaherty showed ritual ceremonies which I believe were no longer part of Samoan life when he made the film. Do you nevertheless see this as presenting the 'truth'?*

JR: I'll answer you not by speaking of Flaherty, but by giving you an example which is more extraordinary for me. The best film on Mexico is Eisenstein's *Que Viva Mexico*. Now, it happens that this film is completely false – it was all created, there wasn't one real scene in it; and the Mexicans themselves recognize it as the truest film on Mexico, simply because the fiction that Eisenstein reconstructed was closest to the Mexican image. I think that's what we have to do. And Flaherty, who is a poet, not an ethnologist, who thought that everyone in the world had a message which was common to all men, applied this method in all of his films by introducing, for example, a child like the child in *Nanook*, the little boy in *Moana*, the boy in *Louisiana Story*, who have this naïve view of the world, and which is Flaherty's view. If you like, you could call Flaherty a 'witty naïve', which is undoubtedly the summit of art . . .

GRL: *Let me ask you what you think about Grierson's definition of documentary: 'the creative treatment of actuality'.*

JR: I think that to make a film is to tell a story. An ethnographic book tells a story; bad ethnographic books, bad theses are accumulations of documents. Good ethnology is a theory and a brilliant exposition of this theory – and that's what a film is. That is, you have something to say. I go in the subway, I look at it and I note that the subway is dirty and that the people are bored – that's not a film. I go on the subway and I say to myself, 'These people are bored, why? What's happening, what are they doing here? Why do they accept it? Why don't they smash the subway? Why do they sit here going over the same route every day?' At that moment you can make a film.

For example, in *Night Mail*, the hero is very probably the train, or the train's battle against the ascent. There's no postal clerk or conductor as hero. That's going the limit. Look at all of Flaherty's films, there's always a hero, there's always someone who is personalized, whom you recognize. If you compare the films of Rasmussen [*The Wedding of Palo* directed by F. Dalsheim and Knud Rasmussen] and Flaherty on the Eskimos, the difference is Nanook, who is someone, who is a man. When we meet people, we're men – even if you're doing work in the social sciences, you're someone. And perhaps the best films of the Maysles and Leacock are based on that, the portrait of someone in a given situation, whether it be Kennedy [in *Primary*] who is the hero, the lawyer in *The Chair* . . .

GRL: *Do you know* Titicut Follies *[1967, directed by John Marshall and Fred Wiseman]?*

JR: I like John Marshall enormously, but I must say that I react to this film with horror.

GRL: *Why?*

35 *Camera as catalyst.* Chronicle of Summer *(1960).*

JR: Because, if you like, there's no hope. Finally it's a film of despair. There's abolutely nothing positive in it. Nothing. It's a totally negative certified report about a situation.

GRL: *But if you see it as the truth?*

JR: Then you have to speak, you have to say it. I would like him to say something, say what the thesis is. Does it mean that we have to suppress this police system? That you have to be in a mental hospital? Does it mean that this particular hospital is a disgrace? It's not obvious. Perhaps it's obvious for Americans, but it's not obvious for foreigners.

GRL: *Perhaps it's not his fault then. He is American, and finally he made it for Americans.*

JR: Perhaps it's not his fault – I understand that. But it's a little as if you went into a hospital for retarded children and showed nothing but that. There's a fascination with horror here. For example, a horrible film like *Nuit et Brouillard* [Alain Renais, 1955] is a profoundly human film precisely because the commentary is there, because there's a guiding hand. In *Titicut Follies* there isn't any, it's a certified report, which could perhaps be interpreted as a cynical and sadomasochistic report.

Jean Rouch
INTERVIEWED BY JAMES BLUE

Much of the theoretical objection to the American Direct Cinema movement concerned the film-makers' downplaying of the distorting effect that the presence of the camera has on the reality which it is trying to capture. In this short interview excerpt Rouch not only admits this distortion but, unlike his American counterparts, argues that the result makes the person being filmed more self-revealing.

JEAN ROUCH: You know very well that when you have a microphone – such as the one you are now holding, and when you have a camera aimed at people, there is, all of a sudden, a phenomenon that takes place because people are being recorded: they behave very differently than they would if they were not being recorded: but what has always seemed very strange to me is that, contrary to what one might think, when people are being recorded, the reactions that they have are always infinitely more sincere than those they have when they are not being recorded. The fact of being recorded gives these people a public.

At first, of course, there is a self-concious 'hamminess'. They say to themselves 'People are looking at me I must give a nice impression of myself.' But this lasts only a very short time. And then, very rapidly, they begin to try to think – perhaps for the first time sincerely – about their own problems, about who they are and then they begin to express what they have within themselves. These moments are very short, and one must know how to take advantage of them. That's the art of making a film like *Chronique d'un Été* . . .

Do you remember Marcelline? The Jewish girl who walks along La Place de la Concorde recalling aloud her memories of being taken to a concentration camp during the occupation? That was the first scene we shot with Michel Brault as cameraman. We had brought him in from Canada and with him came all his lightweight equipment. All of a sudden we felt 'liberated'. We could go anywhere. So we thought we would try out the new material on La Place de la Concorde.

Now, Marcelline was always talking about having been deported and each time she brought it up, she had this sort of exhibitionism that many deportees have when they want to make you feel the horror of it all. And faced with the apparent indifference of those of us who don't know how to reply to her, all we could say was 'yes, you don't say?' – she would make it even more horrible. So we absolutely wanted something of that in the film to explain the character of Marcelline, but we didn't know very how to put it in.

But at that time – it was the 15 August 1960 – there were some film-makers out shooting scenes of that, you know, 'Occupied Paris' genre, so we said – 'let's go to the Place de la Concorde. There will surely be some German soldiers and then we can ask Marcelline to tell us about her experiences.' But we all got up too late that morning, and when we to La Place de la Concorde, there were no more 'German Soldiers'. Nothing. So I said – 'it makes no difference. Marcelline, you hang the tape recorder over your shoulder and take the neck-tie microphone, and you just go for a walk around the Place de la Concorde – (which was empty) – and you say anything that comes into your head.' And she came out with this monologue, which I think is extraordinary, where she just talks to herself – no one could hear her. We followed with the camera. And then I stopped the scene, Marcelline said– 'I haven't finished yet.' So we went to Place de l'Opéra, but nothing seemed to happen. Then by chance we came upon Les Halles [the market place of Paris with a large steel hanger-like structure over the street]. It was empty, so we had her walk through that. And she said whatever she wanted.

And when Morin and I saw that, we were very moved. I thought it was extraordinary. And what seemed so important was that someone could speak so sincerely while walking. And what was even more impressive was that what she said me really involuntarily! And that's what I like so much about this kind of cinema: anything can happen! You never know! All of sudden she began to talk – not of the camp – but of her return! Why? Because Les Halles resembles a railroad station. And you see, by association of ideas, she immediately began to talk of her return when her family came to meet her but her father wasn't there. That was something miraculous. Something aboslutely unplanned! We didn't know what would happen. I thought it was a miracle . . .

Well, when we projected this scene to Marcelline, she said that none of that concerned her! Now what did that mean? She meant – 'I'm an excellent actress and I am capable of acting that!' But that's not true. Morin and I are persuaded that when she said those things, it was the real Marcelline, terribly sincere, who was speaking of all that – exactly as she felt it, as she was.

JB: *So after having revealed herself, she refused the revelation by saying she was just acting. What were the consequences on the rest of the film? Did she freeze up?*

JR: After Marcelline had seen those sequences, she felt that she had to play that role! . . .

JB: *So to sum up – first a 'hammy' artificial self-conciousness; then a reflection upon oneself and a revelation of a hidden aspect of oneself of which one was not aware perhaps; then the more or less conscious attempt to play out a role defined by this revelation and an attempt to resolve the problems of it on the pretext that this is only a film.*

Source: *Film Comment*, Vol. II, No. 2, Spring 1964

Narration Can be a Killer
ROBERT DREW

In this piece Robert Drew (born 1918), the founder of the Direct Cinema movement, outlines his objections to documentary narration. Like his associates, he considered it anti-filmic and reductionist.

One of the few *vérité* films which does use voice-over – and to great success – is *The Search for Locations in Palestine for The Gospel of Saint Matthew* (1965) by Pier Paolo Pasolini, a director not usually associated with documentary. Pasolini's spoken track sounds so spontaneous, so 'direct', that it appears to be an on-the-spot reaction to cut sequences of the film as they play on the Steenbeck.

Narration has always seemed the great friend of the documentary producer. There are producers to this day who find that controlling narration gives them a satisfying way to control the editing, on paper, in advance.

Where would CBS *Reports* or NBC *White Paper* be without narration? For programs like those, narration props up weak film, justifies aimless film, rationalizes disjointed film, unifies disparate film, adds intelligence to dumb film.

Where would *National Geographic* be without narration? Where would travelogues, industrial films and educational films be? For them narration provides the thread to hang the pictures, the opinions with which to colour the pictures, the facts, reasons and measurements that give the pictures their logic. Probably more than ninety per cent of the documentary films produced today are formula films aimed at special audiences, in which narration is key to the formulas.

There is one area of serious contention about the use of narration. This is in documentary films that work, or are beginning to work, or could work, on filmic-dramatic principles.

The production of such films is miniscule. But it may hold an answer to hopes shared by many film-makers; the wish to reach large, general audiences; the desire to generate more power in their work.

Film-makers can see the power to do that, churning away out there in reality. They can see the promise to transmit that power, shimmering away in the films that do reach general audiences – the movies. Whatever else movies do, they invite viewers to think for themselves, without intermediary, narrator or correspondent. They invite them to be puzzled, confused, surprised and to find their own way through an experience with characters.

Films that tell stories directly, through characters who develop through action in dramatic lines – these have the possibility at least of allowing the power of film to build. This kind of film can soar. Beyond reason. Beyond explanation. Beyond words.

Words supplied from outside cannot make a film soar. Exposition, whether narration or voice-over from characters, may maintain a certain level of interest but it can rarely build. To do that, a film must generate power from within. The film itself must provide the thread, the viewpoint, and the logic, which must be dramatic logic. No amount of word logic or propping-up or justifying or rationalizing from narration can do that.

But the verbal traditions are ingrained in documentary films. Whole generations of audiences, managements, assignment editors and critics have been trained to expect those narration formulas. Yet, the general audience – the big audience – too, has been trained. It telegraphs, 'Dull', 'This will be good for you', 'Tune Out'.

Narration not only signals large sections of audience to tune out but it changes the character of the audience that remains. Give viewers the signal, 'Here comes narration', and the program is shunted to the right side of the brain, which sits back expecting to listen to the documentary. Give the same viewers another signal, 'Here comes a story for you to see for yourself' and up comes the other side of the brain, leaning forward, expecting somehow to participate.

Documentary films that begin to develop real film power are extremely vulnerable to mishandling. A few words of narration in the wrong place can put the audience in a mode not to see. An audience that is already sitting back listening may not be persuaded to sit forward and see for itself. An audience that is sitting forward may be put off completely by the sudden onset of words that break the spell.

Some of the most delicate decisions about narration seem to be called for to avoid mystifying or confusing the audience. We must be more willing to mystify, more conscious that narrating a point can cost the whole film. When we do narrate we must be more careful to support dramatic development rather than try to lead it or substitute for it.

If serious and fundamental questions about the use of narration persist, then it could be that the film simply will not work as a film. In that case, narration may make it possible for the film to work for particular audiences. Producing a narration film that works to the maximum extent possible according to its nature is a lot better than producing a film without narration that doesn't work at all.

Last year I made a ninety-minute documentary entirely without narration, *Fire Season*, and I wrote a narration that covered more than half of a one hour program, *Herself, Indira Ghandi*. I do not consider that one film was more successful than the other for its purpose, just that each was of a different nature with different possibilities and requirements.

For most documentary film-makers, narration remains a benign and useful tool for making the kinds of films expected by their audiences. But the documentary film is changing. It is shifting away from formulas based on lecture logic to more filmic forms based on dramatic principles. For film-makers on the leading edge, narration can be a killer. Few film-makers can expect to work on the leading edge all the time, but while they are, it can be true that 'Narration is what you do when you fail.'

Source: *International Documentary*, Summer, 1983.

Gimme Shelter
PAULINE KAEL

Here the trenchant Pauline Kael puts the boot into the Maysles brothers' and Charlotte Zwerin's *Gimme Shelter*. This 1970 film of The Rolling Stones performing at Altamont became notorious because it captured on camera one of four murders which took place at the event. Kael accuses the film makers of hypocrisy because they 'hit the *cinéma vérité* jackpot' yet didn't take at least some responsibility for what happened.

The issue of the ethics of documentary and the film-makers' responsibilities to their subjects run throughout the form (see, for instance, Flaherty on *Nanook* on p. 36 and the criticisms of *Hoop Dreams* on p. 303). That *Gimme Shelter*'s murder is seen three times in the film, raises the question of whether it is milking the gruesome scene in the manner of a snuff movie.

When Mick Jagger is seen in *Gimme Shelter* pensively looking at the Altamont footage – run for him by the Maysles brothers – and wondering how it all happened, this is disingenuous movie–making. One wants to say: Drop the Miss Innocence act and tell us the straight story of the background to the events. What isn't explained is that, four months after Woodstock, Stone Promotions asked the Maysles brothers to shoot the Stones at Madison Square Garden. The Maysles brothers had done a film on an American tour by The Beatles, and Albert Maysles had shot part of *Monterey Pop*. When, as a climax to their American tour, the Stones decided on a filmed free concert in the San Francisco area, the Maysles brothers made a deal with them to film it and rounded up a large crew. Melvin Belli's bordello-style law office and his negotiations for a concert site are in the film, but it isn't explained that Porter Bibb, the producer of *Salesman*, was the person who brought in Belli, or that Bibb became involved in producing the concert in Altamont in order to produce the Maysles film. The sequence in Belli's office omits the detail that the concert had to be hurriedly moved to Altamont because the owners of the previously scheduled site wanted distribution rights of the film. *Gimme Shelter* has been shaped so as to whitewash the Rolling Stones and the film-makers for the thoughtless, careless way the concert was arranged, and especially for the cut-rate approach to keeping order. The Hell's Angels, known for their violence, but cheap and photogenic, were hired as guards for five hundred dollar's worth of beer. This took less time and trouble than arranging for unarmed marshals, and the Hell's Angels must have seemed the appropriate guards for Their Satanic Majesties, the Stones. In the film, the primary concern of the Angels appears to be to keep the stage clear and guard the Stones.

. . . When the self-centred, mercenary movie queen of *Singin' in the Rain* talked about bringing joy into the humdrum lives of the public, we laughed. Should we also laugh at Melvin Belli's talk in *Gimme Shelter* about a 'free concert' for 'the people' and at the talk about the Stone's not wanting money when the concert is being shot for *Gimme Shelter* and The Rolling Stones and the Maysles brothers divide the profits from the picture? One of the jokes of *cinéma vérité* is that practically the only way to attract an audience is to use big stars, but since big stars co-operate only if they get financial – and generally, artistic – control of the film, the *cinéma-vérité* techniques are used to give the look of 'caught' footage to the image the stars are selling . . .

This film has caught [Mick Jagger's] feral intensity as a performer (which, oddly, Godard never captured in *One Plus One*, maybe because he dealt with a rehearsal-recording session, without an audience). It has also captured his teasing, taunting relationship to the audience: he can finish a frenzied number and say to the audience, 'You don't want my trousers to fall down now, do you?' His toughness is itself provocative, and since rock performers are accepted by the young as their own spokesmen, the conventional barriers between performers and audience have been pushed over. From the start of *Gimme Shelter*, our knowledge of the horror to come makes us see The Rolling Stones' numbers not as we might in an ordinary festival film but as the preparations for, and the possible cause of, disaster. We begin to suspect that Mick Jagger's musical style leads to violence, as he himself suggests in a naïve and dissociated way when he complains – somewhat pettishly, but with a flicker of pride – to the crowd that there seems to be some trouble every time he starts to sing 'Sympathy for the Devil'. He may not fully understand the response he works for and gets.

The film has a very disturbing pathos, because everybody seems so helpless. Many of the people at Altamont are blank or frightened but are in thrall to the music, or perhaps just to being there; some twitch and jerk to the beat in an apocalyptic parody of dancing; others strip, or crawl on the heads of the crowd; and we can see tormented tripper's faces, close to the stage, near the angry Angels. When Grace Slick and then Mick Jagger appeal to the audience to cool it, to 'keep your bodies off each other unless you intend to love,' and to 'get yourselves together', they are saying all they know how to say, but the situation is way past that. They don't seem to connect what they're into with the results. Mick Jagger symbolizes the rejection of the values that he then appeals to. Asking stoned and freaked out people to control themselves is pathetic, and since the most dangerous violence is obviously from the Hell's Angels, who are trying to keep their idea of order by stomping dazed, bewildered kids, Jagger's saying 'Brothers and sisters, why are we fighting?' is pitifully beside the point. Musically Jagger has no way to cool it because his orgiastic kind of music has only one way to go – higher, until everyone is knocked out.

Mick Jagger's performing style is a form of aggression not just against the straight world but against his own young audience, and this appeals to them, because it proves to them that he hasn't sold out and gone soft. But when all this aggression is released, who can handle it? The violence he provokes is well known: fans have pulled him off a platform, thrown a chair at him. He's greeted with a punch in the face when he arrives at

Altamont. What the film doesn't deal with is the fact that Jagger attracts this volatile audience, that he magnetizes disintegrating people. This is, of course, an ingredient of the whole rock scene, but it is seen at its most extreme in the San Francisco-Berkeley audience that gathers for The Rolling Stones at Altamont. Everyone – the people who came and the people who planned it – must have wanted a big Dionysian freak-out. The movie includes smiling talk about San Francisco as the place for the concert, and we all understand that it's the place for the concert because it's the farthest out place; it's the mother city of the drug culture. It's where things are already wildly out of control. The film shows part of what happened when Marty Balin, of the Jefferson Airplane, jumped off the stage to stop the Angels from beating a black man and was himself punched unconscious. After that, according to reporters, no one tried to stop the Angels from beating the crazed girls and boys who climbed on-stage or didn't follow instructions; they were hit with leaded pool cues and with fists while the show went on and the three dozen cameramen and soundmen went on working. There were four deaths at Altamont, and a cameraman caught one. You see the Angel's knife flashing high in the air before he stabs a black boy, who has a gun in his hand. You see it at normal speed, see it again slowed down, and then in a frozen frame . . .

It's impossible to say how much movie-making itself is responsible for those consequences, but it is a factor, and with the commercial success of this kind of film it's going to be a bigger factor. Antonioni dickered with black groups to find out what actions they were planning, so that he could include some confrontations in Zabriskie Point. MGM's lawyers must have taken a dim view of this. A smaller company, with much to gain and little to lose, might have encouraged him. Movie studios are closing, but, increasingly, public events are designed to take place on what are essentially movie stages. And with movie-production money getting tight, provoked events can be a cheap source of spectacles. The accidents that happen may be more acceptable to audiences than the choreographed battles of older directors, since for those who grew up with TV careful staging can look arch and stale. It doesn't look so fraudulent if a director excites people to commit violent acts on camera, and the event becomes free publicity for the film. The public will want to see the result, so there is big money to deodorize everyone concerned. What we're getting in the movies is 'total theatre'. Altamont, in *Gimme Shelter*, is like a Roman

36 *Caught on Film at Altamont.* Gimme Shelter *(1970).*

circus, with a difference: the audience and the victims are indistinguishable.

Source: *New Yorker*, 19 December 1970.

Editing as a Four-Way Conversation
FREDERICK WISEMAN

Almost thirty years after making his first documentary (*Titicut Follies*, 1967), Frederick Wiseman remains perhaps the last purist of Direct Cinema. He never interviews, never stages, never uses lights. He continues to shoot enormous ratios on 16mm and insists on long meditative editing schedules. His films – which include *High School* (1968), *Hospital* (1970), and *Near Death* (1969) – are invariably about institutions and usually reflect his liberal politics, but are never obviously 'campaigning'. As this piece makes clear, he has few illusions about the 'truth' or moral superiority of his method of film-making. He has simply chosen Direct Cinema as his discipline and continues to make his movies that way because he likes to.

Maine, 12 August 1992, 6.30 a.m.
I love working in my old barn with the big windows overlooking the Appleton Hills and the brick fireplace waiting for the first cool day of Fall so that it can welcome the dry birch logs stored under the porch. In the basement waiting patiently are my Steenbeck and 425 camera rolls of *Zoo* [Wiseman's film about the zoo in Miami, Florida – ed.]. I have done some editing on *Zoo* but not much – too many interruptions shooting *Ballet* and *High School II* [Wiseman's forthcoming documentary shot at Central Park East Secondary School in the Harlem section of Manhatten – ed.]. I don't like having three unfinished films, but very much like having them to edit. *Zoo* is almost all instinctive animal action and very little dialogue. *High School II* is all talk. *Ballet* is consciously crafted movement to great music. I have to find an editing style appropriate for each film. As usual this is not a problem I can solve in the abstract. I can't start with general statements about editorial style, but have to find my way by learning the material and responding to what I find. Any documentary, mine or anyone else's, made in no matter what style, is arbitrary, biased, prejudiced, compressed and subjective. Like any of its sisterly or brotherly fictional forms it is born in choice – choice of subject matter, place, people, camera angles, duration of shooting, sequences to be shot or omitted, transitional material and cutaways.

Now that the shooting of *Zoo* is over and I stare at the rushes – 100 hours of film hanging on the editing room wall, a different series of choices emerges. This great glop of material which represents the externally recorded memory of my experience of making the film is of necessity incomplete. The memories not preserved on film float somewhat in my mind as fragments available for recall, unavailable for inclusion but of great importance in the mining and shifting process known as editing. This editorial process which is sometimes deductive, sometimes associational, sometimes non-logical and sometimes a failure, is occasionally boring and often exciting. The crucial element for me is to try and think through my own relationship to the material by whatever combination of means is compatible. This involves a need to conduct a four-way conversation between myself, the sequence being worked on, my memory, and general values and experience. The big issue for the moment is can I get myself to sit in the basement and start thinking specifically about the *Zoo* material? Writing these theoretical statements about editing is just a diversion. I've got to go to the basement.

Maine, 13 August 1992
Back at the editing full swing. Started at 6.30 this morning. A short break for lunch and then kept going until an early evening walk. I think or hope that I'm getting somewhere with the rhino birth sequence. This will become a key event in the final film. The rhino was in labour eleven hours. Immediately after the birth the mother sniffed the baby and moved away. The animal curator lifted the still-born baby out of the pen. The vet gave the baby mouth-to-mouth resuscitation, alternating with the animal curator who pounded on the baby's chest, but the baby never began to breathe. The vet cried and the curator and keepers were visibly sad. The dead baby rhino was placed in the back of a pick-up truck and taken to the morgue.

I have just written an eighty-six-word summary (which takes eleven seconds to read) of an event that took eleven hours in real time and of which approximately three hours were recorded on film. My job as editor is to reduce the experience of watching and recording the rhino give birth to a form that works as an individual sequence and that also fits into the rythym and structure of the final film.

Maine, 17 August 1992
My thoughts about the sequences have to be more precise and specific in the editing than during shooting. In shooting, the motivation to record a particular sequence may result from the way someone walks or is dressed; or a hunch, the intuition that something interesting may develop when two people begin to talk. When I have that feeling I've learned to follow it, which is not to say the hunch is always right but rather that in not following it no risk is taken and therefore the risk of missing a 'good' sequence occurs. During the shooting there is no time to do an analysis of the various elements that make the sequence 'good'; attention has to be directed to 'getting' the sequence so that the detailed analysis can be made later. This kind of analysis is retroactively

necessary with all sequences but some, like the rhino birth, are more immediately apparent as an important sequence in the final film.

One aspect of the editing, then, is to confirm or reject the original intuition and to edit, and therefore analyse, the sequence in such a way that it conveys some meaning to a viewer who was not originally present (at, for example, the rhino birth), but to whom the event and its interpretation can be presented in a comprehensible form.

(The diary excerpts jump ahead one year)

Maine, 20 August 1993
Today I worked on the sequence in *High School II* where a fifteen-year-old girl comes back after a six-week absence because she gave birth to her first child. As is so often the case I came across this sequence during the shooting completely by chance. I was walking down the corridor near the principal's office and saw a baby carriage. This was an unusual sight in the high school. I stopped and spoke to the girl who was standing behind the carriage. She told me she was there to talk to the principal and that her mother and brother were with her. I asked all the family whether it was all right with them to shoot the meeting with the principal and explained that I was making a film for public television. The family and the principal had no objection. The meeting went on for an hour and a half and all but about three minutes of it was recorded on film.

The meeting had a variety of purposes. The principal wanted to find out if the girl really wanted to come back to school, what arrangements were made for the care of the baby during school hours, was there going to be a problem between the girl and the baby's father who was also a student at the school but was no longer the girl's boyfriend, did the father accept any responsibility for the child, what was the relationship between the brother and the father since at one time they had been best friends, was the father's new girlfriend bothering the mother and the child, did the mother know that there were other high schools in the city that had nurseries so that the child could be brought to school with the mother, did the mother want to complete high school and go on to college?

The editorial problem was how to give a fair sense of what went on in the meeting without showing the entire hour and a half. I tried to include as many of these issues as I could, attempting to balance complete coverage, suggestion and superficiality so as to give a fair account and highlight the dramatic aspects of the sequence. I now have the sequence down to twenty-two minutes but it still needs more work.

Maine, 21 August 1993
I took another seven minutes out of the teenage mother sequence, mainly by cutting repetitions, shaving the pauses and trying to preserve the dialogue that best explained what was going on. Fortunately, there were enough cut-aways so that I could jump around. If there is one lesson I have learned it's that you can never have enough cut-aways. All those quiet moments when no one is talking, or when you expect someone to talk and they don't, provide you with the shots you need in order to condense and compress a sequence. The idea is to have the audience feel for at least two seconds that what they are watching actually took place the way they are seeing it.

Maine, 22 August 1993
The sequence with the teenage mother may cause me some trouble when the film is released. There may be some people who say that not many students at Central Park East become mothers and that the sequence is not representative of a problem at the school, although it is generally a common enough occurrence. I have no way of determining what is or is not representative in any sequence. It's enough for me that it occurred while I was present and that it fits into the themes I find in the material. I am not interested in ideological film-making, whether of the right or left. I remember being criticized by some on the left when I made *Hospital*. They knew from their ideological positions that white middle-class doctors and nurses exploited poor blacks and Hispanics. Therefore a film like *Hospital* which showed many white doctors and nurses (as well as black and Hispanic doctors and nurses) working hard, long hours to help their patients was ideologically offensive. Film ideologues are not interested in the discovery and surprise aspect of documentary film-making, or in trusting their own or anyone else's independent judgement, but want documentary film-makers to confirm their own ideological, abstract views which have little or no connection with experience. Some documentary film-makers urged on in their self-generated political fantasies by academics and other ideologues, by film barons and bureaucrats, and by all those who form the parasitic platoons fluttering around film-makers, believe documentaries must

educate, expose, inform, reform and effect change in a resistant and otherwise unenlightened world. Documentaries are thought to have the same relation to social change as penicillin to syphilis. The importance of documentaries as political instruments for change is stubbornly clung to, despite the total absence of any supporting evidence.

Sometimes, in his lofty condescension, a film-maker seeks to bring enlightenment to the great unwashed and force feed this or that trendy political pap to an audience which has not had the opportunity, or perhaps even the wish, to participate in either the experience or the mind of the film-maker. This, which might be called the 'Carlos' fantasy, suggests to the film-maker that he is important to the world. Documentaries like plays, novels, poems – are fictional in form and have no measurable social utility.

Source: *Dox: Documentary Quarterly*, no. 1, Spring 1994.

37 Hospital *(1970)*.

Part 4

10 The Cinema of Social Concern

INTRODUCTION

Ask the average person what documentaries are and they're likely to say that they're boring films about striking miners, exploited workers, teenage mothers and other 'social problems'. Although this is prejudiced and clichéd, it is true that fiction film-makers, as a group, tend towards the political right, while documentarists are almost exclusively left-wing. Why is this? Why are there almost no right-wing documentaries being made today?

Is it because documentarists have always been idealists, seeing themselves as intrepid advocates of truth and human rights? Their form became a radical tool, the friend of the individual in the fight against the monolithic and bureaucratic, and, therefore, inimical to the corporate ethos. It seems the closest the right – typified by the corporation – can come to documentary today is the glossy corporate video, an expensive fabrication of soundbites and 'stylish' images, in which no one is allowed to speak in an extended or critical manner, everyone smiles and everything is rosy – propaganda.

Despite its dominance of the genre, the social problem documentary does not seem to satisfy many contemporary documentarists. The newer generation of film-makers have reacted against its perceived preachiness, looking instead for a style that is imaginative, challenging and visually stimulating. The classic documentary of social concern is not in fashion. Television commissioning editors, almost the sole source of money for documentaries now, don't want the down-beat, the depressing and the real on their screens. Audiences switch off.

The following chapter hopes to emphasize that, at its best, the 'traditional' left-wing, social documentary had real aesthetic power and social impact. The documentarist's ambition to change the world was, often, a noble one.

An Interview with Santiago Alvarez

If the Revolutionary cinema of the Soviet Union was all but stultified by the mid 1930s, its spirit was alive and well in the Caribbean thirty years later. Encouraged by the film-minded Fidel Castro, for several decades Cuba turned out the most impressive political cinema in the world.

At the forefront of the Cuban industry was the enormously talented, socially-engaged, cine–journalist Santiago Alvarez (born 1919). In a series of newsreels, shorts and feature-length documentaries, he developed a daring, innovative film-making style, replete with polemic vigour and audiovisual gymnastics that would put most 'pop-promo' directors to shame.

This sympathetic interview appeared in *Cineaste* magazine in 1975.

The importance of the cinema in Cuba can be seen from the fact that the Cuban film institute – the *Instituto Cubano del Arte e Industria Cinematograficos*, or ICAIC for short – was founded in March 1959, just three months after the triumph of the Revolution. From an initially modest program and extremely meagre resources, the Cuban film industry has today developed into one of the most politically and artistically vital cinemas in all of Latin America and one whose films have received international critical acclaim.

Santiago Alvarez is generally regarded as the grand old master of Cuban documentarians. Born in Havana in 1919, Alvarez made two trips to the US, the first in 1939 and a second later to study for a short time at Columbia University in New York City. After returning to Cuba, he studied Philosophy and Literature at Havana University, was a founding member of the *Nuestro Tiempo* cine-club in the 1950s, and actively participated in the underground struggle against the Batista dictatorship. After the Revolution, Alvarez was appointed head of ICAIC's Short Film Department. In 1960 he became director of its 'Latin American Newsreel' and he and his co-workers have produced one *noticero* per week ever since.

From the essentially straightforward, matter-of-fact reportage of *Ciclon* (1963), a report on the devastating effects of hurricane 'Flora', Alvarez's later films demonstrate the development of a fast, free-wheeling editing style combined with a prominent use of music and the utilization of a wide range of materials and methods – live documentary footage, archival material, clips from features and TV programmes, animation, graphics, historical footage, comic books – anything, in fact, to make his point. As Gitlin describes it: 'The incredible energy of Cuban life is echoed in the wild pace and hard variety of an Alvarez film . . . He thinks nothing of playing rock music over a shot of troop mobilization; George Harrison over parched Indian soil; Tchaikovsky's *Piano Concerto* over the Havana skyline.'

In *Hanoi, Tuesday the 13th* (1967), by showing us the daily texture of life in Hanoi under bombardment, Alvarez succeeds in showing us more about the resilience which allowed the Vietnamese to survive and fight their war than the voice-over rhetoric so often used in films on the Vietnam War. In *Take-off at 18:00* (1970), he depicts Cuba at a turning point facing the American blockade, with the Revolution consolidated and the country mobilizing for the sugar harvest, preparing for economic take-off. His recent feature-length documentaries on Fidel's trip to Chile, *De America Soy Hijo Y A Ella Me Debo* (1971), and to the Soviet Union, Eastern Europe and Africa, *Y El Cielo Fue Tomado Por Asalto* (1973), rather than merely recording the Cuban leader's travels, use these trips to expound certain ideas. In the Chilean film it is the idea of Latin American solidarity in confronting the United States and, in *Y El Cielo Fue Tomado Por Asalto*, the notion of Marxism as a humanism and the theme of proletarian internationalism.

Santiago Alvarez is presently in Vietnam where in February of this year he began production on *Year of the Cat*, a feature-length documentary history of Vietnam.

Q: *We'd like to begin with a little personal history about yourself – what you did before the Revolution, how you came to work in the cinema, and so on.*

A: Before the Revolution I was just a film buff, just a spectator like any other spectator from any other part of the world. I belonged to a cultural society *Nuestro Tiempo* [*Our Times*], which had a cine-club where we saw and theoretically discussed the film classics. Other comrades who today work at ICAIC – Alfredo Guevara, Julio Garcia Espinosa, Tomas Gutierrez Alea – also belonged to that cine-club. We also screened some of the classic revolutionary films from the Soviet Union. There was a distributor of Soviet films for Cuba and Mexico and we used to rent them and show them in a small movie house on Sunday mornings. We would get together to show the films and discuss them but it was also a pretext to recruit leftist people and talk about social problems.

Before that, in 1939, I lived in the United States, working as a dishwasher and working in the coal mines in Pennsylvania. It was here in the United States that I started to become politically conscious and when I went back to Cuba I became a communist. American imperialism is the greatest promoter of communism in the world. In fact, it was my experiences here that form the roots of *Now*, my film against racial discrimination in the US. That film grew directly out of my experiences here. It all came back to me one day when I was listening to a song called 'Now' sung by Lena Horne – it's a melody based on an old Hebrew song by an anonymous author. When I started to work on the film at ICAIC, that background, that experience, helped me – I used all the hate I had felt against discrimination and brutality.

I really started learning about the cinema in 1959. After the revolution when the film institute was created – it was the first law about cultural matters that Fidel signed – I started making a newsreel of the first trip that President Dorticos made throughout Latin America. That was the first

38 Los Quatro Puentes *(1968).*

issue of ICAIC's *Noticiero Latinoamericano*. The day that the Moviola arrived at ICAIC so we could do the work it was a cause for celebration. It was a Moviola with only a viewing screen and no sound head, but I still have it and work with it. Every piece of equipment then, like the little pins where you hang the takes in the editing room, was something new for us. We had all talked about the cinema, but we didn't know how to make it. Behind all our ignorance about equipment, though, there was a tremendous desire to move ahead, to fight the reactionary capitalist newsreels that were still being made and disseminating counter-revolutionary propaganda during that period in Cuba.

Q: *As time went on, was there any noticeable evolution in the style of the newsreels? It seems to me that there are a lot of similarities between your films and those of the Soviet film-maker, Dziga Vertov.*

A: Actually, the first newsreels that we made were influenced by traditional newsreels. They were not revolutionary in a formal sense but the content was revolutionary. After we had completed about twenty of them, we started to look for new, expressive cinematic forms for the newsreel.

As for Dziga Vertov, that is a question I'm asked in every interview but I must say that there is absolutely no influence of Vertov in my films. In fact, when I first started making films I hadn't seen any films by Vertov. It is true that the reality Vertov experienced is similar to the one we have experienced and it is this reality, perhaps, which is the common denominator of our films.

In this regard, I think it is important to point out the importance of the Revolution as a powerful motivating force for us – the revolutionary process in Cuba has been the main inspirational muse of all our work. Before the Revolution there was no cinematic expression in Cuba. Every four or five years a North American producer would come to the country and make a pseudo-folkloric or musical film, utilizing exotic elements of our culture in a superficial manner. Sometimes they would use a few Cuban technicians, maybe borrowed from the TV studios, but only a few. So in order for us to begin making films there had to be a revolutionary will, a revolutionary inspiration.

Q: *Specifically, in terms of the application of Marxism in your films, I'm thinking of* Y El Cielo Fue Tomado Por Asalto *where you develop a thesis . . .*

A: Yes, a materialist thesis. The beginning of the film, the introduction, deals with the birth of a child where we show scientific scenes of childbirth as contrasted with Renaissance paintings of children with the Virgin. So we have a juxtaposition of the images of how a child is actually born, scientifically, with those beautiful paintings from the idealist Renaissance world which suggest that the child was born from the Virgin, from all those religious ideas. It's a materialist world view opposed to an idealist world view.

. . . The part of making a film I like best is the editing. My work in the editing room is completely different from that of the other comrades at ICAIC. Many times editors don't want to work with me because they're used to having an easy time with directors who just supervise and let them do the work. But I do all the work myself – I myself break up the material, I don't let the assistant editor do it, I myself hang up the takes in order to see what each sequence is all about. I look at it and look at it and look at it. And I am meticulous, I even choose the exact frame where I want to cut – five frames are five frames, not six, but five. Then, while I am looking at the footage and doing the editing, I start thinking about editing the sound. When I transfer to mag-track, I'm still doing the editing of the sequences because I'm searching for the music at the same time that I'm doing the montage. When I'm listening to the sound I'm thinking about the structure of the sequence and when I'm editing the image I'm always thinking of what sound will go with it. As I'm putting it together and it begins to take on a certain rhythm, I think about what effects, what sound, what music, will go with that image. Fifty per cent of the value of a film is in the sound track . . .

Q: *How successful have Cuban film-makers been in improving public taste? Do Cuban audiences still prefer 'entertainment' films to 'political' films?*

A: We *are* the public, film-makers *are* the public. We start from the basis that we belong to the social reality of our country, we are not foreigners, we are part of the people and our films grow out of a shared reality. If we thought we were a privileged group above the people, then we would probably make films that communicated only with a minority or an élite group. But we are not a group of poets producing abstract or bizarre poetry. One can only be a revolutionary artist by being with the people and by communicating with them.

It has been a challenge for us but we have been successful to some extent in breaking public movie-going habits. Due to the influence of capitalism, even in socialist countries, it has always been the custom to show documentaries only as supplementary material with a feature-length fiction film with actors as the main attraction. But we have been able to show documentaries as the main attraction in theatres. For example, *De America Soy Hijo* which lasts three hours and fifteen minutes and which features as its main character Fidel on a trip, was released simultaneously in seven theatres and there were still long lines of people and they had full houses for two months. Another documentary, *Y El Cielo Fue Tomado Por Asalto* which lasts two hours and eight minutes, was similarly successful . . .

Q: *In conclusion, any thoughts about the future?*

A: I think that in twenty years the cinema is going to disappear, there will be another technology to replace it. There will be new developments in electronic techniques which will completely change the traditional method of making films, not only in Cuba but everywhere. Technology is going to absolutely change everything and the means of communication – for the painter, the musician, the film-maker – will change radically.

I think the individualistic conception of art will change completely and we will no longer continue the practice of the museum or private exhibition of art works as we do now. The creators, the artists in society, will put their energies into making not just one painting but into creating mass art works, into beautifying shoes, homes, factories, everything, the total environment. It will be an anti-individualistic conception of artistic creation where everything will be for the benefit of all humanity.

Source: *Cineaste*, 1975, Vol. 6, No. 4.

History is the Theme of All my Films
AN INTERVIEW WITH EMILE DE ANTONIO

Emil De Antonio (1920–1989) was born into a wealthy Pennsylvanian family and was an early convert to Marxism. After a number of jobs, including barge captain, teacher and longshoreman, he entered films in 1964 with a compilation about the McCarthy hearings, *Point of Order!*

Thereafter he made numerous documentaries reflecting his leftist perspective including *In The Year of the Pig* (1969) about the Vietnam war, *Milhouse: A White Comedy* (1971), which satirized President Nixon, *Underground* (1976), about the radical anti-capitalist Weathermen underground movement and *Painters Painting* (1972), in some senses an uncharacteristic documentary on the post-war New York school of painters. At the time of his death he had just completed the film *Mr. Hoover and I*, a self-portrait through 10,000 pages of FBI reports on him which he retrieved through a law suit based on the Freedom of Information Act.

CINEASTE: *How do you go about making a compilation documentary such as* In the Year of the Pig? *Do you start from a predetermined political thesis that you want to illustrate, or do you do film research first and work out a narrative line from the material available?*

DE ANTONIO: I approach all of my work from a consciously left viewpoint. It's very hard to articulate what it means to be a Marxist today, but it was a little bit clearer in 1967 when I began *Pig*. The film originally grew out of anger, outrage, and passion, but I knew that all of these, estimable as they are as motivations, are wrong if unchecked in a film, because you end up with only a scream, a poster that shouts 'Out of Vietnam!' It seemed to me that the most passionate statement that could be made was to make a film that would treat the history of Vietnam as far back as the footage would take it, to cover the whole history of the war, from its earliest days to the Tet Offensive in 1968, which was the year I completed the film. Compilation film-making lends itself best to history, which is, frankly, the theme of all my films.

The first thing I did was read about 200 books in French and English on Vietnam, because I figured that was one way I could find the images. Many who do compilation documentaries today come from an anti-intellectual generation, or have no historical sense, and they're motivated primarily by flashy images or simple prejudices, when what they should be looking for are historical resonances which are filmic.

Q: *In other words, you're really interested in finding images for a general schema that you've gotten after all your reading, whereas some film-makers feel that they can just rummage through a lot of archival footage and find a film there.*

A: Yes, that's right. I think you've got to do a hell of a lot of homework. I then proceed to assemble a chaotic draft of the subject. I knew that I was going to pursue an historical line, although not necessarily a chronological line. I had a friend who owned a box factory and he used to give me corrugated paper in rolls nine feet high, and I'd tack them up on my office walls. I'd start out by writing 'Han Dynasty', even though I knew I'd never put anything about the Han Dynasty in the film, because the Chinese experience begins there. I would obviously write down 'Dien Bien Phu, 1954, May 8th', and abstract concepts like 'torture', 'inhumanity', and other things that interested me. Sometimes I would also paste a picture into it, so I would have visual images as well as words on the walls.

Once this huge outline was done, I started to do extensive film research. I went to Prague, for instance, where the NLF had a main office and they gave me tremendous footage. I went to East Germany and there I met the Soviets who gave me Roman Karmen's restaging of the battle of Dien Bien Phu. Sometimes it's very sad, by the way, when good research pays off, because most of the people who saw *In the Year of the Pig* thought that really was the battle of Dien Bien Phu. When I lecture with the film today, I tell audiences that, 'You should look more carefully, because if you look at those Vietminh troops, you know they're not actually in combat. They're all so neatly dressed and running at port arms as if some Major were in the back giving orders.' Still, it was beautiful footage, and I think I used it well, because I cut from that to the real footage of all those white faces surrendering to yellow faces, which is one of the symbols of that war.

I met with the Hanoi people in Paris and I was the first westerner to get an extraordinary film called *The Life of Ho Chi Minh*, which is their view of Ho, with early stills of Ho and his family, and great material of Ho joining the French Communist Party in 1922. I love that kind of material. I also got access to the French Army's film library, the greatest collection of Vietnam footage that exists. It goes back to 1902. While there I saw Pierre Schoendoerffer's great footage that nobody's ever seen. He was a sergeant in Vietnam, the head of a camera crew, and got some of the greatest shots of tanks in battle in the jungle that I've ever seen. He later made several documentaries, including *La 317ème Section* and *The Anderson Platoon*. I had acquired a whole bunch of this stuff when one of the two young French sergeants assigned to me said, 'Listen, they're going to pull it out from under you, because now they know who you are, and you're not going to get one frame of this stuff.' There's this beautiful shot in *Pig* of something you can't get in this country. It's Ho Chi Minh with Admiral d'Argenlieu, the French Commissioner of Vietnam, aboard the battlecruiser *Richlieu.* It's the end of talking, a really symbolic scene, because the war's really going to go now, and, as Ho leaves the ship, with the French saluting, he takes the cigarette out of his mouth, and, in that casual way of his, flips it over the side. I had to have that shot, so I said to the kid, 'Listen, I'm going to steal this. Would you mind going out because I don't want you to be implicated in all this.' So I just cut that shot out of the roll of 35mm negative and stuck it into the pocket of my raincoat. I realized that since they knew who I was now, there was a good chance that the guys with the guns at the gate would stop me, and I could have gotten five years for that in France, but I thought it was worth it. Making films is risk-taking.

The thing that staggered me was that even though the TV networks were going on and on about Vietnam, and other people were making films about Vietnam, no one found the footage I did for *Pig.* I located several great scenes no one ever picked up, including one of the film's best scenes, from the 1930s, which is of these absolutely arrogant French men in their colonial hats and white suits being pulled in rickshaws by Vietnamese. They arrive in front of a café where there is a tall Moroccan with a fez – the scene encapsulates the whole French colonial empire – and when the Vietnamese put their hands out for payment, the Moroccan sends them away like trash. To me, that said everything you could say about colonialism without ever saying the word. If anything shows the primacy of the image over the word, what the image can reveal, it's the image of those rickshaws. It's the equivalent of a couple of chapters of dense writing about the meaning of colonialism.

Q: *How do you respond to those who dismiss the film as propaganda?*

A: There is out and out propaganda in the film, obviously, although sometimes I don't know what the distinction is between propaganda and passion, and propaganda and politics. I wanted to make Ho look as good as he could be made to look. It wasn't very hard. Ho was a patriot and a Marxist. There's a lovely sequence of Ho surrounded by a bunch of children and Dan Berrigan says in a voice-over, 'The Vietnamese know what it is to have a leader who leads a simple life.' I used another

39 In the Year of the Pig (1969).

shot they gave me of where Ho lived, which was a small space with a tiny typewriter and one extra Vietnamese suit hanging there, and you knew it wasn't bullshit.

An interesting thing happened when I spoke with the film on Mayday

in 1969 at Columbia University. It was still tumultuous there, even
though it was after the 1968 riots. In the film I have scenes of Sam 3
missiles shooting down American planes, and when the first American
plane flew over, with its insignia clearly visible, and it was shot down,
the whole audience clapped. I thought, 'Jesus, that's weird, isn't it?
What have I done?' I mean, I was in the Air Force, I flew, and, looking at
that scene on the editing table, I wouldn't have clapped. They were
right, of course, except that my reaction was a little more complex.

Q: *What is your approach to editing?*

A: I'm very slow. I mean, I could cut my new film in two weeks, and it
would be OK, but it wouldn't be my film. I work very hard at editing,
I'm never satisfied. I always edit with the whole picture in mind. When I
finish a sequence, I run the entire film from the beginning to see how it
plays. I'll continue working on a scene until I'm satisfied. Finding a
suitable ending to *Pig*, for example, proved a real problem. Originally,
the ending I was going to use was some footage that the Hanoi people
had given me. I had been playing with it for weeks. It was a very quiet
scene of a road in North Vietnam and, suddenly, the brush around the
road gets up, it's the Vietminh, and they come charging out. But I
thought, 'Shit, I'm an American. I mean, I hope the Vietnamese win this
war, I think our position is immoral, and I'm a Marxist, but I'm not
Vietnamese. That would be a suitable ending for a Vietnamese film, but
I'm an American.' I decided to show that, even though we're Americans,
the Vietnamese can punish us, so I got all this footage of dead and
wounded Americans with bandages around their eyes, blinded, being
evacuated. Then I took a shot of a Civil War statue – a young man who
died at Gettysburg – and reversed it, put it into negative, to show, in my
mind anyway, that our cause in Vietnam was not the one that boy had
died for in 1863, and then added a kind of scratchy version of 'The
Battle Hymn of the Republic'. For me that was a suitable ending, a
politically coherent ending . . .

Q: *We understand that Andy Warhol made a film about you. What was
that like?*

A: Andy and I have been friends for a long time, since long before he
was a painter. One day he said to me, 'De, I think we should make a film
together.' I said, 'Come on, Andy, we're friends, but I like to make
political films and you make these *frou-frou* films.' Then one night I saw

him at a bar, when I was drunk, and I said, 'OK, Andy, let's do it!' He said, 'What shall we film?' and I said, 'I'll drink a quart of whiskey in twenty minutes.' I knew that twenty-two-year-old Marines had died doing it, but I knew what I was doing. I'm a very good drinker.

I showed up at his studio with my wife and a drinking companion. They turned the lights on and I sat there cross-legged against a wall and drank a quart of J & B whiskey in twenty minutes. It was boring, nothing happened. I didn't want the glass, so I broke it. I had some ice and I threw that away. Andy was filming with a twelve hundred foot 16mm magazine which runs for thirty-five minutes. When it came time to change the magazine, he was so untrained in the use of the camera that it took him about fifteen minutes to change it. So, by the time the second roll went on, I was on the floor. I mean, I couldn't even get up. My hand goes up the wall, trying to pull myself up, I'm singing Spanish Civil War songs, and shouting, 'Fuck you!' It was unspeakably degrading. I finally walked out with the help of my wife and friend and went home and slept it off. The next day I was sharp enough to call my lawyer and have him call Andy and tell him, 'De never signed a release, so if the film is ever shown, we'll sue.' It appears in Andy's published filmography – it's called *Drink* – but it's never been shown.

Q: *How do you perceive your audience? Who are you making films for, and what sort of political impact can your films have?*

A: A great American, Walt Whitman, said that to have great poetry, you must have great audiences. Since I'm interested in history, I'm obviously interested in what happens to my films over the long haul. Anyone who makes films wants them to be seen, and I would do anything except change my films to reach a larger audience. But in America and most western capitalist countries, film – from its earliest, nickelodeon days up to the most sophisticated mind control today through television – has been seen as an opiate, as entertainment. As the old Hollywood saw has it, 'If you have a message, use Western Union.' Well, all my films have messages, but I don't want to send them by Western Union.

I have never looked upon documentary as an apprenticeship for the making of Hollywood films. That's bullshit. I've always chosen to make documentaries. I love documentary film, I love the political tradition of documentary film, and I love the subjects that documentary film can treat.

Source: From an interview by Gary Crowdus and Dan Georgakas, in *Cineaste* 1982, Vol. 12, No. 2.

Filming Torture Victims
HASKELL WEXLER

Born in Chicago in 1926, Wexler is a noted cinematographer whose numerous feature credits include *Who's Afraid of Viginia Woolf?* (1966), *Bound For Glory* (1976), *Days of Heaven* (1978) and *Colors* (1988). As a director he has made several politically motivated documentaries and the outstanding feature *Medium Cool* (1969). The film which he discusses in this extract, *Brazil: A Report on Torture*, was co-directed with Saul Landau.

When I first showed the rushes [to his documentary *Brazil: A Report on Torture*, 1971] to some friends, I got some interesting comments. Someone said, 'That guy doesn't come off too well in the film. What he's saying doesn't seem sincere.' Well, she was right. One of the guys just had a manner of speaking and looking that was less convincing. But I know he was telling the truth; all his compañeros were there, and he couldn't possibly have invented all those fantastic factual things. So here are real people in a real-life situation, speaking directly to the camera, and we evaluate them like actors. Once it's reduced to a medium – like film or tape we automatically make a theatrical judgment. We made them when we were cutting the film. Even though there's very little manipulation in the cutting – it's just interviews interspersed with some demonstrations of the tortures by the people who had been tortured – we still had to say, 'Well, is it better to have a woman here and a guy there, or should he say this here or there?' In other words, the degree of manipulation, even through the most honest hands, is still considerable. One of the things that showing the dailies did was convince me that when something is reduced to a medium, taken out of reality, it becomes subject to a theatrical evaluation. Nobody gives a shit if it's real anyway, because if you can do it better theatrically you can be more convincing than if you did it actually.

Source: From an interview in *Take One*, July–Aug 1971.

Roger & Me
ROGER EBERT

With *Roger and Me* (1989), Michael Moore broke many of the unwritten taboos of the social documentary by combining irreverence, humour and savagery in a way that had never been seen before. An enormously popular and influential film, it received a successful theatrical release – re-opening after many years the possibility of cinema distribution for documentaries.

Moore has subsequently produced a satirical feature film, *Canadian Bacon* (1994) and a hugely successful series for British and American television, *TV Nation*, which humorously exposes injustice and hypocrisy in high places.

The peculiar genius of *Roger and Me* is not that it's a funny film or an angry film, or even a film with a point to make – although it is all three of those things. It connects because it's a revenge comedy, a film in which the stinkers get their comeuppance at last. It generates the same kind of laughter that Jack Nicholson inspired in that immortal scene [in *Five Easy Pieces*] where he told the waitress what she could do with the chicken salad. It allows the audience to share in the delicious sensation of getting even.

The movie was made by Michael Moore, a native of Flint, Michigan, the birthplace of General Motors. As GM closed eleven plants in Flint and laid off some 33,000 workers, Moore got mad – and this is his response. But it's not a dreary documentary about hard times in the rust belt. It's a stinging comedy that sticks in the knife of satire and twists.

The ostensible subject of the film is the attempt by Moore to get an interview with Roger Smith, chairman of General Motors. We know right away that this is one interview that is unlikely to take place. Moore, a ramshackle man-mountain who fancies baseball caps and overflowing Hush Puppies, wanders through the film like a babe in toyland. He's the kind of guy who gets in an elevator in GM headquarters in Detroit and is surprised when the button for the top floor – Smith's office – doesn't light up when it's pressed. The closest he gets to Smith is a slick, oily GM public relations man who explains why the layoffs are regrettable but necessary. (It goes without saying that the spokesman himself is eventually laid off.)

Denied access to Smith, *Roger and Me* pokes around elsewhere in

Flint. It follows a deputy sheriff on his rounds as he evicts unemployed auto workers. It covers a 'Flint Pride' parade that marches depressingly past the boarded-up store windows of downtown. It listens to enthusiastic spokesmen for Auto World, an indoor amusement park where Flint citizens can visit a replica of their downtown as it used to look before the boards went up. It listens as a civic booster boasts that Flint's new Hyatt Hotel has escalators and 'big plants' in the lobby – just like the Hyatts in Atlanta and Chicago. The hotel and amusement park are supposed to create a tourism industry for Flint, but the biggest convention booked into the hotel is the state Scrabble tournament, and when Auto World goes out of business, the rueful Chamber of Commerce-type speculates that asking people to come to Flint for Auto World 'is sort of like asking them to come to Alaska for Exxon World'. Many celebrities wander through the film, brought to Flint by big fees to cheer people up. Anita Bryant sings, Pat Boone suggests that the unemployed workers might become Amway distributors, and Ronald Reagan has pizza with the jobless, but forgets to pick up the check.

Meanwhile, some resourceful victims fight back. A woman advertises 'Bunnies as Pets or Rabbits as Meat'. Jobless auto workers hire themselves out as living statues who stand around in costume at a Great Gatsby charity benefit. Some local industries even improve – there's need for a new jail, for example. And the local socialites hold a charity ball in the jail the night before it opens for business. They have a lot of fun wearing riot helmets and banging each other over the head with police batons.

Roger and Me does have a message to deliver – a message about corporate newspeak and the ways in which profits really are more important to big American corporations than the lives of their workers. The movie is a counterattack against the amoral pragmatism of modern management theory, against the sickness of the 'In Search of Excellence' mentality.

Michael Moore has struck a nerve with this movie. There are many Americans, I think, who have not lost the ability to think and speak in plain English – to say what they mean. These people were driven mad by the 1980s, in which a new kind of bureaucratese was spawned by Ronald Reagan and his soulmates – a new manner of speech by which it became possible to 'address the problem', while saying nothing and yet somehow conveying optimism.

40 Roger and Me *(1989)*.

Roger Smith and General Motors are good at that kind of talk. *Roger and Me* undercuts it with blunt contradictions. In the movie's single most haunting image, Smith addresses a GM Christmas television hookup, reading from *A Christmas Carol* while Moore shows deputies evicting a jobless GM worker and throwing his Christmas tree in the gutter. A spokesman for GM has attacked this scene as 'manipulative'. It certainly is. But Smith's treacly Christmas ceremony is manipulative, too, and so is the whole corporate doublespeak that justifies his bottom-line heartlessness. The genius of *Roger and Me* is that it understands the image-manipulating machinery of corporate public relations and fights back with the same cynicism and cleverness. The wonder is that the movie is both so angry and so funny. We knew revenge was sweet. What the movie demonstrates is that it is also hilarious – for the avenged.

Source: Roger Ebert's *Video Companion*

Death of a Nation
KEN LOACH

To celebrate its 400th issue, the editors of the French film magazine
Positif asked film-makers from around the world to write something
'about an actor, or a film, or a director who has had a special
significance' for them. Uniquely, Ken Loach chose to write not about a
'great work of art', but about a television documentary.

The film that is most in my thoughts as I write is a documentary by John
Pilger and David Munro called *Death of a Nation*. It tells the story of
the brutal occupation of East Timor by its neighbour Indonesia. Some
of the filming was done in secret, without the approval or knowledge of
the Indonesian authorities. Journalists are not welcome. Two Australian
television teams were murdered in 1975 by the Indonesian Army for
trying to break the wall of silence that the Jakarta régime and its
western allies have built around East Timor.

The silence was to hide the fact that 200,000 people, a third of the
population, have died in this invasion. This has happened with the
complicity of western governments, despite Indonesia's defiance of
many UN resolutions calling on it to withdraw from East Timor. A
British ambassador is quoted: 'We should let matters take their course.'

The military coup that established Suharto's power in Indonesia met
with the approval of the US. The American Ambassador says,
'Washington is sympathetic with and admiring of what the army is
doing.' This is juxtaposed in the film with pictures of Indonesians
uncovering a mass grave of the victims of that same army's brutality.

The story of the destruction of East Timor's emerging democracy is
heart-breaking, particularly as western intelligence knew in advance
every move the Indonesians were making. The archives show appeals by
the Timorese leaders to 'stop the Indonesian isolation of our territory'.
They got no response.

The film shows why in a telling exchange between John Pilger and
Alan Clark, the British Minister of Defence. Britain sold arms to
Indonesia during its attack on the Timorese people.

PILGER: *Did it ever bother you personally that this British equipment
was causing such mayhem and human suffering?*

CLARKE: No, not in the slightest, never entered my head.

The fact that we supply highly effective equipment to a régime like that then is not a consideration as far as you're concerned?

Not at all.

It is not a personal consideration?

No, not at all.

I ask the question because I read you are a vegetarian and you are quite seriously concerned about the way animals are killed.

Yes.

Doesn't that concern extend to the way humans, albeit foreigners, are killed?

Curiously not, no.

Film-makers with access to mass communications have a responsibility to expose the lies and hypocrisy of politicians and the interests they represent. This film is more valuable to us than a hundred self-absorbed movies, however prettily shot.

Source: *Positif* No. 400, 1994. This translation from *Projections* 4½, Faber and Faber, 1995.

On the Rebound: *Hoop Dreams* and its Discontents
PAUL ARTHUR AND JANET CUTLER

Released theatrically and then on sell-through video, *Hoop Dreams* has been the most commercially successful documentary of recent years. This critique comes from *Cineaste* magazine.

As the clock ticks toward zero on the American Century, sports are all the rage. Living in the moonlit Age of O.J., the epicentre of our national identity can no longer be located midway between Wall Street and the Pentagon – as the mid 1950s rubric had it – but somewhere along a televisual circuit that connects the Brown/Goldman murder scene at Bundy, Madison Avenue, and various sites of athletic prowess. The spectacle of pro sports is so thoroughly enmeshed in our frameworks of social analysis and self-promotion that we hardly flinch when ex-jocks get touted as presidential fodder or when the dubious careers of second-rate ice-skaters and prize fighters are cast by hip academics as well as talk show hosts as biblical parables. Meanwhile 'mundane' news is regularly overshadowed by sports strikes and lockouts, the return of the Mikes (Jordan and Tyson), player drug revelations, and baseball PBS style.

In this context, the instant appeal of the documentary *Hoop Dreams* is that of a dramatic 'prequel', an evocative account of the road to potential stardom for two Chicago kids, fraught with all the pressures, deceptions, and heartbreaks that inform the back stories of many NBA icons. Produced as a five year labour of love by grass roots indie film-makers Steve James, Frederick Marx, and Peter Gilbert, *Hoop Dreams* has, like its hopeful subjects, emerged from the cultural 'ghetto' of non-fiction cinema into the glare of a surprising notoriety. Fueled by universal critical acclaim – the choice of over one hundred 'Ten Best' lists – and the controversy generated by its failure to capture an Oscar nomination, *Hoop Dreams* has been elevated to a cause. Not only is it perceived as an antidote to the popular vision of greed and misconduct by millionaire ballplayers, it has fallen victim to forces of institutional blindness and discrimination not entirely dissimilar to those which bedevil its on-screen heroes. Thus the two stories, the filmic and extra filmic, have become so intertwined that they must be mutuallly addressed as refracting and displacing elements in a complex cultural equation.

At the core of that equation are two endearing if not terribly charismatic boyz, Arthur Agee and William Gates, whose physical skills are, if we are to believe the film, their only ticket out of dead-end lives. A three-hour story devoted to black teenagers that does not rely on inflammatory clichés of violence or drugs or sexual aggression is already a rare and admirable undertaking. As augmented by the personal struggles and achievements of various family members, most notably the remarkable Mrs Sheila Agee, the film creates a memorable portrait of supportive urban families for whom emotional ties help compensate for material wants. Moreover, for all the parallels drawn between the two homes and the fledgling careers they nurture, Agee and Gates are granted their full measure of individuality. Although they're both recruited by the same white middle-class suburban Catholic high school – a basketball powerhouse that 'produced' Isiah Thomas – their experiences are vastly different, a fact underscored by their different temperaments, peer groups, and attitudes toward education.

Gates is labeled by scouts, the press, and St Joseph's coach Gene Pingatore as a surefire prospect. When he blows out a knee in his junior year, the school apparently covers his medical expenses and finds him a cushy summer job. The less obviously gifted Agee, on the other hand, is forced to transfer back to a tough neighbourhood school when his parents fall behind on tuition payments (the registrar coolly refuses to forward Arthur's transcript until the bill is paid). This sets up a further contrast between the philosophies of the two coaches, one white and one black. Posing the martinet Pingatore ('William is just too nice a kid. I don't know if he has the killer instinct') against a more sympathetic inner-city coach, Luther Bedford, is dramatic shorthand for a larger, and largely unexamined, system of inequalities and exploitive practices.

Indeed, as *Hoop Dreams* progresses the nuanced elaboration of family dynamics is overwhelmed by the familiar momentum of parallel-edited contests, both on and off court. This thrill-of–victory/agony-of-defeat structure provides the film with rooting interest and a natural climax, but robs it of its earlier strengths. The families continue to appear, on the sidelines or at celebrations, but they are no longer the central focus. In a neat reversal of fortunes, Gates fails to lead his team to victory while Agee sparks a stirring run for the state championship. As Agee sinks clutch free-throws, Gates is ushered to the next level of commercialized athletics by unscrupulous college recruiters.

A commitment to dramatic development and unanticipated outcomes is manifest at practically every level. This is not a film in the *cinéma–vérité* tradition of micro-behavioural observation, but rather a sports movie in the 'grand' Hollywood tradition (reason enough for Spike Lee – who makes a brief and rather disingenuous appearence at a Nike-sponsored all-star camp – to purchase the story's fictionalization rights). In retrospect, everything we learn about the lives of these young men pertains to their passion for roundball. Do they listen to music, watch TV or go to the movies, worry about dating, talk about clothes or crime? *Hoop Dreams* either suppresses this information or treats it as ammunition for surprising plot twists. Without prior warning, Gates is discovered with a girlfriend . . . and a baby. After enrolling in St Joe's, he rapidly makes up four grade levels and seems like a conscientious student but suddenly gets into such academic difficulty that it threatens his offer of a university scholarship. What happened in between?

To be sure, it is neither disreputable nor unusual for documentaries to appropriate tropes and conventions from fiction films (although it may be unprecedented for a documentary publicity kit to urge reviewers not to reveal the ending). Decentred, monotonous works of non-fiction deserve no special moral or political leverage. And a hybrid approach that includes voice-over narration, mood music, interviews, reconstructed events, and manipulated time-sequences can enhance the genre's viability and potential yield of meaning. But in this case, the film's need for cohesive, engaging drama all but blurs the important issues it raises. A street scout named Earl Smith drives to a playground as the voice-over announces, 'Today he spots Arthur Agee', as if the camera has just captured a fortuitous meeting. The film-makers follow Agee's father Bo as he makes a blatant drug buy at a playground court and we wonder if the incident was spontaneous or staged as a 'message' during his later period of rehabilitation. Nothing in the film indicates that Agee and Gates were friends or even knew each other, yet they are shown enjoying an emotional 'reunion' after a championship game.

Such suspicions underscore a more crucial set of gaps and reserva-

41 Hoop Dreams (1994).

tions as the film narrows its 'game' to a numbing courtside litany of performance highlights. In some ways *Hoop Dreams*' voice is aligned less with its adolescent protagonists than with the coaches, school administrators, recruiters, and media vultures it intends to skewer. There are moments when the camera is heedlessly intrusive: it drags Bo into a discussion of college as Arthur rolls his eyes in dismay, and hovers as a doctor gives William a prognosis on his knee.

At a certain point the film's silence about production agreements made with its subjects, and its lack of candor about its own self-interest in a rousing dramatic climax, vitiates the feel-good atmosphere with unsettling questions. When Gates becomes discouraged over his injury and increasingly preoccupied with wife and child, do the pressures exerted by the long-term presence of a camera crew help prevent him from quitting the team? Isn't that continuous presence complicit in the same system of hype that tags him the 'next Isiah', magnifying the failure of each missed shot, and, by the end, souring his inherent sweetness and optimism? As part of its recruiting strategy, Marquette University fabricates an audio tape and newspaper headline with Gates as a last-second hero. We are meant to be horrified by this grossly coercive act, and we are, yet what are we to make of a film that spends less than two minutes on gruelling and endlessly repetitive practice sessions and nearly an hour on drained jump shots and slam dunks?

Just as disturbing are the effects of the film on Arthur Agee, whose dreams of the NBA seem increasingly grim in the face of family upheaval. In a brief item in *Entertainment Weekly*, Agee's college coach at Arkansas State notes that, 'There's no question [the success of the film] has taken away from his basketball and academics.' Agee is clearly more introverted and less confident than Gates. On the eve of starting at St Joe's, he confides that he has 'just never been around a lot of white people before'. He worries that they don't talk like he does and the film hammers home the point with uncomfortable scenes in religion and math classes. His consciousness of racial difference is instructive since for roughly 250 hours he and Gates were followed through black neighbourhoods and housing projects by a couple of white guys with movie equipment. Were relations with the crew ever inflected by their status as white outsiders or was the shoot a miraculously colourblind enterprise? One wonders why a film bold enough to shape its material for dramatic effect – choosing *not* to cloak itself in myths of aesthetic transparency or objectivity – would shrink from an attendant leap: the explication of production-related protocols and tensions directly related to its manifest themes of perseverance and exploitation.

The debate around the imperative of reflexivity in documentary practice has been around longer than Wilt Chamberlain, but in many quarters has yet to sink in. An extraordinary number of daily reviewers seized on *Hoop Dreams*' combination of unusual setting (for a feature release), 'real-life' immediacy, and familiar pay-off, yet ignored its absences and disavowals. It's one thing for mainstream TV critics Siskel/ Ebert/Shalit et al to champion an unheralded independent production, but quite another for the collective film staff of the *Village Voice* to waive its cutting-edge credentials and join the party. Add to the flood of salvific pronouncements, the intimation of an Oscar conspiracy that cheats the film out of its just rewards – a computer search turned up over 5,000 print and media references to the supposed snub – and we are in the realm of cultural hoopla.

As the story gathers steam, baseball man of letters Roger Angell suggests in the *New Yorker* that the values in *Hoop Dreams* should be embraced as the anti-Gump. Oscar host David Letterman opens the award proceedings with a weak *Hoop Dreams* joke and later tosses in another one. ABC devotes its post-Oscar edition of *Night Line* to the raging controversy. Gates, who appeared for Marquette in the NIT playoffs, returns home for the birth of a second baby girl and is interviewed on tabloid television: 'The dream isn't the NBA, it's the process of where we've come from since we were fourteen years old.' On the evening prior to the NCAA championship game, the Fox network airs a new documentary, *Hardwood Dreams*, an eight-month study of five players on a California high school championship team. The next night, during halftime of the NCAA finale, Bill Clinton gets into the act by plugging *Hoop Dreams* and appearing in a video clip shooting buckets with Arthur Agee, 'a fine young man trying to make something of his life'.

What does all this mean and how is it symptomatic of the way at least segments of our society construct positions on African-American males, sports celebrity, and the inner city? Leaving aside scattered evidence of rank opportunism and media feeding frenzy, we can attribute a portion of the response to liberal rhetoric/guilt – that it is simply a good thing in these reactionary times to remind folks of the plight of the underclass. These days survival can be viewed as an accomplishment: the film's most poignant line comes when Sheila Agee points out that 'to get to see eighteen is good'. Another portion of the enthusiastic response no doubt belongs to sports fantasies shared to varying degrees by male and female fans: it is not insignificant that the NBA garners a much wider female audience than any other pro sport.

Limiting the phenomenon to film-critical discourse and its social practices, there are at least three plausible explanations for the apotheosis of *Hoop Dreams*, one or all of which implicitly prop up the humanist critical platitudes. The first is that the film is innovative and accomplished with regard to its theme, which encompasses both the characters and the institutional forces shaping their needs and goals. The second is that the film is innovative and accomplished in its form, in the way it engenders identification with its characters and dramatizes its situations. And the third suggests we ought to respect and encourage the sort of methods and long-term commitments exemplified by this project.

Taking the last justification first, it is probably true that not many social documentaries expend the time and energy necessary to gain the full trust of their subjects or to follow them across years of struggle. Nonetheless, a rudimentary grasp of film history – in particular ethnographic film and contemporary indigenous media – would provide numerous examples dating back to Robert Flaherty. While we could certainly benefit from more engaged non-fiction work, it's not clear that *Hoop Dreams* meets the criteria of self-conscious and responsible visual anthropology.

Accolades rooted in the second argument – the film's formal innovation – are similarly flawed. Many outraged fans surmised that *Hoop Dreams* received no Oscar bid because its advanced aesthetic stance eluded Academy nominating members. But have serious critics ever cheered the Academy's tasteless, capricious, politically-motivated choices? Rather, they're loathe to consider that this year other nominees proved stronger. In fact, *Hoop Dreams* adds absolutely nothing to the current arsenal of documentary codes and techniques.

The first claim – that it presents a unique or disruptive take on the processes of sports commodification and white exploitation of black culture – is the weakest of all, since the film buys into many of the same assumptions it ostensibly condemns. Lacking a fully articulated analysis of social context, failing to provide even simple statistical odds against a high-school player making it to the pros, *Hoop Dreams* settles for vague finger-pointing and individualistic moral distinctions drawn between characters.

Fallen Champ, Barbara Kopple's vastly underrated study of the career of Mike Tyson, is far more politically savvy in its articulation of the dehumanizing effects of media packaging. Journalist Darcy Frey's recent book, *The Last Shot*, travels nearly the same route as *Hoop Dreams* by focusing on a group of budding stars in the projects of Brooklyn; yet it carefully interrogates its own narrational position in the mechanisms of commodification by including discussions in which the principals ask for payment and question the writer on his anticipated rewards. Even NBA commissioner David Stern offers a more concise and telling analysis: 'Disney has its theme parks; we have arenas. They have Mickey Mouse and Goofy; our characters are named Magic and Michael.'

The sports sections of *USA Today* and the *Village Voice* feature annual columns detailing unconscionable exploitation of athletes by major universities; we learn, for example, that the graduation rate for black hoopsters at NCAA powerhouses rarely exceeds ten per cent and at some august institutions is a flat zero. By contrast, *Hoop Dreams* frames its coverage of Agee and Gates's academic difficulties as obstacles to obtaining athletic scholarships. There is no hint that knowledge might be a worthwhile pursuit in its own right, or even provide alternative options for the future. The documentary delivers precious little new understanding of the sports scene and ignores information that could be truly useful to a younger audience.

It would be too easy to conclude that all the fuss over this film results from critical faddishness and self-congratulation. After opening to fabulous reviews and something less than a monster jam at the box office, *Hoop Dreams* has to date generated business of more than six million dollars – roughly the same as the Madonna-motored *Truth or Dare* and far in excess of other recent documentary features. It clearly speaks to a widely and deeply held fascination with the making of sports celebrity. Perhaps its successes will create opportunities for more thoughtful, politicized, and complex treatments. If not, it may very well be viewed in retrospect in the disappointed idiom reserved for a promising rookie clanging a 'three' at the buzzer.

Source: *Cineaste*, 1995, Vol. 21, No. 3.

11 Diversity

INTRODUCTION

As the documentary enters its second century it finds itself less constrained by the ideological and aesthetic dogmas which have by turns driven and hindered its development. At their best, today's documentarists pick and choose from the forms of the past – the observational, poetic, essayistic, investigative or explorational – and produce films which are more varied, imaginative and challenging than anything we've seen before. At their worst they churn out thousands of hours of virtually indisinguishable 'reality TV'.

Two trends in particular have dominated recent innovations. The first is the desire to make films which although educational and informative are also unashamedly entertaining. *Unzipped* and *Crumb* (both 1995) are two particularly notable examples. This in turn has lead to a return of the documentary from the small screen to the cinema.

The second trend is a willingness to challenge the boundaries between 'documentary' and 'fiction' – witness the work of Chantal Ackerman, Errol Morris and Chris Marker. 'Documentary' to them is more a statement of attitude than content. Integral to this movement is a sense that the image itself – which at one time seemed to have a definite and secure relationship with 'actuality' – no longer seems to play such a fixed role in our lives. More and more, screens and images are places where we access aspects of the real world, but also escape or ignore it. Moreover, the photographic or video image, which once seemed to be a straightforward reflection of reality, is now liable to manipulation and distortion through the techniques of digital effects. In consequence, the very 'documentary' quality of the documentary – it's role as 'evidence' – is growing open to question. In its place film-makers are having to look for other justifications for their films.

The Unique Role of Documentaries
KRZYSZTOF KIEŚLOWSKI

Krzysztof Kieślowski (1941–1996) is best known outside his native
Poland for a series of subtle, if occassionally indulgent, art-house films
including the *Decalogue* and the *Three Colours* series. Many Poles,
however, consider the director's finest work to have been the numerous
documentaries with which he started his career in the 1970s after
graduating from the Lodz film school.

Kieślowski's thoughts on some of these films were recorded in the
book *Kieślowski on Kieślowski*.

First Love (1974)
When I was finishing film school I wrote a thesis called 'Reality and the
Documentary Film' where I put forward the argument that in
everybody's life there are stories and plots. So why invent plots if they
exist in real life? You only have to film them. That's the subject I
invented for myself. Then I tried to make films like that but I didn't
make any – except for *First Love*. I don't think it's a bad film.

I had always wanted to make a film about a guy who wins a million
złotys on the pools. That was a lot of money in Poland in the 1970s. A
large villa cost something like 500,000 złotys; a car cost 50,000 or even
70,000. Anyway, it was a huge sum of money, and very few people in
Poland had so much. So I wanted to make a film about a guy who wins
a million and observe him right up until the moment the money
disappears; you could describe it as butter on a frying pan. You put a bit
of butter on a frying pan and it melts, disappears.

Another idea which I had was the one I used in *First Love*. It's the
other side of the coin – it's the idea of rising dough. You put dough into
an oven and it rises of its own accord even though you're not doing
anything to it any more. In this case it was the idea of a woman's belly,
which at a certain moment gets impregnated and we watch it grow.

We spent a long time with the couple – Jadzia and Romek. A year,
because we met them when Jadzia was four months pregnant, and we
stayed with them until the child was two months old. So that was
almost a year.

There was masses of manipulation in this film, or even provocation,
but you can't make a film like that any other way. There's no way you
can keep a crew at somebody's side for twenty-four hours a day. No

way. I say we took eight months to make it, but I think there were no more than thirty or forty shooting days. So during those thirty or forty days I had to manipulate the couple into situations in which they'd find themselves anyway, although not exactly on the same day or at the same time. I don't think I ever put them in a situation in which they wouldn't have found themselves if the camera hadn't been there. For example, they wanted a place to live. They went to the housing co-op, so obviously I had to go there earlier with the camera. But it was their housing co-op. They were trying to get their own apartment and not some fictitious one, and I didn't write dialogues for them.

I wanted them to read a book called something like *Young Mother* or *The Developing Foetus*. So I bought them the book and then waited for them to read and discuss it. These situations were clearly manipulated. They had a tiny room at their grandmother's and they decided they wanted to paint it violet. Right, let them paint it violet. I came to film them while they were painting and this is clear provocation – I sent in a policeman, who arrived and complained that they weren't registered, that they were living there illegally and could be thrown out. I deliberately found a policeman whom I thought wouldn't cause much harm, although Jadzia was in her eighth month by then and the whole thing could have been quite risky – an unexpected visit like that could have induced labour. Everybody was frightened of the police in Poland at the time, especially if they weren't registered where they were living. It wasn't as easy as it is today.

There were a lot of situations like that, but there were also some which resulted from life itself. Like the wedding, for example – we were there with the camera. The birth was the actual birth – we were there with the camera.

A birth, as we all know, takes place only once. For the next one, you have to wait at least a year. So we got ready for it very carefully. We knew Jadzia would give birth at the hospital on Madalińskiego Street, where my daughter was also born . . . Of course, we knew in what room Jadzia would be giving birth. We set up the lights ahead of time, a week before she was due to give birth. The microphones were also set up. Misio Żarneckil was the sound recordist but Małgosia Jaworska recorded sound for that scene so there was a woman present, not a man. As many men were eliminated from the crew as possible. There weren't any electricians because the lights had already been set up and Jacek Petrycki, who was cameraman, had a little chart showing him where the lights were so he could turn them on himself.

Jadzia and Romek didn't have a telephone and we worked it out that the moment Jadzia went into labour, Romek would phone 'Dziób'. Dziób had a telephone and so did everybody who was to be there in the labour room. The rule was that at any one time somebody had to be at home, so if, for example, Jacek, the cameraman, had to go out for a while Grażyna, his wife, would know where he was so that she could get in touch with him and he could rush off to the labour room. We all knew it was a question of two hours and that was it. Or even half an hour. We couldn't be late. We'd already worked on the film for five or six months before the birth so it was obvious we couldn't lose this scene. So Dziób was to phone me, Jacek, Małgosia Jaworska and the production manager. We didn't need anybody else there.

We waited. We waited a week. No news. Every day I sent Dziób off to check if by any chance Romek hadn't forgotten to phone. Then one night, Dziób, who liked to have a drink, couldn't hold out any more and went drinking. He decided he couldn't hang around by the telephone for twenty-four hours a day any more. Off he went and got drunk, Lord knows who with. He didn't know where he went himself and at four in the morning he landed up on a night bus going from Ochota to Śródmieście. He was completely drunk. The night bus in Warsaw goes once every two hours if you're lucky. So Dziób gets on the bus and falls asleep, of course. Sits on the back seat, rests his head on his knees or arms and falls asleep. And makes his way along in this bus. It's four in the morning. Night. It was winter, I think. No, it was already spring but it was cold that night. Suddenly he feels somebody shake him by the shoulders. He wakes up. It's Romek who'd got on the same bus with Jadzia. She had gone into labour that very night. They hadn't been able to find a taxi. They'd phoned Dziób but there was nobody there, of course, because Dziób was already lying drunk on the bus. They'd got on the bus and the only person they saw was Dziób, blind drunk, who immediately sobered up. He jumped off the bus, rushed to a telephone box and phoned me, Jacek and Małgosia. Half an hour later we were all there in the hospital and managed to film the whole birth which, in the end, lasted eight hours so there hadn't been any problem really. But no one was to know. It's like that sometimes. A random incident – like, for example, a drunk Dziób – could have prevented us from filming what we needed.

I still keep in touch with Jadzia and Romek. They lived in Germany for a few years and now live in Canada. They've got three children. I met them not long ago. There was a retrospective of my films in Germany and I persuaded the organizers to show *First Love*. And since I knew that Jadzia and Romek were living in Germany at the time, I persuaded the organizers to invite the whole family to the screening. They all came. The little girl, whose birth we'd filmed, was already eighteen. Of course, everybody was in tears.

Nothing bad came of all this although I was afraid it might. I was afraid it might go to their heads. I was afraid they'd start thinking they were great stars. But then I realized this wouldn't happen. That's one of the reasons I chose that particular couple. I'd noticed that Jadzia, although she was only seventeen, knew exactly what she wanted and was clearly out to get it. And what she wanted was simply to have a child, get married, be a good wife, be a decent woman and have a bit of money. That was her goal, and she managed to get it all, of course. I knew she wouldn't have any pretensions which would change her attitude to life, make her think, for example, that she could be an actress, that she could perform. She knew perfectly well that that wasn't her world, and it didn't interest her in the least.

The film definitely didn't change them. They met with some very good reactions a week or two after it was shown on television. People recognized them in the streets and said hello or simply smiled at them. And that was nice. This only lasted for a short while. Everybody forgot about them afterwards, of course. Other films were shown on television, and other people were recognized in the streets. Other people were smiled at or pointed out. But they had that brief moment when people were friendly to them . . .

. . . Not everything can be described. That's the documentary's great problem. It catches itself as if in its own trap. The closer it wants to get to somebody, the more that person shuts him or herself off from it. And that's perfectly natural. It can't be helped. If I'm making a film about love, I can't go into a bedroom if real people are making love there. If I'm making a film about death, I can't film somebody who's dying because it's such an intimate experience that the person shouldn't be disturbed. And I noticed, when making documentaries, that the closer I wanted to get to an individual, the more the subjects which interested me shut themselves off. That's probably why I changed to features. There's no problem there. I need a couple to make love in bed, that's fine. Of course, it might be difficult to find an actress who's willing to take off her bra, but then you just find one who is. Somebody's supposed to die. That's fine. In a minute, he'll get up again. And so on. I can even buy some glycerine, put some drops in her eyes and the actress will cry. I managed to photograph some real tears several times. It's something completely different. But now I've got glycerine. I'm frightened of those real tears. In fact, I don't know whether I've got the right to photograph them. At such times I feel like somebody who's found himself in a realm which is, in fact, out of bounds. That's the main reason why I escaped from documentaries.

Source: *Kieślowski on Kieślowski*, edited by Danusia Stok, Faber and Faber, London, 1993.

Shoah: Witness to Annihilation
J. HOBERMAN

Made in 1985, *Shoah* is one of cinema's greatest achievements.

Since completing it, Claude Lanzmann (born 1925) has made two further documentaries, *Tu Ne Commetras Pas le Crime* (1991) and *Tsahal* (1994) a long, conventional account of Israel's controversial defence policies.

This article, and the interview which follows it, first appeared in the *Village Voice*.

Claude Lanzmann's *Shoah* is not simply the most ambitious film ever attempted on the extermination of the Jews, it's a work that treats the problem of representation so scrupulously it could have been inspired by the Old Testament injunction against graven images. 'The Holocaust is unique in that it creates a circle of flames around itself, a limit which cannot be transmitted,' Lanzmann wrote in a 1979 essay, ostensibly about the mini-series *Holocaust*. 'Pretending to cross that line is a grave transgression.'

Shoah, which takes its title from the Hebrew word for 'annihilation', doesn't cross that line, it defines it. For much of its nine-and-a-half hours, the film seems formless and repetitive. Moving back and forth from the general to the specific, circling around certain themes, *Shoah* overwhelms the audience with details. For those who demand linear progression, Lanzmann's method may seem perverse – the film's development is not a temporal one. 'The six million Jews did not die in their own time, and that is why any work that today wants to render justice to the Holocaust must take as its first principle the fracturing of chronology,' Lanzmann has written. Although *Shoah* is structured by internal corroborations, in the end you have to supply the connection yourself. This film throws you upon your own resources. It compels you to imagine the unimaginable.

Length aside, *Shoah* is notable for the rigour of Lanzmann's method: the eschewing of archival footage and narration in favour of contemporary landscapes and long interviews (shown mainly in real time) with those who, in one form or another, experienced the Holocaust. 'The film had to be made from traces of traces of traces,' Lanzmann told one interviewer. Like the Swedish *Chaim Rumkowski and the Jews of Lodz* or the Hungarian *Package Tour*, two recent documentaries with less global perspectives on the war against the Jews, *Shoah* embodies a powerful and principled restraint. Like Syberberg's *Hitler, a Film from Germany*, it refuses to 'reconstruct' the past, thus thwarting a conventional response and directing one to the source of one's own fascination.

Lanzmann, however, is scarcely as theatrical as Syberberg. In some respects his strategy resembles that employed by Jean-Marie Straub and Danielle Huillet. The Straubs' 1976 *Fortini-Cani*, for example, punctuates readings by the Italian-Jewish-Communist poet Franco Fortini with long ruminations upon sylvan vistas where, thirty years earlier, the Nazis massacred a group of Italian partisans. Lanzmann shares the same conviction that the past surrounds us, that history is inscribed (if only through its erasure) on the present. In his *Holocaust* piece, he approvingly quotes the philosopher Emil Fackenheim. 'The European Jews massacred are not just of the past, they are the *presence of an absence.*' This is why, while the vast Auschwitz complex has come to epitomize the Nazi death machine, *Shoah* emphasizes Treblinka – a camp built solely to exterminate Jews, a back–country site razed and ploughed under by the Nazis themselves in an attempt to conceal all physical evidence of 800,000 murders.

The landscapes in *Shoah* are no less tranquil than those of *Fortini-Cani*, but they are haunted beyond the mind's capacity to take them in. Piney woods and marshy fields cover mass graves, a brackish lake is silted with the ashes of hundreds of thousands of victims. The camera gazes at the overgrown railroad tracks, end of the line, site of a ramp where a quarter of a million Jews were unloaded and then hurried along with whips to their doom; it considers the postcard town of Chelmno where, one day after Pearl Harbour, the first Jews were gassed in mobile vans, using engine exhaust. What can be more peaceful than the ruins of Birkenau's snow-covered cremos and gas chambers? Of course, not every vista is so scenic. In one unforgettable camera movement, Lanzmann slowly pans down to the brown winter grass covering the rusty spoons and personal detritus that still constitutes the soil of Auschwitz.

What binds these landscapes together are the trains that chug through Europe bound for Poland and the East. Lanzmann even managed to find an engineer who drove the Jewish transports. One of the film's recurring images is that of a train crossing the Polish countryside or pulling up in Treblinka station, with this very engineer, now wizened and boney as some medieval Death, looking back towards his invisible freight. In the argument of *Shoah*, these trains underscore the extent of the bureaucratic organization needed to commit genocide, the blatant obviousness of the transports and, finally, the existential terror of the journey. While the Jews were systematically deprived of water, the railroad crew was plied with drink. Through a translator, the former engineer tells Lanzmann the run was so harrowing the Germans were forced to pay a bonus in vodka. 'He drank every drop he got because without liquor he couldn't stand the stench,' the translator explains. 'They even bought more liquor on their own . . .'

If landscapes give *Shoah* its weight, interviews provide its drama. Over and against these images of present-day Poland and Germany is the testimony of witnesses ranging from Jewish survivors to Polish onlookers to Nazi commandants. But the film is as filled with silence as with talk. Nine hours' worth of subtitles barely makes a comfortably wide-margined book. Pauses, hesitations are often more eloquent than words. The evident torment with which Jan Karski, a onetime courier for the Polish government, recalls two clandestine tours of the Warsaw Ghetto, carries as expressive charge far beyond his pained, halting description. Indeed, his face grey with agony, Karski breaks down and bolts off camera before he can even start.

Moreover, words are belied by expressions. Among the most scandalous aspects of *Shoah* are Lanzmann's interviews with the Polish residents of Chelmno and Treblinka. Although there are exceptions, their blandly volunteered memories and perfunctorily offered concern ('it was sad to watch – nothing to be cheery about') are almost more damning than the casual anti-Semitism ('all Poland was in the Jews' hands') the interviewer has little difficulty in provoking. Real malice only surfaces in tales of 'fat' foreign Jews 'dressed in white shirts' riding to their death in passenger cars where 'they could drink and walk around' and even play cards. 'We'd gesture that they'd be killed,' one peasant adds, passing his finger across his throat in demonstration. His buddies assent, as if this macabre signal was itself an act of guerrilla warfare directed at the Germans.

If the sequence induces the unbearable mental image of trains run by drunken crews, packed to overflowing with a dazed, weeping human cargo, careering through a countryside areek with the stench of gas and burning bodies, jeered at by peasants standing by the tracks, this and more are corroborated by the surviving Jews: 'Most of the people, not only the majority, but ninety-nine per cent of the Polish people when they saw the train going through – we looked really like animals in that wagon, just our eyes looked outside – they were laughing, they had a joy, because they took the Jewish people away.'

As for the Nazis, it's hard to know which is worse, the pathetic evasions of the avuncular Franz Grassler, onetime deputy commissioner of the Warsaw Ghetto, insisting that the Jews knew more about the final solution than did their jailers, or the affable, expansive Franz Suchomel, an SS *Unterscharführer* at Treblinka, expressing a grotesque camaraderie with the people he was killing. Among other things, *Shoah* precisely details the means by which the Jews were compelled to participate in their own destruction. Meanwhile, Suchomel and others, such as the former head of Reich Railways Department 33, demonstrates that genocide – by which the Nazis proposed to have the Jews vanish *without a trace* – posed incredible logistical difficulties, solvable only by a modern, mobilized bureaucracy. It is here that the language of problem-solving takes on a hallucinative unreality. Suchomel allows that at its peak, Treblinka 'processed' 12,000 to 15,000 Jews each day ('we had to spend half the night at it'), a train-load of victims going 'up the funnel' in two or three hours. Unlike at Auschwitz, prisoners at Treblinka were gassed with engine exhaust. 'Auschwitz was a factory!' Suchomel explains. 'Treblinka was a primitive but efficient production line of death.'

You watch this in a state of moral nausea so strong it makes your head swim. Nor does Lanzmann ease you into it. *Shoah* opens at the sight of the Chelmno death camp, with one of the film's few narrative voice-overs observing that of the 40,000 Jews who were sent there only two survived. (Later we meet them.) The film's second part begins with another sort of horror. Suchomel singing the Treblinka anthem.

> Looking squarely ahead, brave and joyous,
> At the world,
> The squads march to work.
> All that matters to us now is Treblinka
> It is our destiny.
> That's why we've become one with Treblinka
> In no time at all.
> We know only the word of our commander,
> We know only obedience and duty,
> We want to serve, to go on serving,
> Until a little luck ends it all.
> Hurray!

Each morning, he explains, the newly arrived Jews selected for slave labour were taught the song: 'By evening they had to be able to sing along with it.' (Even now I can't get this idiotic martial melody out of my head. In Jean-François Steiner's *Treblinka*, it is reported that, after the day's work, Jewish labourers were compelled to stand to attention and repeat these words for hours – as well as sing the anthem as they marched.)

Lanzmann's most detailed interviews are with former members of the *Sondercommando* – the Jews who were kept alive at Treblinka and Auschwitz to stoke the annihilation machine. 'We were the workers in the Treblinka factory, and our lives depended on the whole manufacturing process, that is the slaughtering process at Treblinka,' one explains. Only the naïve or pitiless can call them collaborators. In a sense, these men hyperbolize the dilemma of Jewish survivors in general – it is one of the Holocaust's cruelties that every Jew who survived is somehow tainted. One woman who managed to weather the war hiding in Berlin decribes her feelings on the day that the last Jews in the city were rounded up for deportation: 'I felt very guilty that I didn't go myself and tried to escape fate that the others could not escape. There was no more warmth around, no more soul . . . [only] this feeling of being terribly alone . . . What made us do this? To escape [the] fate that was really our destiny or the destiny of our people.' A terrible fate, an absolute isolation are ideas that recur in *Shoah* again and again.

If the Nazis are all too human, the survivors are as mysterious as extraterrestrials. What is one to make of the urbane, ironic Rudolph Vrba smiling as he describes cleaning the bodies out of the gas chamber, or the beseeching eyes of Filip Müller, survivor of five liquidations of the Auschwitz special detail? (His relentless discourse – an account of undressing corpses, shoving them into the cremo, witnessing the last moments of thousands of Jews, some knowing, some not – is delivered in a tone of perpetual amazement, as though always for the first time: 'It was like a blow on the head, as if I'd been stunned.') Unlike other accounts of the Holocaust, *Shoah* deliberately minimizes acts of individual heroism – to have been a Jew in Hitler's Europe was to have had the most appalling kind of human heroism thrust upon you. 'I began drinking after the war,' the grim, noble-looking Itzhak Zuckerman, second-in-command of the Warsaw Ghetto's Jewish Combat Organization, tells Lanzmann. 'It was very difficult. Claude, you ask for my impression. If you could lick my heart, it would poison you.'

People have been asking me, with a guilty curiosity I can well understand, whether *Shoah* really has to be seen. A sense of moral obligation is unavoidably attached to such a film. Who knows if *Shoah* is good for you? (One hopes, probably in vain, that reviewers will declare a moratorium on the already debased currency of movie-ad hype.) There were many times during the screening that I regarded it as a chore and yet, weeks later, I find myself still mulling over landscapes, facial expressions, vocal inflections – the very stuff of cinema – and even wanting to see it again. The published text can in no way substitute for the film itself: the 'text' of *Shoah* can only be experienced on the screen. On the other hand, the book is quite helpful in grasping Lanzmann's structure. For, if at first, *Shoah* seems porous and inflated, this is a film which expands in one's memory, its intricate cross-references and monumental form only gradually becoming apparent. One resists regarding *Shoah* as a work of art – and, as artful as it is, one should.

Shoah transfixes you, it numbs you, and finally – with infinite tenderness and solicitude – it scars you. There are moments in this film when you simply can't bear to look at another human being, it is something you must experience alone. *Shoah* teaches us the meaning of the word 'inconsolable'. The film ends in Israel (as it has to) with a member of the Jewish Combat Organization describing his fantasy, while searching the empty ruins of the Warsaw Ghetto, of being 'the last Jew'. (After he finishes comes a coda of trains rolling implacably on . . .)

Leaving the theatre, you may recall one survivor's account of a secret trip to 'Aryan' Warsaw on the eve of the Ghetto uprising: 'We suddenly emerged into a street in broad daylight, stunned to find ourselves among normal people. [It was as if] we'd come from another planet.' The horror of it is, that planet is ours.

The Being of Nothingness
AN INTERVIEW WITH CLAUDE LANZMANN

Just sitting down to write about *Shoah*, or do the necessary background reading, I'm experiencing symptoms, alternately irritable and maudlin, subject to queasiness and lower-back pain, assailed by free-floating anxiety, morbid fantasies about my children, and the urge to regale others with tales of atrocities. How, I ask Claude Lanzmann, did he manage to live with this project for eleven years, editing the final version down from some 350 hours of footage? The film-maker is puzzled, then he laughs. 'Yes, but I'm a sick man.'

Lanzmann, the fifty-nine-year-old onetime editor of *Les Temps Modernes*, a crony of Sartre and de Beauvoir, seldom jokes. Tall, craggy and distinguished looking, he exudes an existential melancholy more lushly acrid than the smoke from his Gitanes. Lanzmann's only previous movie was a 1973 documentary on Israel. How did he go about planning a nine-and-a-half-hour film on the Holocaust? 'Such a work is praxis. The concept was built during the work. If I had had a concept at the beginning, the film would be very bad. It would be too abstract. No, I had an obsession . . . I have made the film and the film made me.' His anguish, he says did not disappear when *Shoah* was completed. On the contrary, the finish brought no relief.

Shoah has been running in a Paris cinema for six months. It was hailed at the Venice Film Festival and is scheduled to be shown on West German TV in two parts just as it is in theatres. ('I will never yield another way. I am an uncompromising man.') The film is designed to be experienced as a totality. 'It's not like the Chinese opera – no,' Lanzmann says when I ask him if he feels people can walk in and out. Every minute is purposeful. *Shoah* is 'a film which learns its own memory.' He inscribes a circle in the air and adds, 'It is a world – one has to enter into it.'

Have all the responses been positive? 'All!' Lanzmann emphasizes with a brisk nod. Still, there was an abortive campaign against the film launched by the Polish *chargé d'affaires* in Paris, who asked that *Shoah* be banned from French TV. Then the Polish government put in an official request to see videotapes. Now, because the régime's anti-anti-Semitic faction has prevailed, *Shoah* will be seen in theatres in Warsaw and Cracow, as well as broadcast by Polish TV. 'They realize that their quarrel is not with me, but with their countrymen.'

For Lanzmann, Shoah is *sui generis* – neither documentary nor fiction. In a sense he has sculpted reality. He rented the locomotive with which, in one of the film's leitmotifs, the retired engineer Henryk Gawilowski retraces the routes of the trains to the death camps. (Is it the same type of engine? 'Absolutely. They didn't change.') In one of *Shoah*'s most powerful scenes, Lanzmann arranged for the barber Abraham Bomba to give a haircut in a Tel Aviv barbershop while

42 *Simon Srebnik returns to Chelmno, the site of a Nazi extermination camp that he alone survived, in* Shoah *(1987).*

describing how he cropped the hair of women waiting to be gassed at Treblinka. ('Can you imitate how you did it?' Lanzmann asks at one point.) The situation precipitates Bomba's memories with lacerating vividness. The film-maker similarly brought Simon Srebnik back to Chelmno, site of a murderous massacre that he alone survived. ('He was terrorized as a child and he is terrorized still.') Scenes such as these, Lanzmann says, create 'an explosion of truth. It is as Spinoza said: The truth becomes true!'

Shoah is also sculptural in its use of negative space. The film has to be read for what it cannot say. ('One must speak and hold silent at the same time: knowing here that silence is the most authentic mode of speech,' Lanzmann has written; he praises the French edition of the film's text for its visualized pauses, silence made tangible.) This is not without a controversial aspect. 'You cannot trap me – I know everything about this!' Lanzmann exclaims when asked why the movie makes no mention of the western democracies' indifference to the fate of the Jews. 'Absolutely, purposefully, I leave this aside. I have everything on this! I think it's much stronger from an artistic point of view when you have [Polish courier] Jan Karski say "But I reported what I saw . . . [to the Allies]" The accusation is much stronger if it is simply not said. We know nothing was done.'

In the US and Israel (where it has not yet been released), *Shoah* may be controversial for other reasons as well. Although the film cites the uprisings in Auschwitz, Treblinka and Sobibor, as well as the Warsaw Ghetto, it does not project an image of Jewish resistance. Rather, *Shoah* uses these uprisings as co-ordinates in the mapping of a vast, terrifying landscape. For the Jews of Europe, Lanzmann points out, neither collaboration with the Nazis nor revolt against them could succeed. 'For me,' says Lanzmann, who was a teenage member of the French Resistance, 'it is the same.' The mother who slit her daughter's wrists and then committed suicide while waiting to be gassed is no less a heroic figure than a doomed ghetto fighter.

This is why *Shoah* frustratingly eschews the stories of how its Jewish subjects escaped death: 'Each one survived by a succession of miracles,' explains Lanzmann. 'But this was not my point: I built a structure, a gestalt! I didn't tell one personal story – the subject of the film is the extermination of the Jews, not the handful of survivors.' (It's impossible not to ask, however. So Lanzmann tells me that Bomba escaped Treblinka by leaping through the 'curtain of fire' that rose from the trench of burning corpses. With nowhere else to go, he made his way back to the Czestochowa ghetto where he was again deported. This time, however, he jumped from the train.) Lanzmann considers men like Bomba or the members of Jewish work brigades at Auschwitz 'saints and martyrs and heroes'. These *Sonderkommandos* are 'the direct witnesses. There are only fifteen – no more!'

Asked if he felt that the absence of Jews from Hungary or France or Rumania upset the balance of the film, Lanzmann is indignant. 'I don't deal with places of origin. I deal with the places they arrived.' Still, as he points out, Czech Jews have a special place in the film's complex structure; they were the first to be deported and also the last. So too do the Jews from the Island of Corfu. 'These people made only one trip in their lives . . . to Auschwitz.' Lanzmann was unable to film in the Ukraine or the Baltic republics. Although he would have if he could, he says it makes no difference: 'There are no Jewish survivors of the *Einzatzgruppen*.' (Trying to interview one former member of the Nazi killing squad, the film-maker was beaten so badly he spent a month in hospital.)

Shoah, says Lanzmann, 'starts with the disappearance of the traces, with the difficulty of naming'. There are things which cannot be in the film because they have been totally destroyed. Everything in *Shoah* is literally present. Lanzmann speaks of archival footage almost with disgust; the Holocaust does not belong to the past. 'You must understand. I did not make an historical film.'

Does he have the desire to make other film? 'About what?' About anything. 'It depends, if I go on living . . . or what.'

Source: The *Village Voice*, 29 October 1985.

Appearance and Reality
GABRIELE ANNAN ON MAXIMILIAN SCHELL'S *MARLENE*

The 'celebrity profile' is one of the most debased of documentary formats. Maximilian Schell's film on Marlene Dietrich challenged the normal constraints of the form, and turned an apparently insurmountable handicap to advantage.

This piece first appeared in *The New York Review of Books*. Having briefly reviewed a number of Dietrich biographies, Annan continues:

Every one of the books under review is an attempt in one way or
another to get at the truth behind the Dietrich legend – a carelessly
thrown together document with missing pages and others doubtfully
authentic. By far the most original undertaking is the documentary film
Marlene made by the Austrian-Swiss actor-director Maximilian Schell.
He thought he could get Dietrich to reveal the truth, but all he got in
answer to a direct question was: The truth about me – long pause – is
that everything you read about me is untrue.

Schell was originally chosen by the producer Karel Dirka to do the
interview with Dietrich that was to be the core of the film. It was to be
conducted half in English and half in German. Schell is bilingual and
Dietrich had admired his performance in *Judgment at Nuremberg*
(1961), the film in which she played her last important role. The
director chosen by Dirka was Peter Bogdanovich. Dietrich turned him
down because she did not consider him sufficiently famous, and she
bullied the reluctant Schell into directing as well as interviewing her. So
there was tension from the start.

Like Truffaut's *Day For Night*, Schell's film is about making – or in
his case not making – the film he set out to make. Dietrich refused to
appear in it, and she never does – except in clips from old movies,
newsreels and tapes of her concerts. All you get is her voice on the
sound track. Almost the first thing it says is *Quatsch* – nonsense. She
repeats the word many times during the ninety-minute run, and almost
as often she says *Kitsch*.

Also *Dreck*. To call her uncooperative would be an understatement.
She is dismissive – not only of Schell and the idea of making a film about
her, but of almost anything else that comes up in their conversation:
method acting, Proust, God ('If there's a power above he must be
meschugge'), psychoanalysis, life after death, feminism, women ('I call
them females'), Emil Jannings, and sex ('*Es geht auch ohne*' – one can
manage without). Her disaffected mutter reduces the world to a gray
stretch of ruins, like the aerial shots Schell cuts in of Berlin at the end of
the war. Only a few indestructible people and values stick up from the
rubble: Sternberg, Orson Welles ('You should cross yourself when you
say his name'), Burt Bacharach, Remarque, Hemingway, Goethe, Rilke,
professionalism, self-discipline, generosity with money, not being
sentimental.

Dietrich abhorred the idea of being filmed as an old woman, and
possibly she means it more than many stars do when she says her

private life is nobody's concern, nor even her own: '*Ich gehe mich einen Dreck an*' – an idiosyncratic construction which could be loosely translated 'I'm none of my own shitty business.' Her contract, she repeats in answer to Schell's pleading, was to be interviewed, not photographed: 'I've been photographed to death.' She won't even let them film her flat in the avenue Montaigne, and she won't discuss her films. Schell objects that in that case his film won't be very exciting. 'I'm not contracted to be exciting,' she barks.

Schell interviewed her for twelve hours spread over several days. He had a chance to memorize her apartment and then had it reconstructed in the studio. You see the set being assembled, you watch the lighting and camera crews at work. It is a beautiful film, visually poetic and glamorous, a fitting homage to Sternberg. The bogus apartment is shot through a half-open door against light streaming through muslin-curtained French windows. There are mirrors and console tables and busts. Members of the crew flit by, dark silhouettes with eyelashes showing up romantically *à contre-jour*. Three ravishing young Dietrich look-alikes in tails and top hats lounge and twirl just out of focus. The Schell–Dietrich dialogue and the short-tempered exchanges among the production team are dreamily backed by '*Nimm Dich in acht vor blonden Fraun*' and '*Ich bin von Kopf bis Fuss auf Liebe eingestellt.*'

We move to the editing room where clips from Dietrich's films are run through to comments by Schell and his assistants. With them sits a small old German-Jewish lady, bewildered and bewildering, her presence as unexplained as that of the dark lady glimpsed in Andrei Tarkovsky's film *Mirror* (who is, in fact, the poet Marina Tsvetayeva, a friend of Tarkovsky's parents). But who is Schell's dark lady? The name Anni Albers appears on the cast list (which has only one column, of course, because everyone plays – or is – himself). Can she be the widow of the irresistible Hans Albers, a German cross between Gérard Depardieu and Maurice Chevalier, the raffish darling of the Berlin public before the war? In *The Blue Angel* it is Albers who displaces Emil Jannings in Dietrich's affections. Whoever the old lady is, we can read her as a symbol of the last years of the Weimar republic when Dietrich was in her prime. Her look of displacement haunts and disturbs.

As for the dialogue between Dietrich and Schell, it is a duel – a duel in the sun with Dietrich as the bull. It begins with her in the ascendant, ridiculing, teasing, taunting, refusing, denigrating. He has to coax, persuade, argue, threaten. Gradually her nihilism gets under his skin, though he remains silky, the emollient Austrian baritone contrasting with her Prussian snarl. Like an experienced bullfighter he shows off her ferocity until the moment of putting in the first barb. Then he asks her where in Berlin she was born. She can't remember. But she must remember the name of the street where she lived with her parents. *Quatsch*, of course not; and anyway, who cares? At this point the screen shows a selection of possible residences in pre-war Berlin. It begins with dreary proletarian tenements and gradually works up the social scale, but not very far. The camera lingers at the last frame, a turn-of-the-century apartment block with sunless balconies like cave dwellings framed in baroque whorls of gray concrete. This may be where Dietrich lived immediately after her marriage in 1924 to the young assistant director Rudolph Sieber (their open marriage lasted until he died); or it may just as well be where her parents lived.

By dwelling on her implausible amnesia about her childhood Schell makes the first crack in Dietrich's official self-portrait (he has obviously worked up Marlène D.), which represents a young girl from a rich aristocratic family who trained with Reinhardt only because she had to give up studying the violin because of a wrist injury. Reminded of her nine films before *The Blue Angel*, Dietrich gets cross and brushes them aside – *Quatsch*, those were just bit parts (not true, some were leads).

Schell moves on to the famous audition with Sternberg. Eroticism is something I've never understood, she says techily. It wasn't what Sternberg chose me for. He chose me because he liked my cool – turning up without my music. He chose me because I was *schnodderig*. *Schnodderigkeit* is a Berlin form of loud-mouthed, *je m'en fiche insolence*, and it fits incongruously on to the image of the *jeune fille bien élevée*. Incidentally, Kenneth Tynan agreed with Dietrich about her lack of eroticism: 'She dedicates herself to looking rather than being sexy,' he wrote. How could he tell? Anyway, Sternberg chose her.

So they made *The Blue Angel*, which she despises ('It's enough to make you puke') and which made her famous. And then, indifferent to stardom and caring only about her daughter, Goethe, and cooking, she went to Hollywood, allowed herself to be made into a star, and cynically submitted to all the rites of stardom.

Schell chooses the clips from her Hollywood films with poetic justice – if that expression can mean doing justice to someone's poetry. There is a thrilling scene from Sternberg's *Dishonoured* where Dietrich is about to be executed as a spy. The commander of the firing squad cannot bring himself to give the order to shoot, so a soldier is sent off to find a replacement: meanwhile Dietrich repairs her lipstick. What *Quatsch*, she comments, what *Kitsch*. '*Kitsch und Dreck*.' The only thing she was interested in was getting her fall right. Should it be backward or forward? 'Well, I didn't know, did I? I'd never been shot before.' Another fib, actually: Fritz Kortner had already shot her in 1929 (the year of *The Blue Angel*) in Kurt Bernhardt's brilliant, sadistic, and witty silent, *Die Frau, Nach Der Man Sich Sehnt*. Kortner played a monocled doctor obsessed with Dietrich. She herself radiated – not sex exactly, just radiated. It was quite an achievement in the spectacularly unbecoming clothes she had to wear. Anyway, what she is telling Schell is that the only thing that mattered to her was technique – being professional in her work. It is probably *Kitsch* to feel that Dietrich had a special affinity with the beautiful, brave, and intelligent spy in *Dishonoured*, who declares that she is afraid of neither life nor death. To Schell Dietrich says that she does not fear death – it's life one ought to fear.

Among the rarities Schell has to show is a scene from Orson Welles' *Touch of Evil* (1958), in which Dietrich was only a guest star. She plays the Madame of a Texas brothel, Welles a corrupt, alcoholic police chief on the skids. He comes into the brothel and finds her alone at a table in the hall.

'You've been reading the cards, haven't you? [he says].
'I've been doing the accounts.'
'Come on, read the future for me.'
'You haven't got any.'
'Hm . . . What do you mean?'
'Your future's all used up. Why don't you go home?'

Dietrich's voice is deadpan, but it breaks your heart all right, with a Baudelairean sense of the pathos of human depravity, degradation, and doom.

Welles is falling apart. Schell, in spite of his evident admiration, seems bent on making Dietrich fall apart too. He gets nowhere, though, when he tries to draw her on the men in her life: Remarque, Hemingway, Welles, Gabin – up on their pedestal they disappear behind the smokescreen of her fervent admiration for their genius. About

Hemingway she is quite specific: their relationship was on a plane way above sex. Having sex is what a women does to keep her man – not for pleasure. Can it ever be pleasurable? asks Schell. Oh well, she grumbles, sometimes maybe.

Burt Bacharach, the songwriter, orchestrater, and accompanist with whom she began her worldwide concert tours in 1953, is the only man about whom she uses the world 'love': not in conversation with Schell, but on a tape of one of her concerts. She leads Bacharach to the footlights and declares her love for him (and her admiration, gratitude, etc.). There is a catch in her voice. But so there was right at the beginning of Schell's film, which opened with her farewell performance in Paris. She thanked the audience (in French) for being so wonderful. Dietrich was a mistress of the curtain call with tears choked back. We are watching a performance. And Schell, for his part, deliberately allows – and allows us to see – his film turning into a hide-and-seek between *Sein und Schein*, appearance and reality, 'Then what is real here?' Anni Albers asks. 'You'd better ask the author,' replies the prop girl.

Dietrich and Bacharach split up in 1964, but she went on with her concerts without him well into the 1970s, by which time she was hobbling from various fractures. They did not stop her from being as shamelessly glamorous as ever, slinky and glittering with sequins from a fraction above the nipples to the floor, her hair swinging in a gold lamé curtain, the coils of her white fox cape ramping down into along train so that she looks like a female Laocoön entwined with huge furry white caterpillars.

Eventually, against her wishes, Schell sneaks in a video recorder into the Avenue Mointaigne. But Dietrich refuses to watch her old films. Why? Because, says Schell:

Nessum maggior dolore
Che ricordarsi del tempo felice
Nella miseria

(No greater pain than to remember happy times in times of misery.)

Dietrich's agent slipped him the Dante quotation. So after that, why can't he leave her alone?

Well, obviously, he has to make his film. She gets more and more rattled. 'You should go back to Mama Schell and learn some manners,' she snaps. He hounds her about her deceptions. Why does she say she grew up an only child when there is a photograph of her with her sister who was only a year older? Why does she suppress Friedrich Holländer, who wrote the songs and played the piano in *The Blue Angel*, and was still writing and playing for her in 1948 in *A Foreign Affair*, Billy Wilder's film about post-war Berlin? Once more she was playing a ruthless nightclub entertainer, only now Lola-Lola was upgraded to Erika von Schlütow, an aristocrat down on her luck. Those were the days when Hollywood still preferred foreigners to be, if not peasants, then aristocrats like Boyer and Claudette Colbert in *Tovarich*. That preference seems the most likely reason for Dietrich's slight (and slapdash) upgrading of her origins. Even on the screen she never seriously went in for being a grande dame except when she played the German General's widow in *Judgment at Nuremberg*. She looked like a retired call girl who has married a well-to-do client and been sent by him to his mother's dressmaker. Her performance was phony, though much praised.

I think Alexander Walker [in his 1985 biography *Dietrich*] gets it wrong when he sees her as the incarnation of the Prussian *Junker* spirit. What she represents is the spirit of Berlin, independent, streetwise, sophisticated, and *schnodderig*. Schell understands this and uses his knowledge of what is closest to her heart when he moves in for the kill. It is 1945; a camera flies over Berlin; acre after acre of ruins fills the screen, limitless stretches of desolation. Meanwhile the city's pre-war street songs creep stealthily on to the sound track. Dietrich begins to hum along, entranced by examples of Berlin humour in the lyrics. '*Himmlisch, nicht?*' (Divine, isn't it?), she half chuckles, half sobs. Her voice begins to go out of control; it weaves over the sound track like a drunk across the pavement.

Schell delivers the final thrust. He begins to recite a poem – a very bad poem by the nineteenth century Ferdinand Frelligrath. It was Dietrich's mother's favourite, and Dietrich begins to chant it antiphonally with Schell:

O lieb, so lang du lieben kannst!
O lieb, so lang du lieben magst!
Die Stunde kommt, die Stunde kommt,
Wo du an Gräbern stehst und klagst.

('Oh love, while you can! Oh love, while you may! The hour will come, the hour will come, when you stand weeping over graves.')

They get to the verse:

> *Und hüte deine Zunge wohl!*
> *Bald ist ein böses Wort gesagt.*
> *O Gott, es war nicht bös gemeint –*
> *Der andere aber geht und klagt.*

('And guard your tongue! An unkind word is quickly said! Oh God, I did not mean to be unkind – but the other goes away weeping.')

Here Dietrich bursts into uncontrollable sobs. It makes an effective ending. Shocking. As shocking as a bullfight when the bull is old. It is not just another performance; not appearance, but reality.

Source: *The New York Review of Books*, 14 February, 1985.

The Thin Blue Line
TERRENCE RAFFERTY

Errol Morris's meticulously styled documentaries implicitly question the nature of the relationship between film and reality. In *A Brief History of Time* (1992), an eccentric 'profile' of the physicist Stephen Hawking, for instance, Morris reconstructed on a sound stage the domestic interiors and studies of those he was interviewing. One would never know this from seeing the film – but watching it one does have an almost eerie feeling that everything is too perfect, too well lit, to be 'real'.

Bearing in mind this tangental relationship to reality it is ironic that Morris's best-known film, *The Thin Blue Line*, was an exposé of a miscarriage of justice and had a demonstrable effect on American legal reform.

For many years Morris has tried without success to find funding for feature films.

This piece first appeared in the *New Yorker*.

Errol Morris's documentaries have a luxuriant weirdness, a deep unfamiliarity. In his first two films *Gates of Heaven* (1978), a report on pet cemeteries in California, and *Vernon, Florida* (1981), a loosely assembled collection of tales from a small southern town, told by rambling coots and half-demented good old boys, his choice of material and his fondness for lingering on the cracked discourse of his interview subjects identified him as a true connoisseur of native eccentricity, a hoarder of oddball Americana. His new movie, *The Thin Blue Line*, shows that he's more than an inspired believe-it-or-not artist. Telling the story of a 1976 cop-killing in Dallas, and detailing the process by which a man who is almost certainly innocent was convicted and sentenced to death for the crime (with the likely killer as the prosecution's star witness), Morris burrows into a nightmarish realm of duplicity, faulty perception, and bottomless ambiguity. The movie is both detached and fanatically intense. Its materials have the heterogeneity, the heedless comprehensiveness, of documents in a dossier: there are interviews with the principals, close-ups of key words and paragraphs from the newspaper accounts, courtroom sketches, maps, family-album snapshots of the suspects, diagrams of the crime scene and of the entry and exit wounds in the victim's body, and a series of eerie re-enactments of witnesses' different versions of the murder and the events that led up to it. But this stuff isn't organized in ways that we're used to. *The Thin Blue Line* doesn't have the structure either of *60 Minutes*-style investigative journalism or of detective fiction, though it borrows elements from both; its form is circular, spiraling, its obsessive, repetitive visual motifs echoed in Philip Glass's hauntingly monotonous score. This is documentary as epistemological thriller; Morris seems to want to bring us to the point at which our apprehension of the real world reaches the pitch of paranoia – to induce in us the state of mind of a detective whose scrutiny of the evidence, whose search for the connections between stubbornly isolated facts, has begun to take on the feverish clarity of hallucination.

The movie is a trance like, almost lyrical rendering of a small, messy murder case, the kind of story that's usually found only in local newspapers and, sensationalized, in true-detective magazines – and it's as hypnotic as *Vertigo*. Although Morris himself doesn't appear in *The Thin Blue Line*, he is the film's true detective, the investigator whose insomniac consciousness keeps reshuffling the evidence, generating ambiguous images of the crime from the contradictory testimony of witnesses, swerving constantly between words and pictures, between facts and hypotheses. He came upon the story by accident. In 1985, Morris was interviewing prisoners in a Texas penitentiary for a documentary on Dr James P. Grigson, a Dallas psychiatrist who is known as Dr Death, because his expert testimony in capital cases virtually guarantees that the defendant will be sentenced to death. One of the film-maker's interview subjects was a man named Randall Adams, who claimed to have been wrongly convicted of a policeman's murder. Morris did some digging into the records of the case and the trial, became convinced that Adams was innocent, and wound up on a long detour from the Dr Death movie; the question of how Randall Adams could have landed in jail for something he probably didn't do took over the film-maker's mind. Undoubtedly, the urgent, compulsive quality of *The Thin Blue Line* is, at least in part, a consequence of the film's unusual origin. The subject seems to have seized Morris' imagination unexpectedly – in much the same way that another Dallas murder, the Kennedy assassination, has drawn people, almost against their will, into its labyrinth of half-truths and contradictions, closed files and intimations of conspiracy.

Officer Robert Wood was killed on a cold night in November 1976. He and his partner had stopped a car in a bad section of town just to tell the driver to turn his headlights on; when Wood reached the window on the driver's side, he was shot, several times, by the man at the wheel. Since the crime was apparently so senseless, and since the only known witness, Wood's partner, wasn't very observant (the movie suggests that she may have violated procedure by remaining seated in the patrol car, drinking a milkshake, while Wood approached the killer's car), the Dallas police had no leads and hardly any clues. A month later, they questioned sixteen-year-old David Harris, who had been bragging to his buddies in the small town of Vidor that he had killed a Dallas cop. He admitted to the police that he had been in the car that Wood pulled over, but claimed that the person who had done the shooting was Randall Adams, a hitchhiker he had picked up earlier that day. After interrogating Adams – who insisted that the teenager had dropped him off at his motel a couple of hours before the time of the murder, and who refused to sign a confession – the police decided that they would believe Harris, despite what might have seemed fairly strong circumstantial evidence pointing to him as the killer: both the murder weapon and the car had been stolen by Harris in Vidor; since he knew that the car was stolen, he

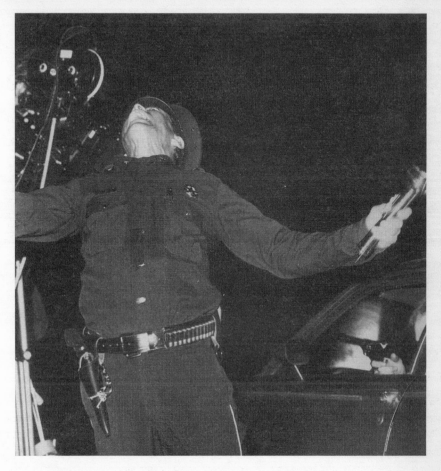

43 *Documentary meets fiction in* The Thin Blue Line *(1989).*

would have had far more reason than Adams to panic at being stopped
by a patrol car; he had a substantial criminal record, and was facing
charges in Vidor at the time he gave his evidence, whereas Adams had no
record at all and no history of violence. So why, the movie asks, was
Adams prosecuted, much less convicted and sentenced to death?

Morris's answers, or suggestions of answers, are complex, and whirl
by us at such speed that we're barely able to keep up. We register one
fact, and then another comes at us, then another and another, until,
finally, we seem to be taking it all in on an almost subliminal level – our
attention is so intensely focused that everything resonates, everything

connects, with a logic we have stopped even trying to articulate. In showing us the lies, the fears, the social pressures, the cultural influences, the unwarranted assumptions, the ulterior motives, the stubbornness, and the plain confusion that combined to produce the case against Randall Adams, Morris – who has a degree in philosophy, and who once worked as a private detective – seems to be investigating not just this squalid murder but the very nature of untruth. It's hard to think of another movie (let alone another documentary) that has such a richly developed sense of the texture of falsehood, that picks out so many of the strands that, woven together, blind us. The Dallas police, their anger stirred and their pride challenged by the murder of one of their own, needed to arrest someone: if they believed Harris, they had a crime with a witness; if they believed Adams, then Harris was alone in the car, and they had nothing. The district attorney, Douglas Mulder, who had never lost a capital case, needed a conviction and a death sentence: Harris, as a juvenile, couldn't be tried for first-degree murder; Adams, who was twenty-seven, could. At the trial, the victim's partner, who was feeling the heat of a departmental investigation of her conduct on the night of the killing and therefore may have been especially eager to co-operate, changed her testimony from her original report: having initially said that there was only one person in the car, she now claimed to have seen two; the driver was now described as having had bushy shoulder-length hair (like Adams), rather than short hair and a fur-collared jacket (like Harris). The judge, the son of an FBI agent, was a man with a passion for law enforcement; he admits that he 'welled up' during the DA's emotional closing argument about 'the thin blue line' of police risking their lives to protect society. One of the prosecution's chief witnesses, sprung on the defence at the last moment, was a woman named Emily Miller, who 'used to watch all the detective shows on TV' and loved to make herself useful to the authorities – particularly in this case, since there was a twenty-one-thousand-dollar reward involved, and her daughter had just been arrested for a felony. (The charges were quietly dropped.)

Morris sucks us into the process by which a man, Randall Adams, becomes a kind of fictional character in a story whose momentum seems unstoppable. Adams, labeled a 'drifter' by the police and the press (although he had been holding down a decent job ever since he arrived in Dallas, two months before the murder), is, when we see him interviewed in prison, a wan, ghostly, soft-spoken man. He's much thinner than the mustachioed hippie we've seen in newspaper photos from the time of his arrest, and he has a flat, weary voice. Although Adams isn't on Death Row anymore – in a complicated legal manoeuvre, the State of Texas commuted his sentence to life imprisonment in 1977 (after the Supreme Court struck down his death penalty), so that it wouldn't have to give him a new trial – he looks and sounds like someone on the verge of disappearing. He seems barely real, a shadowy image animated only sporadically by glints of bitter humour. The recreations of the murder and the events surrounding it have a stronger presence than Adams himself. Even when these scenes are representing accounts that are probably false, they're compelling. We watch the same actions occur over and over again, with slight but significant variations, on the same dark stretch of road – a setting that Morris endows with an unearthly vividness, composed of the piercing beams of headlights, silhouetted figures, flashes of gunfire, the revolving red light on top of the police car, and rich, enveloping nighttime blackness – and we think, against all reason, that one more detail, a different angle of vision, will suddenly reveal the truth, that these reconstructions somehow have the power to take us to the heart of things. Once David Harris had told his story, Randall Adams's life was obliterated, to be replaced by an endless series of constructions and reconstructions of a single moment (a moment at which he was most likely asleep in his motel room). It's as if time had simply stopped for him the instant the image of him shooting Robert Wood lodged in the minds of the Dallas police, and he had been condemned to live the rest of his life exclusively in the minds of others: cops, judges, juries, lawyers, newspaper readers, Errol Morris, audiences watching this movie all of us, for our various reasons, rehearsing that terrible moment, with the figure of Randall Adams flickering in and out of the picture.

Adams's fate is worthy of a Borges hero, one of those melancholy spirits trapped in infinite loops of metaphysical treachery. It's no small feat for Morris to have made a documentary that evokes this kind of existential unease in its audience. There are times, though, when things get all muddy and confused, and that's not because reality is, you know, hopelessly ambiguous; it's because the film-maker's style is too fancy and eliptical, or because he just hasn't bothered to give us information we need. The legal proceedings, in particular, are almost never entirely lucid. The flowering absurdity of Adams's experiences with the courts wouldn't lose its horror if Morris troubled to explain a few crucial points of law. But this is a powerful and thrillingly strange movie, and Morris's occasional excess of artiness shouldn't be taken as an indication of indifference to the reality of Randall Adams's plight. In fact, the film-maker himself uncovered several pieces of new evidence, testified in Adams's behalf at hearings on motions for retrial, and coaxed a near-confession out of David Harris, which we hear, on tape, in the movie's final scene. (Harris has since, in a recent interview with a newspaper reporter, come even closer to an outright admission of guilt. He's on Death Row for another murder, and Adams is still petitioning for a new trial.) Morris, who clearly has a very sophisticated understanding of the relationship between art and reality, did a thorough, painstaking investigation in the real world, and then did something different on film: he turned the case into a kind of tabloid poetry, a meditation on uncertainty and the fascination of violence. If we quibble every now and then with his presentation of the facts, it's his own fault; *The Thin Blue Line* makes us all obsessed detectives.

On 1 March 1989, the Texas Court of Criminal Appeals overturned the conviction of Randall Adams. He was released from prison shortly thereafter, and the Dallas District Attorney's Office announced that it had no intention of trying the case again.

Source: *The New Yorker*, September 5, 1988.

When Documentary is not Documentary
LIZZIE FRANCKE

The dividing line between 'documentary' and 'fiction' has never been sharp, but recent films like *The Thin Blue Line*, with its dramatized reconstructions and noir-like narrative twists, have further blurred the distinction. Not that the seepage has all been in one direction. Fiction films have also enthusiastically appropriated the techniques and stylistics of the documentary – to such an extent that it often seems that 'documentary' is no more than a *style* a director choses to indicate (or mock) authenticity.

Director Kevin Hull could be forgiven for being somewhat dismayed about the press coverage of his documentary *Einstein's Brain* when the

BBC broadcast it in 1994 as part of an *Arena* trilogy on relics for Easter. It wasn't that there weren't enough previews/reviews. Indeed, the film – which followed the picaresque trail of Professor of Mathematics, Kenji Sugimoto as he criss-crossed America in his attempt to locate the whereabouts of Albert Einstein's grey matter which famously disappeared in mysterious circumstances after the autopsy – received a high level of attention. The trouble was that most of the journalists writing about it fixated on its screening date of April 1st (which that year also happened to be Good Friday). From the broadsheet papers through to the tabloids, the verdict was that the film was an elaborate hoax. 'Kevin Hull's film is consistently diverting though the thought occurs that if the BBC is going to perpetrate an April Fool's joke, this could be it,' wrote *The Times*. In typically lurid fashion, The *Sun* attempted to stir controversy by eliciting a response from rival channels about the 'sick spoof'. The consensus was that the documentary about a 'nutty' Japanese professor who hailed from one Kinki University, with only a modest grasp of the English language so that he pronounces Missouri as 'misery' and greets people with a guttural 'harro', could only have been a fabrication. It was cod with an ample side order of red herring, as Sugimoto pursued various leads only to finally catch his first glimpse of his formalin-pickled Holy Grail served sliced up on a chopping board in the dingy kitchen of a medical man who fell from grace and now works in a plastics moulding factory. If this didn't seem a weird enough trip, credulity was only stretched further by the appearance of the writer William Burroughs.

But *Einstein's Brain* wasn't designed to baffle and tease so. If it had been scheduled for April 2nd, one suspects that its authenticity could not have been so easily doubted. Watch Hull's film untrammelled by Fool's Day expectations, and it is a highly perceptive account of how a scientist like Einstein has been turned into a latter-day saint, with Sugimoto the pilgrim whose fervour for the man who defined the nuclear age may or may not have something to do with the fact that he was born only miles from Hiroshima. As such it is a story of strange atonement that in itself interrogates the questing desire for the authentic 'religious' experience. One might point out that even if Hull had invented the whole tale, it would not have been any less valid in terms of its examination of the themes.

It is symptomatic of one's expectations of the medium and form, however, that a television documentary is construed as pure fiction –

and consequently treated lightly – simply because it makes imaginative use of its raw material. The fact that the material might also have an absurd edge to it compounds the problem. Presented with the bizarre, the weird, the odd, the magical stuff that fills the pages of the *Fortean Times* on television and the viewer becomes too easily side-tracked by the disturbing suspicion that one might be being duped. But while Hull's film did not deliberately set out to be so disconcerting – though it does literally swat the fly on the wall in its attempt to redefine what the documentary can do, such refutations or interrogations of the faith are important to a genre which is predicated on the credo, to see is to believe, and to believe is to buy into.

The *faux* documentary exists to fray the thin line between fact and fiction and make sceptics of us all. Peter Greenaway's *Act of God* (1980) is an elliptical case in point. Commissioned by Thames Television as part of their *Take Six* series, it overtly played with the conventions and expectations of the TV investigative documentary. In it a range of people recount their experience of being struck by lightning and how it affected their lives, while mixed in with these often very amusing accounts are a series of apocryphal stories about tempestuous weather. Each of the film's witnesses is highly rigorous in their account, detailing the time and place of the strike, their height, the type of shoes that they were wearing and what they were holding in their hand. They are depicted invariably seated behind desks and tables, but the formal presentation usually (in the late 1970s at least) associated with the straight-to-camera report is rejigged. Several subjects sit with their backs to French windows that have been flung open – the final barrier between them and whatever is 'out there' removed. Meanwhile a woman, who was struck by lightning while on the phone, tells her story down the phone, her disembodied voice crackling through the mouth-piece that the camera is focused on. Such stylistic strategies forge new meanings out of the experiences recounted while as to the 'truth' of these people's accounts, it is left ambiguous.

Films such as *Act of God* are delightfully opaque. More recently, the witness sequences in Wayne Wang and Paul Auster's yap rap movie *Blue in the Face* also occupy the hinterland between the scripted and the genuine. There a series of Brooklynites talk to video camera about phenomena that occupy them, the best being the man obsessed with plastic bags in trees, which he construes to be 'signs of chaos'. Primed poetry or just a wonderful turn of phrase? Wang purloins some of the stylistic techniques of the documentary – the straight-to-camera inter-views (and also in this case the reading of statistics about Brooklyn's population) to make the film seem more immediate and alive. As such *Blue in the Face* can be construed as an anthropological project of sorts – as it scrutinizes – and celebrates – a diverse and odd American culture (in this respect it is not dissimilar to David Byrne's *True Stories* with its small town made up of *Weekly World News*-style peculiarities).

Wang follows in a tradition of film-makers who have used documentary methods to bring a dimension of the 'real' to their projects. In a different vein Warren Beatty and Trevor Griffiths chose to insert straight-to-camera interviews with key veteran witnesses into *Reds*, their shrewd film based on John Reed and Louise Bryant's accounts of the Russian Revolution. The presence of the likes of Rebecca West and Henry Miller shook up the 'biopic' conventions as it shifted between the dramatized reconstruction and the recollections of those who participated in that key historical moment. Meanwhile Ken Loach has famously adopted and adapted the conventions of *cinéma vérité* with the direct style of camera-work and spare use of music (or no music at all) on the sound track giving his dramas a raw immediacy that highlights their social realist intention. Likewise the mobile camera-work used in Oliver Stone's historical epics *JFK* (1993) and *Nixon* (1995) is also meant as some short-hand claim to authenticity.

Conversely from the serious, authoritative style of the anthropologi-cal essays to the instant attraction of the *cinéma-vérité* films, the documentary techniques which can give gravitas to a project also provide much material for lampoon. With the satire boom in the 1960s, the 'parody documentary' came into its own – as witnessed in sketches on such TV shows as *Monty Python's Flying Circus* and later in the US show, *Saturday Night Live*. Meanwhile film-makers such as Jim McBride took a sly swipe at the self-importance of the diary genre with David Holzman's *Diary* (1967), about an anxious young man dedicated to filming his own autobiography which, incidentally, was shot by Michael Wadleigh who would go on to make *Woodstock*. In a more obvious vein, Woody Allen choose the noted documentary narrator Jackson Beck to provide the booming voice-over commentary for his directorial debut *Take the Money and Run* (1969), a spoof sociological study of the retrograde career of the inept crook Virgil Starkwell. Later, Allen would experiment with other documentary styles, shooting the frantic comedy of emotional entanglements *Husbands and Wives*

(1992) in wild, hand-held wobbly-scope, while overtly playing with the format in the sophisticated *Zelig* (1983). There he reconstructed the life of the human chameleon who finds himself fitting in with a gamut of twentieth-century figures from Herbert Hoover to Adolf Hitler, Eugene O'Neill to Dolores Del Rio. Using special effects, Allen fabricated an immaculate history, substantiated by grainy news-real footage and serious talking heads such as Susan Sontag and Saul Bellow who provided the requisite critique (a device purloined from Warren Beatty's *Reds*).

At its most simplistic, *faux* documentary such as *Zelig* draw one's attention to the way that the truth can be so easily falsified (as such they are the flip side of the propaganda films that peddle lies for verities). For this reason directors have been drawn to the form for more overtly political purposes. Robert Altman's television series *Tanner '88*, which he co-wrote with the Doonesbury cartoonist Garry Trudeau, and Altman protégé Tim Robbin's fictional bio-pic *Bob Roberts* (1992) are both satires on American presidential campaigns which have a very particular purpose in the dizzy era of spin-doctors where the campaigns of the real senators themselves seem to run like glossy TV movies while talk-show hosts have designs on the White House. *Tanner '88*, which was broadcast in the US on the cable channel HBO during the run-up to the real George Bush/Michael Dukakis contest in 1988 is the far sharper of the two, with its fictional candidate, an affable, grinning former Democrat congressman Jack Tanner (Michael Murphy), mingling with such real players as Gary Hart, Bob Dole and Pat Robertson. Trailing the legend 'The Future is Now' (in fact the motto of the Washington Redskins), Tanner comes up with the appropriate platitudes while bumbling his way through the make-over process which Altman records on video in vivid, freewheeling style. This is *The Candidate* done as *cinéma vérité* with Altman and Trudeau underscoring the blipvert blurring of politics and showbiz. With Tanner's agit-prop daughter played by one Cynthia Nixon (no relation), the distinctions between fact and fiction become very hazy. 'I believe in Jack Tanner . . . he seems real to me' says the pundit Wayne Jennings at one point. When, on the eve of the Californian primary, HBO decided to run a straw poll Tanner won thirty-five per cent of the 40,000 strong vote, outstripping Bush, Dukakis and Jesse Jackson.

Choosing such a relatively low-profile actor as Murphy to play the lead was astute. He had no persona other than Tanner. With Tim Robbins in the title role, *Bob Roberts* had less of an edge than the Altman project (with which it shared the cinematographer Jean Lepine) in that it was a more obviously a fictional, cautionary tale that charted the rise of another grinning would-be politician, but this time a 1960s beatnik turned into a 1990s scary crypto-fascist who has the corporations on his side. Perhaps Robbins, who first invented his monster for *Saturday Night Live*, decided to play the part because he had no confidence in the audiences' ability to separate out truth from myth.

Robbins cited the 'mock rockumentary', *This is Spinal Tap*, as a key influence and in that lies a cautionary tale. Rob Reiner's hilarious spoof followed a truly awful British heavy metal band – complete with bad hair, whiny guitars and trousers too tight to mention – on the 'comeback' tour of America. Intercutting interviews with the boys in reflective mode, with dramatic confrontational moments – as when the news reaches them that Spinal Tap's *Smell the Glove* LP cover has been banned for being sexist ('sexy – isn't that good?' murmurs one band member) – and clever archive footage pastiches. It's an astute moment on not just the genre of the 'back-stage' rockumentary, but of the music business itself. But while *This is Spinal Tap* was rightfully a box-office success, one begins to wonder how some audiences were construing the film, when not only did the album of the movie begin to sell, but a market was created for 'Spinal Tap gigs'. Unnervingly, as with those who voted for Jack Tanner, for some the bogus band had a rather real appeal.

Meanwhile Hull's *Einstein's Brain* has been receiving good notices as it plays on the international festival circuit – it has gone down particularly well in Japan where it has also been released at cinemas. But revealingly, there Professor Sugimoto finds himself now treated like a film star as the factual takes a most fabulous turn.

Source: This piece was written especially for this collection.

Nick Broomfield: The Fly in the Ointment
ALLISON PEARSON

Nick Broomfield is that rare beast: a celebrity documentary film-maker. His handsome face and ingratiating voice are known to millions of

television viewers because he has appeared – with what is either characterized as 'boyish charm' or simple vanity – in all the documentaries he has made since the early 1980s.

Broomfield readily admits that he was not the originator of the self-reflexive documentary style, in which the questing film-maker appears on camera, sharing his filming difficulties with the audience, and cites the precedence and influence of Michael Rubbo's 1974 film *Waiting for Fidel*. Nevertheless, Broomfield has made the style his trademark.

Recently, however, the formula has been wearing thin and Broomfield's films of the 1990s became unconvincing. What started as iconoclasm and honesty had become little more than a convention, another stylistic trope. Thankfully though, *Heidi Fleiss: Hollywood Madam* (1995), is a return to form; a complex, noirish tale of vice and dysfunction set in Los Angeles and peopled with memorable characters.

This piece first appeared in the *Independent on Sunday* to coincide with the transmission of *Tracking Down Maggie* (1994).

Chapter One
Containing such grave Matter, that the Reader cannot laugh once through the whole Chapter, unless peradventure he should laugh at the Author.

Thus Henry Fielding in *Tom Jones*. Here is the authentic voice of the picaresque – bibulous, full of tall tales scoffing at others but even more at himself. It summons up a whole host of reckless, often alliterative heroes who make a plot out of their own adventures. So whatever happened to Roderick Random and Peregrine Pickle? Did the road-novel rakes simply die out? I used to think so until I turned on the television one night and saw a man dangling a microphone the size of Cyrano's nose under the foaming beard of the Boer leader, Eugene Terreblanche. 'Why are you late?' thundered the neo-Nazi. 'Er, we were getting some tea,' said his rueful interviewer. Yes, Nicholas Naughty is alive and well and making documentaries.

Nick Broomfield is arguably one of Britain's foremost documentarists – although the only ones doing the arguing are seething rivals – and certainly the most visible. Documentary-makers are traditionally as invisible of television as prompters are in theatres; their voice should be heard only in emergency, and even then it should barely be audible to an audience which must, at all costs, have its illusions kept intact. The grandest illusion of the fly-on-the-wall school is objectivity: we can't see the producer leaving key witnesses out because they won't co-operate, or because they say things that don't fit the thesis or are just plain ugly, and so we get the idea that the programme must be telling it like it is. Broomfield has snookered that one by doubling as sound-man and reporter, forever popping up in front of his own camera. He has become what Peter Moore, his fond but exasperated boss at Channel Four, calls 'the fly in the ointment'.

Critics say Broomfield is vain (he was known as Pretty Boy Broomfield while at Central Television), a megalomaniac who makes films about his ego rather than his subjects. Broomfield says: 'Why pretend you're not there, when everyone knows you are?'

A Broomfield documentary is like Rodgers and Piano's Pompidou Centre: cheeky and with the workings on the outside, it riles the purists and makes a lot of people smile. He shows us the parts other directors will not, such as the sordid, frustrated attempts to get past a pair of mercenary minders to interview a condemned woman in *Aileen Wurnos – The Selling of a Serial Killer*. Bumbling into kitchens, bars and offices, Broomfield can imply things that documentaries locked into formal narratives would be afraid to. He tails his subjects with such abject doggedness that they make the mistake of thinking they have the upper hand. Chico Twata, the roguish black South African star of *Too White for Me*, telephones his shifty Afrikaner partner and says: 'I have no choice. I have to bring them along. They are sitting in the lounge right now. They are following me everywhere I go. Except the toilet.' Of course, Broomfield's haplessness is a fruitful fiction. Producer and psychotherapist Udi Eichler says of his friend: 'Nick has a total ruthlessness, a nose for trouble and an extraordinarily low boredom threshold. Not to mention a profound shamelessness to keep poking in where anyone else would retreat in embarrassment.' In *The Leader, His Driver and the Driver's Wife*, Broomfield deliberately turned up late to meet Terreblanche, prompting a tirade of venom far more revealing than any formal interview.

The technique is well suited to his latest quarry. One of the best scenes in *Tracking Down Maggie*, an inevitably doomed quest to find 'the real Margaret Thatcher' shows a chance meeting in Chelsea with a dowager who admits she once pinched the former PM's lavatory from a skip. Other documentarists might have recorded the lady's rambling reminiscences; only Broomfield would have followed her home for the

44 *The documentarist as his own subject: Nick Broomfield.*

coup de grâce – the toilet displayed with a 'Mrs Thatcher sat here'
plaque.

' 'Scuse me. 'Scuse me, can we just get a shot of Lady Thatcher?' is
Broomfield's constant cry as he follows her on her US book-signing tour,
allegedly trying to secure an interview. In fact an official meeting would
have spoilt the fun. Barred from all Lady Thatcher's speeches,
Broomfield peeps at her through cracks in doors like a naughty boy
afraid to be caught smoking in the bike-sheds. He doesn't tell us

anything we don't know from Denys Blackeway's magisterial *The Downing Street Years*, but he captures her creepy hauteur, the fear she inspires in others – and him. 'She thought we'd play the traditional game,' says Broomfield, 'that if she ignored us we'd just evaporate. I don't think she expected a guerrilla action to start up.' It was a stroke of genius to make a comic film about a woman who, as her best friend confides to Broomfield, has absolutely no sense of humour.

Broomfield played by the rules once. *Who Cares*, his poignant first short-film about the destruction wrought on a Liverpool community when they were moved from back-to-backs to a tower block, made while he was still a student at Essex University, was classic, grainy *vérité*. In his next film, *Proud to be British*, he conducted a deadpan inquiry into Home Counties hunting and debutantes. The equally deadpan *Buckinghamshire Advertiser* noted: 'It was difficult to avoid the conclusion that it was a film about private schooling, the Church and the conservative party, made by a left wing, pro-comprehensive atheist, though Mr Broomfield said this would be an exaggeration.'

From 1975–1985, Broomfield and his then wife, the gifted American camerawoman Joan Churchill, made a series of the kind of films that try to change society. *Juvenile Liaison*, the first films they made together after leaving the National Film School, exposed Blackburn police's excessively harsh treatment of children, including a boy who was taken to a cell for nicking a cowboy suit. (It was never broadcast because timid liberals at the BFI caved in to police pressure, says Broomfield; because Nick didn't get the proper release forms from the parents, says the distinguished documentarist Roger Graeff), *Soldier Girls* tackled basic training in Georgia, *Chicken Ranch* penetrated a Nevada whorehouse. In 1985, he and Joan co-directed a film about Lily Tomlin. The comedienne insisted on a flattering portrait: they demurred, she sued; they counter-sued. Broomfield calls it 'the most humiliating experience of my life: the best stuff was left on the cutting room floor.'

When his next project, the recording of the progress of an all-black musical in New York, started to go hideously wrong, he adopted the view taken by Woody Allen pondering the seduction of Diane Keaton in *Play it Again Sam*: 'If it doesn't work, I'll pretend it was a joke.' The result, *Driving Me Crazy*, saw Mercedes Ellington hit on the head by a camera, an emergency finance meeting held in a broom cupboard and the director turn to Broomfield and say: 'I no longer find you adorable.' From then on, Broomfield was to drive everyone crazy on purpose . . .

Chapter Two
Wherein Nicholas Naughty tries to show the terrible Truth about
Baroness Thatcher and her son Mark but, Thwarted, makes much sport
of Mr Wheen at his Pianoforte.

I meet Nick Broomfield at the peeling 1930s mansion block in Highgate
that doubles as office and London pad (he also has a house in Sussex
and Jane Fonda's old beach place in Santa Monica to be near his son,
Barney). Rita Oord, Broomfield's producer, is working in the back
bedroom which betrays signs of the chaos Peter Moore claims is the
outfit's guiding principle. The budgets written in crayon still rankle with
Moore ('Can't he get a bloody typewriter?'), but he has reconciled
himself to Broomfield's proposals ('three scribbled lines on a bit of A4')
since he approved an idea for a film about a South African black-white
encounter group and it turned into *The Leader*. Its gentle hints about
journalist Jani Allen's involvement with Terreblanche landed Channel
Four in the High Court and the tabloids ('Drunk Nazi wore green
underpants with holes'), but it also landed the Royal Television Society
Award for Best Documentary.

'A film by Nick Broomfield', as his works are always billed, is actually
a film by Nick, Rita and their superb cameraman, Barry Ackroyd. 'Rita
is the slave, Nick is the maestro' is how one observer sums up the
arrangement. I ask Rita if she minds Nick calling her 'my assistant' in
the films as if she were a conjuror's moll. 'Things are looking up,' she
laughs. 'In the Thatcher film he calls me "my colleague".'

Rita has also learnt to take Broomfield's perfectionist rages in her
stride. Udi Eichler, who commissioned Nick and Joan to make *Marriage
Guidance*, had told me that if Joan got a less than perfect shot Nick
would practically grab her by the hair and fling her round the editing
suite. Did that sound familiar? Rita said it did, but that he doesn't dare
do that to Barry and if he tries it on her she threatens to take the next
plane home. 'That's his *Jekyll and Hyde* thing – Hyde for work, Jekyll
for home.'

Broomfield and I go for lunch at a genteel café round the block. He
insists I chose first, then orders just tea and water. While he sips
reflectively, muggins is left trying to eat paté and toast without making
crumbs in front of the coolest man for miles. He is wearing his
trademark shirt – as white as the legendary loose grin – and a black
leather jacket. At forty-six the boyish charm is spookily intact. With

olive skin, snub nose and wistful eyes, he has a look of Oliver Tobias before Joan Collins wore him out.

The Thatcher film is still buzzing round his brain; he says it was the most difficult to date: six different edited versions, never realized her security would be that strict. Was she more frightening than Terreblanche? 'Absolutely.' Any regrets? 'Well, leaving out the interview with the Archbishop of Canterbury. He said that when he talked to Lady Thatcher about the Bible she was very up on the Old Testament – vengeance, eye for an eye stuff – but didn't have a clue about the New Testament – learning from the poor, charity, that kind of thing.' Why did that bit have to go? 'Well, he didn't fit in with the cast terribly well.'

Does he really think adopting a bumbling persona gets the best results? 'Well, I always delight in buffoony kind of people and I think it's much more important that the audience laughs at you than the people you're filming. I definitely feel there's an Inspector Clouseau feeling to this film.' There is, helped along by Rolf Harris's 'Two Little Boys' on the soundtrack (Lady Thatcher's choice on 'Desert Island Discs') and Broomfield's totally straight account of increasingly hostile encounters with her staff: 'Sadly, my relationship with Elizabeth had deteriorated visibly by now.'

After Broomfield and Churchill split up, it became clear that it had been Joan who had had the Social conscience. Nick admits his attraction to places like Liverpool was a 'romantic, Jack London thing'. As his work grows ever more entertaining, he has attacked preachy, didactic documentaries. I put it to him that his films still convey a strong feeling of right and wrong: 'Yeah, I think there's a clear sense of why you're making the film which is hopefully different from telling an audience what to think – treating them like stupid, inferior people that you need to teach. I think it's more a question of taking them on the journey with you.' . . .

'People say you're a fantastically vain film-maker?' 'Vain?' 'Vain.' 'I find it funny. Stupid. I mean you don't call Alan Whicker vain for being in his films, do you?' 'Yes.' 'Ah, well, I'm clear why I got into it. Because you're a player, a major mover of the action, you have a lot more control. You can use yourself as a battering ram.' They also say you get away with things because you fix people with this look of sweet surprise when they get angry with you. He fixes me with a look of sweet surprise.

Chapter Three
Containing little more than a few odd Observations.

A few days ago a documentarist I know who is struggling to get people to say on camera the interesting things they say off it, suddenly shouted out: 'God, I wish I could do a Broomfield.'

'A Broomfield,' says Roger Graeff, is descended from that day in the sixties when James Baldwin went to interview Ingmar Bergman for *Esquire* magazine. He waited and waited, but he never did get to meet Bergman. Instead, he wrote a hilarious article about not interviewing Ingmar Bergman. The New Journalism was born.

In 1992, Nick Broomfield was caught by a photographer grinning outside the High Court after the Jani Allen verdict: 'Look at all the fun we've had. Everyone had a good old giggle at the expense of a bunch of neo-Nazis. I can't think of a better use of our time.'

If Nicholas Naughty had a coat of arms, its motto might well read: 'Tis better to travel entertainingly than arrive with the viewer half asleep.'

Source: The *Independent on Sunday*, 15th May 1994.

Hearts of Darkness: A Film-maker's Apocalypse
ROGER EBERT

'Making of the movie' documentaries are usually little more than obsequious PR puff, but there have been two notable exceptions: Fax Bahr's *Hearts of Darkness: A Film-Maker's Apocalypse* (1991), about the making of Francis Coppola's *Apocalypse Now*, and Les Blank's *Burden of Dreams* (1982) about Werner Herzog's *Fitzcaraldo*.

Both had unusual access to unusually fraught productions helmed by obsessive, even megalomaniac, directors. Both are fascinating portraits of human creativity in extremis, depicting their director-subjects as flawed, over-reaching, but ultimately heroic.

The making of a film has never been documented with more penetration and truth than in *Hearts of Darkness*, which chronicles the agony and the ecstasy of Francis Ford Coppola's *Apocalypse Now*. That is because no other documentary has ever had access to materials that are normally off limits: shots that were never used, scenes that were abandoned, private arguments between the director and his actors, cries for help and confessions of despair, and even conversations between Coppola and his wife that she secretly tape-recorded.

The film strips Coppola bare of all defenses and yet reveals him as a great and brave film-maker. It also reveals the ordeal he put his actors and crew through, on location in the Philippines, and what he endured at their hands. We see a drunken and bloodied Martin Sheen improvising a breakdown while the room is charged with the possibility that he will attack Coppola or his camera. Sheen being given first aid after a serious heart attack. Coppola screaming in outrage that Sheen's condition has been leaked to the trade papers and the news could pull the plug on the production: 'Even if he dies, I don't want to hear anything but good news until it comes from me.' Dennis Hopper, his mind adrift on drugs, unable to remember his lines and yet improvising brilliantly. Marlon Brando, at $1 million a week, turning up without preparation and engaging in endless debates with Coppola about his character. Brando beginning a scene, then wandering off while the camera is still running, and mumbling, 'and that's all the dialogue I can think of today.'

Apocalypse Now premièred in 1979 at Cannes, shared the Palme d'Or, and went on to become one of the great mythic productions in film history. It told a story about Vietnam that was inspired by Joseph Conrad's great novella *Heart of Darkness*, about a journey up the Congo River in search of a man named Kurtz. In the film, Sheen commands a Navy patrol boat that penetrates a Vietnamese river in search of Colonel Kurtz (Brando), who has set himself up as the god of a tribe of jungle Indians.

Apocalypse Now is one of the greatest films ever made, and legends have grown up around it. Coppola, at a tumultuous press conference at Cannes in 1979, famously said, 'My film is not about Vietnam. My film is Vietnam.' He also confessed he did not think the ending worked. Now we see what he was talking about.

The script, written by John Milius and originally set to be directed by George Lucas, went through so many changes that finally Coppola was writing it as he shot it, and actors were improvising. The production was bedeviled by monsoons, destroyed sets, huge cost overruns, health problems, and logistical nightmares, as when the Philippine government of Ferdinand Marcos tried to rent Coppola the same helicopters it was

using to fight rebels ten miles away. Brando put Coppola under-
enormous pressure by turning up without having read *Heart of
Darkness* and refusing to be shot except in shadow.

And Coppola, in conversations he did not know were being recorded,
shouted in despair to his wife, Eleanor: 'I tell you from the bottom of my
heart that I am making a bad film.' And again, 'We are all lost. I have no
idea where to go with this.' Yet Coppola's vision somehow remained
secure. Milius, flown to the Philippines by a desperate United Artists to
try to bring sanity back to the script, remembers that he walked in
prepared to convince Coppola that the war was lost and they had to
salvage what they could. After ninety minutes, he says, 'Francis had me
convinced this would be the first film to win the Nobel Prize.' *Hearts of
Darkness* written and directed by Fax Bahr and George Hickenlooper,
is based on documentary footage that Eleanor Coppola shot at the time,
and on recent interviews with both Coppolas, plus Milius, Lucas, and
actors Martin Sheen, Frederic Forrest, Robert Duvall, Dennis Hopper,
Timothy Bottoms, and Larry Fishburne, who incredibly was only
fourteen when he played one of the patrol boat crew. Eleanor's secret
tape recordings were also made available, and the result is fascinating,
harrowing film history. We feel for once we are witnessing the true story
of how a movie got made.

Source: Roger Ebert's *Video Companion*.

The Rise of Camcorder Culture
PAUL BARKER

Undoubtedly the most significant development in documentary in the
last decade has been the rise of the camcorder. Just as the invention of
lightweight cameras and sound equipment in the early 1960s lead to the
explosion of *cinéma vérité*, so the advent of cheap, high-quality
camcorders has opened up a whole new range of possibilities for the
documentary.

The cheapness of shooting on Hi-8 (the best quality camcorder
format) means that film-makers can continue to shoot for much, much
longer than they would usually be able to, so they can follow a story for
as long as it takes. Another benefit is the increased sense of intimacy
these cameras allow, because they are unobtrusive, unintimidating, and

easily operated by non-professionals. A good Hi–8 documentary (like those in the early BBC series *Video Diaries*) could not be done in any other way.

Because camcorders are so easy to use, virtually anyone can now become a film-maker. Consequently, a series like *Video Diaries* gives airtime to a whole set of experiences that have never been on television before and a voice to sections of the public who have been ignored by professional film-makers.

Unfortunately, television commissioning editors have been all too keen to see camcorder documentaries as a cheap way of filling screen time, with the result that the form has rapidly become debased. Without long shooting and editing periods, tight editorial control and most of all a really good story to tell and the skill to tell it, films will not be any good, no matter on what format they are originally shot.

This article first appeared in *The Times* in 1992.

Steve Feltham decided to follow his dreams. He gave up his job as a burglar alarm salesman in Dorset, sold his house, and set off to the Scottish Highlands in a converted mobile library van. Since the age of seven, he had been fascinated by the Loch Ness monster. Now, at twenty-eight, he would be a full-time monster-hunter, encamped on the shores of the loch.

He had everything a monster-hunter needs: a wind generator whirring on the roof, for electric power, a pair of good binoculars; a strong dose of incurable optimism; but, most important of all, a portable video camera. This was not just to capture evidence, if he saw the monster emerge from the mysterious deep. It was to chronicle his entire quest, successful or not – to make a video diary. BBC2 broadcasts it on Saturday under the title *Desperately Seeking Nessie*.

It's a do-it-yourself light comedy. Mr Feltham, obsessive or not, knows a joke when he sees one. Surrounded by thick winter fog, he confides to the camera: 'Some days are better than others for monster hunting.' He often addresses his camera as 'you'. It has become his friend and companion like Long John Silver's parrot.

His programme is an entertaining blip in the usual pattern of BBC2's *Video Diaries*. Many of them come closer to DIY psychoanalysis than to DIY comedy. In last Saturday's *Searching For a Killer*, for example, Geoffrey Smith went back to Haiti to try to come to terms with the day, in 1987, when he was caught up in a polling-day bloodbath. A maverick (or CIA sponsored?) gunman sprayed bullets all around. Haitians were killed as they tried to vote. A friend of Mr Smith's was shot dead at his feet. Mr Smith was shot in the leg.

An Australian based in London, he came back to Britain. But he could never get the recurring nightmare out of his mind. With the BBC-supplied camcorder on his shoulder, he went back into the real nightmare of Haiti, and faced fresh fear and danger – and the nightmares left him. 'The camera was my only companion,' he said. 'I needed a friend that would listen. It is a cathartic device when you use it in the right way. I said to it: "I hate all this." But I became attached to the thing. I buried myself in filming.'

Or you can *find* yourself through filming, as Willa Woolston did. She is an American-born portrait painter, also living in London. In the first series of *Video Diaries*, in 1990, she used her camcorder to get back to her American family, to come to terms with the torment – torture, really – that she suffered as a child at the hands of her stepmother. She has now gone back and videoed a second diary (to be transmitted in September) about how they have coped with the knowledge they disinterred. For her, the camcorder was a kind of exorcist, driving out demons. 'It was extremely distressing at first,' she told me. 'A painted portrait is objective. Here you were being subjective. I was unaccustomed to looking at myself like that. One is accustomed to glossing over what is difficult in life; explaining it away.' After her first programme, she set up a Child Abuse Survivor Network because so many viewers rang in.

These video diaries are produced by the BBC's community programmes unit. They are the sophisticated end of the video culture that is galloping up on us, unawares. The trigger for the series, back in 1990, was the arrival of a small but high-quality camcorder.

Trade may be crashing around most shopkeeper's ears, but camcorders are booming. The market analyst, Mintel, say that sales began to take off in Britain in 1985. In that year, 60,000 were sold, at an average price of £1,250. Last year, it was 475,000, at an average of £710. Amstrad's new 'king of the budget camcorders' sells for £499. The business is so alive with innovation that 'everything is outdated within weeks', says Jeremy Gibson, the editor of *Video Diaries*. He gave his current diarists a Dutch camcorder, from Philips, because it was easier to edit with. 'But I decide each year-end what we'll use next time.'

Diarists get some training in, he says, 'the grammar of television'.

Editorial discussions help them keep to the point. At the end, there is a huge editing job. But the diarist has the right of veto. 'This little camera,' Mr Gibson says, 'shows up the unfortunate methods of most fly-on-the-wall TV: the kerfuffle, the time, the crew. You can use this without threatening other people.'

A camcorder records the emotions of the user, as well as those of the people filmed. Perhaps even more so. Watching videos, you begin to wonder about the hand that shakes the camera. Shops find, in fact, that camcorders are mostly bought to record emotive moments. 'Baby's first words, a wedding, a once-in-a-lifetime holiday,' says Paul Wheaton, the photography manager at Dixon's Marble Arch branch.

Professional photographers are beginning to feel wary. 'The problem is what we call the Uncle Henrys – the relative with the camcorder,' says Pete Randall, a north London wedding specialist. 'For now video is an "also". Photographs are more accessible.' But Mr Randall has a camcorder for the high points in his own family's life.

About a million viewers watch each Saturday night edition of *Video Diaries*, with (in Mr Gibson's words) 'its sociological deconstruction of TV power: the power is in people's own hands.' Almost a million and a half watched BBC2's *Teenage Diaries* variant in June and July. But Granada's *You've Been Framed*, presented by Jeremy Beadle, is playing the game to different rules.

It has reached 18.7 million viewers for a single programme of video-captured mishaps. It is entertainment. It is close to the way most people use their camcorders. 'Dixons and Currys rub their hands with glee when a series goes out,' says Jane Macnaught, the producer. Mr Wheaton, at Dixons, confirms that it helps. The appetite for video grows by what it feeds on. Ms Macnaught is busy now on the third series, for the autumn.

The idea for *You've Been Framed* came from America's *Your Favourite Home Video*, the programme President Bush is said to like the best. In America, video voyeurs can now enjoy *Witness Video*, a primetime programme from NBC which shows videos of real deaths and disasters and which invites viewers' offerings.

British taste, according to Ms Macnaught, is still for shots of animals, children, sport: 'cats with balls of wool'. Tapes reach Ms Macnaught by the vanload. This year she expects between 40,000 and 50,000. Her four full-time viewers play them all.

'It's spontaneous family slapstick,' she says. 'There's the recognition factor. It brings back the times you said, "I wish I had a camera".' The swift spread of camcorders has broadened what is sent in. 'It used to be always wedding clips, and children's first birthdays. But now we have decorating mishaps: dad laying the patio. Or graduation ceremonies. It's a moving piece of family history. And if I ever see another skiing fall . . .'

Viewers don't send her much sex or nudity: 'Our most notorious video was one and a half hours of a man decorating his bedroom with no clothes on.' No doubt in the world outside Beadle, camcorders (like Polaroid cameras before them) follow their owners into the bedroom. Mintel say that one British home in twenty has a camcorder now, they expect one in seven by 1994. In Japan it is already one in five. Two years ago, Sony created the tiny, lightweight 'palmcorder'. As its price drops, it may become the camcorder equivalent of the Kodak Brownie, which sold in every Woolworth's in the 1920s and 1930s and created the family snapshot business.

Sales of everything photographic have been cut back by the recession – except camcorders. They are usually made by electronics companies, not the traditional camera firms. They have already crippled home cine and slides. For family snaps Kodak fights back this autumn with a roll of camera film that can be processed on to compact disc, and played (like video) through your television set, frame by frame.

Camcorders are also destroying old interpretations of photography. For the critic Susan Sontag in her book, *On Photography*, the essential thing about a photograph is that it captures one moment in time and freezes it. Its techniques of composition often bear some relation to fine art. But the images of videos' walking, talking snapshot take place in real time. Not every photo tells a story, but every video does. It is a new folk-narrative.

Michael Langford teaches photography at the Royal College of Art. 'Video is such a draw,' he says, 'because people end up as stars on their own television sets. They're up there with their heroes.' Geoffrey Smith says that, in *Video Diaries*, 'We are watching life exactly as it happened.' But 'life' sometimes needs prompting towards the demands of television. In Haiti, 'I found myself doing things for its sake, rather than simply recording what I was doing.'

The usual family video tape is kept, just as it was filmed, unedited. A Slice of Life in a box. But things never stay that simple. Ian Campbell, editor of the buff's monthly, *Camcorder User*, has been judging the

British amateur video awards. They included elaborate excursions into solo film-making and acting. 'In the 1970s,' he muses, 'new film directors emerged from commercials. In the 1980s it was pop videos. In the 1990s I think we'll see directors who began at home with a humble camcorder.'

Four adults out of five have a camera already, which they are not going to throw away. Mr Langford says: 'Most people still want things in frames and albums, to dwell on. But video is more of a personal eye view. If the composition isn't perfect, the action will carry it through. There's greater freedom.'

The video culture is penetrating everywhere. We are becoming a species in love with its own moving image. In Mr Feltham's video diary on Saturday, he often interconnects with other cameramen. He becomes, he says, 'an overnight success in Japan', when a Japanese news team arrives. He observes David Bellamy, the ecologist, followed by an entire camera crew, creeping along the Loch Ness foreshore in search of supposed spoor from the monster. When a coachload of tourists disembark next to him, about half seem to have their own camcorders. With his BBC-issue Philips Explorer, he videos them videoing. Instead of the old funfair Hall of Mirrors, we increasingly inhabit a video hall of lenses.

Source: *The Times*, 27 July 1992.

Drawing it Out
MICHAEL EATON

In 1995 among the small number of documentaries which received cinema distribution, two very different films attained remarkable popularity and box office success: *Hoop Dreams* (see p. 303) and *Crumb*. For almost the first time since the Lumière brothers a century before, audiences seemed to be willing to pay to see documentaries.

The screenwriter Michael Eaton wrote this piece on *Crumb* for *Sight and Sound*.

In an address to art students in his home town of Philadelphia Robert Crumb declares the feature-cartoon of his *Fritz the Cat* an 'embarrass-ment' and its director Ralph Bakshi a schlockmeister; towards the end of this documentary (made by friend, publisher and long-time collaborator Terry Zwigoff) Crumb roundly insults a young Hollywood producer when the producer dares to suggest that he knows where Crumb is coming from by saying 'Hey, I'm your kind of guy, we're talking toilet, I love it.' So Crumb hates Hollywood: but is interesting to speculate how Hollywood might have turned his life into a classic mythological biopic – if only to free one's mind from the disturbing traces left by this film.

The first act would have shown a sensitive child from a humble background (although such pictures tend to exaggerate the unpromising surroundings the great artist sprang from, here no such hyperbole would be necessary). Misunderstood by an overbearing father, bullied by brutish good-looking high school jocks, he discovers through the careful nurturing of an older brother the one thing at which he can excel: drawing cartoons. The epiphanal moment: through his pen he can express all his suppressed rage and wreak revenge on those who put

45 Crumb *(1995)*.

him down. He is freed from the pressure to be normal and sets out to find a society conducive to his individuality.

Second act; arriving in San Francisco at the height of Flower Power he finds that though he in no way shares in the psychedelic excesses around him, he can nevertheless *draw* his way into society – his pen makes him rich and famous, he becomes the friend of rock stars, hippie chicks lie down before him. But it is not enough. After an intense and revealing transcendental experience he is transformed, he returns to consciousness entirely in touch with his deepest desires.

Third act: redemption in the arms of a loving, mature woman who appreciates and encourages his talents; withdrawal from the world to an idyllic country retreat with his wife and a beautiful daughter who inherits his talents, recognized by the world for the great artist he is, he can live at one with himself, his demons exorcized, his past hurdles surmounted by an integration of art and life. California Dreaming!

In the very first sequence of *Crumb*, the artist reveals that he has no idea what he is doing when he is drawing, that he gets suicidal when he cannot draw and suicidal when he does, and that he only started drawing because of his elder brother's obsession with comics. Thus are most of the major themes of the film laid out. Under prompting from the director, the artist phones his mother's house and requests that they come over to do an interview with this brother Charles. This request is refused. If it had stayed that way – if Charles had continued in his refusal as Crumb's two sisters Carol and Sandy continued to refuse – then this film would have turned out very different if indeed it had turned out at all.

And so we are taken into the heart of the Crumb family, a lower-middle-class American Gothic milieu with none of the Addams' family's saving aristocratic graces. We also realize why this film is presented by David Lynch, who could only envy and never hope to invent such grotesque psychosexual dysfunction.

The Crumb *paterfamilias* was some kind of salesman, clinging desperately to white-collar conformity in McCarthy's America – he was the author of a manual entitled *Training People Effectively*, though he signally failed with his three sons. The mother, who became addicted to amphetamines as a side effect of 1950s weight-loss mania, is still with us, living in reclusive squalor with Charles. Charles it was who 'discovered' the *Treasure Island* of cartoon fantasy – but now he never leaves his room and has been on medication for the past twenty years.

Maxon, Crumb's younger brother, lives as a transient in a San Francisco flop house. Neither the coherence with which Charles speaks of his detachment from the human race, his narcissistic, suicidal tendencies and his mother's denial of the strangeness of her strange brood, nor the cogency with which Maxon analyses the sibling rivalry of the household and its effect on his life, can disguise the fact that Crumb's brothers are condemned to be forever bizarre, depressive people.

At this point in the proceedings we've seen Crumb enthusiastically received by a college audience, present at a gallery opening of a one-man show, feted by an internationally famous art critic who sees him as a successor of Brueghel, Goya and Daumier, and enjoying his record collection in his country retreat with his wife and daughter. So we may have been suckered into feeling that he has escaped the curse of his genetic blight, turning his artistic talent into something that can communicate with the rest of the species. We may even suspect we're in the presence of another piece of 1960s propaganda in which the drug- and/or counter-culture underground emerges as the salvation for the children of a repressed, buttoned-down post-war America. But Zwigoff's film – which at first seems so commonplace in its docu-mentary construction – is far too cannily and insidiously structured to grant an audience any such stereotypically wished-for relief.

Robert Crumb's favourite music is the ragtime, blues and traditional jazz he collects in fragile 78s – a restrained, dignified, rule-governed, harmonious slice of American nostalgia. It is a world away from the freeform, acid-inspired improvisations of The Grateful Dead with whom, as legend seems to have it, he lived in the Haight-Ashbury days. Truth is, Crumb never liked hippie music, or clothes, or indeed hippies. He only hung out with them in the hope of getting some of that Free Love they kept talking about. The movement with which his work is most associated, and iconic of, is one he never felt a part of. The self-portrait familiar to all his readers – of a nerdy, uptight geek – is not cartoon caricature, but documentary realism. Except if anything, as this film so graphically demonstrates, the reality is far more grotesque and disturbing than the cartoon.

One aspect of Crumb's character that marked him off as an oddball in the eyes of his erstwhile colleagues in the underground comics movement was that he didn't even have to think twice before refusing the offer of hundreds of thousands of dollars to appear on the *Tonight Show* or to design a Rolling Stones album sleeve. While the rest of his generation were turning on and tuning in the better to sell out, Crumb devoted himself to the graphic depiction of his dark side. While those around him were parroting the slogan 'Let it all hang out', Crumb took it literally. It is the resultant horrorshow that the middle of the film concentrates on.

In the male corner: Robert Hughes, the art critic of *Time* magazine. For him, Crumb's work is in a fine misanthropic tradition, a passionate Rabelaisian carnival of lusting, suffering humanity and imaginative gaze that is painfully disturbing because it refuses to shrink from the truth. This is graphic art as social satire, unappreciated in America because of the ruling ideologies of Utopianism and Puritanism. In the female corner: Deirdre English, former editor of *Mother Jones*, the left-wing magazine, and Trina Robbins, cartoonist. For them, Crumb's work may start out as satire but by exposing the underbelly of American life results in a self-indulgent, misogynist orgy of his own, personal fantasies becoming a species of pornography, revealing nothing more than Crumb's own arrested juvenile development.

The argument really hinges not on *art* – all commentators are in no doubt (who could be?) about Crumb's graphic brilliance – but on *communication*. If Crumb's dystopia somehow illuminates the world we live in, then his lubriciously available Amazons (with overdeveloped thighs and underdeveloped heads, or none at all, some in the shape of birds and beasts) is social commentary. If it merely gives vent to his own solipsistic, masturbatory fears of impotence, it is case history. If it is put before the public it is irresponsible incitement: in revealing his own warpedness he validates the expression of depravity in others. When the unrestrained male libido hangs out maybe its time to shove it back in. Maybe civilisation's none too comfortable with its discontents.

Crumb himself seems sublimely removed from this debate: he is content to let loose his fantasies and be as surprised as the next man or woman when they emerge with such consistent regularity. They're out in the open for better or worse, and if they display a deep-seated racism or sexism, then that's precisely because such feelings are deep seated in the white male American psyche. His wife Aline says that he reveals his id in undiluted form; his hostility to her gender seems to pose her no threat.

Perhaps the most psychoanalytic response comes from the most unlikely mouthpiece: Dian Hanson, a career pornographer and editor of *Leg Show*, is shooting a cheesy photospread of Crumb surrounded by a bevy of models who put flesh on his fantasies – an experience he seems to relish without irony. For her, men who are obsessed with the lower half of women's bodies have never grown up, and are still powerless children overawed by their gargantuan mothers. Men's propensities for fetishistic fixation makes them easy to manipulate. Crumb , ever the pissed-off outsider, replies that women fixate on power – a remark which acknowledges his hatred and his fear all at once.

But just when we think we know where we are with this film, just when we feel most comfortable with the terms of an insoluble debate on the psycho-structure of male sexuality, Zwigoff undermines any audience complacency by revealing aspects of the Crumb family history that seem unbridled by any account. As with the wedding at Cana, the heaviest brew is saved till last.

From Charcot to Oprah the photographic image has turned its gaze on weirdos. Crumb, too, is fascinated by outcasts – perhaps his most realistic, most empathetic sketches are of bums on the street (from life), and of nineteenth-century inhabitants of female lunacy wards (from photographs). But nothing in the Salpetière gallery comes close to the brothers Crumb. Words cannot convey the horror of this family of compulsive drawers.

When we visit Maxon again we are privileged to see not only his collection of oil paintings of the female form (which even so generous an apologist for masculine fantasy as Hughes would be pressed to justify) but also his self-made bed of nails on which he assumes the lotus position of self-mortification – though not when begging in the street, as the city types of the business district find it hard to accept. After this it comes as no shock to learn he has a history of molesting women.

When we see Charles for the final time we are granted a peek at his artistic development: and at the way his narcissistic crush on the *Treasure Island* character Jim Hawkins, surrounded by pirates, evolved into total graphomania, the line being abandoned for ever tinier and more incomprehensible words. After this it is almost a relief to discover that he committed suicide after the film was shot. His mother is presumably still being pursued by her invisible enemies.

Crumb's response to his family is a pained, unbelieving laughter: 'Haw, haw, haw. Jee-sus!' His only normal relationship is with his daughter – and he's teaching her to draw cartoons!

The cumulative effect is to demonstrate that human beings can have total awareness of their own psychopathological tendencies without in any way being able to overcome them. Psychological insight does not lead to transcendence. Crumb operates as a howling 'No!' to the Californian therapist's 'Affirmative!' If the operative myth of contemporary America at its most extreme in its most westerly state, is that bodies, noses, lives and souls can be continually remodelled through liposuction, rhinoplasty, psychobabble and whateverology, then this film is as anti-American as any communist front.

But this is not a satire on the Utopianism that Robert Hughes mocks, even though Crumb's California is an eternal Haight Street populated by pissed old hippies with hardly a brain cell between them, and by young tourists with minds entirely colonized by consumerism. Crumb cannot escape his background through his art; rather through his art he is condemned forever to relive it. His next stop is the South of France.

Crumb is a rare instance of a film which has no unconscious, it refuses any reading which it does not itself supply, and second-guesses our responses before we can make them. Using the apparently formless, haphazard technicalities of observational cinema (albeit a species of that genre which recognizes the existence of the camera) it offers up a structuring of a tiny slice of reality which is as dense, as textured, as disturbing as its subject matter. A man who has been available only through his work up to this point is now laid out for all the world by the prying eye of a camera wielded by a friend. One thing is for sure: after living through this document the viewer may well wish to see or read no more of Robert Crumb and the dysfunction that surrounds him. *Crumb* may be unique in the history of documentary: a film which tells us more about its theme than we need to know, a film which completely exhausts its subject.

Source: *Sight and Sound*, Vol. 5, No. 7, July 1995.

12 The Burning Question

We asked a selection of prominent documentarians, old and young, to answer two questions:

1. What in the most general terms do you try to achieve in your documentaries?
2. What is the future of the documentary?

The second question was also asked of a handful of television executives.

These are the replies we received:

Nick Broomfield

Nick Broomfield's documentaries include *The Chicken Shack* (1983), *Driving Me Crazy* (1988), *The Leader the Driver and the Driver's Wife* (1991) and *Heidi Fleiss: Hollywood Madam* (1995). He has directed one feature film, *Diamond Skulls* (1989) and is at work on a second, *Original Sin*, from a screenplay by Joe Eszterhas.

1. In my films I try to communicate my own fascination and enthusiasm for the subject to the audience. Feature films may be taken more seriously, as works of art and as pieces of entertainment, but only the documentary can really capture the spontaneity and immediacy of real life. I find that endlessly thrilling. Because of the way I make my films, there is never an opportunity to do a second take. The crucial encounters are very quick and unscripted and they give me an enormous flood of adrenalin.

My style of personal intervention is not original to me – I think Michael Rubbo was the first to do it, in a film called *Waiting for Fidel* – but I have honed it down. Although I have adopted much from the traditional 'observational' documentary style – small crews, long takes and immediacy – I hope that I am moving the argument forward a bit further.

2. I think people are much more interested in documentary today than they ever have been. The films being shown on BBC2's *Fine Cut* and Channel Four's *True Stories* are better than most of what was made in the 1960s and 1970s. Not only that, but mainstream feature films and TV series are enormously influenced by the documentary aesthetic – you only need to look at *NYPD Blue* or *Homicide* and 'real-life' shows like *Cops*.

Perhaps the more traditional documentaries we've been accustomed to seeing on the BBC will disappear – I hope so. You know the kind of thing: talking head, cutaway, talking head . . . They just illustrate a thesis. But the power of documentary is spontaneity, 'realness'.

It's encouraging that more documentaries are being released theatrically. Because they're shown on the big screen they have to take on a bigger, more epic quality, both thematically and visually. Television is a very undiscerning medium with an enormous appetite. Every week it chomps up hundreds of hours of film and then spits them out. A documentary made for the cinema has to have a broader frame of reference, it needs to be better executed. Ultimately, those films will last longer and mean more to future generations.

Molly Dineen

Molly Dineen's film's include, *Home From the Hill* (1989), *The Ark* (1992) and *The Company of Men* (1995).

1. What I try to achieve in my documentaries is a familiarity, an intimacy with people, in the hope that audiences will *respond* to them as human beings rather than dismiss them as stereotypes. I think that by focusing on the human drama and trying to tell a story through character rather than communicate facts through interview and voice-over, you can portray more of life's inherent complexities and contradictions. If audiences are immersed in a situation and the characters involved, (accentuated by the camera contact, because the interviewer [me] is behind the camera) they will be more open to the ideas/ metaphors inherent in the material.

A favourite editor of mine tells me this is too optimistic and idealistic, that television simply reinforces people's prejudices.

I can't say where documentary is going but at the moment it is fast becoming soap opera in order to keep its place in the schedules (I know this because I'm guilty of it too!). Relatively simple stories or ideas are being stretched over weeks in order to build up an audience, and the subjects chosen tend to be vehicles for excitement and violence, e.g. the armed forces, the police, customs men, security companies. There is a pressure on us to be sensationalistic in order to compete with drama.

However, I am optimistic that the documentary will be kept very much alive in Great Britain, largely because of the commitment of a few key people in television (Alan Yentob, Michael Jackson, Paul Hamman, John Willis etc.), who have actually ended up providing a 'haven' for documentary makers world-wide who cannot get financed in their own countries.

Hi-8 is an exciting technical development which allows shooting in otherwise impossible circumstances (e.g. at war or climbing a mountain!). It is also exciting because it *can* lower production costs. But I feel – possibly rather pompously – that at the moment broadcasters are looking at it as a means of getting rid of crews and production values, and, in my eye most immorally, using it as a deceitful way of gaining access. Hoping the home-movie scale of the camera will lull subjects into a false sense of security which will may later be betrayed. If we do not abuse Hi-8 and misunderstand its advantages, then I think it breathes new life into certain areas of documentary and – the great consideration at the moment – makes things *cheaper*.

Nicholas Fraser

Nicholas Fraser is Editor of BBC2's prestigious 'Fine Cut' Documentary strand.

Two things can be reliably predicted about the fate of documentary films. The first is that while more and more are made each year, people will continue to say, mysteriously, that the form is dying. The second is that wherever juries, television executives or film-makers gather together you will find them disagreeing, often acrimoniously, about the definition of 'a documentary'.

I came more or less by accident to documentaries, after writing journalism for much of my career; and it has taken me a while to understand the debates surrounding documentary reality. Documentaries are different from news reports, to be sure, and they aren't quite the same as educational programmes. They may use reconstructions, or actors, as if they were drama productions; but usually they don't. Sometimes documentary makers are reduced to 'cheating' – getting people to redo, or represent events out of order, but for the most part, they are truthful, disdaining mock-ups on the grounds that they are less than honest, and in any case, easily detected.

Academic criticism is the death of the documentary impulse. Is the image genuinely annexed to reality, or is it part of a societal code? Do all messages carried in the film format contain their quota of non-explicit bias? Does anyone care? Good documentary-makers are bad liars; my experience shows them to be touchingly non-relativistic, attached – literally in most cases, as a consequence of the physical demands implied by the process of making films – to the most old-fashioned, literal-minded notions of truth-telling. There really is nothing complicated to be said about people who make non-fiction films. They use cameras – once they were restricted to 35mm, now super 16, 16mm, Beta and Hi-8 are available. They are almost always demon-possessed, usually manic-depressives, who panic in the middle of the night, but who are capable of manipulating their subjects into doing things that they would disdain under any other circumstances; and they tend never to die rich. Documentary film-makers are the mendicant friars of our times, visiting one forlorn hell hole after another in a vain effort to correct the growing view that everything is no more than virtual. They are our epistemological nags and scolds, our empiricist consciences. To say (another refrain from critics, right-wing ones, Lord Rees-Mogg for one) that they are immoral in their pursuit of harrowing or sensational images seems quite unfair. How else do we want to take our 'reality' but raw?

Documentaries must surely be regarded like non-fiction books or journalism – anything should go in the matter of technique, and the only real criterion for a good film is whether it tells the truth or not.

I watch hundreds of documentaries a year. What do I look for? Well, regrettably, it's easier for me to say what I don't look for. I'm afraid I've all but abandoned experimental documentaries, particularly highbrow French ones. I do like Chris Marker's films, but they stand isolated like primitive menhirs, as a reminder of what, in more leisured times, people thought could be done with the form. Such films, coming out of Godard via the wretched, garbled pretensions of 1970s cultural studies, represent the old Academicism and, to my chagrin, they still find favour with the state organizations staffed by well-meaning cultural bureaucrats, particularly in France, world centre of subsidized aestheticism.

But I also resent, increasingly, the New Voyeurism, which is our end-of-the-century growth industry. So many films I watch suffer from having received no investment whatsoever on the part of their makers. You can catch them any night, on any American network, and the affectless style is now spreading to Europe; it is hard to distinguish them from each other, or from the surrounding ads or drama series. They are cold to watch, presenting reality under half-blackened glass, like watches at duty free shops, or piles of over-priced, half-frozen sushi. You can tell such fakes by the labels affixed to them – hidden this, secret that. We don't have real investigative journalism any more; instead we have the illusion of disclosure, conveyed electronically by eyeball-crushing graphics and one second cuts. The scale of such banality is, literally, numbing and disorienting. I also wish that I didn't encounter waves of films made on the same subject, equally incompetently – dolphins were in vogue some years ago, then we had transvestites, now socio-sexual tourism is back in vogue, and concern is displayed in documentaries via many scenes of small, emaciated black children feeding off rubbish tips. Such films invite cynicism and disaffection by their casual, perfunctory sense of half-engagement with the subject – they turn the heart to stone.

Lastly, and I suppose most of all, I dislike The Great American Wind Film. This comes from PBS, usually, or Discovery. It deals with a historical subject, almost invariably American and excessively well-known; and reverence is written into the script courtesy of an earnest, pseudo-authoritative commentary, and a lustreless score featuring bassoons, hautboys, *cor d'ennui*, from the school of Andrew Lloyd Webber. In the old days Grand Figures taken from the environs of Mount Rushmore peopled such efforts – now the genre has fallen into the hands of the folk whom Robert Hughes called practitioners of the culture of complaint: minority rights claimants, plangent orchestrators of the under-privileged sensibility. I would like to be able to sympathize with the plight of the Plains Indians; ruthlessly, however, the films dedicated to their memory extinguish my capacity for collective remorse or grief.

'You can have too much of everything at the end of the century,' says Umberto Eco. 'Even food and sex, taken to excess, tend to confuse the mind.' One can say the same of documentaries, certainly; but I have a shortlist of people whose work seems to me to be indispensable.

Barbet Schroeder created the techniques of seduction and betrayal, later cunningly exploited by Nick Broomfield; his 1974 'self-portrait' of Idi Amin remains without peer for me, one of the greatest black farces of our century. I am still entranced by Louis Malle's *India* films; they are his favourite work, and they show him in a different light than that of his sometimes over-structured feature fllms, as a man who has warmth (rare for a French intellectual on public display) as well as doubts. Among American films, I like Barbara Kopple's work very much, all of it; and of course *Hoop Dreams*, the three-hour long, five years in the making Chicago epic of Steve James, Peter Gilbert and Frederic Marx – a remarkable film which deserves all the credit it received. The three British documentary-makers whose work I like most at present are: Molly Dineen, Phillipa Lowthorpe, and Clive Gordon. The latter's *The Betrayed* is the film which most captures the horrors of the future for me, *à la* Chechenya – war after war until the end of time rendered with wholly apposite, but somehow appalling brio, set to music not courtesy of Sir Andrew, but Russian heavy metal, itself part of the violence in the film. I enjoyed Toichi Nakata's astonishingly intimate *Osaka Story*, about his father and family. I love the work of Viktor Kossakovsky, a St Petersburg film-maker. *The Belovs*, made in black and white, consisting of Gogolesque dialogues between a drunken old man and his sister, featuring many farm animals, is the only documentary film I can think of in terms of the greatest feature films of the twentieth century.

But there are other kinds of films which are hard to make, and which are truly endangered. These are the expensive, thoughtful series, about painful but important contemporary subjects, which take a long time to make, score moderate or low ratings, and demand much of their audiences. Nowadays, a Marcel Ophüls wishing to make a three-hour film about a difficult contemporary or historical subject from the most rigorous investigative perspective would be politely shown the door. I'm glad that it's still possible to make series such as Norma Percy's *The Second Russian Revolution* and *The Death of Yugoslavia*. I hope that television executives won't tire of such efforts. I won't, certainly.

Clive Gordon

Clive Gordon's films include the two BAFTA award-winners *The Unforgiving* (1994) and *The Betrayed* (1995) about Bosnia and Chechnya respectively.

1. I try to tell a human story, which I hope will move people. The story must have a purpose; the film, a point of view. I'm not interested in giving 'information' but in creating an emotional response in the audience. It's a kind of manipulation, I suppose. In some ways I try to create something like a feature film, but inhabited by real people. The whole thing is fuelled by a kind of passion in the making, a commitment to the subject – a commitment shared by the whole team – and the 'manipulation' is achieved not on location, where I never interfere with the course of events, but technically, in the cutting room. I use a lot of music and no, or hardly any, commentary – in other words, the minimum of intellectual barriers between the film and the viewer. There is a strong central story and a lot of intercutting: an emotional mixture, which cannot be paraphrased or summarized. It is (I hope) – uniquely – film.

2. I wish I could say something about how documentaries will change in the future, but I've really no idea, other than to say that there has been in Britain in the last few years a slight shift towards a more 'filmic' and less journalistic, less fly-on-the-wall style. But this concerns only a small proportion of documentary output. In the end 'documentary' covers such a wide range of style and approaches that the question is, I suppose meaningless – at least to me! Sorry.

Mike Grigsby

Mike Grigsby's films include *A Life Apart* (1973) *The People's Land* (1976), *Living on the Edge* (1987), *Thoi Noi* (1992) and *Hidden Voices* (1995).

1. My driving force in documentary has been trying to find a way to give a voice to the voiceless. Increasingly people have become isolated and fragmented. In addition to scrutinizing society, I believe we should

be trying to guage emotional resonances and listen to those hidden voices.

I am also passionate about the imaginative possibilities of documentary. So my other cornerstone has been Grierson's original definition of documentary as the 'creative interpretation of actuality'.

This allows me to liberate the imagination, freeing audiences to identify with the characters and the situation on several levels. I believe audiences are always open to new ideas and fresh approaches.

I had a graphic example of this after the screening of my film *A Life Apart* – a documentary about deep-sea fishermen. I received letters from all over the country. Significantly many of them came from non-fishermen saying, 'Thanks for giving us a voice.'

I've never forgotten that!

2. If documentarists possess vision, passion and commitment, there is nothing to stop them producing personal and original work. However, inspired directors need inspired producers and sponsors. People who are prepared to take risks, back adventurous film-makers, back exciting new blood.

The reality in television today is that the chances for self-expression in documentary are being whittled away very quickly. There are few outlets now where one can exercise independence and self-expression without being confined to the formulaic demands of a particular strand. It is assumed that audiences always want more of the same. This tells us more about the insecurity of the broadcaster than the imagination and sensitivity of the audience.

The pressure in television for a fast turnover and fast profits are a reflection of our society – a society where care and compassion are being usurped by greed and the short term gain. But film-makers have to be realistic and optimistic. We have to understand what is happening and then findways to beat the system!

In addition to challenging television, we should look at the possibilities of theatrical backing, screening and distribution. We should get together and lobby the relevant bodies and companies.

Let's explore every way of turning our dream into reality.

Michael Jackson

Michael Jackson is the Controller of BBC2.

Factual programmes on television have rarely been as strong or as varied.

Documentaries, both as single films and as series, are as popular as ever and they remain a core component of all the terrestrial channels. Series like *H.M.S. Brilliant* and *Family Therapy* and strands such as *Modern Times* and *Cutting Edge* regularly reveal unfamiliar worlds to wide audiences.

Film-makers of considerable distinction, including Phil Agland, Adam Curtis, Molly Dineen, Pawel Pawlikowski and many, many others, continue to produce remarkable work. The last twelve months alone have given us *The Death of Yugoslavia*, *The House*, *The Gulf War*, *In The Company of Men*, *The Factory* and many more.

It's no surprise that commentators have referred to there being a 'golden age of factual television'. Nick Barker's *From A to B* and *Signs of the Times*, Adam Curtis's *Pandora's Box*, Molly Dineen's *The Ark* and *In the Company of Men* are all supreme examples of the BBC's own documentary-making tradition at its original and inventive best.

And yet there is sometimes a feeling that every subject and every story has been told more than once before. The range of approaches invariably adopted are also limited, so that most of the films we see have strong narratives and strong characters and are centred on social concerns in a domestic context. Yet the world is becoming more open, more complex, more confusing and more fragmented, and to reflect the many new realities, new documentary forms may be necessary.

These new forms may draw on neglected aspects of the British documentary tradition, including the too often forgotten poetic and analytic approaches. The documentary poems achieved by Humphrey Jennings in the 1930s and 1940s and subsequently by Philip Donnellan are neither as familiar as they should be nor have their lessons been built on and developed. Equally, the analytic film-making of a director such as Robert Vas is rarely echoed in contemporary television.

New forms too may come from assimilating the achievements of film-makers working in alternative traditions abroad. Older figures like Jean-Luc Godard and Chris Marker, as well as younger directors like Stefaan Decostere and Ian Kerkhof, have quite distinctive visions of the world. And these visions, whilst not immediately attractive to a wide audience, have much to offer. Hence on BBC2 we have put considerable resources into our new arts documentary strand *Tx*. It has included brave and remarkable work by directors like Marc Karlin (on painter Cy Twombly and much more); David Hinton (on the Chinese conservatoire) and Deborah Warner (*The Waste Land*). We have commissioned *Tx* to encourage new ways of telling stories in order to look at the world with fresh eyes. And *Modern Times* has surprised with films like Lucy Blakstead's *The Lido* and Dan Reed's *The Partners* (about John Lewis), both human films with a wry and surprising approach.

We need to recognize the possibilities of developing technologies. These never determine new forms of film-making, but they can offer original avenues for exploration, just as 16mm cameras and sync sound did around 1960, and as camcorders and desktop editing systems are doing now. We are already seeing how low-cost cameras can reveal the world in new ways in projects such as *Video Nation*, which I believe has been one of the great achievements of the past couple of years. *Russian Wonderland* an Anglo-Russian collaboration, also on Hi-8, gave extraordinary insight into contemporary Russia and offered very different understandings to those which might have been achieved by conventional methods. The honesty and clarity of these simple and direct records must push us all to think of more subjective possibilities for documentaries in the future.

Digital imaging, too, will become increasingly important. The wide availability of systems offering seamless and instant manipulation of both still and moving images is seen by some as a threat to the traditional truth values of photography and the documentary. Yet used responsibly such systems may help creative artists achieve what documentaries have always sought to do – to reveal not 'the' truth about the world around us, but 'a' truth which is original and provocative.

Claude Lanzmann

Instead of directly answering our questions, Claude Lanzmann (see p. 316) has asked us to print the following piece, in which he compares his own work with that of the Japanese documentarist Noriaki

Tsuchimoto. 'I think that my own intentions and hopes for the documentary are obvious from it,' he says.

Tscuchimoto has made many films about the Japanese coastal town of Minamata, where a local factory has contaminated the fishstocks with mercury effluent, causing sickness, deformation and death among the inhabitants.

Tsuchimoto invited Lanzmann to a joint retrospective of their work in Tokyo in May 1996.

How to express my feelings! At the other end of the world a film-maker whom I had never met, whose films I had never seen, whose name I didn't even know, asks that I be invited to Tokyo and associated with a celebration organized for him, demanding that *Shoah* be screened at the same time as his own films, that the two works – his and mine – be discussed and confronted by him, by me, in public, before an audience, with our questions and theirs.

This co-celebration – which is all at once recognition and generosity – overwhelms me: Noriaki Tsuchimoto saw *Shoah* last year in Tokyo and, straight away, with the eye and experience of a great artist, with his profound vision as a fighter and political militant, understood what ties of creative kinship existed between us, which identical problems of an ethical, aesthetic and technical nature we had had to confront, each for himself, which same pivotal questions we had asked ourselves, which answers we had provided: how to transmit, how to instruct, how to interrogate, how to remain dispassionate while, as we each desperately strove to do, methodically unveiling a hell; how to remain calm in the face of grief and tears, without letting oneself be carried away by the emotion which would preclude all work, how to denounce in the truest manner injustice and crime? A thousand questions, a thousand paths!

Today I have the right to say – I can state advisedly – that Noriaki Tsuchimoto is a great artist because, since February, since I received the letter of invitation, I have been locked into a long and attentive tête-à-tête with two of his films (two only, alas, because I had no more at my disposal): *The Message of Minamata to the World*, in English, and, above all, *Victims and their Universe*, in Japanese, without subtitles. What an event! Of course, I had closely studied the documentation that I had been able to gather on the illness of Minamata and its history – this other crime against humanity – but Tsuchimoto is such a marvellous film-maker, such a rigorous creator, that I followed the film passionately, without ever losing the thread, from the first image to the last. I did not understand the words, I heard the calm, precise voice, both human and neutral, of Tsuchimoto himself; and every time I was about to have doubts, to hesitate as to the sense of what was actually being said, the image intervened to comment, support, underpin, assist the words and, literally, illuminate them.

Images, in Tsuchimoto, do not chatter, as is the case in so many of today's films, where they proliferate in order to mask the emptiness of the thought – they are rare, precious, heartrending and enigmatic with beauty, always meaningful. I am thinking of the opening shot of the film, a long, fixed silent shot of a fishing boat, motionless on a smooth, hard sea reverberating flashes of sunlight. That boat is both close and far from us: its distance from the camera, the centring, the duration of the shot are of such perfect accuracy that the imminence of disaster is immediately perceptible. Deceptive image of peace and beauty, this sea is dead, this sea is deadly. I could not, of course, refrain from conjuring up in my mind's eye the opening scene of *Shoah*: not a fixed shot, but a slow panoramic one which glides with the small boat of Simon Srebnik, the child singer, on the calm waters of a Polish river, transporting us, from the very first minute of the narrative, to the boundaries of the world to step through the doors of Hades and make us enter the Kingdom of Death.

But there are so many more unforgettable images in Tsuchimoto's film, the last one, for example, an intricate jewel of enormous clouds in black, grey and white, a cancroid growth which spells out the interminable menace; or else the flight of the bird, imprisoned as far as the horizon by the camera, a pure arrow in the sky; or the curve of the bare shoulders of the old fisherman of octopi from Minamata bay, sunk into the sea up to the armpits, who, through a wooden framed primitive mask, watches for his prey and suddenly spears it with a single stroke of his archaic Neptunian trident; the same, straightened up, with the brilliant smile of the universal proletarian despite the wrinkles of life and worries engraved on his face, who walks up the shore, neck and waist belted and garlanded with tentacular octopi, forming a train behind him like the quivering mane of hair of Boticelli's Venus.

But, in Tsuchimoto, there are not only 'images of beauty', beautiful images. There are also boom mikes, faltering travelling shots, insistent, brutal zooms of a camera completely immersed in the action, combat camera, didactic tool which obeys a single law: instruct, teach, show, prove, convince, mobilize, denounce, describe. Camera of a topographer and a land surveyor, preoccupied with the most exact details, espousing here again the thought-processes which were mine during the eleven years of the making of *Shoah*.

The theme of the festival which will, in a few days, reunite us in Tokyo is: *The World of Noriaki Tsuchimoto and Claude Lanzmann*. It is a vast subject: it would be necessary to dedicate not just a few pages to it, but a whole book. Several perhaps. In front of the attendance in Tokyo, with the help of Tsuchimoto and that of our films' audiences, I will speak at some length on the subject of *Shoah*. You must realize that here, while talking mainly about him, I have also spoken about myself. He knows it: he has recognized me, I have recognized him. We have, without knowing each other, centrally recognized one another as brothers through and in our works: we both speak the same language, that of the cinema, of truth and of justice. Truth and justice which demand the work of art, all its power and subtlety, in order to be summoned and transmitted, so that each human being can bear witness to it.

Sublime work of Tsuchimoto, patient examination of martyred bodies and faces, close-ups of faces caressed, hollowed out, scoured – mostly horizontally – by the camera (I was thinking of Eisenstein or Pudovkin): the mad eyes, rolled upwards, of the adolescents of Minamata; the heartbreaking compassion of the mothers or 'rehabilitators', magnificently caught by the eye of the director, a look of anger and of kindness.

And the joy, the creative force, the absolute necessity to create in order to tell the truth, to relive if necessary (as such a film is not, cannot be, a mere 'documentary' which confines itself to a simple reproduction of 'events' or a dull recording of 'what's happening'), in a word to stage (*mettre en scène*) since lost occurrences, when one embarks on such undertakings, do not repeat themselves nor are they ever recaptured. Thinking about my own work during the shooting of *Shoah*, I called this form of direction 'fiction of reality' (*fiction du réel*) and I declare with pride that ordinary fictions – those which the professionals of the film industry, specialists of settled categorizations, call 'fictions', contrasting them with 'documentaries', are poor compared with ours. No 'director' of fiction will ever achieve the force and imaginative inventiveness, the empathy displayed by Tsuchimoto as he transforms the status of the characters in his film from protagonists in the real story to actors of the acted story, re-acted; nor will such a director ever achieve Tsuchimoto's precision in directing scenes, the true hallucination in which he plunges himself and plunges us with him, crossing all the borders which separate reality from the imaginary. I have in mind these extraordinary sequences of confrontation, in a huge amphitheatre, between the victims of Minamata and the sinister bevy of the tie-wearing managers and directors of the Chisso conglomerate, those responsible for the crime, of the storming of the bosses' rostrum by the fishermen who demand all at once their rights, the recognition of the fault committed and reparation for the irreparable. So violent an attack that it sweeps away, jostles and madly knocks about the director's camera. The camera, literally, becomes crazy because Tsuchimoto, to show us the truth, has dared to take the risk of giving up control.

I will close therefore on this scene which is unparalleled in the annals of the cinema. In a few days, I will know Noriaki Tsuchimoto, an admirable man, my brother, of whom, three months ago, I knew nothing. I do not apologize for this: since 1973 I have been steeped in the world of Claude Lanzmann. The world of *Shoah*. Another world. The same world.

See you soon Noriaki. See you soon, in Tokyo. See you soon, in Minamata.

Richard Leacock

Richard Leacock (see p. 251), one of the founders of the Direct Cinema movement, has worked exclusively on Hi-8 video for the past decade. His recent films include *Les Oeufs à la Coque de Richard Leacock* (1991), *Rehearsal: The Killings of Cariola* (1992) and *A Celebration of St Silas* (1994).

My greatest fear in life is boredom. I have a passion for experiences; good experiences; bad experiences. The more vivid an experience, the greater my need to share it. As a child, sent from our home on a banana plantation in the Canary Islands to the dank confines of boarding school in darkest winter England, I had a compelling need to tell my chillblained, snivelling schoolmates where I came from. At age eleven our innovative school showed us a silent film on the building of the

Trans-Siberian railway, *Turksib*, directed by Turin. I said to myself, 'I can do that' and three years later I completed *Canary Bananas*, a 16mm silent film which, in fourteen minutes, tells you all you need to know about growing bananas. Since then I have moved consistently in the direction of conveying what it is like to be someplace, rather than how to do things or how to improve the world.

It was this need that drove me to develop portable synchronous sound equipment. Sound: not just any sound; not music, not voice over, but THE sound, the actual sound to go with the actual pictures was what obsessed me. Equipment that is smaller and more sensitive, allowing one to observe with the least possible impact on what is taking place. Both action and dialogue captured, not directed, captured from observation, never repeated on demand.

This is how I like to work. It has nothing to do with specious arguments about 'objectivity'. I select in shooting, I select in editing. I like to play with my ingredients and sometimes I am pleased at the feeling of 'being there' that is achieved.

2. Documentary films were once shown in cinemas to large audiences who had paid good money to be entertained for about ninety minutes. These films were therefore in competition with the thrills, murders, sex and passion of just plain old movies. They seldom won. They were very expensive to make and 'sponsors' had an axe to grind. Then came television and documentaries had to compete for audiences not of thousands but of millions. I have worked so hard for so long to make films that went 'on the air' and vanished 'in millions of homes' – a sickening feeling.

Robert Flaherty used to tell me that there should be a way for us to see 'what we want, when we want, where we want at a reasonable price' which, of course, is true of non-fiction books. I think we should now take book publishing as our model. No one reads books at a single sitting. Ridiculous! Well within a year we can put documentary film on DVD's (Digital Video Discs) about two-and-a-half hours of quality, full-screen video plus all the text and stills you could wish for.

Originate the video in the new Digital-8, which can cost amazingly little, distribute whatever combination of text and video you find equitable on DVD, published like books and sold either on their own or together with a traditional book, to an audience who will look and look again; who will think about it, who will talk to their friends about it, write reviews, keep the disc in their library! An audience not of millions but of thousands of thinking people. Yes, there is hope! And like writers we might even earn an honest living.

Kim Longinotto

Kim Longinotto's films include *Dream Girls* (1993) and *Shinjuku Boys* (1995).

I want to make films which create a situation where the audience gets close to another individual, often from a completely different background, and feel a shock of understanding. I want the whole experience to be a strong and emotional one. I set up the filming in as relaxed a way as possible so that people can express themselves freely within it. I'm also trying to make documentaries that are engrossing and fun to watch, so there has to be a sense of story or exploration. In the latest film, *Shinjuku Boys*, which is about three women in Tokyo who are living as men, we were lucky in that they were as desperate to make the film work as we were. So it was a question of taking their passions and energy and trying to give the film a sense of movement and discovery. I think the brilliant thing about documentary is how you have to often be incredibly flexible and quite humble really as the story can take on a life of its own, and at the same time keep very clear what you're trying to do. The other thing which I'm probably trying to achieve, but this is a more underlying feeling, is to question structures and authority. I like films which subvert and make fun of established power. My first film was about the boarding school I went to where most of the rules were crazy and the régime was brutal. It was a place that was all about breaking your spirit. I'd love to make films which could reaffirm in a small way what the powerful are often trying to crush.

Philippa Lowthorpe

Philippa Lowthorpe's films include *Three Salons at the Seaside* (1994) and *Remember the Family* (1995).

1. The trouble with thinking about what I'm trying to achieve in my

documentary film-making is that it reminds me of all the things I've failed to achieve!

Anyway, here are some thoughts.

I think people are the heart and soul of the kind of documentaries I make, and I suppose what I struggle towards achieving in my films is a space where ordinary people can be themselves and say what they want, whether it's about losing a father and mother in the bomb in Enniskillen, or describing a handbag lent out for funerals in a Blackpool hairdressers.

Looking at human beings, their lives and relationships is endlessly fascinating. I'm not particularly interested in politics or current affairs. I'd rather examine the big universal questions of life through the small, everyday things that everyone can relate to – the minutiae of life.

To me, a documentary should be as visually arresting and inventive as a piece of cinema. In my films I try to think hard about the form and style. I don't agree with the purists who say true documentary has to be fly on the wall or 'natural', or that any visual style is just the director showing off. I don't think documentaries have to be like this to get near the truth or be insightful. And what's the point of having a visual medium if you don't use it?

I think the 'eye' of the director is very important. I try to develop a form and style for each film which will give emotional and aesthetic coherence.

I get enormous pleasure when a film I've made moves people or makes them laugh. In the end I think this is what I'm most trying to achieve.

2. I hope more people making documentaries get the opportunity to make films with an individual voice. I'm fed up with the identikit, off-the-peg films we're getting on the TV all the time. These bread-and-butter type documentaries have their place, of course, but I'd like to see more documentary strands where film-makers have a chance to experiment with style and form so they can find their own voice.

Chris Marker

Chris Marker (see p. 241) is currently working on *Immemory: The Ultimate* CD-ROM.

Writing is always a nightmare for me. Writing about my difficulty to write doubles the nightmare, especially when I'm supposed to express it in a polite way. So I warmly thank you for making matters easier for me by asking questions I simply can't answer (frankly, I doubt that anyone could answer the first question sincerely). I practised cinema just as I practised other, less visible, things, and I never thought it necessary to brood over them. Never explain, never complain . . .

Besides, I don't feel I belong to the realm of documentarists.

Sorry to disappoint you . . . But I'm sure you'll understand. My best wishes for your book: rarely has Reality needed so much to be imagined.

Peter Moore

Peter Moore is commissioning Editor for Documentaries at Channel Four

Channel Four's documentary policy is to give expression to a diverse range of documentary authorship from a broad group of independent film-makers, whilst also acknowledging the concerns of a general television audience.

Channel Four was the first broadcaster to make an avowed commitment to the awkward scheduling requirements of feature-length documentaries. The series *True Stories* has underpinned that commitment for ten years, showcasing the work of exceptional documentary talent. The series has supported and exhibited the work of Fred Wiseman: *Near Death* and *Miami Zoo*; Yuris Podniek: *Hello, Can You Hear Us* and *Homeland* and Bob Connolly's *Joe Leahy Trilogy*.

However, five years ago, alongside *True Stories*, we launched a new initiative with a very different agenda. *Cutting Edge* was to have a fixed point in the peak schedule and celebrate the artful observation of everyday life. From privatized dustmen and Eton school, to shoplifting at Marks and Spencer and the tribulations of Graham Taylor (the

England Football Manager), the series deliberately took as its yardstick
the preoccupations of contemporary Britons. The overview of the
Series Editor constrained the complete freedom of film-makers to
explore their creative preferences, but made a stronger connection with
a wider audience's experience and fascinations. The popularity of the
programmes usefully complimented the more idiosyncratic *True
Stories*.

But both series underlined the message that good documentary rests
on strong authorship. Whether the creative inspiration is indebted to
the observational tradition of Flaherty, Grierson's constructed
approach, or a photo-journalistic imperative, and whether the intention
is to report, investigate, subvert or entertain, a strong sense of purpose
ought to characterize our film-making.

Building on the explosion in new technology which has already
influenced the possibilities for documentary work, we pioneered and
persisted with an inventive documentary form, *Undercover Britain*,
which uses the small hidden cameras to explore the dark underbelly of
society. Employing the advances in new camera technology, with a
diarist's approach, allows the film-maker to provide eye-witness
accounts of conditions, and experience the world as well as report it.

The documentary has been in a permanent state of revolution, as it
should be. Invention in style, advances in technology, changes in
investment and opportunity will pull the genre in competing directions.
The observational documentary has undergone an exploitative phase,
Broadcasters quickly recognized that voyeuristic factual programmes of
the ambulance-chasing variety were cheap to make and successful with
audiences. This has undoubtedly diminished the reputation of the
observational approach. But this preoccupation by some broadcasters
shouldn't wholly distract us from present achievements.

The documentary is in crisis, certainly, as ever and some traditions
are healthier than others. There are new stresses. The numbers of media
graduates grows each year, their hopes and expectations may not be met
by the explosion in TV channels whose output of low-budget
programming to fill airtime will provide less fulfilling work and less
choice for viewers. But work that we can all acknowledge as intelligent,
inquisitive, powerful and creative continues to be made. Authorship is
alive, innovation in form and approach will continue.

Marcel Ophüls

Marcel Ophüls's (see p. 224) most recent film was the two-part study of war correspondents in Sarajevo, *The Troubles We've Seen* (1995).

The chickens are coming home to roost. In the Short and Happy Life of the Cinema, I think the Great White Hunters of fiction have been far too modest, and the documentarians far too pretentious. Now we are paying the price for both of these attitudes.

The great directors of the Hollywood Golden Age (Hawks, Ford, Hitchcock, Lubitsch, Wilder), in part for reasons of expediency or tinsel-town diplomacy, in part also because of the traditional Anglo-Saxon attitudes inherited by showbusiness people, were notoriously reluctant to let themselves be called 'artists'. In interviews with French *auteur* theorists, they could invariably be counted upon to downplay the very notion of cinema as an art form, even if only as a popular art form. In the Hollywood I grew up in, the company town of my father's day, there could be no greater insult than to have one's films labelled as 'artsy-fartsy'.

Remember? Right. More than Louella Parsons and William Randolph Hearst were necessary to drive Orson Welles into the wilderness. It was that poisonous epithet that really turned the trick. Perhaps the time has now come to confess: curiously enough, even my old man, that eccentric European virtuoso of tracking shots, always thought there was a good deal of truth in the accusation. The fact is that my father belonged to a generation of great film artists who seemed, on the whole, to feel quite comfortable and content with the idea of mere 'entertainment'.

The result is that now, some thirty years later, we must all pay the bill for this strange and frivolous self-disparagement, for this curious mix of reticence, opportunism and false modesty. In these days of relentless TV ratings, box-office blockbusters 'top fifties' ideology, and *Dallas* cynicism, any attempts not to conform to the degenerated, latter day standards of popular 'entertainment', any efforts to use film-making as a means for individuals to address other individuals, are considered an intolerable, élitist attack on the ideals of western Democracy, a shameful plot to subvert free-market values and impose suspicious and subversive foreign tastes on ordinary, self-satisfied consumers. Every survivor of the various blacklists I've ever met, every battle-scared veteran of the

old studio days, seemed anxious to tell me that compared to yuppie
decision-makers and contemporary programme controllers, the hypoc-
risies of Louis B. Mayer and the Ghetto kid vulgarities of good old
Harry Cohn were downright *gemütlich*. Zukor's motto 'The public is
always right' was not a notion entirely inimical to the great masters of
the silver screen. I think they understood it, quite rightly, to be taken as
nothing more than a good-natured invitation to come and enjoy the
show without worrying their 'pretty little heads' about complicated
issues of content and form. 'Leave it to the experts,' seemed to be the
general consensus. Now it turns out that what goes on in the heads of
those wonderful members of the public is neither little nor pretty. Of
course, at heart we always knew this. All we had to do was delve into
the darker corners of our own little heads. Even so, for the better half of
our movie-making century, we managed to suppress most of that
knowledge. Was that such a bad thing to do? Now we are confronted
with evidence. The writing is own the wall in big, black letters: 'NO
MORE HAYS OFFICE MEANS NO MORE LUBITSCH.' Can films
survive for long without some kind of Lubitsch touch? Perhaps, yes. Do
they deserve to survive without it? Frankly, I think not . . .

So, while I've come to feel that the great masters of fiction movie-
making contributed to the mess we're in by their excessive modesty, at
the same time I've also become quite convinced that the most famous
documentarians of the past contributed to it by their outrageous
pretensions.

The modesty might have been false in many cases. We can probably
assume that John Ford knew himself to be a major film artist, no matter
what he had to say about it to the *Cahiers du Cinéma*. On the other
hand, I fear that the pretensions of the documentary film-makers were
and still are quite genuine. Much as I admire Robert Flaherty's genius,
his Irish lyricism, it sometimes seems to me that even his claims to the
achievement of the sacrosanct 'authenticity' of life in the raw, or to the
pure, unadulterated poetry of sheer imagery don't always stand the test
of time. Worse, listening to our good friend Ricky Leacock, the other
day, recollect his experiences working as a young cameraman for the
great man on *Louisiana Story*, I surprised myself wondering, perhaps
not for the first time, if even that legendary reputation wasn't just a bit
overrated. *Nanook*, yes, *Man of Aran*, no? Would such a reassessment
still be considered a crime of *lèse-majesté*? I'm not sure. A little later,
standing in the lobby of the Hollywood Academy theatre, sipping tepid

champagne out of paper cups, I remember Ricky asking me: 'Do you really think Orson Welles was a great film-maker, Marcel?' I told him I thought *Filming Othello* was a damn good documentary. Christ! What else could I have said without seeming extremely rude? What I became quite sure of, right then and there was that in filming *Taboo* as a fictional love story, rather than as a documentary tribute to the native nobility of the Polynesian savage, Murnau had been entirely right, and Flaherty dead wrong. I was also reminded of a conversation I had many years ago while filming *The Memory of Justice*, with a celebrated and thoroughly charming Nazi war criminal, the late Albert Speer. He told me with a smile that, after having served his sentence in Spandau, he had become an icon on what he called 'the Nazi College tour'. He claimed that his house in Heidelberg had now become a major tourist attraction for American students, 'a bit like those movie star mansions in Bel Air'. Then he added: 'And you know what? The students always happened to be either on the way to see Leni Riefenstahl or just on their way back. Every once in a while, I feel like speaking the truth. Every once in a while, I tell them that *we* provided the decor, that *we* provided the crowds, that *we* provided the costumes and the action, the *mise-en-scène* and the choreography. All *she* had to do was to place the cameras. So why is that considered such a big deal?' I don't know the answer to that one. Do you? Why is it?

I'm also reminded of the time I skied down a slope at sundown, in Robert Redford country, right behind Cathy Wyler, William's charming daughter. We weren't going very fast, the slope was gentle and unencumbered. At one point, I called out to her: 'How come your dad turned out *The Memphis Belle* just with his left hand, when the rest of us have such a hard time on a full-time basis?' She didn't even turn around: 'A sense of structure,' she called out. Right again!

So what's all this I still keep hearing about reality in the raw, the exclusive claims to 'authenticity' of the true documentaries, about the sheer, unadulterated poetry of the lens, and all the rest of the stale, puritanical credo still being put out by the old aficionados of *cinéma vérité*, and the theologians of direct, free cinema? Glaaak! Bring back Harry Cohn to see if his ass still hurts.

Left in the wake of bygone modesties and bygone pomposities, left to shift for ourselves in a wasted landscape of totalitarian schlock, what can documentarian survivors still do for their fellow man? Damn little, if you ask me. One thing they could do is to get rid of their self-righteous pieties and shibboleths. These are as dead as the dodo. Like the Neanderthal man, these are prehistoric, obsolete and ungainly old bachelors, condemned to live and die without progeny. Another good idea might be to watch a lot of television news and reportage, if only in order to learn how to react against its silly norms, against all those managerial notions of deadly pseudo-objectivity.

Movie-making, even at its very best, was probably only a minor art form, and documentaries a very narrow, very bleak corner of that particular harvest. But what we can still do, at the very least, is to resist the dictates of mass consumerism. How? By developing an audio-visual style of essay writing. Never mind, perhaps, the poetry of images. '*Il ne faut jamais péter plus haut que son cul*', as we French are fond of saying. As a literary model, Orwell should be good enough for us. Let's face it, fellows: in today's world, Shelley and Rilke are far beyond our reach. Why don't we learn to live with that?

Fred Wiseman's doctors and nurses, in the long haul, might become 'authentic' enough, once they 'forget about the camera' while seriously discussing the fate of their near terminal patients in the hospital corridors in *Near Death*. The feelings being conveyed to an audience in the process are indeed beyond the scope, ambition and format of any normal TV documentary. Even more interesting, mysterious and challenging, it seems to me, is Wiseman's relaxed and patient approach, when recording and putting into context the language of broken phrases, gestures and mysterious signs, which modern choreographers use in communicating their teachings to a young ballet dancer. That is truly exhilarating, that is constantly surprising, eternally attractive. If that isn't 'art', what the hell is? And never mind if the late Harry Cohn's godamn ass still hurts in the grave. If any future is left for documentaries, those are the regions we should try to stake out and claim as our territory, build a wire around it, dig in . . . and RESIST!

Pawel Pawlikowski

Polish-born Pawel Pawlikowski's prizewinning documentaries include *Vaclav Havel* (1988), *From Moscow to Pietushki* (1990), *Doestoevsky's Travels* (1992), and *Tripping with Zhirinovsky* (1995). He is currently developing feature-film projects.

1. It seems to me that in a world where video cameras are omnipresent and where everything is being filmed all the time, it is essential that the film-makers concentrate on the film-making as opposed to recording. The thing that can salvage the documentary amid the increasingly meaningless glut of images is Form. More important still is the personal vision of the director.

Most documentaries claim to be simply recording reality. I make no bones about manipulating my subjects. I do it through choices in photography, sound, music, editing and narrative devices. Indeed, I go as far as setting up entire scenes. For me the point of making films is not to convey objective information about the world, but to show it as I see it and to find a form which is relevant.

The choice of the subject is crucial. The two films of mine that are still closest to my heart are those where I was lucky enough to come across a subject which struck a deep chord inside me and where the process of making the film became also a process of spiritual and formal discovery.

For me making a documentary involves a degree of schizophrenia: I try and enter the subject, see the world through its eyes, accept its logic, while at the same time maintaining an aesthetic and often ironic distance from it.

If the electronic media tend to flatten reality, make everything reassuringly the same and easily explainable to the laziest viewer, documentary films ought to disturb and show reality to be surprising, ambiguous, paradoxical, tragic, grotesque, beautiful . . .

I like films that force me to think – not through words or rhetoric, but through their very form.

Challenging the viewer doesn't necessarily mean being didactic or boring. The documentary, like any other film, should try to seduce and entertain its audience, if only for the sake of its own survival.

2. As for the future of the documentary, it doesn't look good. The basic paradox is that nowadays the documentary needs TV for its survival and yet it is TV that is killing the documentary.

Television is a fast-developing mass industry. Its bosses need to fill more and more screen-time for less and less money.

Most of the people who commission documentaries for TV are journalists with no time for film–making (although they like their films to be 'visual' or 'well-put-together'). They tend to be more interested in voyeurism (ratings) or political postures and intellectual packaging (critics) than in the way films are made. Their professional lifespan is usually short, their mentality institutional. What they need are not films that will stand the test of time, but instant visibility, high ratings or kudos among other media people.

From the point of view of a TV commissioning editor the cheapest and safest bet is a film which involves planting cameras in interesting places: hospitals, prisons, army barracks, police stations, customs offices, taxis, court rooms and filming the events as they unfold.

Vérité film-making may once have been novel and refreshing. Now that cameras are everywhere and our society gets more and more narcissistic, it has become the line of least resistance. All you need is to win people's trust and get unreserved access. For prestige reasons a lot of such films are still shot on film, but as TV channels go on multiplying and budgets shrinking, television will mass produce its *vérité* material on video.

Whether we like it or not, this type of TV documentary is the future. It's not only cheap, but also popular with the viewers. Most people watching TV don't really think of documentaries as films. What they want to see are things they're not supposed to see, witness real human dramas as they unfold, watch people like themselves when they feel unobserved.

There's a more 'ambitious' approach which I've observed on the documentary film festival circuit. It consists in film-makers from rich European countries (where nothing much happens) going off to exotic locations or wars to bring back colourful, dramatic tales of the struggle between good and evil. Their budgets are huge by local standards, but usually too small to allow the film-makers the time to enter the spirit of the place, let alone learn the local language. As a result, the wars, social conflicts and the locations keep changing, but the stories remain curiously the same. The images of corpses, massacres or suffering may be disturbing, but the ready-made morality of the film-makers is always reassuring.

The most successful documentaries nowadays seem to be those made by people with a lot of time on their hands, people who can stalk their subjects for five or ten years or however long it takes them to distil a 'human story' which then works as a kind of cheap feature film. As this approach takes time and involves big risks, it doesn't really suit TV. However, some of these films made it to the cinema screens and feature-film producers are getting in on the act, so maybe these feature documentaries do have a future.

The other source of interesting documentaries (which rely more on formal ideas than on 'human stories') are the countries of the former Eastern Block, where documentary film-making is still taken seriously as an art form and is still practised by some fanatical film people with ancient 35mm cameras on the ruins of the state-owned studios.

3. One of the reasons I made documentaries rather than fiction films was because they give you more freedom and fun. They were much cheaper to make and you don't have nervous producers and accountants breathing down your neck.

But over the last few years television (which financed my films) has become increasingly industrial. From the point of view of the accountants who are running television the ideal documentary is a six part 'fly on the wall' series about a children's hospital or a portrait of Pavarotti or at least a film about some high-profile issue. This atmosphere is not conducive to taking risks. Producing documentaries has become as big a pain in the neck as making feature films.

I must admit that, spoilt by a long and cushy relationship with TV, I am no longer prepared to operate in the wilderness and make films over years while constantly having to raise finance.

Anyway, I see the films I'm working on at present as a continuation of my documentaries. I have always treated documentaries as films above all. The feature films I've most admired, on the other hand, had their roots in neo-realism. What I liked about films like *Germany Year Zero*, *A Blonde in Love*, *Black Jack*, *Kes* or the first three films by Emir Kusturica, was their documentary texture, their use of real people and places, their moments of truth. They managed to tell touching stories without theatricality and literary dialogues. Whether there is any place for such films today remains to be seen.

D.A. Pennebaker and Chris Hegedus

A founder of the Direct Cinema movement, D.A. Pennebaker's films include *Primary* (1960), *Crisis* (1963) and the Bob Dylan profile *Don't Look Back*. Since the late 1970s Pennebaker has worked in partnership with Chris Hegedus, sharing all aspects of film-making, camerawork and editing. Their films together include the award-winning *The War Room* (1993).

Why can't we have a true theatre of documentary (non-fiction) film-making that entertains and excites rather than explains; why not a dramatic documentary, instead of a promotional one. As big and bright as any narrative fiction film, it would be filmed from reality not scripts, and its protagonists would be the villains and heroes around us that we only come to know through the press, as deceitful a ritual as can be conceived. Instead of pedantic charades on wildlife and government prudence we could, by turning a few film-makers loose in the world, create a new and different sort of theatre that searches for its plots and characters among the real streets and jungles of our times. Instead of editing testimonials to our more virtuous citizens we could watch those around us get through or attempt to get through their complicated, normal lives, and leave to newsprint the narration of obituaries, an artform for which it is far better suited. If a new generation of film-makers is ever going to be interested in a film form called 'documentary' for any reason other than present day career opportunities, it will only be because it can throw off new sparks, not old news. Documentaries could do what the industry dollar guzzlers can't, because that industry doesn't know how, nor would it really serve them to find out. Comparatively speaking there's no money there. These films are the 'little impudent verses' about which Ezra Pound sang, that, 'jangle the doors of rich people and merchants, do no work and live forever.'

And they might also lead us to what Heisenberg once called the 'new harmonies'.

Acknowledgements

This book would have been a near impossible undertaking without the resources of the British Film Institute Library, in particular the brilliant "SIFT" database of periodical articles. Long may the Institute continue to recognize the vital importance of its research facilities.

We are immensely grateful to Kevin Brownlow for screening a selection of early factual films from his private archive, Erich Sargeant for locating and screening a new subtitled print of Vertov's *Enthusiasm*, Milestone Films in New York, a wonderful distributor of rare films, including many documentaries, who generously supplied us with video tapes of expeditionary films of the 1920s, Nick Fraser who let us ransack his address book and the Drambuie Edinburgh Film Festival which made its fax and phone available to us.

In making our selection, we received invaluable suggestions and advice from Kevin Brownlow, David Robinson, Kevin Gough-Yates, Ian Buruma and Richard Leacock.

Particular gratitude must go to all the documentarists who took the time to contribute to the book's final chapter.

Apologies to Tat Lund, who put up with Kevin working on this book for a year of weekends.

At Faber and Faber we'd like to thank Justine Willett and Vanessa Unwin for copy-editing with skill and tact under restraints of time and circumstance and Walter Donohue, who edited the book.

The editors and publishers gratefully acknowledge permission to reprint copyright material as follows:

The Estate of Lindsay Anderson for 'Only Connect: Some Aspects of the Work of Humphrey Jennings'; Paul Barker for 'The Rise of Camcorder Culture' from *The Times* (27 July 1992. Copyright © Paul Barker, 1992); Erik Barnouk for 'Iwasaki and The Occupied Screen' from *Film*

'Tackling Social Problems'; Universal Press Syndicate for *Roger Ebert's Video Companion*; University of California Press for *Kino-Eye: The Writings of Dziga Vertov*, trans./ed. Annette Michelson. Copyright © 1984 The Regents of the University of California; Dai Vaughan for 'Night Mail' from *Portrait of an Invisible Man* (British Film Institute); Frederick Wiseman for 'Editing as a Four Way Conversation'.

Every effort has been made to contact or trace all copyright holders. The publishers will be pleased to make good in future editions or reprints any omissions or corrections brought to their attention.

Index

Page numbers in italics refer to illustrations